THE KENYA PIONEERS

THE KENYA PIONEERS

BY
Errol Trzebinski

W·W·NORTON & COMPANY
NEW YORK · LONDON

ISBN 0-393-02287-0

W. W. Norton & Company, Inc.
500 Fifth Avenue, New York, NY 10110
W. W. Norton & Company, Ltd.
37 Great Russell Street, London WC1B 3NU

Printed in Great Britain
2 3 4 5 6 7 8 9 0

CONTENTS

In loving memory of Jack Block,
the son of one of Kenya's pioneers,
whose contribution to
Independent Kenya is infinite.

LIST OF ILLUSTRATIONS

✧

FOREWORD

The biggest problem in trying to record the activities of an entire generation is to decide what to leave in and what to leave out. Every family which pioneered had equally fascinating tales to tell and each member of the family a number of unique anecdotes. Not only that but the child-in-arms at the turn of the century lived to see British East Africa through three radical changes; Protectorate, Crown Colony and Independence. Africa is the only place in the world that has changed from primitive culture to western civilisation in the span of a man's lifetime. The decimation of the game and tribes and the undermining of tradition within each tribe was the price paid for European settlement. But it is futile to wring ones hands and bemoan the fact that the white man ever took his civilisation to Africa. That cannot be undone.

The missionaries never doubted that they were special to their religion and chosen by God to play their role, while in the ranks of the rest of the pioneers could be found the restless, the enterprising, the unfortunate, the ambitious, the damned and the discontented. They were chiefly young, some barely in their twenties, and their common conviction was that they were exchanging an old life for a new one full of promise and opportunity. Leaving technically advanced countries behind, their scenes of departure were filled with bustle and panic and a sense of finality as mothers, fiancées and wives mopped their swollen eyes and imagined that the dark continent would swallow their loved men, without a trace. But Africa became indelibly shaped by the advent of the white men as they made it their home and strove to fulfil their dream. For many, the dream did not last for as long as they had hoped. This book is not so much for the older generation who have experienced it and have no need of explanation but for their grandchildren (black and white) who cannot possibly know of the underpinnings of the society in which their forefathers pioneered.

Originally the book was to have been dedicated to those grandchildren, and to their children, but Jack Block's tragic death occurred as my manuscript was in the final stages of preparation for delivery to the publishers. Since he loved and has done so much for Kenya and was born of pioneer parents it seems fitting that the book should stand as a lasting tribute to him for he was one of those babes in arms to live through the three radical changes and contributed so much to Independent Kenya. Also I think it fair to say that all who knew him, black or white, young or old, felt it to be a privilege.

E. T.

AUTHOR'S ACKNOWLEDGEMENTS

One can never adequately thank the numerous people who contribute in so many different ways during the research of a book such as this. In the past five years people have talked to me about their own experiences or those of their parents, given me hospitality and time, allowed Doria Block or myself to tape-record interviews, delve into diaries and letters, given me photographs, put me in touch with those who might help me and encouraged me in my quest. I am grateful to all of them and could not have attempted this book without that help. In particular, however, I would like to thank Doria Block who has given her time and support unstintingly as my research assistant and as a friend; Dylis Rhodes, whose encouragement and practical help supported me during the research phase; my father, who taught me to use a micro-word processor; Mrs Doris Rose, whose gift made it possible to write the book in a room of my own; Roland Gant, my editor whose guidance is valued; Elspeth Huxley from whose book *White Man's Country* most of the information on Lord Delamere has been drawn; Danie Steyn, whose generous donation of papers on the Boers has been helpful; my husband Sbish and my children, Bruce, Tonio and Gabriela, whose tolerance and understanding of my committal has been remarkable; and last but by no means least my thanks to A. T. Matson for generously putting the Johansen manuscript at my disposal, as well as some of his own papers, and for checking my draft manuscript with patience and care.

It is hoped that the remaining contributors will understand if I simply list their names in alphabetical order; to them I nonetheless express my deepest gratitude.

Alec Abell, Alison Abell, Mrs Barbie Adcock, Mrs G. C. Aggett, Clive Aggett, Taj Ahmed, Miss B. E. Ainsworth, the late Mrs Gertrude Alexander, Reggie Alexander, James de Vere Allen, Fergie Allison, Peggy Allison, Mr D. Anderson, Dr Gerald Anderson, Robin Anderson, Mr Lars Askar, Mrs Joan Ayre, Mrs Joan Bagehot, Mr Hugh Barclay, Commander Herbert Barry, Mrs Battley, the late Mr Leo Beck, the late Mrs L. Beecher, Mrs Yvonne Bell, Margaret Bentley-Buckle, Bruce Berman, Mrs Kate Bicknell, Anthony Block, the late Jack Block, the late Sarah Block, Tubby Block, Mr A. A. W. Blowers, Mr Alan Bobbe, Pollie Bodgener, Connie Bowker Douglass, Miss Lois Bulley, Mr Frank Bullowes, Mr Sonny Bumpus, Mr Brian Burrows, Mr D. G. Buxton, Mrs Diana Cadot, Juanita Carberry, Rabbi Julius Carlebach, Mrs Rose Cartwright, Mrs W. H. Case, Dr R. Cashmore, Mrs Irene Channer, Mrs Sally Church, Delia Craig, Mr R. R.

Creighton, Mr Arthur Cole, Marion Cole, Mr Mervyn Cowie, Mr Eddie
Davis, Ivor Davis, Mrs Cecily Destro, Sandy Dickinson, the late Mr Sidney
Downey, Mr Ian Dundas, Mr Dunn, Rose Dyer, Tony Dyer, Christopher
Eames, the late Dicky Edmondson, Mr Fred Ellison, Mr David Epstein,
Anna Falck, John Falconer, Mrs Leda Farrant, Peter Faull, Eleanor Fazan, Mr
Micky Fernandes, Mrs Margot Fernandes, Charles Fisher, Mr Finne, David
Forrester, Miss Peggy Forrester, James Fox, Dr Foy, Miss Olga Franklin,
Lyn Fuss, Tibor Gaal, Mrs Hazel Gage, Terence Gavaghan, the late Mrs
Geater, Mrs Winifred Gethin, Margaretta Gichuru, the late Mrs Jean Gill, Mr
J. B. Glen, Mrs Dorothy Glynn, Mrs Elsie Goodram, Mr P. J. Gough, Janice
Gott Kane, Mrs Eileen Grant, Mr and Mrs T. G. Gregory, Mrs H. Grenfell
Hicks, Stephen Grimes, Mr H. K. Grogan, Mr Adamalli Gulamhussein, Mr
Andrew Hake, Lady Claude Hamilton, Gay Harper, Professor Malcom
Harper, Jan Hemsing, Mr Jacob Hirschfeldt, Mrs Molly Hodge, Hazel
Holmes, David Hopcraft, the late Jack Hopcraft, John Hopcraft, Mr W. D.
Horne, Peggy Howden, Mrs Margot Howerd, Kathy Hurd, Dr Pascal
Imperato, Brian Jenkins, Mrs G. Jensen, the Late F. S. Joelson, Mrs Glennis
Jones, Mr Fred Jordon, Mr Bernard Kampf, Mrs Pat Kenealy, the late
Donald Kerr, Betty Kiggan, Mr Ben Kipkorir, Mr Rex Kirk, Mrs Edith
Klapprott, Cynthia Kofsky, the late Mr M. P. C. Krarup, Dr David Lee,
Mrs Yvonne Lewin, John Lonsdale, Kurt Luedtke, Mr A. J. MacDonald, the
late Mrs I. MacDougall, C. J. MacIlvain, Joan MacKinlay, John MacKinlay,
Minnie McKenzie, Mr Jim McQueen, Beryl Markham, Mr Harry Markus,
Mrs Sybil Mattison, the late Helen Mayers, Mr Ray Mayers, Mr Mervyn
Medicks, Mr R. R. Meinertzhagen, Roger Mennell, Bonnie Miller, Mrs Iris
Mistry, Maeve and Barry Mitchell, The late Alban M. B., Alban Mitford
Barberton, Mary Mitford Barberton, W. L. K. Morson, Miss Kay Mortim-
er, Molly Mortimer, Colin Newsome, Miss Mollie Newton, Barbie Night-
ingale, Mr George Nightingale, Mr and Mrs James Nightingale, Nigel
Nightingale, Mr Charles Njonjo, Mollie Noon, Myra Oates, Titus Oates,
Mrs Phylida O'Brien, Desmond O'Hagan, Pam O'Hagan, Ian Paseka, Miss
D. Payne, Mrs Philip Percival, General Phillips, Mrs Dorothy Pittaway, Eve
Pollecoff, Tristram Powell, Brian Havelock Potts, Mrs Dorothy Powell, the
late Mr Will Powys, Mrs Vic Preston, William Kilpatrick Purdy, Ruth Rabb,
Mr G. E. Ramsay, Mrs Freda Rawson-Shaw, the late Mervyn Ray, Michael
Redley, Dr Ayres Ribeiro, the Rev. John Riddell, Janice Robertson, Edward
Rodwell, Olivia Rodwell, Mrs Olga Rogers, Grahame Rose, Mrs. M.
Roseveare, Mr J. Rowlands, the late Eddie Ruben, Mr Jock Rutherfurd, Mrs
Josephine Sandhu, Miss Pam Scott, Teresa Seawright, Anthony Seth-Smith,
Mrs F. Sexton, Mr Peter Shepherd, Mrs Norah Shipley, Mr Donald Simp-
son, OBE, Sylvia Simpson, Mr Bert Sparrow, Lady Stella Spry, Mr James
Smart, Xan Smiley, Mr J. Stanley-Smith, Danie Steyn, Mr Alan Stocker,
Mrs May Stocker, Odin Sunde, Sonja Sunde, Mr Hobo Swift, Miss Hazel
Taylor, Mrs Kit Taylor, Barbara Thorpe, Pip Thorpe, Anne Thurston, Mrs
Margaret Thurstan, Jean Tomes, Tom Twist, the late Mrs Elaine Tyson, Mr

W. H. Udall, Rosemary Van Dyk, Mr C. G. R. Van Someren, Dorothy Vaughan, Mr John de Villiers, Mr Donald Vincent, the late James Walker, Dr Richard Waller, Mr John Ward and Mrs Pam Ward, Mr and Mrs G. A. Webb, Sam Weller, Luise White, Michael Williams, Phyllis Williamson, Richard Wilson, Mr Henry Winterton, Ole Wivel, Mr M. Woolf, Mr Brian Yonge.

Establishments: In particular I would like to thank the Royal Commonwealth Society Library staff for their helpfulness and for allowing me access to the Langridge papers and the letters of Arnold Paice, also Anglo-Jewish Archives; East African Newspapers (Nation Series) Ltd; The East African Railways and Harbours 'Railway Museum', Nairobi; *The East African Standard*; The Imperial War Museum Photographic Library; The Jewish Colonisation Association; The Jewish Historical Society; Kensington Public Library; Kenya National Archives; The University of Birmingham Library; The University of Nairobi Library; The Nairobi Library; The Public Records Office; Rhodes House Library, Oxford; Ringwood Library; the Royal Geographic Society; The World Zionist Organisation.

E. T.

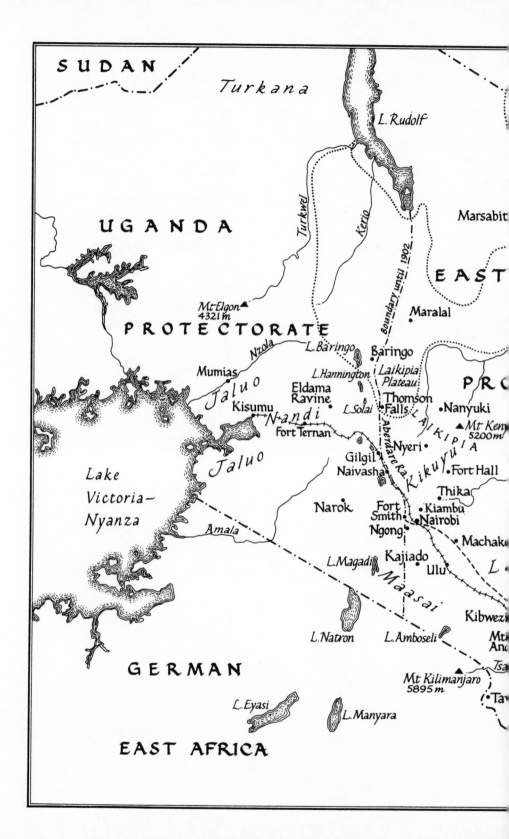

BYSSINIA

Lugo

ITALIAN

Juba

SOMALILAND

Wajir

AFRICA

ngare Uaso Nyiro

Lorian Swamp

Lak Dera

TORATE

Tana

Kismayu

*I n d i a n
O c e a n*

m b a

Witu Lamu

Sabaki

Malindi

*Tibi
Desert*

Takaungu

Mombasa

Vanga

**THE EAST AFRICA
PROTECTORATE**
c. **1900**

+++ Uganda railway Mombasa to
Port Florence (Kisumu)
- - - McQueen, Wallace, Boedeker route, 1896
.... Lord Delamere's route from Berbera
to Eldama Ravine

0   100   200 km
0   50   100 miles

CHAPTER 1

✧✦✧

The Stepping-Stones

'. . . that men may rise on stepping-stones
Of their dead selves to higher things . . .'
Tennyson, *In Memoriam*

Man made his entry into silence and the stones that he honed for his own use have gradually betrayed his existence. Since the beginning of time, rain and wind and drought have played their role in shaping evolution. In Africa it is the elements which continue to shift this great continent forward subtly but irretrievably, despite the white men's schemes for its future. Just as time and necessity smooth the boulders which precede a bridge over water, their worn surface proves that the bridge was needed. In this context the Kenya pioneers may be compared to stepping-stones, being a means of new, of different progress in a country where today every modern benefit is underscored by the memory of hardships.

Before the turn of the nineteenth century the white man's destination was more often fixed in his mind than on a map, for his route was unlikely to be charted; the land mass of Africa was referred to still by three words . . . The Dark Continent. On the day's march across the bush a man's chief concern was to reach a good place so as to pitch his tent before sundown and, in his determination to move on, perhaps by arranging a few stones to get himself over a stream, he might also unwittingly change destinies. For behind the mist and sun and the thorn-branch-blur of each new day, there already lay one and a half million years of unrecorded civilisation.

On the African plains and in the bush, barring the fact that night follows day, everything is uncertain. Those stones of which we speak may not even withstand the force of the stream swollen out of all recognition by the downpours of the next rainy season. Occasionally, despite all the rules, fate and nature itself are defied. The swamp and surrounding plain from which the city of Nairobi grew in less than half a century is a prime example.

In 1896, shortly after the building of the Uganda Railway had begun, Dr

Boedeker, one of the earliest pioneers of British East Africa, skirted the area. He had walked from Mombasa up-country to Fort Smith with his wife and two other adventurous couples. Later, in the temporary role of a Medical Officer, his opinion of the siting of Nairobi was 'the worst possible choice for any sort of urban centre by virtue of its swamps alone, for even among the early caravan leaders the site had always been recognised as an unhealthy locality swarming with mosquitoes.'[1]

To those white men and women who went out to pioneer and settle, British East Africa was the promised land. Having been urged overseas to take up land there that was dirt cheap, they did not pause to think that what was offered belonged to somebody else because, to the European eye, there was so little evidence to suggest that it did. Many of those who went to Africa stayed on because they liked their African existence better than the life they had led at home. They found that they preferred to ride a horse than drive a car and would rather warm their hands over a camp fire under the starlit sky than upon a radiator within the security of four walls.

From 1896 until the First World War all manner of white men, bad and good, had found in East Africa a chance to make a fresh start. After slavery colonization was the most crucial event in African history, and since the past very much affects the present, if any value is to come from it, it cannot be ignored. The colonial period and its influences, which in so many ways gave the Third World its present shape, is now treated as an almost irrelevant interlude, more often ignored than attacked. This is a dangerous distortion of truth, for whether a human being is black or brown or white, each colour tag carries within it a responsibility, a meaning and a penalty.

Accountability, for example, in the choice of ruling elders and chiefs, was swept aside as chiefs were appointed in all districts by a foreigner because that foreigner approved of them and the traditional check on the leader was slowly removed as the Africans lost their initiative to the white men.

Given the benefit of hindsight, the Africans displayed an extraordinary level of human tolerance towards the peculiarities of white men during those exploratory years. For the pervading dream of all outsiders who enter Africa has been to change it. The white concept of education seems to be to make others over in the same mould, carbon copies of people who faithfully reproduce age-old mistakes. Today in the wake of the eager foreigners who scrambled over Africa's contemptuous surface, it may seem to offer a reshaped promise to its own people. But equally, tomorrow that promise could be withdrawn for it is altered now by European encroachment and ways. This continent of brooding, fundamental values takes everything back into itself. In this primeval fashion there is no waste.

The completion of the Uganda Railway altered everything. In December 1901 a rail track ran for 582 miles through virgin country from Mombasa on the Indian Ocean to Port Florence (at that time still part of Uganda) on the shores of Lake Victoria. But quite suddenly, once it was built, the Uganda Railway represented less of an achievement than an uneconomic backbone traversing unexploited land. It seemed, as Henry Labouchère had forecast six years before, indeed a 'Lunatic Line'. Somehow the expenditure had to be justified to the British taxpayer. The total came to a staggering £5,500,000. The assumption that trade follows the flag had cost the British Government £10,000 per mile of track without a jot of evidence to support it. Habitually adept at the art of muddling through, the Foreign Office then used the land flanking the railway as bait to attract white settlement.

Much of it eventually was converted into farms. Gradually tiny, administrative bomas of one thatched hut expanded and formed the heart of one-street villages. A handful of these became towns, the largest of which was Nairobi. It grew from a tented camp at mile 327 and a cattle boma. This scruffy knot of tin shacks took fifty years of sweat and toil and misunderstanding to become a city. It was built on the flat and was unremittingly ugly. When it rained Nairobi became a swamp, and the black cotton soil, which was the colour and texture of coffee grounds, turned into a quagmire. But when the sun shone for months on end, the earth was little better than dust and was responsible for an ailment known to the white men in the dry season as 'Nairobi throat.'[2]

The pioneers' farms were made out of nothing and everything—as all farms are originally made. They were hacked out of bush and rocks; they were coaxed out of new earth and forests and experimental crops parched for want of rain. They were made out of sun, which also ruined them, and from patience during fanatical droughts when the pioneers discovered that in Africa the seasons were halved and, if not quite upside-down, the sun ruled by a system unimagined by them before. They were made from noise to ward off invasions of locusts and out of ignorance and innovation, sharp practice, skill, luck, dogged persistence and, by no means least, by humour and heartbreak. Lack of administrative continuity also played its part in development, a result perhaps, of the most serious flaw in the British Colonial system. The District Commissioners, their ADCs and the District Officers were always being moved on to a new post just as they got to know those whom they were administering. Their pet schemes, such as building a dam, setting up a clinic or some other facility to improve conditions might then be abandoned by successors in favour of a different amenity such as a bridge or a road.[3] Boundaries too were frequently adjusted to ease administrative pressures, causing even more confusion.

Against this raw backdrop, there lived hundreds of pioneers whose humble but vital contributions to the founding of modern Kenya have largely gone unsung. The reason for this is simple. Like Kipling's lost legion, they were a phantom regiment that was never listed, carried no crest or colour but which split up almost invisibly against the vastness of Africa into a thousand fragments to break the ground for the rest.[4] Men and women from all walks of life were attracted by the campaign for white settlement, not just from England but from all over the world. But they shared one common bond. Having decided to make British East Africa their home, their committal was fundamental to their way of life. They were people who could shrug their shoulders and adjust to circumstance. They carried within them a certain flexibility and, in their instinct to migrate, the willingess to make long treks on foot into the unknown. This impulse for adventure is an essential part of pioneering. The resulting discomforts and uncertainties were often inexplicable to relatives left behind. The lure, above all, was a sense of freedom. In 1919 Lord Francis Scott drew a Soldier Settlement farm in a lottery. His wife kept diaries and as late as 1922 touches on this attraction in her journals. They built their home, 'Deloraine', north-west of Nakuru at Rongai. Hitherto they had lived in grand style in India and before inspecting the land they had drawn near Nanyuki Lady Francis Scott had to be taught to ride astride for she had only ridden side-saddle. She writes of her doubts as to the wisdom of 'living out here, being a drudge and meeting no-one except delightful farmers . . . then, I order a pony and gallop up the hill in the sunshine and stand at the top gazing over the limitless spaces of Africa with the glorious wind blowing the delicious mimosa scent against my face and wonder if I haven't got the best possible kind of life after all . . .'[5]

There was a feeling of unequalled nobility in this freedom, a greatness which overpowered the white men who were new to Africa; once they had experienced it they would never settle for less.

They were days of great romance. Days when the stockade of a village was kept in constant repair. It was an unwritten law, when travellers used one of the bomas formed by high thorn fences against lions, in which they could safely outspan their oxen for the night, that the men would repair any weak spots with good, strong branches before moving on. They were days when the Kikuyu fought the Maasai* *moran*, the warriors who went out on cattle raiding forays. The white men kept kegs of explosive in the store for an emergency, when the old Martini rifles would be dished out. At night lion could be heard outside the tent or gunny sacking door, a coffin was kept as a matter of course in the rafters, and a trader such as John Boyes, a cobbler's son from Hull, though of dubious repute could appoint himself king over the entire Kikuyu tribe.

In the period before the First World War, newcomers called themselves settlers but were unquestionably pioneers. There is a basic difference between those who settle in a wilderness, establishing a new society, and those foreigners who arrive only when a country's laws, customs and language are fixed: really immigrants. In the case of British East Africa the first white men who came out, apart from missionaries, may also be divided into two categories: settlers and officials. Each group considered itself superior to the other, and both were bound by the common opinion that they were better than those who arrived after the Great War, in spite of the fact that they were

---

* The spelling of the word Maasai throughout the narrative is the one favoured by the modern school of Africanists. In the strictest sense, 'Maasai' means 'speaker of the language, Maa'. There are two distinct groups of Maa speaking peoples; those who lead a semi nomadic and pastoral life, who may be regarded today as the Maasai proper, and the Samburu.

almost always in disharmony with one another. The great 'Settler *v* Official' matches played out so often on cricket pitches all over the Protectorate at weekends were merely sporting extensions of battles waged resolutely during the week. After the war the tempo of development altered again. The Soldier Settlement Schemes brought yet another type of person and a different lease of life into the country.

The white pioneer phase of Kenya's history spans the twenty-four years from September 1896—when three couples, the Boedekers, Wallaces and McQueens started an arduous walk from the coast—to 1920 when the Protectorate became a Crown Colony. It is a history not just of the rich, though some individuals became very wealthy, or of the literate middle-class but of the poor and courageous in their infinite variety. In many ways the women were more remarkable than their men. They were liberated females long before the catch-phrase was dreamed of. Cara Buxton,* a gentlewoman from Norfolk, walked all the way (apart from a small trip down the Niger in a canoe) from the North African coast to Nairobi. She did not know Swahili or any tribal language and suffered from malaria frequently. She had taken quinine with her but as most of it was given to her porters she had run out of supplies by the time she reached the Congo. When she got to BEA she decided to settle: she ordered a timber house in sections to be made for her in Norwich and this was shipped piecemeal to Mombasa. It was sent up-country by train to her nearest station from whence she took it in stages by ox-wagon to Kericho south of the railway. She called her home Kipsaas. Eventually it was sold and became a tea store after she built a proper house at Kedowa, north of the line, where as a spinster she lived for the rest of her life.[6] Cara Buxton farmed but chiefly made money out of training teams of oxen for the farmers who settled near Kedowa. One of her letters 'home' reveals her unconventional living conditions, echoing again the prevailing sense of freedom which Africa gives. It is dated 6 November 1913: 'I live with a spirit level in my pocket and dream about corrugated iron. So far I have only been building a big shed to put all the stuff into as it comes up from the station. That's hard enough work. I saw so awfully badly but hope to improve . . . Tho I'm so happy in a tent I don't much care if the house is never finished. There is not much game here and when one shoots, it is because one is hungry . . . I had a thrilling leopard hunt but didn't get the leopard. I even have to do the cooking sometimes as my boy can't cook. I made quite a good tart one day. There is lots of wild fruit here . . . I might someday get poisoned but so far its all right. I've bought ponies, goats and cows . . . Its really a bore having to worry about food when I've so much else to do.' Scribbled on the back of

---

* 1875–1936. Grand-daughter of Hannah Gurney, one of the 'The Gurney's of Earlham'—the well-known Quaker family—and Thomas Fowell Buxton, whom she married. Cara Buxton was the daughter of their son, Mr S. Gurney Buxton of Catton Hall, Norwich. In 1910 she descended from Cairo and travelled all the way up the White Nile and on to Victoria Nyanza. In 1911 she made an expedition into the Sudan and thence to Abyssinia making her way from Cape Town, visiting Nyasaland and German East Africa.

her next letter is 'Great excitement last night a lion came and frightened us and bit one of my donkeys very badly.'[7]

Cara Buxton was writing twelve years after the completion of the railway, yet she still describes a land of extremes. It was a land that dictated the lives of the pioneers as it had shaped that of the Africans before them. The difference was that thousands of years of exposure to hazard had already adjusted the African temperament to the assault of the unexpected. Mentally he had come to terms with fate by learning to bow his head to it; in consequence he was bold, fearless and equally unsurprised by pain or death. This acceptance or lack of sentiment would often be misconstrued by the European as heartlessness. It was the sort of courage that was witnessed with disbelief at first by Dr Boedeker and the medical men who came after him. They were astounded by the way a Maasai stood without flinching as a wound was sewn up without even the aid of the old 'rag and bottle' means of anaesthetic.

In complete contrast the European had concentrated for hundreds of years on protecting himself against discomfort and the unknown, from the bitter taste of medicine to the vagaries of the weather. The pioneers had been forewarned about the dangers of the sun. Everyone, young and old alike, wore either a sun helmet or double terai from 7 am until sunset as well as a spine-pad lined with red felt as a protection against its damaging rays. Another generally expressed fear was that altitude would never entirely counteract latitude and for that reason the future of white settlement was highly precarious.[8]

It was not easy. In Africa, hostility tended to rise to the surface, in the form of dust storms, in the form of lions, in the form of snakes, in the form of malaria or black-water fever and siafu. These are the dreaded man-eating ants of Africa, which, left to themselves, as Karen Blixen once wrote, 'would eat you up alive.'[9] A baby in its cot might be devoured as ruthlessly as a flock of turkeys. Siafu march mostly at night or in the rainy season and if when crossing their path they happen to crawl onto the body, there is nothing to be done but to tear off the clothes and pull them out of the flesh.

Moreover those pioneering Europeans had to adjust to the Africans. The white men were startled, for example, not to say disgusted, to find that in place of the ritual of handshaking by way of introduction, spitting was the form of greeting among some tribes; it was intended to mean 'go in peace'. Not unnaturally such behaviour was repellent to Westerners who interpreted the custom as the highest possible insult. Then there was the discovery that some African females were circumcised; the Europeans were appalled to learn of the savagery of this infibulation or sewing up.

The Administration, too, were puzzled by what they saw as the African's indifference to the lure of money. Even after the almost biblical scourges of rinderpest—(a disease of cattle) and locusts culminated in the famine of 1897–9, the Africans still could not be induced to work for gain on the construction of the railway. The white people had no inkling of the strict undertakings within each tribe to ensure survival. In general, the men acted as protectors, responsible for the safety of their villages, women and children and ever watchful for marauding tribes and animals. Consequently it was the women who laboured, working in the *shamba* where they cultivated their crops. They provided meals and bore children and loads with seeming indifference. In the European male's eyes, used to women who were cosseted and not allowed to lift a finger, these customs were shocking. Yet here was a system which had worked for thousands of years and so natural to the Africans that they saw no reason to alter it.

Furthermore the wheel had not been encountered here. The bush was unsuited to it; the land was not approachable until tracks were worn by feet and hooves. Loads, limited to 60 lbs, were borne on the heads of long crocodiles of porters in the slave and ivory trading caravans for hundreds of miles; and this repeated use, single file inland and back to the coast, etched the first paths into the monotonous surface of the bush. Later, these were the tracks followed by the European explorers. As Charles Miller wrote in *The Lunatic Express*, '. . . these ivory and slave caravans were the real pioneer of African exploration. The Europeans who made the so-called discoveries of the nineteenth century followed trails which almost without exception, had been blazed for them by Zanzibari Arabs and Swahilis.'[10]

As late as 1904, by which time the great hissing engine pulled into Nairobi station from Mombasa twice a week, when wagons, rickshaws and bicycles had become a familiar sight beyond the settlement, the wheel was still not taken for granted by the African. Tradition dies hard and he had centuries of his own to follow. For example, the Morson brothers were setting up their sawmill, 'Romolo', at Limuru at that time. Their labour was untrained and had been recruited with difficulty from miles away in the Fort Hall district. The first task at Romolo was to shift tons of earth. Sam Morson, thinking he would make their work easier by providing them with wheelbarrows, rode down to his wagon works in Nairobi and had them sent up to the sawmill by train. When he returned a week later he found that the labourers were using the barrows, but after filling them instead of wheeling them to the dumping area, they were carrying them on their heads.[11]

In 1896, the coin was as enigmatic as the wheel and in addition was more of a nuisance than a reward. Barter and trading followed a complex African system, shaped by tribal need and culture, and since the African did not wear trousers, he had no pockets to put the coin in. He was far more attracted by the glitter and its potential for ornament.[12] This is why beads were used for trading and why forty miles of copper telegraph wire disappeared during the first Nandi Rebellion in 1900. Passing caravans occasionally helped themselves to small lengths of wire too, once they discovered that it was useful for barter.

So wherever the pioneers decided to settle, they had to do everything for themselves until they had persuaded and trained people to work for them. Employees had to be taught to lay tables and make beds, to use picks, shovels and wheelbarrows and to inspan teams of oxen and drive them before the plough. This required great patience from those doing the teaching. Western tools were as alien to the African as were the people trying to communicate by signs and in an unknown tongue.

As the white men and women trekked across the land, dwarfed by the feeling of limitless sky and bush, looking for somewhere to make a new start, the wait-a-bit thorns confirmed their nervousness, as they tore at clothes unsuited to the scrub. The land's improductiveness, the sheer distances, directed each day as they crossed it like ants, each step vital to some private, individual plan or dream. But it was not a dream; the alternatives were too often basic—to go on or to turn back. Even that decision was dictated by the nearest point at which water could be found. For what alternative did a newcomer in those days have if he found himself several hundred miles up-country with only a horse and a tent and a handful of sovereigns tucked into a money belt?[13]

This is not a chronicle of supermen. It is the unvarnished tale of the trials and struggles and successes of a group of human beings who came from all walks of life, whose failings and virtues were as inseparable from their nature as was their courage to start a new life. They were not necessarily avaricious or cruel; some were land hungry but above all they were opportunists. Their belief in themselves, their certainty that what they were creating was right—this was unshakeable. Their ideal is reflected in an extract from a speech made by the President of the United States, Theodore Roosevelt, in Nairobi in 1909. His opinion both flattered and encouraged the pioneer. 'You young people are doing a great work of which you have every right to be proud. You have brought freedom where there was slavery. You are bringing health where there was disease. You are bringing food where there was famine. You are bringing peace where their was continual war. Be proud of yourselves, for the time is coming when the world will be proud of you.'[14]

But Roosevelt was not quite right; the years passed, then with ever increasing virulence the settlers were told that they were merely exploiting that which was not theirs and that the Africans were the real owners of the country. They were puzzled and hurt by this attitude. When Cranworth wrote in 1958, 'this is the most outstanding change that I have seen in the fifty years, and I find it as unpleasant as it is unexpected'[15] his was the reaction of the majority. They had been proud, self-respecting people genuinely involved with their contribution to the building of an empire and they felt no need to apologise, whether they were raising the Union Jack, issuing medals for patriotism and bravery or meting out flogging for punishment.

CHAPTER 2

Somewhere in Africa . . .

Love heeds not caste,
Nor sleep a broken bed,
I went in search of love
And lost myself.
A Hindu Proverb

Dr Henry Albert Boedeker and his bride sailed from Tilbury on 6 June 1896 bound for Mombasa; beyond their decision to leave Scotland, they had decided little except that they hoped to make a home 'somewhere in Africa'.

By the end of August they had docked at Mombasa and on 3 September Mrs Boedeker wrote in her journal: 'Found Europeans in Mombasa very hospitable and friendly; on the whole we had quite a gay time. We started our march up-country, having a good number of porters and having 20 donkeys waiting for us at Mazeras. There to join the McQueens; enjoying tent life immensely so far . . .'[1]

The white ants have chewed through most of Mrs Boedeker's diary with her descriptions of the adventures that followed, as they have consumed so many records of the early lives of the pioneers. 'Silver fish' by tens of dozens have added their quota of destruction. The voracious appetite of both insects is answerable for the disappearance of letters, journals, documents, photograph albums and even floorboards and foundations of old houses. White ants relished the flour and water paste with which wall-paper was applied and managed to consume the entire backing unnoticed to leave only a brittle façade. The few pages from Mrs Boedeker's journal to survive give odd clues as to what the historic safari entailed but there is little to indicate that she was different from any other newly married white woman setting out on an adventure with her partner for life. In her reference to their welcome from the Europeans in Mombasa however lies an inaudible sigh of relief, for while she was the daughter of a knight, not only was her husband a Parsee by religion, he was Eurasian by birth, small in stature and his skin was almost black.

McQueen were newly married too and the three-hundred-
walk ahead of them was part of their honeymoon.[2]

r was planning to farm as far as possible from the stigma of
l. He had studied, trained and qualified as a doctor at Glasgow
d it was here that he fell in love with his wife, the daughter of Sir
law of Tillicoultry. Their relationship was considered scandal-
question of a permanent union even more outrageous. He spoke
Engl... eccably but neither the fact that this was one of his most attractive
qualities or his medical expertise had had any palliative effect on the
disapproval.[3]

Just as they were searching for a chance to start a new life, an article
describing Kikuyu country as a land flowing with milk and honey appeared in
a British newspaper and this convinced them that they should emigrate to the
British East African highlands. They set about ordering large quantities of
'candles, matches, soap and tinned goods', and a 'great deal of clothing' for
Mrs Boedeker who was almost painfully aware of her clothes and
appearance.[4]

Tips for the uninitiated going to British East Africa at the turn of the
century included a stern warning to travellers against alcohol and a caution
against taking 'innumerable boxes of bloaters' because, being too much in
harmony with the African sun, they would not do the liver any good.
Dickeson and Stewart of Victoria Street in London were highly recommended as advisers on safari provisions who could be relied upon to dispatch
everything 'according to instructions', whilst tents and camp furniture could
be 'procured from Benjamin Edgington, Duke Street—most obliging.'[5]

The dangers of the sun could not be emphasised enough. Wool was the
watchword for all who valued health because it was difficult 'for the Britisher
to believe that the sun was here before him . . . Men who indulged in the
luxury of walking out in a cricket cap and swagger dinner shirt that has often
seen mutton but never wool, (sic) . . . put missionary societies, business
houses and Government Departments to needlessly premature funeral
expenses.'[6]

Mary McQueen and Mrs Boedeker did not have the benefit of such advice,
being two of the earliest women to travel to British East Africa. Mary
McQueen was a practical Scotswoman, who later made her children's clothes
from old flour-bag linings. But Mrs Boedeker was a romantic creature, a
different type entirely. Her boxes contained a large variety of hats, not of the
protective sort, but wide-brimmed and small, trimmed with osprey and
veiling to match a selection of gowns in the high fashion of the day. None was
suited to travelling in the bush but she was one of those women who kept up
standards despite everything. Into her cabin trunks in 1896 went piles of
exquisite laces, velvets, silks and muslins; the high-necked dresses with
leg-of mutton sleeves were without doubt quite unbearable for marching
along in the dust and the heat.[7]

Within ten years a classic safari outfit for women emerged which, if just as hot as Mrs Boedeker's, was more sensible and was made from a heavy, thorn-proof material with a red thread interwoven to keep out the air and protect the body from the rays of the sun. The best—from Burberry—were already fitted with spine pads and consisted of a coat, tailored blouse and a divided skirt under which breeches and high leather boots were worn.[8]

Dr Boedeker had been more perceptive as to their needs than his frivolous bride. His luggage included a mould-board plough, so called because of the curved plate which turned the furrow and the first, as far as is known, to arrive in British East Africa. They sailed on the s.s. *Goorka*, a slow boat which called at every port for food and water. Sheep and cattle were bought in Mediterranean markets, taken aboard and slaughtered when required. At Aden, the Boedekers transhipped to the s.s. *Goa* when, after the excitement of seeing flying fish for the first time, 'a frightful passage' ensued. They were relieved to come ashore at Mombasa.

Few who arrived by ship ever forgot their first impression of it for nature has ensured that the approach to Mombasa would never be less than beautiful from the sea. Time and development have failed to alter its impact. Once ashore, despite the stink of dried fish and the humidity, Mrs Boedeker felt that she had arrived at the Garden of Eden.[9]

The ship first had to pass through the *mlango*, an opening in the coral reef which, treacherous though it was to craft, also protected the waters within from sharks. The enchantment began as the ship turned south west and approached the atoll towards what today is the Old Harbour. Here the black-ringed lighthouse on Ras Serani Point could be seen against a backdrop of brilliant but natural colour. Beyond sparkling clear waters in every shade of blue, lush green foliage was lit by the sun. Gigantic and legendary baobabs, for the greater part of the year their purplish branches unclad, provided a dramatic contrast to this humid vegetation and the feathery palms surrounding them. In the distance, what appeared to be a spick and span Arab town edged onto the channel. A little to the right of the lighthouse stood Kilindini House,* squat, unpretentious and white. Occasionally the Union Jack flew from it, depending who was in residence. The Acting Commissioner and his wife, Mr and Mrs Crauford, occupied it in 1896.[10] Towering beyond were the pink battlements of Fort Jesus built by the Portuguese between 1593 and 1595. It had seen many battles and bloody sieges. Scarlet, unequivocal against the blue sky from the highest bastion of the Fort, the flag of the Sultan of Zanzibar provided a constant reminder that the island of Mombasa and the entire strip of coast ten miles inland, though held by the British, were under lease from Sultan Barghash.

The old Arab houses of stout, irregularly shaped walls with flat roofs were ever pleasing to the western eye. They stood at least three storeys high with shutters barred against the sun. Clustered together and divided by a network of sewage-gutters and courtyards the houses provided welcome channels of

---

* Later Government House until Independence in 1963.

shade. Two narrow alleys served the town. Of these, Vasco da Gama Street was the main thoroughfare and led up an incline from the wharf. The only other that could be called a street was known as Ndia Kuu.

Two Government buildings existed then—the European Hospital standing where it has always stood—and a small bungalow at the lighthouse itself, occupied by Captain Pidcock, the first Port Officer. The Court buildings were near the Fort and there was also a small wood-and-iron house in which Mr Powter, the first Treasurer, lived.[11]

The famous Mombasa Club in the shadow of the Fort Jesus was already under construction and opened the following year. Its forerunner was functioning in 1896 and consisted of two rooms above Mr M. R. da Souza's shop in Ndia Kuu. The mess occupied one, a bar and a billiard table the other. The proprietors were Messrs Boustead and Ridley, general merchants who had run their business in Zanzibar for 18 years before coming to Mombasa in 1892. The Boustead brothers were already old hands compared with most of the Europeans living in Mombasa and London firms recommended them as chief suppliers of porters, head men, brass wire, beads and other trade goods to ensure newcomers a peaceful journey up-country.

The six-week safari for travellers on foot was an endurance test for all. Originally there were eight in the Boedeker party intending to walk to Fort Smith.* Besides Mary and James McQueen, who was a blacksmith from Dumfriesshire, were two Wallace brothers, (one was a doctor) and their wives. The bulk of the expedition had been financed by Dr Boedeker and the Wallaces but at Mombasa, when Dr David Wallace's wife fell sick, this pair abandoned the project and returned home. Subsequently the other Wallaces went ahead of the rest of the party and reached Machakos on 23 September, where they stayed with John Ainsworth, then the Sub-Commissioner of Ukamaba.

Some weeks later along the same cayenne-coloured path flanked by tropical vegetation, the Boedekers trudged uphill towards Mazeras where they collected their donkeys and joined the McQueens. On the way they witnessed the packing-up and transportation of the now famous s.s. *William MacKinnon.*[12]

Named after the founder of the Imperial British East Africa Company,** Sir William MacKinnon, it had been built in the shipyards of Great Britain, broken down and shipped piecemeal to Mombasa. It was now on the point of being carried 500 miles to Uganda by human porterage. In 1935 Dr Boedeker described this incident in a series of lectures about his first experiences in the country that he gave at the McMillan Memorial Library.*** His observations, though brief, are interesting because what he was witnessing was the setting-up of a caravan that was unique, though he did not realise it at

---

* A tiny frontier garrison in Kikuyuland, named after its first commandant, Major Smith; it was the next stopping place after Machakos on the caravan route to Uganda.
** See Chronology.
*** Built to commemorate a wealthy American pioneer Sir Northrup McMillan by his wife.

the time. The s.s. *William MacKinnon* was a small steamer, destined for the Uganda Protectorate . . .' James Martin, an illiterate Portuguese, was in charge of recruiting the porters and at his camp at Kilindini overlooking the Makupa ferry could be seen an extraordinary collection of various parts of the steamer, including heavy iron plates which were to be carried on stout poles with two porters at each end. After leaving Rabai, however, the unwieldy loads of steel plates utterly defeated the porters who dumped them by the wayside. In later years, when the *William MacKinnon* was completed, she had to be almost wholly duplicated with a new outfit from 'home'.[13]

'Home', meaning Great Britain, was a word to which the pioneers would cling no matter how many houses they built or harvests they reaped from African soil and it was part of Colonial jargon. The persistence with which the word was used seemed almost to offer a tacit escape route by which, if things went too badly wrong, they could return, and the practice of sending children, especially sons, 'home' to boarding school, caused much hardship and affected an entire generation, subjected to long separations for 'their own good'. Few partings were as difficult as those for a mother sending her children to Europe to be educated. They might not meet again for four years after which they were like strangers to one another and often the children were misfits in Europe too. In these protracted absences they became sick at heart. They were always being foisted on to relatives who, though well-meaning, could not understand what their charges pined for. Not having been born in Africa, let alone visited it, how could they know that their nephews and nieces felt deprived of freedom. That the wearing of shoes and heavy winter clothes was like a form of imprisonment; that the sight of fences after open plains offended them or that they craved the warmth of the sun on naked limbs. They felt trapped, like wild animals suddenly caged. Later, those who had experienced it swore never to put their own children through the ordeal.

But if Britain was referred to broadly and often as 'home', almost as if to redress the habit, newcomers soon began to use Swahili words in place of simple English words and phrases not only when speaking but in the written language too. Diaries and letters 'home' were peppered with expressions picked up as 'kitchen' Swahili was learned from the Africans. Illustrating this point, Mrs Boedeker shortly wrote in her diary that, 'Mr Francis Hall, the District Commissioner at Fort Smith lent me a *Suferia*—a little beauty with a cast-iron lid, in which I can makes cakes nicely.'[14] *Suferia* is Swahili for pan, which would have been quicker to write but the Swahili language has a music of its own. It appeals to the European under the spell of Africa and is one way of becoming part of, closer to it. Such words as *chai* meaning tea, *kuku* for fowl, *kuni* meaning wood or *duka* for shop (which was borrowed from the Indian coolies) once adopted remained in the vocabulary for life. In many ways Swahili words simplified things. Children grew up, safe in the knowledge that all they had to say to the *ayah*, their African nanny, was *dudu* for insect, whether referring to a harmless sugar-ant or a scorpion found in the dust in which they had been playing.

The crossing of the Taru desert, as Joseph Thomson the explorer had discovered, was the most arduous part of the Boedekers' and McQueens' safari. Temperatures here reached over 100 degrees F and, being waterless, there was no need to stray from the dusty path in order to perish. Without due precaution it was easy to die of thirst alone. It was also strangely quiet with few birds apart from the hornbill whose desolate note, so often heard in the waterless wastes of Africa, drifted across the dry scrub. Every drop of water had to be carried across a route that all the caravans had dreaded and avoided if possible. Thomson described its featureless miles in his book, *Through Masai Land* published in 1885: 'a "skeleton" forest. Weird and ghastly is the aspect of greyish-coloured trees and bushes . . . The wind . . . raised only a mournful whistling or dreary croaking, "eerie" and full of sadness, as if it had said, "here is all death and desolation."'[15]

Years later when Mary McQueen's children begged her to describe this safari she usually recalled the joy of reaching Kibwezi where a small river ran cold from the mountains, the relief of dangling her stockingless feet in the water and of how she carried their father part of the way after he had sprained his ankle. Fortunately she was strong and, being six feet in height, taller than her husband. She explained how she cooked their meals on a piece of flat iron perched on three stones. Tinned meats and pigeons varied their diet from freshly-killed goat, which Mrs Boedeker described as 'tough enough in all conscience'. Mary McQueen never talked much about the problems of the walk. Yet, as if crossing almost fifty miles of the vicious bush thorn was not enough, the party was harassed by petty thieving in the Taru as well. Food and blankets were stolen and, to her husband's outrage, his cut-throat razor disappeared with them. He was a quick-tempered man and swore in his fit of anger, that he would never shave again. Nor did he for his remaining forty years and in Nairobi where men were more often bearded men than not in the early days, McQueen was easily distinguishable from the rest by his waist-length black beard.[16]

Dysentery next afflicted the small cavalcade. The Europeans recovered but many of their porters died from it. The loss meant that the two Muscat donkeys which had been purchased for the women to ride now had to be used to carry loads instead. Other porters defected after they had been paid in advance.

For Mary Wallace and Mary McQueen in particular, the historic journey across those blistering miles of heat in 1896 was an exercise of great fortitude because they were both expecting babies. Mrs Wallace was seven months pregnant when she arrived at Machakos.[17]

There has always been confusion as to who was the first white child born in Nairobi. Some argue that it was the Wallaces' son, others that it was one of the McQueen children. The discrepancy in these claims seems to lie in the location of their births in relation to that of the town and its growth. One must remember that Nairobi did not exist except perhaps in the eyes of the Maasai at that time. Francis George Kikuyu Wallace was the first white child to be born at Fort Smith, now known as Kabete, in December 1896. He was named after the tribe which predominated the area as well as after District Commissioner Hall,* who happened to be posted to Fort Smith at the time. John McQueen's birth followed and, like his five brothers and sisters, he was delivered by his blacksmith father. But it is Jean McQueen, the first daughter who, by virtue of being born at Pangani in November 1899, has generally earned the distinction of being the first white child to be born in Nairobi itself even though her arrival was three years after the two boys.[18]

Whilst these first settlers were making their way up-country the rail track was being bullied from the land. It was hacked and blasted into existence and began slowly, winding its way over ravines from Mazeras to the Rabai escarpment two thousand feet up. Survey and construction advanced more or less together and, though they were impeded by great difficulties, at times the builders were in danger of overtaking the map-makers. A more precarious means of constructing a railway could hardly have been devised. The engineers, George Whitehouse, J. H. Patterson and Ronald Preston were the best known men in charge of this feat. The first four or five miles represented in reality a second attempt, that is, up to Mazeras. Here, signifying earlier defeat, the upturned ends of a smaller set of railway lines protruded from the red earth.[19] It was all that was left of the narrow-gauge Central African Railway which the Imperial British East Africa Company had attempted to build.

The Uganda Railway construction trains rumbled their way up to Mazeras and back, shuttling the labour force imported from India to and fro. When Africans showed no interest in or aptitude to the work labourers had been brought in from Bombay by the thousand. The trucks were crammed with clerks, carpenters, masons, draftsmen and coolies who created squalid camps as they progressed towards the highlands. Hovering among the dhoti-clad workers, bearing shovels, mattocks and the inevitable bed-roll were the camp followers, prostitutes and small boys, their eyes furtive, greedy, always focused on the main chance.

The Indians' contracts registered the condition that they must be given the opportunity to remain in the country on completion of the railway if they wished. But it stipulated too that if they did so they forfeited their return passage to Bombay. In December 1901, when the line at last reached the lake, only a handful of them settled in British East Africa. Out of a total of 31,983, only 6,794 stayed. It is a wonder that even those few remained, for the track was not built without considerable loss to life or good health; 2,493 died during construction and over 6,000 were permanently invalided.

Since the problems of citizenship of the Indian community in general

---

* Ironically, five years later Francis Hall gave his name to Fort Hall where in the course of administrative duty he died of blackwater fever. Fort Hall is today known as Marunga.

would raise so much acrimony in Kenya and Britain years later, it is as well to remember that without their help, their sweat, their fear for loss of life through lions, dysentery, malaria and septicaemia, without their particular skills as artisans the construction of the railway at that time could never have taken place. And British East Africa, as will be seen, owed its birth to the Lunatic Line.

It was not an easy birth. The coolies may have been familiar enough with dysentery and malaria, plague, cholera and even heat but they had not encountered lack of water or man-eating lions before. Nor had they met the tiny pestilential 'chiggers' or jiggers—Latin name *Pulex irritans*—which often so damaged toes that they had to be amputated, and lame men got no pay for the days they did not work. The jigger was no respecter of class, creed or colour. It needed little introduction, once newcomers had been in the country for more than eight weeks. Sir Albert Cook, the famous missionary doctor, on his journey to Uganda a month after Dr Boedeker's party, came across jiggers at Machakos for the first time. Later he recalled, 'we were to know its terrible ravages very well in Uganda where it left a trail of gangrene toes and ulcerated feet . . .'

The first sign of infection is a terrible itching in one or more of the toes. Closer examination reveals a fine black dot in or near the edge of the nail. Careful insertion of a large sterilised needle would dig out a tiny sac or capsule full of eggs. But it was seldom as easy as that, and as most Europeans were to discover, the Africans were wonderfully skilled at dealing with them: 'care must be taken not to burst this sac; native boys are often very expert at this job and save one the agonising efforts to extract it oneself. A drop of pure carbolic on the end of a wooden match dropped into a tiny pit left, will then safely end matters but if the capsule is burst by rough extraction and the eggs are scattered over the little wound, suppuration will follow and perhaps serious ulceration.'[21] Jiggers, favoured by drought and dusty conditions, became so prevalent in Nairobi and Kiambu in 1906[22] that, as a precaution against them, the white pioneers held daily 'jigger parades'.[23]

In *Permanent Way*, Mervyn Hill wrote that 'it seemed as if the very spirit of Africa resented the intrusion of the railway', which does not seem to be too sweeping a claim, for Africa's climate and topography appeared to be in control of every advance.[24] Drought was one problem. The long rains were another; they washed away newly built viaducts and bridges; the downpours were torrential and the air became so humid that it fostered perfect conditions in which putrefaction and amoebic dysentery could spread. The official rainfall for the coast in the month of November 1896 came to 27½ inches.[25] There are years when the short rains emphasise their arrival in no uncertain terms and these continued until the end of January 1897.

Here was a prime example of the unpredictability of Africa. Not only should the rains have been lighter, they should have ceased by the end of December. The drenched Indians in their equally drenched tents waited for them to stop; they only did eighteen days of work that November. During the other twelve, not a fishbolt could be secured, nor a rail laid, nor even a sleeper put on to the sodden ground. And in the puddles which were more like ponds, the mosquitoes began to breed; outbreaks of malaria followed. By Christmas, over five-hundred workers were immobilised through disease.[26]

When the rains stopped, the fierceness of the sun took over and brought thirst. From mile 38 to Voi River, there was not a drop of water for the best part of sixty miles, and the coolies required 10,000 gallons daily for their needs. Waterholes in which catchments of rain had stood for months contained little better than slime. To make it drinkable the Indians soon taught the others the trick of straining this unhealthy ooze through turbans. Animals and men alike suffered from drought; that was exceptional too and lasted for three years.[27]

In 1899 Dr Boedeker enjoyed, for the first time, the luxury of riding in a goods train. (He had walked everywhere since his arrival.) Railhead had reached Kibwezi by then and on his way to the coast he met Dr Rose, the medical officer in charge there, who told him how the petrified labour force were haunted by the likelihood of being taken by a man-eater during every darkened hour. The lions played havoc in the railway camps.[28] The knowledge that nothing but thin canvas lay between themselves and death from 'devil-lions' deprived the labourers of rest for months. Twenty-eight Indians perished in their jaws, and the African victims, said to be well over a hundred, at a conservative estimate, were never even accounted for.[29] One European superintendent on the railway, C. H. Ryall, was devoured by a lion that leapt into the carriage which the man shared with two others, dragging him from it at night.[30] One of Ryall's companions, Parenti, who was a trader and Italian Vice-Consul at Mombasa, tried to fight it off while the other, Huebener, could do little but watch. Paralysed with fear himself he had no room to manoeuvre let alone escape.[31]

Though they did not apparently encounter any man-eaters, it was with some relief that the Boedekers and McQueens entered Kikuyu country in October 1896. They were footsore after the miles they had covered, not to mention the discomfort, hardship and toil the pioneer women had endured. How welcome was the surrounding country, so fertile and green after the bleached thorn desert where the heat parched the throat and foxed the mind with mirages of lakes beyond. The cool wooded patches were balm to them, after the miles of grassy Athi Plains where, for all the abundance of wildlife, it was not easy to find shade from the diamond light. Dr Cook, who marched up-country behind the Boedekers and McQueens, mentions some of the discomforts: 'our khaki knickers and shorts were torn to ribbons by wait-a-bit thorns, and our boots had the very soles slashed and half torn off, by walking over sharp and jagged rocks . . . Happy were those, who, with a fine and infectious courage, made light of their troubles.'[32]

At Fort Smith, the sun was less consuming. The mornings were dewy with promise, the trees gave real shade, their leaves diffused the sunlight in dapples which were more in keeping with the Victorian notion of summer, and the evenings, if brief, were restful and cool. At night it was cold enough for a fire.

On the march, their fires had been built for cooking on three stones but were also essential for warding off predators. Travellers found little comfort either as they glimpsed a silver-backed jackal whilst gathering kindling at dusk. It suggested that they might be being stalked. People soon learned that what the lion shunned, the hyena scavenged leaving the bones to be picked clean by jackals and vultures.

In European terms, at Fort Smith, travellers came upon the first proper house to be built up-country. It had been designed by Captain Eric Smith after whom the Fort was named. It was thatched and the brick walls were of local clay which were fired in a kiln Smith had made in 1892. This station was considered one of the loneliest of the thirty-five staging posts between the coast to Uganda. In those days it was said that to walk 200 yards from the door invited certain death.[33]

Despite its reputation quite a little community of Europeans was already established there by the time that the Wallaces, Boedekers and McQueens arrived. Francis Hall was largely responsible for making it a safer place, succeeding in getting the Maasai and Kikuyu on to reasonably peaceful terms here, and planting a tree to commemorate the pact. Within several hundred yards of the 'Peace Tree', Kikuyu grazed their cattle now and a food depot and camping ground had been set up for the Boustead and Ridley caravans. Opposite them but a little farther up on the other side of Captain Sclater's newly widened road to Uganda*, stood Smith MacKenzie's trading depot which was being run by a man called Trefusis.[34]

Temporarily responsible for building and running the Boustead and Ridley outfit was an Irish woman with hair as red as the soil of Kikuyu, a temper to match, and her second husband, John Walsh. Mary Walsh gained notoriety with Europeans and Africans for her ferocious nature. To the white people she was 'Pioneer Mary' but it was her Swahili name that evoked her character. The Africans called her 'Bibi Kiboko' on account of the rhino-hide whip she always carried and never hesitated to use if she was crossed.

One wonders what Mrs Boedeker thought of this fiercely energetic woman, reputed to be the first female pioneer in Rhodesia as well as one of the earliest in British East Africa.[35] Her dress was as unorthodox as her attitudes; usually she wore men's puttees, and in her skirts she concealed a pearl-handled revolver. In her strong Irish accent, she said to her friends, 'Put on my gravestone that Africans and keys caused my death'[36] but when she died in 1922 she was buried in an unknown spot. In the course of her life she ran

---

* Captain B. L. Sclater was appointed to make the road to Kedong, a distance of 130 miles, when the Foreign Office decided instead to extend the road from the coast which terminated at Kibwezi. Sclater had had considerable experience in Nyasaland and selected his team of assistants from the men who had served with him there. His second-in command was Lieutenant G. E. 'Uganda' Smith and he also chose five NCOs of the Royal Engineers. These were Corporal Ellis, 2nd Corporal Clarke and Lance Corporals Smith, Simmonds and Brodie. Work on the road began in 1895 and was completed in about 18 months, something of a record—even for a road of earth construction—in those days. A fraction of it, running through the modern suburb of Westlands, is still in existence on the outskirts of Nairobi today.

dairies, tea-rooms, raised and traded cattle, set up bakeries, built trading stores and trekked up and down the country running a transport business with donkeys and trading with the Africans. It was she who built the house at Naivasha which later became the Bell Inn.[37] In a way she was the female counterpart of the Yorkshireman, John Boyes, who appointed himself King of the Wakikuyu.

Mary Walsh left Ireland as a bride of seventeen to go with her first husband to the Australian outback. They intended to sheep-farm and, like all those who sought a fortune, hoped to find it in the goldfields of Western Australia.[38] Far from making money, fate dealt her poverty and sadness. In twelve years, she lost her husband and their two children, one died from a snake bite and the other drowned. Next she moved on to try her luck in Rhodesia where she met John Walsh, whose wanderlust matched her own. They trekked up to British East Africa together. Possibly the Australian, Tom Deacon, another resident at Fort Smith, arrived with them. Certainly all three were at Kikuyu in 1896. It was Tom Deacon and John Walsh who, early in 1902, pegged and acquired mining rights to Lake Magadi but towards the end of the year they transferred their interests to the East African Syndicate Ltd, in return for 20% of any net profits which might be obtained by the sale or working of soda deposits. The East African Syndicate had spent more than £39,000 in prospecting for minerals in British East Africa and every expedition had proved disappointing. On 22 November Walsh transferred all their rights and interests at Kisumu, to Commerell M. Cowper Coles, a mining engineer, 'for and in consideration of the sum of £15.00'. He was giving away a fortune. Five days later, by Indenture, registered at the Department of Lands, Cowper Coles transferred the interests to the East Africa Syndicate who had both the knowledge and funds to exploit its possibilities. Lake Magadi proved later to be an inexhaustible supply of soda worth millions of pounds. It is still supplying the world with soda today.[39]

However the willingness to gamble is inseparable from pioneering and, to Mary and John Walsh and their partner Tom Deacon, risk was a way of life. Unencumbered by the chattels of comfort they were at liberty to please themselves, always free to move and to trade when opportunity and necessity presented itself. 'Pioneer Mary' was small and weatherbeaten from the miles she had travelled on foot and by the time she was thirty as tough as the *kiboko* she brandished. She sold handkerchiefs, mirrors and combs, oranges, bananas, eggs or cooked chickens to anyone who would buy them; she changed her occupation according to the profit to be made. Sometimes she just drank; from time to time she was given to wild, drunken binges, perhaps to blot out the pain of recollection of the loss of her children. When this happened, she kept the bars open and amused her companions by riding her mule sitting back-to-front.[40]

Her more disorderly escapades brought officials to her door but she did not give a fig for the constabulary. If she was served with a summons, she would tear it up, sending the poor askari off with a thwack of her *kiboko* for good measure.[41] John Walsh seems to have been overshadowed by his wife; when they were not working together he went on quietly trading cattle and goats between Kikuyu, Machakos and Kibwezi.[42]

Tom Deacon started without capital and lost whatever he had managed to make several times over. His first land, near Donyo Sabuk, was acquired through settlement of a gambling debt that had been incurred two hundred miles away. Before accepting it in lieu of the £10 he was owed in a card game, he had trekked up-country to inspect it. In the course of fifty years it was transformed from uncultivated bush into a valuable coffee farm but his daughter was the person who benefited. Deacon hardly made a penny[43] but, in 1950 Florrie Deacon, who ran the farm after her father's death, refused an offer of £250,000 for Mutuu Estate. The same story could be told over and again by many of the pioneer families. The struggle to achieve the worth of that piece of land took Tom Deacon all his life. He tried raising pigs to begin with but they all died of swine fever; next he experimented with wheat. Marketing proved virtually impossible, and harvesting was as bad owing to the incursion in the district of game which trampled every crop. He started to plant coffee when it was still in its experimental stage and this, after five years of husbandry, produced a promising yield. In the end, it was what he concentrated upon and developed. Ultimately his farm became one of the finest plantations in the country and after Independence became the property of the late President Kenyatta.[44]

The acquisition of huge tracts of land was to cause bitter contention between those literate Africans who had grown up accustomed to coinage and their contemporaries, the adult children of the white pioneers. The Africans were convinced that their fathers and the Chiefs had been tricked, that the farms, by then vastly different from virgin bush, were on virtually stolen land, that no payment had taken place at all. This was not true. The formalities, if seen as unorthodox by later generations of Africans who by then had been schooled in European ways, were nevertheless appropriate to the time and were concluded to the satisfaction of the Chiefs. Matters were strictly observed under the supervision of District Officers, in this instance, Francis Hall.[45]

According to Dr Boedeker, for example, Smith MacKenzie was the first company to 'purchase' land from Africans under Government approval. Those Kikuyu involved were consulted with regard to the price for the land and asked to be paid in cattle and trade goods rather than money, which represented less value in 1896; there was no question of coercion to bring this transaction into force. The land in question was inspected by both buyer and seller in front of Mr Hall. The natives specified exactly what they wanted in exchange for the land, the boundaries were agreed and finally deeds of purchase were drawn up and witnessed by Mr Hall at Fort Smith in the hut that served as his office. The Chiefs made thumbprints in lieu of signatures. The question of signing the papers never arose because the Africans were illiterate still. After completion, the documents were sent to John Ainsworth at Machakos for registration.[46]

It was the same story three months afterwards, when Dr Boedeker approached Chief Kinyanjui for land upon which he could build a house and start to farm. Rumour has it that Kinyanjui was not born a Chief. He was a crafty old man with a fine manner and much greatness to him and allegedly the English had made him a Chief when they could no longer get on with the legitimate ruler in that district. It is not beyond the bounds of possibility that Kinyanjui's reputation as a co-operative man stems from his transaction with Dr Boedeker, for he was offered not one but the choice of three plots and Kinanjui insisted on giving it to him.[47] It is not unreasonable to suppose that this gesture was made out of gratitude rather than generosity, perhaps in return having saved the life of one of Kinyanjui's sick relatives. Boedeker was known by the Africans as 'Daktari Kabisa'[48] meaning a doctor through and through, and Kinyanjui would have respected his skills, bearing in mind that he was as black as himself yet manifested all the traits of a white man including marriage to a European. But Francis Hall warned Dr Boedeker against accepting this gift, and Kinyanjui agreed to trade the land, specifying that he wanted eight bales of *americani*, unbleached calico, as well as four head-loads each of beads and brass wire and the sum of five pounds.[49]

Like so many of the pioneers, the doctor and his wife built their first house in the Kikuyu style. It included the use of fig-tree branches, about which the tribe is highly superstitious. Within the simple mud hut the three 'mugumu' staves took root and sprouted. Fifty years later at the Veterinary Department, Kabete, long after 'Harvey Hill' had crumbled, the exact spot was identifiable by three immense wild fig-trees growing closely together.[50]

Now the mould-board plough with which Dr Boedeker broke the ground for the first time was demonstrated for Chief Kinyanjui's benefit by Francis Hall. Those Kikuyu who were present had never seen anything like it and, in the doctor's words, were 'incredulous at their first sight of oxen turning over the soil.'[51]

Before the white men had shown otherwise, the *'ngombe'*—a cow or bullock, had been a provider of meat, skins and milk or, in the case of the Maasai, of blood which is taken from the jugular vein, mixed with milk and drunk. The animal could be used for trading purposes or its hide could be tanned. Or perhaps its worth shown as a bride-price or to ascertain a man's social standing but never had they thought that a bullock could replace the *jembe*, an African hoe. An even more outstanding event on the same theme was to follow in the October of 1897, when a man called Feltham reached Fort Smith from Mombasa with two Cape wagons loaded up with trade goods and provisions for Messrs Smith MacKenzie. These were the first wagons to arrive in the country from South Africa and with them Feltham brought eighty cattle and a number of Cape boys, efficient and experienced in the running of wagons and the training of huge teams of oxen, for which the Boers were renowned.[52] It was to the South Africans and Boers in the widespread community that the English would turn for supplies of trained oxen and advice on inspanning when white settlement quickened after 1904, for they had had no experience of handling teams themselves, but unfortunately Feltham's cattle fell victim at Kikuyu Station to rinderpest.

The rhythm of the country changed with the arrival of the wheel in British East Africa. Before long, rolling stock would be making full use of the shining, new track, easing transport facilities beyond recognition. Hitherto, the shortage of porters, due to the fact that the railway authorities had commandeered the greater number of them, delayed the progress of Europeans travelling up-country, sometimes for weeks. Safari supplies, at that time, were calculated to last for three years at least.[53] This meant that caravans were cumbersome for individuals and disproportionately long for their actual needs on the safari.

But if the wheel eased the passage of the white man, it was a revelation in itself to the African who had never seen wagons, bicycles or wheelbarrows before. The first rickshaws were brought in by Dr Cook in 1896: 'prams or miniature hansom cabs, two-wheeled, with little cushioned seats'.[54]

After Boedeker had broken and cleared enough ground at Kabete, he sowed the coffee beans that John Patterson of the Church of Scotland Mission had given to him when they had stopped at Kibwezi on the way up from Mombasa.[55] The first *Arabica* seeds are alleged to have been stolen from Aden in 1893, a fortunate if crafty move[56] and not the last time that the founding of an industry in the Protectorate depended on theft. In 1907, the first sisal bulbils were stolen too, from just over the border of German East Africa.[57]

Apparently, all the early coffee originated from John Patterson at Kibwezi, whose first crop fetched ninety shillings per hundredweight in Europe in 1896. Patterson presented it to the French priests of the Community of the Holy Ghost at Taita as a gift from the Scottish Mission, where the first recorded coffee was growing in 1895. Because coffee growing is a long job, the chalky white blossom heralding promise of the first crops was to be as deceptive as a mirage, as the pioneers soon learned to their cost. Patterson's harvest had been a fluke; Kibwezi proved as unsuitable for coffee growing as the Ngong area, where Karen Blixen bankrupted her company in 1931 for having stubbornly tried to fulfil a dream for seventeen years.[58]

More sensibly, Patterson abandoned efforts at Kibwezi and much, much later grew coffee at Mitubiri, where it throve.[59] He was apparently generous with the stolen seed, for he also gave coffee to Charles Kitchin, who was the first white man to grow coffee at Kikuyu and represented Smith MacKenzie's Coffee Syndicate at Donyo Sabuk.[60] Nevertheless the major credit for the founding of the coffee industry still rests with St Austin's Mission a few miles beyond Nairobi. Here the Roman Catholic fathers sold seedlings from their nursery in 1900 and it was to them the first real coffee farmers turned for plants and seed as white settlement gathered momentum. In the year 1910 these pioneer farmers managed to produce 2,239 one-hundred-and-twenty-pound bags of it. Ten years afterwards, when they had acquired a bit more knowledge of the best conditions under which coffee would grow, the annual figure had increased to 40,950 bags.[61]

In 1896 several missionaries had already pitched their tents, and within ten years there were eighteen missionary societies established in the Protectorate. The Reverend Stuart Watt, was living with his wife and several small children at Ngeleni, Machakos, close to the Government boma. In his time it was a stopping place for caravans but fifty years later Machakos would be regarded as the orchard of Kenya. Its success owed much to the missionary Watt even though he was a thorn in Ainsworth's side. It was he who planted the first fruit trees, as well as eucalyptus and black wattle, both of which had been brought from Australia where he had lived until 1893.[62]

Wattle is a member of the acacia family and is grown almost entirely for its bark which is rich in tannin. In 1912 the East African industry was thought to be one of the most promising in which to invest, comparing favourably with those of Natal and Australia. Those lucky enough to live near the railway line often secured contracts to supply the wood also as a fuel.[63] Though John Boyes believed it was he who introduced wattle still further upcountry, Watt is more likely to have grown it first because Boyes was at that time much on the move.

It was amazing that the wattle seed germinated for this was a time of drought followed by a famine known to the Africans as '*Ngaa Nere*', the great hunger. It wiped out thousands of Kikuyu, Wakamba and Maasai people and it is now believed that between 1898 and 1900 some 25,000 Africans perished from drought, starvation or smallpox. *Shambas* that had been under cultivation lapsed back into bush and misled white men into believing that no human life had existed in the area before. In Limuru and Kiambu 70% of the African population was wiped out.

Missionaries could and did bob up in the most unexpected places. Dr Arthur Donaldson Smith who preceded young Lord Delamere into the country from Berbera in 1896 had not seen a sign of human or animal life for months when a missionary appeared on the waters of the Tana; he was floating along in an African dug-out canoe, under the shade of a pink umbrella.[64] Parties of them called at Machakos and Fort Smith on their way up to Uganda as a matter of course. Their approach was heralded by the strains of such hymns as 'Onward Christian Soldiers'.[65] The women among the party were severe and dedicated creatures who in their dark uniforms looked 'unspeakably mournful.'[66] But newcomers soon learned that in pioneering countries hospitality is a necessity of life. In British East Africa it became almost as legendary as the game. Travellers brought news to those in lonely places, and whether it was good or bad it fed the minds of the isolated, possibly for months to come. The visitor asked little more than shelter for the night and perhaps a simple meal and water for washing and drinking but what he received was far beyond necessity. It was balm to the weary and as unimagined by the footsore as it was unforgettable before they went on their way.

Unexpected visits turned into social occasions. At Fort Hall, musical evenings of a sort were possible: Dr Boedeker would bring out his violin after dinner, and was accompanied by two Goanese clerks and another resident, a Captain Dugmore, who played the organ. Food here was delicious and fresh in contrast to dry, safari rations. Mrs Boedeker made meals with vegetables grown in the experimental *shamba*, and improvised to cope with quantities of guests by using washing-up basins for salads and stews. On one occasion, when her African helpers put flower-filled chamber-pots on the dinner-table, she was embarrassed but touched by their willingness to help.[67]

The year, 1897, was that of Queen Victoria's Diamond Jubilee. It was the year of the Uganda Mutiny, the time when the lions held grisly reign over the workers on the railway at Tsavo and was also when Lord Delamere set eyes upon the 'white highlands' for the first time. Jubilee celebrations were held even in this far flung corner of Queen Victoria's realm. At Machakos, the Protectorate's first race meeting marked the occasion. Every nag available was raced and afterwards 'dinner jackets and finery graced the evening'. John Ainsworth even presented a silver cup to Francis Hall, whose horse, Tempest, had beaten Dr Boedeker's mount, Sparklet. Prompted by an exhausting walk of thirty miles to attend to a sick man, Boedeker had imported a pony from Aden.[68] He had come out to farm but was constantly in demand as a doctor and it had not taken him long to realise that, with such long distances to cover, his patients were usually dead or recovered by the time he reached them. Africa reawakened a sense of immediacy and perspective in the European when it came to wounds and sickness. A man could die from a few hours of indecision or delay. Gangrene from the maulings of lions or leopards moved fast and was common then. By 1899, the Administration had asked Dr Boedeker to accompany a caravan to Uganda as Medical Officer and then offered him a permanent post which he accepted, returning to live at Naivasha until 1903. It was here, in order to save a man's life, that he once used a brake-van at the station as a temporary theatre and a hand-saw to operate.[69]

On 25 August 1897, a few weeks ahead of Delamere, a remarkable caravan arrived at Fort Smith. Trekking across the barren wastes of Somaliland from Berbera, the safari entered the cool glades beyond the Rift Valley from the north. Their large number of camels were laden with game trophies of every description but chiefly with ivory. The leaders were two young sportsmen, Lord Hartingdon's nephew Cavendish and a friend who brought tales of an active volcano at Lake Rudolf; and they also spoke of the handsome profit they expected to make in Zanzibar from their haul of ivory.[70]

Ivory, with its reward of gold, was a temptation that few could resist. Both black and white men succumbed to it. Before the turn of the century, the great elephant hunters, Arthur Neumann, Sutherland, Karamoja Bell and Bill Pickering whose names became legendary in their field, were already dedicating themselves to obtaining it. The finest ivory in the world came from the Protectorate and Zanzibar was the great centre of the trade.[71]

Although it was illicit for them to do so, a number of Administrators, as well as many pioneer settlers, took the chance of earning extra money out of a pair of tusks. In fact, by 1903 gun-running and ivory hunting were being practised in tandem successfully by an Arab trader, a fat rogue called Mohamedi bin Abdullah to whom ivory was being supplied by over a hundred ruffians like himself. His second-in-command was Juma Mkamba and their business was so lucrative that they went to great lengths to set up permanent camp a hundred miles from Mumias on the Turkwell River where they secreted a huge pile of ivory.[72]

In Zanzibar, which was easily reached by dhow, the middle-men seldom asked questions about the ivory's source. Arab, Swahili and Baluchi ivory traders journeyed to and from the northern deserts to obtain it. By the turn of the century it was fetching £1,000 per ton.

For all the profit there was genuine risk involved in bagging it. Pickering, for example, had his head torn off by an enraged bull elephant. The head was found later perfectly intact and caught in a bush not far from where his body lay. Young Cavendish almost paid with his life near Lake Rudolf where elephant were to be found in abundance. His escape is legendary. He wounded an old bull that charged as he was trying to get the cartridge home in the barrel for a second shot. Once it jammed the only alternative was to flee and as its enormous shadow overtook Cavendish, he flung himself aside. The elephant overshot him. He lay motionless but it swung round quickly; for so large an animal, an elephant is able to turn with surprising nimbleness even when wounded. It came back and prodded him with its tusks. Using incredible discipline, Cavendish managed to wriggle back under the elephant's chin so that its tusks could no longer reach him but, for twenty minutes it endeavoured to pound him with its knees. Luckily it failed to get its enemy fair and square. In the meantime a Somali 'shikari', who thought that his employer was already dead, went to fetch another rifle to finish off the wounded beast. After he had pumped several bullets into it, it moved off and dropped seventy yards away.[73] Then, to the astonishment of his Somali bearers, what they had imagined was the 'corpse' of Cavendish got up and walked away without so much as a broken bone. He was in a state of shock but after several days' rest in camp, he moved on to Eldama Ravine to tell the tale of his miraculous escape.[74] It was repeated over many camp fires to come, for in terms of kudos in the eyes of the Somali, a man who killed an elephant was worth forty men and, when he lived through an attack such as this, was almost supernatural.

Lord Delamere survived an equally close encounter with a lion. The quest for adventure and a tremendous zest for life are the qualities which drove Hugh Cholmondeley of Vale Royal, third Baron Delamere, to travel from the age of eighteen. After Eton, the red headed young man had visited Corsica after which each subsequent year brought him new horizons. He toured Australia and New Zealand and in 1890, when he came of age, decided to visit Africa. This was to be the first of five shooting expeditions to

Somaliland. He was twenty-seven when he entered the no-man's land of the north-east, unclaimed by anyone yet but later to become part of the East African Protectorate.[75] One hundred and twenty-two miles of rail track had been laid when on his third visit to Africa, he gazed first upon the land which would later become known as the White Highlands. He had trekked south-ward from Somaliland crossing a fearsome stretch of desert whose nomads were as inhospitable as the land itself. He was the fourth white man to attempt the journey but, unlike the American Donaldson Smith, Cavendish and his friend who preceded him and were merely travellers, Delamere and his companion Dr A. E. Atkinson, became pioneers.

The inclusion of the newly qualified doctor in Delamere's 1897 safari party should be explained. He had been reading for his final examination for the Fellowship of the Royal College of Surgeons, when Rowland Ward, the London taxidermists, recommended him to Lady Delamere who believed that her son would stand a better chance of surviving another expedition to Africa if she could find a companion for him, preferably a doctor. All his life Delemere was accident-prone and his boisterous nature and quick temper invited scrapes. Even as he planned the route for his 1897 trip to Somaliland he was confined to bed, recuperating from severe concussion of the spine having been thrown from his horse while hunting.[76].

Lady Delamere had every right to fear for her son. On his trip to Somaliland in 1894 he had been knocked over by a lion which charged and mauled him, gripping him by the ankle. But for the expedience and bravery of his gun-bearer, Abdullah Ashur, he would have died. To save Delamere, the Somali had thrown himself upon the lion, grasped its mane and tried to seize its tongue. The attack diverted the lion long enough for Delamere to recover his rifle and shoot it. Abdullah's arm was mauled badly too in the struggle and how either of them managed to evade gangrene and death is remarkable in itself. Delamere later attributed this to the fact that he had lain absolutely still where he had fallen, on his back, for five days, preventing the poison from spreading. His loyal Somali staff sheltered, fed and nurtured him and when he felt that he could be moved safely, they carried him on a stretcher to Berbera. He had also suffered typhoid at the beginning of the safari so that by the time he reached England he weighed only eight stone. His damaged leg was clamped into irons but it was too late to prevent a permanent limp. To disguise this he wore a blocked boot for the rest of his life.[77]

Abdullah Ashur's courageous action, when he had so much to fear, sealed Delamere's admiration for the Somali tribe. He rewarded Abdullah with a life-pension and when the Somalis came under fierce criticism later in the Protectorate it was Delamere who stood up for them. Once, when the English skipper of an Arab-owned cattle boat showed his objection to having Abdullah on board by kicking him in the face and calling him a 'nigger' Delamere knocked the man overboard.[78]

Delamere and Atkinson, with a photographer and a taxidermist, left

Berbera in December 1896 with a caravan of 200 camels laden with traditional beads, bolts of *americani*, provisions, ammunition, rifles and tents. The trading goods roped into position ensured a peaceful safari among the punitive Abyssinians. The group headed south-west, taking three months to reach Lugh.[79]

In the territory they crossed the air seemed hotter, drier and thirstier than any amount of rain could ever satisfy. It almost defied the existence of the shrubs and cacti that provided meagre shade yet somehow survived in furnace-like conditions. They halted at Lugh, an Italian trading post on a bend of the Juba River, where Delamere took stock of his supply of trade beads and *americani*. Before going any further they needed replenishing. Luckily a Captain Ferrandi who was in charge of the trading post happened to be proceeding to the coast for European leave; he suggested that Atkinson go with him and ensured a passage to Zanzibar on an Italian gun-boat. Delamere now scribbled one of his most famous notes and gave it to Atkinson to present to the manager of Cowsaji Dinshaw, a merchant in Zanzibar. In pencil he wrote, 'Kindly oblige bearer with whatever he wants up to £1,000.'[80]

It was at Zanzibar that the full impact of just how much profit was to be made out of ivory hit Dr Atkinson, a man reputed to possess great charm of manner and physique but with a nefarious streak, and in the bush there were few prying eyes to keep temptation in check.

Atkinson left Zanzibar by dhow with beads and cloth, sailing before the south-west monsoon to Brava, a voyage which took six days when the wind was favourable.[81] He and Delamere planned to push south towards Lake Rudolf, which, as Elspeth Huxley explains in *White Man's Country*, was labelled on French maps of the day as, '"Grande plaine avec des nombreuses montagnes isolees". Lake Albert was another blue blot to the west . . . with the observation: "Les elephants y sont très nombreux"'.[82]

In May 1897 they left the waterholes of El Mado[83], lying on the regular route between the north of the lake and Lugh, their camels tied jaw to tail. Laden anew with goods for barter they made for Lake Rudolf. At Marsabit, which they reached in August 1897, Atkinson shot his first elephant. There were so many to be had that he asked Delamere for extra time to hunt them. Delamere possibly welcomed the delay for he was engrossed in compiling a Swahili dictionary rather than shooting, which he had largely given up. In any case he agreed to Atkinson's request and they remained there for three weeks and the doctor shot twenty more elephant in as many days. The forty-two tusks fetched £1,100 at the Mombasa ivory auctions and he offered to contribute some of it towards the cost of the expedition.[84] But Delamere refused to accept any part of it though whether this was on moral grounds no-one can say. Perhaps he did not need the supplement. According to the observations of the British Commissioner for Uganda in 1899, Sir Harry Johnston, Lord Delamere ended up with almost £14,000 from ivory himself. Johnston was a painter and naturalist as well as an administrator and from

Uganda in 1900 wrote, 'The fact is Lord D who secured £14,000 on ivory in the Baringo District by shooting elephants with a maxim-gun, was exceedingly annoyed on returning to his old hunting ground, to find that I had created Baringo Game Reserve which was intended to preserve elephants from Lake Baringo to Lake Rudolf until such time as we were able to establish a station to control so-called sportsmen.'[85]

Delamere and Atkinson had travelled a thousand miles on the safari from Lugh to Lake Baringo, lying in the Rift Valley and separating Abyssinia from British East Africa. After camping the first night at Baringo, they were confronted in the morning by a runner bearing a letter. It read, 'Sir, Please take note that you are now on British soil. Any act of aggression on your part will be sternly resisted.' It was signed 'J. Martin'.[86] The sender was illiterate and one of the most unlikely candidates that the British East African Administration ever employed for he knew only how to sign his name. His cousin, a Goan named da Silva, had written the message. He was employed as Martin's clerk. Also, ironically enough, James Martin, as he usually signed himself, was in the thick of illicit ivory trading whilst acting as Her Majesty's Collector of the Baringo District of Uganda. That too was illegal. No member of the Administration was allowed to own land or indulge in any form of trading for personal gain. He organised a network of supplies in the Baringo territory and in the six years which he spent there it is estimated that he pocketed between £12 and 15,000 through his deals. Sir Harry Johnston and Sir Frederick Jackson put a stop to it after they caught him red-handed when he was somewhat naively using his shamba boy's hut as an ivory store. When questioned, the gardener obligingly took the officials straight to it. The only way to stop the corruption was to transfer James Martin away from the Baringo District to the Ssese Islands where no such temptation existed. Prosecution would have embarrassed everyone.[87]

Curious at the tone of the letter, Atkinson and Delamere decided to ride the fifty miles to meet the sender. To reach Ravine they had to climb the Kamasia escarpment, and it was here, with understandable disbelief, that Delamere was to discover one of the most beautiful parts of the Protectorate. The men had experienced months of shading their eyes from the glare, becoming accustomed to the monotony of stone and the muted greys of thorn and cactus in the desert. Now, in breathtaking contrast, the views that lay before them encompassed forest, lake, thicketed valley and green, moist grass where cattle might graze, evoking memories of a summer's day in Europe. As Elspeth Huxley put it, 'He saw it from the first, as a country of great latent wealth only waiting for development.'[88] His imagination imposed on the wild country before him, farms and fields planted out with grain. This wilderness contained promise. It could be changed into pasture for ranching and given the sort of geometric order in which the European eye delighted and found comfort and security. Delamere was so captivated by the magnificence and potential of the untouched land below that it inspired new ambition in him. From this point he largely abandoned his pleasure-seeking life, using his energies for his dream of converting this part of Africa into a white man's country. His faith never wavered and his allegiance to Kenya bankrupted his English estates. Delamere was the Rhodes of Kenya and the settlers followed him both politically and spiritually.

The two Englishmen spent the night with 'Bwana Martini' as Martin was known to Africans from the coast to Uganda. After his death in 1924 many Africans named their children after him.[89]

Antonio Martini had been born in 1857 and was Maltese by birth. As a sail-maker he had been to many parts of the world but, though he learned to read a compass he had never actually been a sailor. Then, in Bombay, he joined an American ship which was bound for Zanzibar. The skipper, who was part-owner of the vessel, was as much of a drunkard as his crew. Because Martini was teetotal he frequently became responsible for steering the ship. Zanzibar was sighted whilst it was in his charge. The inebriated Captain had instructed him to keep a certain course without reckoning on the tide which was then at half-flood. Nor had he taken into consideration a ship that was lying concealed in a creek on the look out for slave dhows. Luckily for Martini, the British officer and his blue-jackets saw the vessel run aground and boarded her. The officer-in-charge assessed the situation and ordered the Maltese sail-maker onto his own boat for safety. The American ship was anchored to prevent it going further aground and as the tide rose they warped her off and took her into Zanzibar.[90] Next, Martini found himself giving evidence before Naval Court, after which the authorities, fearing that Martini's ex-shipmates would cut his throat, dispatched him to Freretown, in Mombasa. Freretown was the headquarters of the Church Missionary Society. Under the Anglicised name of Martin, he became their handyman; he built houses, sank wells and cared for the s.s. *Highland Lassie*, which plied between the island and the northern mainland. In 1883 when Thomson the explorer needed an interpreter he took Martin with him on the journey that brought Thomson fame as the first white man to cross Maasailand. Thomson had already performed a remarkable journey to Lakes Nyasa and Tanganyika and now he went with Martin over Laikipia to Victoria Nyanza, discovering Lake Baringo on the way. Dr Fischer, the German naturalist, had discovered the Rift Valley and Lake Naivasha the year before.[91]

An iron constitution and Martin's devoted nursing saved Thomson from death from dysentery and fever on the Kinankop during the return journey. Though still too feeble to walk he recovered enough to travel by stretcher and, at the summit of the Rift Valley's eastern escarpment, he had himself 'held up to view this grand landscape—probably unsurpassed anywhere—and, weak and weary as I was, I surveyed the glorious panorama with infinite delight, though also with a spice of awe.' By the time the two returned to Mombasa in May 1884 they had walked three thousand miles in fourteen months.[92]

After Thomson's departure Martin began conducting caravans to Uganda. In between these safaris he acted as second-in-command to the Sultan of

Zanzibar's troops. He was enormously proud of his full-dress uniform which was stiff with braid and cord 'gymnastics', as he called them; he also wore very wide bell-bottomed trousers and a helmet with a large gold badge on the front. The effect was completed by a big curved sword with an inlaid ivory handle. Every Friday he attended the review of troops in the square at Zanzibar before the Sultan's palace and would bring up the rear as they marched off the parade ground, having blazed away many thousands of blank cartridges in a display that was extremely comical, not to say grotesque.[93] This jack-of-all trades next became an officer in the IBEA Company. His European contemporaries were Hobley, Bagge, Jackson, Ainsworth and MacKinnon and, like them, he joined the Government when the Company was taken over in 1895. It was Frederick Jackson (later Governor of Uganda) and Dr Mackinnon who taught Martin to write his signature.[94] Before he had been a civil servant for long, James Martin had risen to the rank of Collector at Ravine and was forty years old when he, Delamere and Atkinson met for the first time.

Even if his literacy had progressed no further, Martin's skills as a caravan leader were unsurpassed. His superiors recognised his ability to recruit and, more importantly, control large numbers of men and get a good day's work out of them—a more valuable asset in the bush anyway. He understood and could write numbers so that he could make records in his caravan book before he was allowed the services of da Silva. But when it came to contents— various cloths, beads, wire etc., they were represented with hieroglyphics of his very own invention, a series of noughts and crosses and pot-hooks. He was also adept at substituting words for those which he could not pronounce, and often told of how the Maasai resented Joseph Thomson's use of a theodolite about which they were most suspicious. He explained, 'It would have been all right if Mr Thomson had not insisted on using his damned hurricane light.' Because of his other qualities Martin eventually rose to the rank of District Commissioner with the full magisterial powers accorded to that post.[95]

Ironically it was not Martin's administration so much as his illiteracy which is remembered. He had a delightful way of hiding this (or so he imagined) from strangers and friends alike, particularly when he was entertaining at the Mombasa Club. The club chit system might have been created to overcome his problem. He would hand the order to his guests, saying, 'What will you drink? You write it down. I'll sign.'[96]

Now in 1897 after Martin had entertained Delamere, Atkinson and their photographer at Eldama Ravine for twenty-four hours they left for Fort Smith. They met the Boedekers and Wallaces and stayed here but Delamere seems to have pushed on alone to Machakos where he met Ainsworth on 22 September. In recording this Ainsworth wrote, 'Delamere called at 3.30 pm. He looks extraordinary. He has a leather shooting suit, all patched up etc. His behind is all sewn over with hide etc . . . his hands are bandaged . . . he looks a remarkable sight. I cannot understand why such people wander about in such a state. I am sure it cannot be any pleasure and it is, to say the least of it, not a very pleasing object lesson to the natives etc. It is curious why such people, whom I suppose have every luxury at home seem to enjoy the greatest of discomforts out here.'[97]

All of them, traders, ivory poachers, missionaries, railway employees and travellers like Delamere and Atkinson were unusually interdependent. Paradoxically the bush which separated them was the very thing that held them together. The early pioneers and administrators lived mostly alone. Few men had white female companionship or domestic ties. They were free to travel, at liberty to mock authority, to take an African girl for the night and remain as anonymous as they wished. They could pan for gold or peg for minerals or they could experiment with crops without emerging from their '*shamba*' for years. Their lives were their own to put at risk and sometimes they died as a result. The possibility that Africa would swallow them up without trace was always present; a dozen or more men vanished over the next thirty years. A few men turned into eccentrics, others became drunkards; but they cannot be dismissed as nonentities simply because they carried a rifle in one hand and a whisky bottle in the other, or were hungry for land, or because they took an African wife. Today, in Maasailand there live African traders by the name of Dick directly descended from the one white victim of the Kedong Massacre.[98]

Countless numbers of Africans overcame their instinctive distrust of the *Mzungu*, as they called the white man. (*Wazungu* being the plural.) A Swahili dictionary published in 1909 defines the word as 'one who wears European clothes' whilst another, *A Handbook of the Swahili Language* dated that same year, explains that the word means 'a strange or startling thing'. Whatever the true definition, against the wishes of the majority of their tribe, a number of Africans tried to communicate with the pale-skinned beings traversing the land with increasing frequency. But the white man was so alien a breed that many Africans were too frightened and either hid themselves or ran away at their first glimpse of a European. The primitive eye, accustomed only to seeing dark-skinned people, likened the white men to an unfinished foetus which should not yet have left the womb; the colour of their skin was unnatural and evoked some premature creature whose lack of pigment proved that it was not ready for birth. Change was as ominous to them as it was invisible and now the wheel of it had started to turn, there was no stopping it.

In July 1895, the British Government had taken over from the Imperial British East Africa Company which had administered the country since 1888; now running the country became the responsibility of the Foreign Office and it was necessary to appoint Consular Officers to attend to the requirements of British subjects living or trading there. Thus Ainsworth was one of Her Majesty's Vice-Consuls before he was made Sub-Commissioner of Ukamba. Machakos was the first inland station of the Company and one of the three places at which trading caravans could stop for long periods between the coast and Uganda. The others were at Kibwezi and Fort Smith. Expeditions involving as many as two thousand porters could purchase food at Machakos. But suddenly in 1892 Ainsworth was advised that it must be sacrificed in the name of economy. The Company's failure to attract more funds from the City to support its finances was directly responsible, but the restrictions imposed by human and animal porterage as the sole means of transport had hardly augured well for large profit margins in the first place. Ainsworth, whose bulky form bespoke a persevering nature, refused to quit his post. He had already started a garden here and preferred to carry on the work he had begun without a salary rather than abandon the half-finished Fort. Thus Machakos became the headquarters of the Ukamba Province and Ainsworth was later appointed the Chief Native Commissioner. His stubborn conviction illustrates the true spirit of the pioneer. Since his arrival in 1889 he had proven his involvement beyond the course of Company duty and his committal was as much steeped in the land as Delamere's would shortly be. To understand this one has only to read Ainsworth's personal diaries, which were written between his struggles to exert some influence over the Wakamba tribe, his efforts to lay out a garden and the interminable waits for runners to bring in news. They include such everyday occurrences as records of the seeds he planted, battles between the Maasai and Kikuyu and his expressions of relief at the fact that some missing traveller's corpse had been found. They show his courage in his bachelor solitude and his stamina, neither of which had anything to do with comfort or material gain. His garden drew admiring comments from those on their way inland. The orderly rows of peas and lettuces, cabbages and beans created a small oasis in the bush with plants that had never been seen in this part of Africa before. He managed to reap wheat and barley there, distributing the seed to all those who called in to see him on their way up-country before the railway was finished, with the result that most of the resident settlers and missionaries in the country by 1900 were eating bread made from locally grown wheat.[99]

When his consular duties were done, he recorded by the light of a Dietz lantern the minutiae of East Africa's colonial history. 'April 2nd, 1898: Laid out the first shop in the bazaar: May 9th, 1898 . . . First day that rupees were issued instead of beads and cloth and posho to the men . . . ; July 19th . . .' Haslam* killed by the Sudanese . . . he had fired all his and his askari's ammunition away . . . body very mutilated and hardly any left. October 1898: Locusts . . . Lord Delamere has been leaving his camels all along the road. There are now eight from the bridge to Bondini Camp. He should be ashamed of himself . . .'[100]

Ainsworth naturally disapproved of Delamere's lack of responsibility in abandoning his pack camels as he neared the coast and the goods for barter diminished. Transportation was notoriously difficult. Three years before,

---

* Captain A. J. Haslam, the Army Vet who was speared and killed some way from Fort Smith. His gravestone was later on J. C. Judd's farm, Kabete.

the murder of two traders, Andrew Dick and his assistant West, had crippled trading along the Uganda road.

Andrew Dick was a Scot who had come out as the IBEA Company's first Chief Accountant. After gaining experience at their expense, however, he decided he could trade more profitably on his own. Being of a querulous nature, he was unable to sustain for long good relations with anyone and when later, in 1900, Sir Charles Eliot, HM Commissioner, criticised the behaviour of some of the early arrivals, Dick was one who was largely to blame for Eliot's comment that, 'the methods of pioneers are sometimes summary and it is beyond a doubt that several tribes have become hostile to the white man merely because they have been alarmed by the conduct of unscrupulous traders.'[101]

'Trader Dick' as he was known, had been granted a five-year concession at Mumias and Ravine along the road to Uganda. This consisted of eleven plots from which he could run transport centres and with as much land adjacent to them as he could cultivate. The concession enabled Dick to work the supply of goods and victuals to caravans along the entire length of the Uganda road which was being widened and improved at that time by Captain Sclater. He was a violent man and believing, wrongly, that some members of the Nandi tribe had looted cattle from one of his caravans, retaliated by having beaten two Nandi whom he encountered at Kipkarren River. When the Nandi warriors heard of this offence, they took revenge by attacking a mail caravan and, though it was heavily armed, caused considerable loss of life.[102]

The situation was horrific. The power, the manner in which the white man conducted himself in front of Africans and the respect he commanded were considered to be of paramount importance; to the individual, in terms of unquestioned authority, it could be vital. It followed that the most worrying factor of the success of the Nandi attack was not so much the number of people they had killed as the discovery that the white man's strength was far from impervious to primitive attack, for all the ammunition he carried.

Nor were matters helped by an employee of Dick's, Peter West, who after Dick's departure had stupidly amassed his arms in front of his tent. The Nandi, watchful and as silent as the landscape which had seemed so devoid of human life, crept down the escarpment and stole them before killing him. The ensuing Nandi Expedition, a punitive campaign, was drawn out painfully over the next eleven years in an attempt to bring the Nandi to heel.

Meanwhile at Fort Smith Thomas Train Gilkison, an officer in charge, had dispatched a large caravan for Eldama Ravine, but it had gone off without a European as none had been available to take charge. This was unheard of when as many as eleven hundred porters were involved. Instead, Gilkison chose a Swahili headman whom he felt could be trusted but who, strictly speaking, was too young for the job, particularly as the porterage was unbalanced tribally. There were only one hundred and five Swahilis while the rest of the men were Kikuyu. The caravan reached its destination safely but on the return journey the porters at the rear of the column got out of hand;

they entered a *manyatta*, a Maasai village, in the Kedong Valley, stole some milk and molested some Maasai *nditos*, virgins, with whom they tried to take liberties. Next a Swahili askari shot a calf and in defence a *moran*, or Maasai warrior, speared one of the Swahilis and then all hell broke loose. Ninety-eight of the Swahili porters were killed.[103]

News of the fray and what followed reached Ainsworth on 30 November 1895, by runner from Fort Smith, who brought in Gilkison's report written four days before. Ainsworth wrote that 'The bodies are horribly mutilated, some disembowelled . . . the village reduced to smoking ruins. Gilkison . . . received information that the whole of his caravan from Ravine has been cut up by the Masai (sic) at Naivasha and he anticipated trouble with the Wakikuyu on account of them attacking the Masai at the Fort in which case he expects the Wakikuyu to attack the Fort . . . things are looking bad all round.'[104] By 2 December another runner brought news that the death toll was higher than feared. One hundred and eighteen Swahilis and nine hundred and twenty Kikuyu had perished in a clash between tribe and trader. Dick had also been slain. Despite warnings from Gilkison, not to go down by the Kedong where the *manyatta* stood, Dick had seized the chance at the outbreak of fighting to annex a few Maasai cattle for himself.[105]

As Ainsworth recorded, 'Another casualty is the death of Mr A. Dick who was killed by the same Masai . . . It appears that Dick had started on a trip up north for the purpose of trading and while encamped at the first camp after leaving Kikuyu, he met the survivors from the disaster in the Kedong and he sent back to the District Officer in Kikuyu for an escort to see him through.' This was sent and was accompanied by three Frenchmen who had been staying at Fort Smith, Monsieur Versepuit, Baron de Romans and Monsieur Sporc who had worked their way up from Kilimanjaro on a shooting expedition. After joining Dick they eventually met the Maasai and 'fired at them and managed to take a lot of cattle and donkeys with which they were returning when the Maasai attacked on all sides. During the attack Dick, with six askaris, got separated from the rest and the next time that the Frenchmen saw him was at the moment that a Masai pierced his heart from behind with a spear. They reported Dick to have died instantaneously. They were unable to recover his body and had to retreat for the Masai were coming and surrounding them in large numbers.'[106]

There had been open butchery from the point where Dick died to the foot of Mount Margaret. It became known as 'Skeleton Plain'. Sir Frederick Jackson passed along the road five weeks later and found skeletons everywhere. The dusty road was strewn with basket-work hampers and lids, stools, dressed leather garments (all loot) and small loads of *karia andus*, the white china clay with which the Kukuyu ornamented their shields and their bodies for *barazas*, or dances.

Three years later when Ronald Preston was reconnoitering for a camp site for the plate-laying gangs on the floor of the Rift Valley, and making his way through the *leleshwa*, a low and pungent shrub with silvery-green branches that grows in profusion there, he was trying to assess the ground. Suddenly his attention was caught by the sight of hundreds of ostrich eggs on the bank beyond a small stream. On closer inspection these turned out to be human skulls. These relics of the Kedong Massacre unnerved the railway builders, even though the Maasai were, by then, orderly. The men refused to move camp until Preston had obtained enough corrugated iron with which to build a tin boma, to protect themselves against the possibility of attack by the Maasai hurling spears.[107]

But by then John Ainsworth was stationed in Nairobi. He remained at Machakos until 1899 where he married Ina Scott, the daughter of an American missionary whose father, Peter Cameron Scott, headed the Africa Inland Mission near Nziu. Ten Europeans, chiefly missionaries, attended the ceremony at Machakos on 3 November 1897. The Minister was 'an exceptionally nice fellow' called Reverend Hubbard and troops flanked the pathway from the Fort gate to Captain E. G. Harrison's house where the couple had their wedding breakfast. Ainsworth and his bride had arranged to marry only the day before but, as Ainsworth commented, 'the whole affair passed off very satisfactory (sic) . . . And afterwards Mr Hattersley took some photos.'[108] Probably it was the first European wedding ceremony to be performed up-country.

The single redeeming factor to emerge from the Kedong Massacre was the friendship and trust that grew between Ainsworth and the Maasai chief, the *Laibon*, Lenana, as days of tactful and patient discussion and negotiation followed the disaster. But Lenana's negotiations with Ainsworth were misconstrued by his brother, Legalishu, a minor *laibon*. A split was created among the tribesmen because Legalishu saw Lenana's friendliness with the white man as a defection of loyalty and disapproved of it. The Maasai began taking sides, favouring one rather than the other brother. Some moved north of Ngong, others remained at Naivasha.

It took the Administration until 1904 to reach a temporary solution which, was an agreement that caused vacillation until just before the First World war. In 1904 the tribe undertook to move into two Reserves, one lying south of Ngong and the railway, the other north, upon Laikipia Plateau which were reserved 'so long as the Masai Race shall exist'.[109] The Government also promised them a half-mile wide road linking their two reserves but this never was fulfilled on account of quarantine against disease in cattle.[110]

Lenana emerged as spiritual leader over Legalishu and continued to negotiate with the Colonial Government over further Maasai moves until his death. Meanwhile Legalishu upheld the story that his brother had succeeded as *laibon* by trickery. It was said that Lenana's mother heard at the deathbed of their father Mbatian, that Legalishu, the favourite and son of Sendeyo, another wife, was to be appointed *laibon* when Mbatian died. Knowing that her husband was almost blind, Lenana's mother brought him to his father's side so that his powers were passed to her son, rather than Sendeyo's, without realising it.

The tale seems to be true though because nothing was written down and African history has an oral tradition, tales tend to lose focus, altering as language itself does with the passing of each generation.

From the day that Dick was murdered in the Kedong Valley, as the number of white cattle traders increased and passed with their herds through Skeleton Plain, seeing others place a stone on the flat rock where Dick had perished, they adopted the habit. Until quite recently, there was a similar tradition in Ireland, everyone adding a stone where a man had died. Hence the word 'cairn'. But it is also the Maasai custom of *ndalingo*, honouring the spirit of the dead.[11] Skeleton Plain became farmland eventually, after two pioneer farmers settled there. One was Russell Bowker, who came from South Africa and gave his name to Bowker's Horse, a platoon set up in Nairobi at the outbreak of the First World War; in 1912 part of his land was bought by Frank Greswolde Williams, an Englishman who had lost an eye in an accident caused by a defective gun. He ran over a thousand head of cattle at Knight-wyck, as he called his farm,[112] and was one of the infamous 'Happy Valley' crowd, supplying them with the fashionable drugs of the day, cocaine and morphine, which he obtained from Port Said and then plied openly at Muthaiga Club in the 1940's.[113]

The Kedong Massacre illustrates the terrible contradictions which in Africa lie between the form and character of wild beauty, and savagery and ignorance. Hundreds of years may yet still have to elapse before a balance is regained and upheld. For the old traditions, varying within each tribe, are still battling for survival. During eighty years of European influence their ethnic values and rituals have been corrupted, jumbled by another culture, which does not mix well with their own. As for Christianity, the African converts could shed it as easily as a pair of shorts. The Kikuyu approach to death was, for example, quite beyond any European pioneer's understanding. The Kikuyu did not bury their dead. It was against their creed to allow a person to die in the home or to handle a corpse. Instead the sick, elderly or mortally wounded relative was carried out into the bush as he neared death so that predators could deal with the remains. The early Europeans reaching Nairobi were appalled to discover that coffins were unheard of and found the custom not only heartless but unhygienic.

At Nairobi John Ainsworth had organised a camp for new arrivals just a little farther upstream from where the Norfolk Hotel would stand, and, as people hunched round their fires at night, they used to hear the most terrible screams coming regularly from the nearby Kikuyu village. Here sentries were posted outside the doors of the huts whose job it was scare off the jackals, leopards and hyenas which had become used to their nightly prowl here for carrion. It was not so much a question of human flesh being more appetising than that of animals, it was more readily available to the predators living in the forest behind the village, saving them the need to hunt for food.

Helen Sanderson, the wife of Nairobi's first town clerk, was camping there in September 1904. She recorded in her diary how one of the men, 'found a pair of black hands one morning close to us here. Wherever you go you come upon skulls and human bones, out on the plain they lie in heaps. The Kikuyu huts are in quiet, hidden places and they never keep fowl for fear the noise would lead the terrible Masai to them.'[114]

Dick's murder was soon forgotten but the pile of stones continues to grow today. Until quite recent times the track was frequented by those bringing stock on the hoof to Nairobi, jacks-of-all-trades exchanging the role of farmer, wainwright or professional hunter with stock trading as became necessary for survival. To mention a few, there was Fred Roy and his partner Frank Bullows the founders of Bullows and Roy, Freddy Ward who helped to establish Muthaiga Club and with Jack Riddell started the Boma Trading Company, Will Judd the hunter, Count Hornyhold (alleged to have purchased his title), Seth-Smith, Viscount Colville, Arnold Paice—all farmers, the redoubtable Dr Atkinson and his ivory-hunting companions Smith and Vincent, the Honourable Denys Finch Hatton, Fred Raper, 'Fatty' Garland, Cardovillis and Salibrakis, two Greek horse-traders, Baron von Blixen and John Boyes and many, many more. But out of all those one could list and the varied and unforeseen turns their lives took in Africa, perhaps none was as surprising as that of the young Lithuanian, Abraham Block, who in 1927 founded his hotel group by exchanging an empty plot of land and £500 for the now world-famous Norfolk Hotel in Nairobi.[115]

CHAPTER 3

❦

Nyrobe

I pine for the roar on the edge of the clearing;
For the rustle of grass snake; the bird flashing wing in the heath:
For the sun shrivelled peaks of the mountains to blue heaven rearing;
The limitless outlook, the space and the freedom beneath.

William Hamilton, 1704–54

'Nyrobe' was born with the twentieth century and, in its unsuitability as the site of a town, may be looked upon as the illegitimate child of the railway. Sickness dominated its conception. On 30 May 1899 when the Railhead Club, which travelled up the line as construction progressed, reached the plain, many of the coolies were in any case too ill to move.

The name of the spot originated from the Maasai *'Engore Nyarobe'* meaning place of cold water and Sir George Whitehouse had ear-marked it in 1897 when he had travelled on foot from railhead with his wife Florence to look for a suitable site for the railway headquarters. He decided that supplies and base camps could be organised from here before tackling the construction across the Kikuyu escarpment and the drop into the great Rift Valley.

During their reconnaissance safari, he and his wife came across Delamere who was encamped in the shelter of a huge rock at Lukenia and was on his way home after an absence of two years. His clothes and tents were in the last stages of dilapidation but he was leaving with the skins of two lions he had shot the day before besides 'a wonderful collection of trophies'.[1]

The wealth of animal life on the Athi Plains was remarkable then, thick with all kinds of game roaming across the yellow grass. Ronald Preston, in charge of the plate-laying gangs, reflected later, 'To describe what we saw in the way of game, would be put down today as exaggeration, but . . . wherever one looked it was nothing but a moving mass of Hartebeeste, wildbeeste, zebra and the smaller antelope. The clang of the rails and steel sleepers would frighten the game within about five hundred yards radius so as to make the number greater and denser at the edge of the circle.'[2] In 1904, the impact was no less. Robert Foran, one of Nairobi's earliest police officers, exclaimed 'Ye Gods, what a truly amazing show . . . The graceful Grant's and Thomson's gazelle, reedbuck, duiker . . . were in their uncountable thousands . . . Flocks of handsome cock and drab hen ostriches stalked leisurely in springing strides, as if stepping on red-hot cinders, among the feeding animals. A black rhino dozed comfortably beneath a lonely tree . . . Time was when I would have been written down as a colossal liar.'3 Even Marcuswell Maxwell, the American photographer who twenty years later tried to capture the splendour on film commented, 'Here is the eighth wonder of the world . . . no zoo can offer a spectacle so impressive.'4

The game was more profuse in 1897 but strangely enough the 'prowling animals' did not frighten the chief engineer's wife Lady Whitehouse: 'one feels quite comfortable with a good fire . . . tomorrow we reach our future dwelling place Nyrobe. Our porters have done very well so far. There have only been four deserters. I am afraid the mules will never get through to the Lake and back. Two are lame already and the tonga is terribly heavy and trying for them and they are perfectly idiotic.'5

Though as disappointed as Preston was in Nairobi, her impressions contrast with his because she saw it first at the end of the dry season when the land aches for rain. 'Everything is so burnt up and on the east side of the river where our bungalows must be, on account of the station offices, the country is very bare with only a few scattered trees. The other side is wooded and very pretty. The stream . . . below the camp is thoroughly English with lovely ferns on the banks . . . the Chiefs came to pay their salaams. V scanty clothing but plentifully besmeared with red clay and castor oil. What clothes they do wear are also made thick and warm by the same mixture. They are fine looking people with very good features. They look like bronze statuary. Yesterday we drove out in the tonga to see Mrs McQueen and her baby . . . They have a miserable house . . . tumbled down wood but . . . seem to keep quite well. George set up the site for the houses this morning. It was too far away for me to go. He says there is a lovely view and a few blue-gum trees will soon take away the bare look . . .'6 Of that same spot in October 1899, Preston wrote, 'a bleak, swampy stretch of soppy landscape, windswept, devoid of any habitation of any sort except thousands of wild animals of every species. The only evidence of the occasional presence of human kind was the old caravan track skirting the bog-like plain.'7

The extremes of wet and dry season had not hindered the rapid spread of tents and shacks. Ainsworth's administrative quarters had been transferred from Machakos to the mound above the 'thoroughly English stream'. A flag pole and tin shack were put up and from here for a while the country was ruled. At sundown when the Union Jack was lowered, the strains of the Last Post drifted towards the distant Athi Plains over the cluster of canvas and tin roofs in the hollow. The Sub-Commissioner could have commanded a fine view over the plains from his new dwelling but he preferred to face the forest. Whitehouse's presence dominated the settlement. Ainsworth disliked him so much that he could not tolerate the thought of having the Chief Engineer's house in sight every day on the far hill from his window.[8] Instead, and to control the crossing of the Nairobi River, Ainsworth overlooked the recognised boundary between the Maasai and Kikuyu above some stepping-stones that were used by both tribes for raiding.[9] In 1900 Ainsworth had replaced these with a flimsy wooden bridge to connect the road from the railway station to the area behind his. This was intended for residential settlement and was named Parklands.

The early layout of Nairobi was based upon segregation of colour and class. Olive Grey, an ex-Salvation Army major with a bent for journalism describes with some bitterness how—'The sticky morass of the railway headquarters contrasted with the palatial residences in the hearts of men, that no plausible speech can eradicate.' Eighty years later, with a population exceeding one million, Nairobi has retained its original social shape. Olive Grey, who was living with a Eurasian railway employee to whom the white community referred as 'that black man', was understandably conscious of the barriers. But it was nevertheless true that when the rains were heavy the black cotton soil, upon which the tents and shacks were pitched below the hill dominated by Whitehouse's residence, was little more than a quagmire.

By contrast in the dry season the dust got into everything. The river dwindled to a trickle which gave no clue as to the volume of water and sediment that flowed along its banks in the long rains. The rains were acclaimed by the time they came. For weeks they were heralded by distant thunder, the horizon shaped by lightning so that when the first fat drops of rain fell they seemed like a benison but they brought problems too. In 1905 John Ainsworth's bridge was washed away twice. People managed before it was rebuilt by crawling over the sleepers of the railway bridge farther up.[10] Eventually the Public Works Department replaced Ainsworth's Bridge with a permanent structure which, unlike most landmarks named after European pioneers, has remained unchanged. The site from which John Ainsworth administered was surrounded by a beautiful garden that he had made, for from 1899, when he left Machakos, Ainsworth strove seriously for horticulture and agricultural innovation. In between his duties as a civil servant he planted blue gums to help mark out the streets and provide shade. About his home he cultivated exotic shrubs and trees, many of which stand clumped round today's Nairobi Museum. He became the first Secretary of the Agricultural Society and eventually introduced cash-crop agriculture on a large scale in the Nyanza Province. He was convinced that sisal, ramie*, cotton and rubber, the non-edible fibres, would play an important part in the prosperity of the country. If he was wrong about ramie and rubber he was right about sisal and cotton, both of which were grown originally in his own garden.[11]

In 1900 it was unsafe to walk after dark between the railway line and what

---

* China-grass which was used in the east for ropes, cordage and lamp-mantles.

was known as the Hill where Whitehouse lived. The whole valley was a series of game pits dug out by the natives who lay in wait for their prey, firing poisoned arrows as it passed.

Lions were plentiful in the papyrus swamp stretching almost from the station to below Ainsworth's hut and was a perfect breeding paradise for mosquitoes, crickets and frogs. At night the chorus of croaking drowned the hiss of the lanterns throwing gentle, distorting shadows on tin and canvas walls.

Four hundred yards from Ainsworth's door stood a Kikuyu village. The forest stretched far beyond and was impenetrable, magnificent. Here elephants, baboons, colobus monkeys, buffaloes, lions, leopards, rhinos and hyenas and bushbucks followed their own secret paths, revealing themselves occasionally in the glades where patches of sunlight penetrated the foliage. By day the innumerable, brightly coloured butterflies entranced those pursuing them with nets. The wild flowers and indigenous shrubs fascinated horti-culturalists. But by night the walk from Nairobi to Parklands was nerve-racking.[12]

As it grew, Nairobi's squalor was chiefly because there were no lavatories or proper drains. Open trenches which were supposed to be adequate for storm water took care of the flow of sewage but not the stench. In the badly lit streets people often fell into these at night. The Nairobi River was used for all purposes including drinking water. After sundown, waste from the community was collected in buckets. These were placed on wagons called 'lavender carts' which creaked their way down to the river when the lions did not take the bullock on duty.

A. M. Jeevanjee, a very rich Parsee and shipowner who headed a firm of contractors and general merchants, had constructed Ainsworth's permanent house. It was a modest job but led to many profitable enterprises including the acquisition of much land in Nairobi itself. A. M. Jeevanjee was a stalwart of a large family of Bhoras and was a keen racing enthusiast. He cut a graceful eastern figure with his grey beard and golden turban and was always clad in immaculate white and easily picked out among the European fraternity with whom he mingled.[13] His was the first horse to win at Nairobi Racecourse in 1903.[14] His family set up Jeevanjee Market, the first of its kind in the town[15] and in 1906 it was he who presented Nairobi with Jeevanjee Gardens, complete with a statue of Queen Victoria. He also started the first newspaper, *The African Standard*, in Mombasa which was bought by Anderson and Mayer for £50 in 1902.[16] Together with Allidina Visram, an established trader, Jeevanjee became to the Indian community what Delamere was to the European.

Many other Indians and Goans played key parts in the Protectorate's development beyond the vital role of the coolies who built the railway and by 1903 there were already several thousand of them settled in Nairobi. They were commercial men or petty traders, many of whose forebears had traded at the coast for generations and had financed the caravans which travelled inland and had brought currency and trading to the interior. More importantly as the railway progressed, rupees took the place of beads and wire which had hitherto occupied the place of money among Africans. While trading in beads and wire had fallen off considerably by 1899, cloth, soap, iron and tobacco showed a good increase all of which was due to the Indians and in fact, Sir John Kirk, a former Consul General at Zanzibar whose knowledge of the Protectorate was extensive, told the Sanderson Committee in 1910 that but for the Indians the Europeans would not have been in BEA at all.[17]

While their success in business is motivated by a deep rooted self-interest, Indians should be credited for opening *dukas* where no white man would have lived. Besides ensuring supplies of enamelware, cotton goods, beads, wire and blankets they also formed a natural and very necessary social bridge between the sharply defined shades of the black and white communities. Hajee Noormohammed visited Allidina Visram and was then employed by him, and in 1900 had *dukas* at Eldama Ravine and Hajee's Drift (named after him). Visram, small in stature but a powerful, well established trader, had opened for business at Bagamoyo in 1877.[18] At the turn of the century he had forty-three *dukas* between the coast and to the Nile district, a highly successful trading chain. He was so rich that he was regarded by some as the uncrowned King of Uganda.[19] The other great Indian merchants like him, Suleman Virjee and Alibhai Sharif, eventually built small villas, with balustrades, columns and much ornate plaster work on the outer reaches of Parklands. They were painted in fondant colours like heavily iced cakes and contrasted sharply with the squalor of their dukas in the shabby Indian bazaar.

The first European resident in Nairobi was always thought to be Corporal George Ellis, one of the Sclater's Road party, who had given the Reverend Fisher tea in his tent on the bank of the Nairobi River in 1898 at Martin's Camp.[20] But it would hardly have been named that had James Martin not camped there before Ellis. Now there is evidence that Martin spent ten days at Nairobi River Camp, as it used to be called in 1896. He was engaged in recruiting Africans to carry out the earthworks for the railway for Whitehouse at the time. It was after this exercise that the camp took Martin's name.[21]

The McQueens were perhaps the most self-sufficient members of this early and scattered community. But they had taken longer to settle than the Boedekers and Wallaces, moving briefly to Pangani and even trekking to Uganda before choosing land at Mbagathi, twelve miles from Nairobi near Ngong, not far from where Karen Blixen farmed coffee when she arrived from Denmark in January 1914. They called it Rhino Farm—later Rhino Park—because there were so many. Morning and evening the tank-like creatures came to drink from the Mbagathi River or wallow in the mud near the slope from which the McQueens drew their water supplies. McQueen built the house. He made all the hinges, nails, shutters and doors himself and encircled it with a thorn boma to keep the leopards and bothersome rhinos away. Water was taken up in old paraffin tins slung over their donkeys' withers. Three stones and an improvised Dutch oven made from the baked clay of Kikuyu formed Mary McQueen's kitchen. The same flat griddle she had brought from Scotland was used for frying for as long as she lived. Food was cheap. McQueen shot birds and game for the pot. Before long a Somali butcher opened from whom they bought local mutton. Occasionally they killed a steer and pickled it in brine and the salt beef kept them going for months. Bananas could be exchanged for the foul-smelling iodoform, which, ever since John Boyes had introduced the ointment to the Kikuyu, was much valued by them in the prevention of septicaemia from wounds. A large bunch of bananas could be traded with them for as much iodoform as could be placed on a pice piece the size of a silver sixpence.[22] The McQueens lived at Rhino Farm until the blacksmith died in 1944. Mary McQueen educated her children by reading to them from her family Bible or *Pilgrim's Progress* before losing her eyesight prematurely.[23]

Oddly enough McQueen's own relations with the Africans were good despite the fact that he took no pains to hide his conviction that 'they must remain cheap labour and slaves'.[32] But his wife would not allow an African servant in the house; her one concession was to employ a *dhobi* boy who laundered their clothes by pounding them in the water of the Mbagathi.

John, Jean, Madge, Minnie and Jim McQueen kept tame gazelles and saw nothing unusual in rhino drinking from their stream. Other children reared cheetahs, monkeys, lion cubs, mongooses or hyraxes which were accepted no less than white mice as pets. The McQueen children conversed with one another in Kikuyu and played tribal games learned from their helpers. The most favourite and bizarre of these was to steal beads which they would commandeer from the dying women as playthings before the hyenas did their undertaking. Neither they nor their parents thought anything of it; it never crossed their minds that they could be causing offence.

Possibly as often as every six months the McQueens walked to Nairobi on a shopping expedition. Newcomers were surprised by the strange cavalcade headed by the blacksmith whose wife dwarfed him, and each child walking one pace behind the last. They never wore shoes and had travelled so many native tracks barefoot through the bush that, as with the Africans themselves, it had become second nature to walk single-file in order to avoid the wait-a-bit thorns, even when in town. Unlike other Europeans then, the McQueens never wore spine-pads or pith helmets though shoes were introduced when they went to 'proper' school at the age of ten.[25]

From the time Eliot was appointed, those arriving in Nairobi had a changed identity, an altered sense of purpose. Mingling in the streets with the railway personnel were artisans, Colonial administrators, speculators, hunters, traders, collectors, missionaries, and soldiers, most of whom carried guns. The railway employees predominated however for, as Charles Miller points out in his *Lunatic Express*, 'the railway had its own Administration, law courts, police, fire, health depot, telegraph and all land touching on right of way or used in any fashion for railway purposes was the property of the railway committee. In certain respects Whitehouse could almost be said to have owned Nairobi.'[26] No wonder that Ainsworth and Whitehouse crossed one another with their different administrative motives.

In the glaring noon of the British Empire, the crazy shacks steadily replaced tent-pegs and canvas. In February 1900, Dr Rosendo Ayres Ribeiro, Nairobi's first private medical practitioner, made his appearance. His tubby, Goanese figure became familiar as he rode his tame zebra about the Bazaar or along Station Street. He pitched his tent where the bakery later stood in Whitehouse Road. Wearing a stetson, his black beard trimmed neatly, his buttons looking as if they would pop off his waistcoat at any moment, Dr Ribeiro visited the sick among all communities. He became famous in Nairobi for his special malarial cure, which he patented and was sold to an international pharmaceutical company eventually. For six months he and his assistant, Mr C. Pinto, shared a tent as home and practice. In the evenings, by the light of a candle and a kerosene lamp they made up prescriptions of the young Goanese doctor's invention.[27] He cured many grateful settlers of fever with his nameless, grey powders; the first dose induced vomiting which produced a lot of green bile but that was the extent of discomfort. After completing the course his patients were assured of freedom from fever for many months.[28]

As the Indian Bazaar expanded Dr Ribeiro moved into more luxurious quarters and their next surgery was built from the packing cases in which his drug supplies had been shipped from England. A tarpaulin, borrowed from the railway, provided temporary cover and when it was reclaimed he practised with no roof, like Aesculapius in the Sacred Groves, receiving many a tough native chicken in lieu of payment for his cures. It was Dr Ribeiro who, in 1902, had diagnosed bubonic plague in two Somali patients and reported it.[29] The Medical Officer of Health, with no experience of tropical diseases, panicked at the news, ordered the Indian Bazaar to be evacuated and burned it to the ground. Dr Ribeiro's surgery went up in flames with the rest. This drastic measure cost the Government £50,000 but Dr Ribeiro fared rather well out of the disaster.[30] He was compensated for the loss with the gift of a domestic plot near the station. There he built the usual 'Dak' bungalow on stilts, from which he carried on with his work and, in 1903, was given a concession of sixteen acres behind Victoria Street* by the Government in recognition for services rendered over his report on the plague.[31]

The shops in the Indian bazaar mainly catered for the African trade. They bought spices like ginger and cardamom here and the Kikuyu became very partial to these exotic oriental flavours. In the rainy season the bullocks and carts turned the bazaar into a black, oozing mire and the *duka-wallahs* put down bits of packing-case by which shoppers might get across the glutinous

* Campos Ribeiro Avenue was named after Julius Campos and Rosendo Ribeiro. Campos, another Goan pioneer bought half Ribeiro's land.

mud. While it was small enough, the bazaar was moved to drier ground when it got too bad.

The first Municipal Meeting had been held in 1901 on 24 July but it took years for any council to improve matters. The greatest trial was the water. Even in 1904 it was still carried up from the river which was 'small and creeping and lying in pools'; the Kikuyu from the nearby village washed themselves and their clothes at the spot from which the water was drawn, leaving it cloudy. One only seemed to get dirtier by washing in it and no matter how long it was boiled it never tasted clean.[32] Dr Freddy Henderson, the newest recruit of the East African Medical Services in 1904, had been warned before he left England that he would be lucky to survive six months in the country. Insurance Companies looked upon his application for life insurance as the request of a madman and told him so. One firm, in Scotland, out of those approached, was prepared to take the gamble even though he was a doctor himself.[33]

When they were living in South Africa, G. W. Anderson had tied a scarf over the eyes of his Belgian wife, Maia, turned her around three times and asked her to stick a pin into a map of Africa on the table before her. When the blindfold was removed she saw she had stuck it against Kismayu and the destiny of the Anderson family was set. Dr Gerald Anderson, her son, remembers sailing into the old port of Mombasa in January 1901 and looks back on the eighty years he has lived in the country without a shred of regret for the hardship or poverty they endured: 'we started from naught and were part of the creation of something new and inspite of everything, every evidence of disease and difficulty we were proud to be involved with it. Our fellows died of plague, dysentery, typhoid, pneumonia, blackwater and malaria.'[34]

In Nairobi, the early inhabitants slept at night under mosquito nets as sounds of the swamp creatures filled the air. By day, at Tommy Wood's Hotel—sometimes called the Victoria Hotel because the street in which it stood was Victoria Street—customers sat on cases of Lifebuoy Soap or condensed milk when the chairs ran out. Over beer or tea, their shirt-sleeves rolled up over sun-burned arms, they discussed the prospects for the future, picked up useful gossip or cooked-up deals for business of every description as they might in any frontier town. Before the Norfolk Hotel opened it was the acknowledged centre of wheeling and dealing. It was here that the first political meetings took place, and the settler banner waved against the officials once Lord Delamere returned—a cause for which he became famous.[35]

The two-storey wood-and-iron building was owned by A. M. Jeevanjee and, as it was near the station, Tommy Wood had seen its potential in 1901, rented it and turned it into an hotel. Wood came from Sheffield and was an enterprising character with a penchant for sitting on committees. Having spent eleven years in South Africa, he no longer wanted to live in England and in 1900 had chosen Nairobi instead, and soon emerged as the undisputed leader of the commercial sector developing along Victoria Street.[36] He founded the Colonists' Association, became a member of the Labour Board and Nairobi's first Mayor. He knew everybody and everybody knew him. Abraham Block, with whom Wood became firm friends, stayed at his hotel when he first arrived in Nairobi.[37] It occupied the first floor above the shop which stocked everything from agricultural implements to suiting. Wood ran the post office and a messenger service for those who could not get to railhead. Since there were no banks and he had the only safe in the town it was here that money was deposited. Thus, it was here too that the first exchanges of land took place as well as the animated discussions over prospective agencies and markets. As in village life, few matters could be kept private for long. Eavesdropping was a favourite and often profitable pastime for the quick-witted among the pioneers, as the decisive young Block discovered before he had lived there long.[38]

Abraham Lazarus Block was born in Vilna, the capital of Lithuania, on 15 April 1883, the year in which Thomson and Martin crossed Maasailand. His father, Samuel Block, was a farmer from the village of Kirkle, who moved to Vilna at the marrying age to find himself a wife, Ethel, who bore him three daughters and a son.[39] Abraham was their second child. He and his elder sister Annie and the two younger girls, Lily and Freda, grew up in the shadow of the pogroms. Brutality and fear dominated their lives and, like countless other children of that generation, they came to know the sounds of aggression. First came the clatter of many horses' hooves and raised voices to be followed by the burning of the rye harvests. Nevertheless economic pressures during this period (since referred to as the new Diaspora) were as much responsible for Jewish emigration as the pogroms themselves.

When Abraham Block was eight years old, Samuel and Ethel Block decided that there must be a better life elsewhere and Samuel went alone to South Africa to investigate the possibilities for the young family he had left behind. It was not an easy move because central to the creed of Judaism is the home and family life. Years of separation followed, for the eldest children, Abraham and Annie, went to England to stay with their uncle, Rabbi Sinson in Leeds while Lily and Freda remained in Vilna with their mother.

Though Africa seems a strange choice for a Slav to have made when thousands like him had flocked to America, perhaps Samuel was influenced by the fact that the Jewish colony in South Africa, dating back to the first quarter of the nineteenth century, seemed to be flourishing.

Lily, her father's favourite child, claimed that her father had not left voluntarily but had been forced to flee Vilna. In an interview given as an old woman, she stated that he had been wanted by the secret police and that Ethel Block and her daughters were at first sheltered by relatives after Samuel Block's departure and their possessions sold off to pay for necessities. There is no-one alive to gainsay these claims, so it will never be known whether her recollections are accurate or whether her father's leaving was dramatised by a young and lively imagination. Without giving dates Lily maintains that when she was seventeen, like her father, she fled political pressure. Some foreign pamphlets and magazines were discovered in her school desk at a time of unrest and suspicion and decided to flee to England. In the middle of winter she made for the German border with a group of friends.[40] Somehow they escaped the notice of the patrols and Lily arranged for a passage to England on a cattle boat sailing from Essen. She had been looking forward to being with Abraham and Annie once more after two years' separation but she was to be disappointed. Neither was with the Sinson family when Lily reached Leeds. Annie had married and Abraham had gone in search of their father in South Africa.[41]

Though her aunt and uncle were much loved and respected members of the Jewish community, Lily learned that Abraham had not been happy there. Though neither had met these relatives before, in contrast to the way in which, through their kindness, Lily was able to recuperate after the trauma of leaving her mother and sister in Russia, the family connection, kindness and well-meaning attitudes had provided Abraham with no comfort at all.

He had gone to live with Annie for a while but her husband's efforts to ease his young brother-in-law's feelings of discontent had not helped much. Annie's husband worked for the Rakusen family who owned a matzo factory and had asked them to give Abraham a job too. But Abraham loathed it and during the short time he worked there, longed only to escape the routine and the smell of baking biscuits.[42] He was restless by nature and, as his later life showed, was happiest when he was on the move.

Abraham Block's wages were too poor for him to think of saving for a passage to South Africa. He worked his way on a cargo ship bound for Cape Town from Hull instead. The Boer War was already in its second year and he believed his father to be in Johannesburg but before Abraham could make the next stage of the journey he had to earn more money. In those days Cape Town was a transit port for cold meat storage for which casual labour was always required; cash for humping carcases was earned quickly and easily and probably while doing this he picked up a smattering of the craft of butchering which he later exploited in Nairobi. At Cape Town he earned enough money to get him to Simonstown, the next port. By 'port crawling' as this system was known he progressed in stages to Port Elizabeth, East London and Durban, picking up work where he could until he had enough money to get him to Johannesburg.[43]

How he finally managed to trace his father is not known but shortly after they were re-united Abraham Block enlisted in a Boer Commando unit. He was just eighteen when on May 1902 the final meeting of the Boer delegates took place with the British at Vereeniging and surrender terms were signed at Pretoria, bringing the Boer War to an end.[44]

Block, whose terms of survival could be described as winning at losing, got through the following months by 'schmussing', gathering the tufts of wool left on barbed wire and shrubs or the hurdles of sheep pens.[45] In the next fifty years he would sell everything from pigs to Persian carpets but until

January 1903, when he heard Joseph Chamberlain talk about British East
Africa, he sold wool sack by sack, earning enough to keep his ponies and
himself in East London, a great wool-buying centre. In Kenya it is rumoured
that he also worked as a tinker.[46]

At the end of 1902 Mr Joseph Chamberlain, Secretary of State for the
Colonies was touring British East Africa with his wife and they were on their
way to South Africa. Chamberlain was to report on progress in BEA since
the completion of the railway to Lord Lansdowne.

Sir Charles Eliot, who had been appointed HM Commissioner in 1900,
became the forefather of white settlement in the Protectorate and that
December was plunged into formalities connected with Chamberlain's
visit.[47]

The unpalatable truth, as Chamberlain discovered, was that the Uganda
railway was losing more and more money and in 1902 its income totalled less
than one-third of the Protectorate's expenditure. A few settlers had taken an
interest in the country but Eliot urgently needed more, and, to avert disaster
it was necessary to attract them in droves.

It was chiefly towards South Africa that Eliot turned for potential settlers.
Already in April, a month before the Boer War had ended, the first application for land had come in from a company in which financiers belonging to
the Chartered Company of South Africa held interests also. Calling themselves the East African Syndicate, they sought a grant of five-hundred square
miles and they had acquired Lake Magadi from Commerell M. Cowper
Coles to whom Deacon and Walsh had relinquished the rights and were given
a direct lease by the Foreign Office on 300,000 acres of land in the Rift Valley.
The allocation of this land, where the Maasai were concentrated, is worth
remembering because not only was it a classic example of the problems the
man on the spot encountered constantly in his dealings with the men in
Whitehall, it caused Eliot's resignation.[48]

Chamberlain supported Eliot's need for pioneers and made it known that
he was going to speak in Johannesburg about the country.[49] The impression
Chamberlain preferred to give was that of the cool, imperturbable administrator. A self-made man from Birmingham, he viewed the British Empire
through his monocle with as much responsibility as the portfolio of his
Foreign Office colleague, Lord Lansdowne, would allow. But his Jewish
sympathies were open and there was another side to him, not often displayed
in public. He could be moody, emotional and impulsive and possibly in this
last mood he made that speech in South Africa. At any rate Block looked back
on hearing him as a turning point and claimed that it changed the whole
direction of his life.

England's policy towards Jews was comparatively liberal. But even so the
natural concern for the livelihood of the ordinary workman, possibly now
threatened by the influx of Jews into Britain, led to repeated attempts by
Balfour's Government to pass an Aliens Bill to protect British Trade Union-
ists against cheap Jewish labour. Consequently when Chamberlain first saw

the empty tracts of land requiring development in the Rift Valley, his opportunist mind contemplated the possibilities that BEA might offer which would at one stroke benefit the young Protectorate and give asylum to the persecuted Russian Jews. He wrote in his journal there and then, 'If Dr Herzl were to transfer his efforts to East Africa there would be no difficulty in finding land for Jewish settlers but I assume this country is too far removed from Palestine to have many attractions for him.'[50]

So it was as early as December 1902 that the seed for the idea of a Zionist Colony within the Protectorate was sown. Chamberlain was impressed by Dr Theodor Herzl, the Jewish leader for whom the effort to present Jews as a nation, rather than as dispersed groups of alienated wanderers with religion as a common bond, had become a way of life. Zion was his dream. Chamberlain had been influenced too by his friend Nathan Rothschild, the first practising Jew to be made a British peer, whose concern over the anti-Semitic pogroms in Russia, Roumania and Poland were well known.[51]

In Johannesburg Block urged five friends to go with him to Nairobi and they made plans to leave for Mombasa as soon as possible. Four were farmers. Their names were Sulsky, Hotz, London and Moscow—the fifth remains unknown. Finding the money for the passages was difficult because Block was determined not to leave his ponies behind. As a farmer's son he also thought it sensible to take something to grow so a bag each of peas, linseed, beans and Early Rose potatoes went with him and, besides the Basutos, £25 in cash, which, with a gold watch and a change of clothes, were his total assets. In March, the six friends boarded a small Austrian trading vessel at Delagoa Bay.[52]

That Easter, just as they disembarked at Mombasa, a singularly brutal pogrom was taking place in Kishinev, Moldavia. Some 2,000 Jewish families were wiped out. The horror of it reverberated round the world and, perhaps not unexpectedly, it also catapulted Chamberlain's private ideas on the problems of what to do about the persecuted Jews into the limelight of political issue.[53] Shortly after his return from South Africa, he and Theodor Herzl met in London. Once more they discussed Herzl's dream to secure an 'ante-chamber to the Holy Land, a place of apprenticeship that would serve to fit the Russian Jews to enter into their inheritance, an equivalent to the wilderness in which the followers of Moses spent forty years preparatory to settlement in the land of Canaan.' Chamberlain, with Eliot's urgent need for increased white settlement very much in mind, suggested the possibility of creating a refuge for the Jews of Russia in British East Africa where there was plenty of unoccupied land. Before long, serious negotiation for such a scheme was under way.

On 15 April, four days before the Kishinev pogrom, Block spent his birthday in Nairobi. Unfortunately there are no photographs in existence that give any clue to his looks before those taken on his wedding day in 1914. These reveal a short (almost squat) and serious young man, with pale eyes. His darkish hair is parted in the centre and swept back from his wide forehead in two waves, in a style worthy of any actor out of a silent motion picture, except that Block never grew a moustache. This was unusual in Nairobi in those days when most young men sported a set of whiskers. When Block started looking for work in the ugly little town where he made his fortune, it was just three years old. [54]

Mayence Bent, who figured later in Block's life, ran the millinery department of Tommy Wood's shop. But she quarrelled with him and, closing her haberdashery store in umbrage, decided to set up the Hotel Stanley farther along the street. [55]

Mayence had come to Mombasa from West Africa in 1898 as the wife of W. S. Bent, a railway employee, who had worked on the Nigerian Railway. She was capable and ambitious by the time she was thirty in 1901, was Nairobi's first dress-maker and milliner. She had an infallible instinct for what women wanted and needed, from a flowered toque to a muslin dress, coming into her own once there were regular fixtures for race meetings. Despite the daintiness of her trade however, she was not above emptying the chamber pots from the balcony of The Stanley into Victoria Street to save herself a journey downstairs to the sanitation ditches. She was also very frugal and when fire broke out in 1905, dropped the new enamel chamber pots one by one into the street rather than give them up to the fire. [56]

The railway not only provided a great strand of communication from coast to lake, many of its European employees remained and settled after their contracts had expired. These valuable pioneers had already gained experience of the country's conditions. Having grasped them at a basic level they were able to contribute first-hand knowledge to the economy; among these were the founders of Gailey and Roberts, J. H. Gailey and D. O. Roberts (both were surveyors), Reginald Barton-Wright destined to become Land Officer, the plate-layer, Ronald Preston who founded the Nairobi Exchange and W.D. Young, the official photographer who opened the Dempster Studio, Nairobi's earliest commercial camera house.

Most of the aristocrats, whose stamping ground became the Norfolk Hotel, arrived slightly later. Many came out first on safari, either to shoot or stay with friends. A few would be persuaded by Lord Delamere to join him in the great experiment purely on speculative terms and many of these had money to invest. Because they were able to envisage development on a larger scale than the majority already in Nairobi in 1901, they could get things done with their useful contacts among those in power commercially and at Government level at home. Like the battle of Waterloo, said so often to have been won on the playing fields of Eton, their achievements were based chiefly on the old-boy network. Many a friendship begun at Harrow, Marlborough and Winchester ended up in partnership in Nairobi and beyond. Their wives became weary of teaching the African domestic staff the same simple tasks over and again. Despite the fact that the early servants had had no training or even a smattering of knowledge of European ways, the Memsahibs took certain standards for granted. Often they were uncompromising, and with their high-pitched criticisms seemed both impatient and unreasonable to the Africans, particularly where household management was concerned. The exasperation creeps through the list of hints to prospective settlers' wives which Lady Cranworth wrote in 1912, 'I would add house management were it not that the supervision of native servants is an art in itself. One could not, for instance, learn by experience in England when is the right time to have a servant beaten for rubbing silver plate on the gravel to clean it, and this after several warnings.'[57]

Herbert Binks, a chemist, came to East Africa when his proposal of marriage was rejected. He became a turn-your-hand-to anything individual who, as a settler, played the roles of farmer, prospector, hunter, contractor, astronomer and photographer.[58] His impression of Nairobi was that it did not exist at all. Admittedly he had arrived after the Indian bazaar had just been burned after the 1902 outbreak of bubonic plague. The nameboard alone on the platform told the twenty-year-old Yorkshireman that he had reached his destination. Binks had enquired at the station, 'How far is the town?'

'This *is* the town' was the reply.

On the voyage out Binks had struck up friendship with another settler Stephen Bagnall. Both young men were speechless as they gazed at the wilderness of grass, dotted by a few iron shacks. Suddenly they saw the funny side of it. They had intended to settle in a town, to supply it with the things a town needs but now it appeared that they would have to build the town first. Nairobi's shortcomings did not put Binks off. After seventy years, aged ninety-one, he was buried there but the unfortunate Bagnall was snatched from his tent on the Athi Plain by a lion leaving only his boots as evidence of his existence in 1905.

Like so many other elderly pioneers, Binks had few regrets but in speaking of the early European community admitted 'we were a profligate lot'.[59] Sir Harry Johnston of the Uganda Administration used more restraint about them in a letter to Captain Sclater, 'The majority of settlers are a lot of scallywags, grumble if they are not given what they ask but do nothing on the land given them, spend money at Wood's Hotel etc . . .'[60]

Considering that the British Government had deliberately founded its economy on settler enterprise, and the thirty or so white settlers already resident in 1903 had obtained land in areas which were uninhabited and where labour was all but impossible to obtain, Sir Harry's remarks are pompous and carping. At heart pioneers may be visionaries but they need solid encouragement too. If colonists were to be attracted in any number, more tempting terms than those in existence were required. Yet Johnston's attitudes were precisely those which prompted ill-feeling between the officials and settlers, when the last thing needed in the name of progress was antagonism.

Distance undermined everything. There was no continuity in the Administrative system and the delays due to the Foreign Office having to make every decision in London were more than frustrating. Not only were those in

Whitehall totally ignorant of local conditions, settlers' requests could not be met quickly either. No-one could occupy his land until it was surveyed and there was only one surveyor to carry it out. The transporters Smith and Vincent had applied for 5,000 acres at Elmenteita as early as 1898 but had been turned down on the strength that all applications for more than two acres had 'hitherto been refused by Her Majesty's Commissioner for Uganda'. Boedeker and Stuart Watt's requests were granted because the Foreign Office had still been in a state of suspension, waiting for the rail-track to reach the lake before making decisions on granting larger acreages to anyone. To say that the handling of land grants between Nairobi and London was 'confused' is an understatement.

Added to these problems were those which the pioneers ran up against while waiting for land titles which were more often delayed than not.[61] For example, price anomalies made it almost impossible to budget. It was quite common to see large tins of porridge costing 24 rupees next to small tins of caviar for 4 rupees at George Stewart and Company. This was the only European shop in competition with Tommy Wood and was run by two sepulchral looking brothers in a tin hut who sold the usual medley of goods. Tinned jams, sardines and paraffin crammed their make-shift shelves. Cartridges cost the equivalent of eighteen pence each but beer was five shillings a bottle.[62] Such discrepancies persisted for years and were due to the fact that, when they were imported, porters' wages on a six- to twelve-month safari varied in accordance with the size and weight of the goods to be transported and were affected also by the remoteness of the *duka* for which they were destined. Prices therefore were either ridiculously high or low and bore little relation to the simplicity or luxury of the item on sale.[63]

But by the time the Uganda Railway had been completed and Florence Preston had driven home the final key in the last rail on December 20th 1901 at Port Florence,* Sir Charles Eliot had already had a year in which to assess local conditions. He understood the problems, knew that to attract settlers was vital but more importantly realised rules and regulations at the Land Office must be adjusted, and that the mishandling of its affairs was being carried out by officials who were as inexperienced over land settlement as the people applying for it.

In 1897 the Foreign Office had laid down tentative land regulations allowing the Commissioners to make grants of land of an unlimited size on twenty-one year leases, but the conditions to which applicants must agree to obtain it were restrictive. Knowing nothing as to the suitability of the land and ignoring the question of grazing grants completely, the Foreign Office insisted that a quarter of each allocation be planted up within five years with 'coffee, cocoa, indigo rubber or other plants approved of by the Commis-

---

* Though it has generally been assumed that Kisumu, when it was known as Port Florence, was originally named after Ronald Preston's wife, it had actually already been decided by George Whitehouse that it would be named after his wife on their safari when Lady Florence Whitehouse reached the lake with him in 1898.

sioner'. Since they had no notion as to what would grow, these suppositions were based on the little they knew about the climate.

In 1902 it was easier for the commercial and professional men than for the farmers. Nairobi's first lawyers, B. G. Allen and his partner Osmond Tonks, had already started up their practice in Victoria Street.[64] Allen arrived in 1902 with only £300 but was worth £150,000 when he died in 1920.[65] The farmer, in contrast, had little chance of getting anything calculable by way of a return from his land for several years. The market, the climate, health conditions and even the humblest of crops such as the potato were unknown quantities. Nothing was certain but the red tape confronting every would-be settler and making the acquisition of land more of a gamble than a security.

For example, rules governing the use of timber read, 'all timber is the property of the Crown; the settler may not sell any except with the permission of the forest officer and may not clear except for cultivation . . . Tenants must be prepared to import their fencing, as the Government will not ordinarily supply timbers from the forest for this purpose.' Another rule ran: 'In consequence of the destructive habits of goats in relation to vegetation, no settler would be allowed to keep any goats without special permission.'[66]

Twenty-two very impatient Europeans had met at Tommy Wood's Hotel in July 1902. They had had enough of the lethargy of the Administration and its tardy methods. The idea behind the meeting was to elect a committee to give encouragement to white settlement. Three issues, land, labour and opposition to the Indians, formed the theme of the resulting letter they sent to Sir Charles Eliot. They asked for government support in granting freehold land; they expressed the need for the setting up of experimental farms and forestry departments; mining laws should be passed and, on the thorny question of labour or, more accurately, the lack of it, they suggested that 'natives should be more amenable to supervision'. They also pointed out that the Asian community was detrimental to the European inhabitants generally. Just before he went on home leave Eliot faced the committee and assured them that HM Government intended to encourage white settlement despite evidence to the contrary. By telling them that the Highlands were 'positively distasteful to the Hindu' he hoped to pacify them on the Indian issue.[67]

The Acting Commissioner, Mr Frederick Jackson, now took Eliot's place. The Crown Lands Ordinance of 1902 had been followed in November by a prohibitive set of regulations governing the disposal of land and under this the Land Office opened its doors for the first time.

Two years of practical experience was enough to sour Eliot's vision and temper his opinion. In his final despatch to the Secretary of State he wrote with irony, 'No doubt on platforms and in reports we declare that we have no intention of depriving natives of their lands. But this has never prevented us from taking whatever land we wanted for Government purposes or from settling Europeans on land actually occupied by natives . . . Your Lordship has opened this Protectorate to white immigration and Colonisation and I think it is well that, in confidential correspondence at least, we should face the undoubted issue: viz that white mates black in very few moves.' A clear-cut example is the case of Atkinson, Smith and Vincent, who were brought to trial and whose plea was fixed beforehand so that the white man would not lose face before the black. The transporters from South Africa had been waiting for their grant of land to come through but they turned to ivory hunting when their application was denied and were experienced ivory dealers by the time they inveigled Dr Atkinson into joining them. After Delamere's departure, Atkinson had acquired land and started a farm of sorts five miles out of Nairobi at Karura. He had already imported a Berkshire Boar and Delamere had sent him a gift of a Shorthorn bull in 1901,[68] but he knew there was more profit from ivory than pigs.

Greed for more and more ivory led Smith, Vincent and Atkinson into questionable dealings in the Rendile country and news of their activities leaked out through their porters, who had not been paid.[69] The don-like Eliot, unused to mixing with riff-raff, also held unfashionable but frank opinions on big-game shooting, which he disliked. Indeed he had a natural abhorrence of violence of any sort. So when, on 30 July 1902, this unpalatable gossip reached his ears he ordered one of his District Officers at Fort Hall, H. R. Tate, into the area south-east of Lake Rudolf to find out if what he had heard about Smith, Vincent and Atkinson was true.[70] Tate was instructed to gather every scrap of evidence that might be used in court against the three ruffians. Eliot had been told that the three white men had been elephant hunting in the Rendile country near Mount Kulal and Horr but, besides shooting for ivory had murdered some tribesmen in order to get it. The explanation of how this came about was pieced together afterwards. Apparently, having bagged ivory for themselves, they then began negotiations to buy a great pile of it from a Rendile chief. But when the time came to pay for it, Atkinson decided that the price was too high; days of haggling followed, everyone lost patience and the chief and his retainers became cantankerous with the three white men and threatened them. At this point Atkinson decided to resolve the situation drastically.[71]

By 1902 ammunition and trade guns known to the Africans as 'Fataki' were in great demand; these were a musket type of smooth-bore which were very cheap, usually manufactured in Birmingham. They were fired by a percussion cap, loaded from the muzzle, with a measured charge of black powder. Gunpowder, bullets and caps had subsequently become easy trading items, taking the place of beads with the traders of the northern area of the Protectorate and southern Abyssinia, Rendile and Boran, who were quick to recognise that they could bring huge profits traded against elephant tusks. As a matter of course traders began to carry kegs of gun-powder, shot and caps to sell to the owners of 'Fataki' guns which in turn ensured greater hauls of ivory for themselves.[72] Dr Atkinson had seated himself on one of these kegs during the final harangue over the ivory but had attached a slow fuse to it, ready for lighting. Giving his last price to the chief he asked the group of

Rendile to draw near as the keg contained their payment of Maria Theresa dollars, the Abyssinian currency. Without their realising what he was up to, he lit the fuse and walked away from them as if to relieve himself in the bush; they had been talking and gesticulating excitedly over the money when the keg exploded. Nearly all the men present had been killed or so badly wounded as to be ineffective.[73]

Atkinson, Vincent and Smith left the scene of carnage at once with the ivory which was borne on the heads of their 200 porters. Tate travelled 1,050 miles in eighty-five days gathering evidence, and as a result the men were arrested for dacoity* and charged with murder, the wholesale slaughter of elephant and raiding in the Rendile country. Tate's report, submitted that October, contained enough evidence to hang all three, but the Africans were so terrified of the repercussions if they spoke up in court that they would not give evidence.

The Administration managed to bring three witnesses 'with the greatest reluctance' for the prosecution, one of them the elephant hunter Arthur Neumann. According to Jackson, who referred to Atkinson as 'that well-known filibuster' and was acting in Eliot's absence, the European jury, which included Government servants, 'would not convict the men; the plea was fixed "because they feared they were going to be attacked." '[74] Smith and Vincent were deported and Atkinson retired to his land at Karura, where he applied his energies to experimental potato growing. And there he stayed until Delamere returned in 1903 by which time the scandal had died down. There is a strange sad echo to the story however. In 1907 when the Boma Trading Company was opening up trade routes to the north, one of its employees camped at Neumann's Boma. The famed and once respected elephant hunter had died in May the same year. 'Neumann is the man who shot himself in England about three months ago for reasons unknown,' the young man wrote. 'Information gathered from the natives, I only wonder his conscience did not prompt him to do away with himself before. It would not be advisable to say too much in a letter, even though the man is dead, but I will reserve for a future occasion.' Neumann's secret seems to have died with him; possibly the fact that he perjured himself in the Atkinson trial added to his self-annihilating guilt, though it is unlikely that his suicide will ever be explained now.**[75]

Such individuals exist in any society; there is nothing exceptional about the bad apple in the barrel. The worst of them were dealt with by the Police, often under the Distressed British Subject's Act commonly known as 'DBS'. On the whole, when the offenders were unable to satisfy the Court as to their past record or financial resources, they were imprisoned in Fort Jesus for six months, then deported by steamer to Bombay and forbidden to return to the

---

* Robbery with violence committed by a gang originating from the word *dacoit*, one of a class of robbers in India or Burma who plunder in gangs.

** A commemorative plaque set in the wall of Mombasa Cathedral records that Neumann died in London on 29 May 1907.

Protectorate. Their passage money was deducted from earnings from work done in prison and usually the country was glad to see the back of them, but it was a bit hard that India should be saddled with British East Africa's white dross.[76]

John Boyes was not only arrested for dacoity but, unlike Atkinson, imprisoned for it. By a few, Boyes was thought to be 'an awful little man', yet almost every single one of the early pioneers did business with him at one stage, including such visiting dignitaries as the American President, Theodore Roosevelt.

Lord Cranworth describes him in his memoirs as 'a most remarkable early settler, coffee grower and Legion Frontiersman'. Despite the uncouth language with which he peppered all conversation, delivered in a strong Yorkshire accent, the disgrace attached to the charge of dacoity, his imprisonment, his sharp deals and his bragging nature, when Boyes died in Nairobi in 1951 all the great men in the Colony walked in the funeral cortège to mourn the passing of an extraordinary man.[77] Indeed by 1909 he was as respectable a member of the pioneer community as Dr Atkinson. By then Boyes was running a livestock business from the Norfolk Stores where Martin's Camp had once stood. From here he provided the local community with vital supplies of mules and camels which were driven down from Abyssinia. He had also acquired a 1,000-acre farm, 'Kasarini', which had been given to him as a reward for help given to the Administration in quelling a clan of raiding Kikuyu.[78]

Boyes had sailed into Mombasa on a dhow in 1898 at the age of twenty-three. The clothes on his back were his only possessions and he had been on the move constantly for ten years. His father was a bootmaker in Hull and Boyes had run away from school to sea. At the age of thirteen he had walked to Liverpool, signed on as crew and sailed to Brazil, moving on in stages to India, Port Said and the West Coast of Africa. Here he contracted yellow-fever which impaired his eyesight for life and though he attempted to join the Royal Navy at one stage, was rejected because of his defective vision. Boyes seemed to be attracted by disturbance itself and involved himself first in the Matabele Rebellion and then the Uganda Mutiny. The army paid well for the transport of food and Boyes leapt at the chance to earn money shortly after reaching Mombasa, by delivering supplies for the troops from the coast to the lake.[79]

His earnings exceeded all expectation. The £200 he received was the largest sum of money he had ever had in his life but if he imagined the transportation would be easy he was wrong.[80] He suffered malaria during the safari and became delirious on the road. After losing consciousness for three days he came round to see vultures circling over him in their calculating way. Vultures glide on the rising thermals, remaining aloft all day, flying high in search of food. They were waiting for his death. Many of Boyes's donkeys fell prey to tsetse fly. He left their carcases for the predators, ignored the loss and instead used their drivers to take the loads. Not surprisingly they deserted

him. Boyes was determined not to be defeated by this seemingly insur-
mountable obstacle. He reasoned that he must have been preceded along
Sclater's road by other caravans which had suffered similar setbacks. If he
waited long enough the porters who had deserted them would, like his
drivers, make for the coast. They would have to pass him on the road and he
might be able to tempt them to work for him. His instincts proved right and
after persuading some deserters to join him, he proceeded as planned to Lake
Victoria.

He was eager to repeat his success, but his experiences had convinced him
that there must be a nearer source of supplies of food than Mombasa. When
he realised that the Kikuyu were an agricultural rather than a pastoral tribe he
decided to tap their resources first. The Administration tried to prevent
Boyes entering Kikuyu country but in his characteristic way he ignored
them. With seven porters and an interpreter, risking their lives as well as his
own, he crossed the Aberdares. He was captured by Kikuyu warriors from
Chief Karurie's tribe but through an interpreter suggested that rather than kill
him, which they were all set to do, they take him instead to the ruling council
of their village. Luckily they agreed; days passed while Boyes did his best to
persuade the chiefs to release him and trade food with him but no amount of
glib talk could lure them into accepting his suggestions. It was fortuitous
during the little Yorkshireman's campaign for friendly co-operation that a
rival clan of Kikuyu attacked Karurie's village. This gave Boyes the perfect
opportunity to illustrate his powers as a healer. After the fray, while they
were tending their wounded, Boyes produced his pot of iodoform and
applied it to the worst injuries.[81] The *Kiama*, a Kikuyu council of elders, was
so impressed with the result of the ointment that Boyes won his imaginary
crown and title 'King of the Wakikuyu'. More important, he had broken
down the negative attitudes of this particular clan and become accepted as
their friend and protector. His involvement was frowned upon by other
Kikuyu. Just as Lenana had been mistrusted because of his association with
John Ainsworth, Karurie suffered too for his co-operation with Boyes; much
jealousy and suspicion arose from other clans. All the same, Boyes was now
able to buy all the food he wanted. In exchange for enough iodoform to cover
a man's thumbnail the Kikuyu provided 20 lbs of flour. By the time Boyes
had settled this agreement the railway had progressed as far as the Kikuyu
escarpment. The thousands of coolies engaged in its construction required
food and now became his principal customers. Boyes' three years of patience
had paid off handsomely. He capitalized on his friendship with Karurie while
the going was good. He taught the young warriors how to handle guns and
the tactics he himself learned during the Matabele rebellion. Karurie's clan
became invincible, feared by those who still fought with bows and arrows.
They overpowered one village just after it had looted an Arab caravan of its
guns and, without losing one man, acquired an armoury of their own. When
Karurie defeated the Chinga, his most feared and bitter enemies who had
murdered three Goanese traders, he openly acknowledged Boyes as their

'king'. But while Karurie's trust in Boyes was understandable, it was also ill-advised for he was a slippery customer.

And, after this cheerful rogue had inveigled Karurie into forfeiting a great store of ivory, one cannot help wondering how much the Kikuyu chief regretted his faith in his relationship with the white man. The Administration interpreted Boyes's action as theft. He was charged with dacoity and brought to Nairobi for trial. The formalities were a farce from start to finish. The askari who collected Boyes gave him the folder of charges so that he could keep it for safety. Bands of warriors turned out in full regalia to salute him as they marched through the villages, such was Boyes's reputation by now among the Kikuyu. The escort became so nervous at this enthusiasm that Boyes was sent ahead to pacify each village lest they were attacked. Even the officials in Nairobi were unprepared to receive the prisoner. But, after some dithering, Boyes was dispatched by train for imprisonment in Fort Jesus. His case came before a judge but, on the grounds that the evidence was flimsy and conflicting, was dismissed.[82] Boyes was released, went to Europe and joined McMillan's White Nile expedition in 1902.

Northrup McMillan was an American millionaire who brought immense wealth to the Protectorate in 1904 and was knighted in recognition for his efforts after the First World War. In 1902 he had mounted an expedition with his friend, an athlete named Charles Bulpett and besides John Boyes Mc-Millan took his aide with him, a nineteen-year-old Venetian, John Destro who had already visited America with him. The group took two years to travel down the Nile by steamer, camel and on foot to Nairobi. In 1904 at Donyo Sabuk, McMillan established Juja Estates and made Destro his farm manager.[83] Northrup McMillan weighed twenty-five stone and his size so impressed the Africans that they called him the largest *msungu* in the world. His income, from rubber estates in Malaya and oil fields in Roumania, made him a valuable pioneer. His companion, Charles Bulpett who lived with McMillan and his wife, became known by everyone in Nairobi as 'Uncle' and claimed that the famous courtesan, La Belle Otero had ruined him financially. Among his athletic achievements was included swimming the Hellespont. Like Sir Northrup and Lady McMillan, Uncle Charles Bulpett, along with Delamere and the Cole brothers, would one day appear in the pages of Karen Blixen's classic *Out of Africa*.[84]

The first large lease of land in Nairobi had been granted to a European married couple on condition that they supplied Nairobi with meat, so that in effect Mr and Mrs Sandbach Baker became Nairobi's first butchers. It was John Ainsworth who recommended the arrangement to Eliot, who gave them 5,000 acres of land at Muthaiga. They called it 'Homestead Farm' and before long, Sandbach Baker, a former merchant of the cotton industry, was supplying beef instead of native mutton for sale; 6 lbs of beef cost only 1 rupee. Soon they were selling the first fresh butter to Nairobi residents as well.[85]

In 1904, in the face of keen German competition, Mrs Sandbach Baker won nine first prizes for her dairy products at a show in Mombasa. By 1908 she had bred between three and four hundred milking cows and by 1909 'Homestead Farm' was supplying Nairobi with butter, cream, milk, Stilton and other cheeses from the cattle raised at Muthaiga.[86] Today, Gertrude's Garden,* the childrens' hospital, stands on the site of the original farmhouse in the exclusive residential suburb of Nairobi.

But as has been seen, not all those early arrivals were as desirable as the Sandbach Bakers. Richard Meinertzhagen who volunteered for service in Africa and had arrived from Burma in April 1902, looked upon his brother officers as regimental rejects. Most were heavily in debt and he was amazed at the casual way in which they brought African women into the mess where 'talk centered round sex and money and is always connected with some kind of pornography'. As a Lieutenant with the First Battalion of The Royal Fusiliers, Meinertzhagen kept diaries. One of his motives behind their publication in 1957 was, he stated, that he wanted his readers to understand the contrasts of life in Nairobi for young subalterns then which, fifty years later, 'oozed with respectability'.[87]

That contrast was not confined to the mess; 'going native' was forgivable so long as one did not get caught. This attitude was a reflection of life in embryonic Nairobi generally. Meinertzhagen felt he had been too junior in 1902 to complain against the flaunting of protocol reserved by other white men, for twilight in the bazaar when, 'almost every man in Nairobi was a railway official and everyone keeps a native girl, usually a Masai.'[88]

Meinertzhagen was doubtful about the success of the settlers' dream, 'I cannot see millions of educated Africans—as there will be in a hundred years time—submitting tamely to white domination. After all it is an African country, and they will demand domination. Then blood will be spilled and I have little doubt about the eventual outcome . . . sooner or later it must lead to a clash between black and white.'[89] He was wrong only in that it took just half that time.

Nairobi had been 'en fête' to greet its first visiting VIP, Joseph Chamberlain in December 1902. Bunting and Union Jacks fluttered above the main thoroughfare from the station as Eliot welcomed the Secretary of State for the Colonies and his wife. Frederick Jackson, his assistant, had thoroughly disapproved of the guest list for the first luncheon to welcome them. He accused Eliot of excluding the 'good settlers', favouring instead people who had been most unsuited to meet a visiting dignitary, among them, '. . . a well known drunkard who . . . left the tent during lunch to relieve himself in front of the ladies . . . Mrs Grey who lives with a black man; Young the photographer and drunkard; Anderson of the Grand Hotel and a rogue of the first water and Tiller, the drunken editor of a native newspaper.'[90]

These were the reporters covering the official visit. Olive Grey was the

---

* Gertrude's Garden was built at Muthaiga by Ewart Grogan after the Second World War in memory of his wife.

ex-Salvation army immigrant turned journalist; Palmer, her Eurasian common-law husband was an ex-employee of the IBEA Company now working
for the railway. Young, of the Dempster Studio, recorded much of Nairobi's
pictorial history with his camera and Tiller was Mayer and Anderson's editor
on the *African Standard* which they had just bought from A. M. Jeevanjee.

Paradoxically it was the distinguished guest who was destined to cause far
more embarrassment than a few bibulous pressmen. Within six months the
result of Chamberlain's tour caused such a disturbance in Nairobi that the
flurry can best be compared with the overturning of an ants' nest.

CHAPTER 4

⊱⊰

White Mates Black in very few Moves

Here in a large and sunlit land,
Where no wrong bites to the bone,
I will lay my hand in my neighbour's hand,
And together we will atone
For the set folly and the red breach,
And the black waste of it all;
Giving and taking council each
Over the cattle kraal.
          Rudyard Kipling, *The Settler*, 1903

In a sense, everything for which Eliot was striving in the Protectorate in 1903 was being undertaken in the wrong order. The trail-blazing role should have been carried out by a handful of adventuresome men and, in time, a railway would have followed. Established settlements would then have been linked to each other once prospects for substantial returns on capital expenditure were certain. Exactly the opposite happened in British East Africa. The railway blazed the trail for the settlers who followed. The land on offer was not even surveyed.

Even so 1903 and 1904 were probably two of the most significant years in its pioneering phase. Several names to become notable in Kenya history emerged when the second Agricultural and Horticultural show was held in February 1903.[1]

John Ainsworth, the Sub-Commissioner, had instigated the event the year before in Nairobi, hoping that it would become an annual fixture.[2] Eleven months afterwards, twenty-six settlers were confident enough to form a Planters' and Farmers' Association. They met on 26 January 1903 at Tommy Wood's. He was made treasurer and W. J. King was appointed secretary and also became the agent for the first crops of potatoes soon to be dispatched with such high hopes of the South African market.[3]

Modest in size though the early shows were, the important thing was that they generated confidence for the future in spectator and producer alike. Not only was the orderliness, effort and enthusiasm behind the displays evident, value lay in the fact that there were enough competitors in 1903 who were willing to take the trouble to walk so many miles to Nairobi to participate.

Delamere had not yet committed himself to settling, but had returned to BEA on a second visit with his wife, Florence, leaving their eighteen-month-old heir at Vale Royal in the care of his nanny. The Delameres attended the 1903 show as guests of honour. Eliot was anxious to draw their attention to the variety and quality of the produce exhibited by those growing experimental crops.[4]

The prize for maize was carried off by E. W. Kreiger, an American missionary who was already growing potatoes as well as trying to raise pigs and cure pork for bacon at Kiambu. Stuart Watt, the missionary from Machakos, won the first prize for fruit; Mrs Oulton for butter. The Oultons* lived at Ngong and vied fiercely with the Sandbach Bakers over the quality of their dairy products at these early shows. By 1904, apples, cotton, castor oil, simsim,** linseed, coffee, poultry, sugar-cane, potatoes and garden produce of all kinds would be displayed.[5]

To assume that the pioneers came only from England would be wrong; they came from Scandinavia, Australia, New Zealand, Russia, France, Austria—from all over the globe. But the majority arriving in the next two years were culled from South Africa's depression following the Boer War. Among them were names which as time went on proved important to the growth of the Protectorate—Ewart Scott Grogan, Russell Bowker, A. C. Hoey, Newland, the Tarlton brothers, the Harries, Stocker and Cowie families and Abraham Block.

Of those names that emerged Delamere and Grogan were the visionaries who wielded power; they became successful spokesmen, landowners, troubleshooters and notable policy makers among the white contingent. Delamere was outspoken and impulsive. Grogan was calculating, a born orator with a sense of the theatrical which he seldom failed to use in his own favour. Few were so well to do that, like Delamere and Grogan, they could make reconnaissance visits before committing themselves. But those who did, such as William Smith and Russell Bowker, carried back their favourable impressions after deciding to take up land, acting as Eliot's disciples by urging relatives, friends and countrymen to follow suit.

Bowker's enthusiasm knew no bounds. In South Africa he described the Nairobi climate as 'one of perpetual summer' where 'cabbages as big as bicycle wheels, turned the scales at thirty pounds; ostriches could be had for

---

* Mr J. T. Oulton is listed in the Kenya Society of Pioneers as having arrived to settle in 1899 and was a telegraph sapper in the NCO. His wife joined him in 1900 and they ran a dairy at Ngong, on land which was later sold to Bror von Blixen. The birth of their first son, Harry, is believed to have been the first European birth registered at Nairobi. Oddly enough in 1985 the site for filming Universal/Pollack's *Out of Africa*.

** Simsim: (*Sesamum Indicum*). The Sesame shrub is native to Ceylon and its oil is used in cooking and medical purposes. It grows three to four feet high, has white flowers which are followed by oil-bearing seeds high in protein and mineral content. The mature pods open at the merest touch; hence the saying 'open sesame'.

the trouble of catching them; there was a comparative absence of stock diseases . . .'[6] His opinion brought forth an immediate response. A flood of applications arrived at Nairobi's Land Office. It was Bowker who was directly responsible in 1904 for the emigration of the Cowie and Harries families who, by a quirk of fate, between them founded the pineapple industry eventually at Thika.[7]

In 1901 the East Africa (Lands) Order Council had tried to place the alienation of land to Europeans on a firm basis by laying down that any land alienated must be Crown Land, that is, land not already occupied by Africans. Next, the Council laid down terms upon which Crown Land could be alienated and thus the Land Department was created. Chiefly its workings were based on the Canadian system though the clause prohibiting the raising of goats came from Cyprus.[8] Once the Department had produced an Ordinance after the Canadian formula for land control, Europeans were able to purchase land whereas before they had only been able to lease it; this immediately proved attractive to would-be settlers although in other respects the Canadian system was not ideally suited to East African conditions.[9]

What the settlers could not buy they made and they learned to make everything, from soap out of zebra-fat to saw-mill belting from buffalo hide. When they had no candle-sticks they cut potatoes in half; they learned the training of oxen from the Boers, and bushcraft from the Africans. The Maasai taught them to make poultices out of dung to apply to wounds closed by thorns. Innovation became second nature to them. Each fresh dilemma was met head-on; every abandoned scheme was replaced by a new one. Necessity made them into a generation of amateur inventors, Heath Robinsons in their own right. Block made needles out of bicycle spokes; Odin Sunde's wife melted down her brass candle-sticks to make bearings for their saw-mill. Farmers used the sawn-off bough of a thorn tree as a harrow and every house contained furniture made from the discarded boxes in which cans of paraffin were shipped.

In Africa, servants became part of the Europeans' existence too. Even those who had never had such luxuries at home employed them and before long it became unthinkable to live without a retinue. As Africans were trained there were cooks and houseboys, dhobies to do the laundry, gun-bearers, syces, labourers and *totos* to help them.

The new grants of land were divided into three classes. There were 'farms' which was a misnomer for a start; in reality they were nothing but 5,000 acres of bush intended for combined pastoral and agricultural purposes of which 1,000 acres was freehold at a penny per acre per annum. The balance was held on a 99-year lease at a half-penny per acre annually. The next category were homesteads of 640 acres (Block and Binks each acquired one of these) which were destined purely for agricultural development on equally favourable but slightly different terms. Lastly there were small business or residential plots which ranged between one and ten acres in proclaimed township areas.[10] Absentee landlords were prohibited but a good deal of 'dummying' went on.

But there were no maps. Prospective settlers were sent off into the blue to choose land and then they were supposed to register their claim. Charles Harries walked 400 miles with one of his sons before applying for land at Thika and Naivasha; William Smith chartered a ship to bring his own large family, a number of friends and their animals from South Africa in 1907 to settle, and walked even farther. On a reconnaissance safari in 1905, Smith enlisted the help of the Chief Blankot as interpreter and guide through the Nandi country during which he and A. C. Hoey covered a thousand miles on foot before applying for land on the Loita Plains.[11] Smith undertook to return from South Africa with twenty more settlers, which helped push through his land grant, and the Government saw that he got 10,000 acres in return for his co-operation but even so the deal took two years to complete.

The same story was repeated over and again. When land had not been registered, and mostly it was not, a crude sketch would be made by a draughtsman in the Survey Office and the applicant's name registered as the provisional owner. He was then free to camp on the area in question *if* his claim happened not to overlap with someone else's. The result of this situation was that it often took months before a clear title could be granted. First a survey had to be carried out at the applicant's expense. The shortage of surveyors (in the course of duty, one of them, a man called Ortlipp, drowned while crossing the Morendat River and his papers were taken by a python, slowing down the process even more),[12] and the great distances that had to be covered caused formidable delays. Month-long queues of would-be settlers waited in limbo for completion. Once the survey had been completed, legal title to the property could be issued after payment off the freehold price, as well as registration and survey fees, on top of the leasehold rent for the first year.

The confusion, the overlapping and all the disadvantages brought about by the way the Land and Survey Department worked, meant that boundaries caused contention between pioneer neighbours in years to come. And they were still 'neighbours' even though, in some cases, they lived as far as twenty-five miles apart. Beacons would be difficult to locate and the unscrupulous took advantage of a problem common to many farmers, claiming a few extra feet of land that was not actually theirs by law.

Meanwhile a social 'upper crust' was establishing itself in Nairobi. Residents jockeyed for invitations to dine with the Commissioner on the Hill. Formal dinners were now given several days a week by Eliot whose ADC would see to it that no-one was left out.[13] Black tie was worn; etiquette was observed carefully; female guests were expected to converse with the gentlemen on their right before the fish course and to those on their left after it.

Behaviour round Eliot's dining-table contrasted sharply with the realities of being out at night. Male guests travelled by mule or bicycle while women were occasionally transported there and back sitting upright in an ordinary chair which was carried by four Africans. The roaring of lion could be heard throughout dinner (it was quite possible to find a snake neatly coiled under one's seat)[14] threatening the life of anyone out after dark. Dusk is brief in Africa and sundown barely lasts half an hour.

The presence of lions was not taken lightly and they were just as evident by daylight and often rested in the shade of the houses on stilts. If one chose not to leave it could and did keep the inmates imprisoned for hours. In 1904, the Post Master, Dan Noble, emerged through his front door one morning to find a young lion sleeping on the wooden steps. They were regarded as vermin and poison was put down in the hope of controlling their numbers. Horses could not be left out as they were a prime target for mauling. As for men, there were already seven headstones in the tiny cemetery, erected in memory of the Europeans who had been killed by lion by 1903. Lions were not the only hazard. Herbert Binks was returning home via the McQueens at Mbagathi after the Agricultural Show and was chased by two rhinos on the nine-mile walk. At Dagoretti he was obliged to light matches and fire off his revolver alternately so as to reach his destination safely.[15]

Such was life in Nairobi when Lord and Lady Delamere were living there in 1903. But why Delamere, who never was content with less than bold experiments, first sought a post in the Administration before applying for land on his own account, is puzzling. Having decided he wanted to take an active part in the opening up of the country, his first idea was to become a Game Ranger.[16] He discussed the feasibility with the Provincial Commissioner, Mr J. O. Hope, but as is shown by remarks made in a letter from Sir Harry Johnston to Sir Clement Hill, the Under Secretary for the East African Department of the Foreign Office in 1903, members of the Administration were already wary of Delamere's sulphurous temper. 'Hope won't make Delamere a Game Ranger as he will make himself a confounded nuisance in any capacity. I wouldn't trust him. He and that other blackguard Dr Atkinson are as thick as thieves.'[17] Denied that post, Delamere asked instead for the even more powerful role of Land Officer.

Eliot had confided in Delamere that often his officials were inexplicably against the incoming settler and had confessed that their general attitude was obstructive enough to suggest that they viewed white settlement with disfavour and distrust. Delamere replied that in contrast his own sympathies lay entirely with the settler, and, if he got the job, he ventured that he would give as much time as possible to listening to the grievances of the settler community. With Eliot's full support, Delamere applied for the post of Assistant Collector and Land Officer on 16 April which was approved four days later by Sir Clement Hill. But on 27 April a note made against Foreign Office records states that the appointment was cancelled.[18]

It seems likely that Delamere's third serious accident was responsible for that annotation. His pony had stumbled into one of the numerous pig-holes on the Athi Plains and he was carried back to Nairobi on a stretcher in severe pain. In the event, Barton-Wright became Acting Land Officer, though his post was not confirmed until 1906.

For the next four months, Delamere lay flat on his back encased in plaster-of-Paris in a thatched hut near Ainsworth's house while Lady Delamere looked after him.[19] It was at this point that Block and his friends from South Africa arrived.

At Mombasa disembarkation took place mid-stream in 1903, so that reaching the stone causeway below the Customs shed in the old town was somewhat precarious. The waters were warm and clear but notorious for sharks which were reputed to follow the ships as they navigated the *mlangu* in the reef.

After the anchor went down, the gang-side was quickly approached by hordes of small craft while, on the other side, lighters moved in to unload baggage. Dug-outs bobbed about among the rowing boats which were manned by Swahili oarsmen, smart in uniforms of white with red cummerbunds. All were clamouring for business. Passengers descended by a companion ladder pressed against the steep and rusting sides of the ship. At the bottom they scrambled aboard a boat, sat upon white cushions and waited, under the protection of a scarlet-lined awning, for every seat to be filled.[20]

It was Swahili custom to chant as they rowed; the lyrics were made up around each boatload and lent an air of festivity as the new arrivals were welcomed by song. Muscled Africans lifted them across the last few wavelets to the island; the impact of heat was fierce with neither breeze nor shade for relief.

Over the side of the ship, Block hailed a *ngalau*. A fisherman's dug-out was the cheapest way to get to shore. In the shallows he was lifted on to the shoulders of a black porter who waded to the causeway with Block's short, thick-set figure clinging to his back.[21]

Luggage was brought off by lighters which took packing cases and animals to a small wooden jetty nearby where it was unloaded by a hand-cranked crane. Block's ponies were crated in improvised horseboxes, like all the early, larger livestock. Smaller animals were usually transferred in baskets by this one crane until it was replaced by steam-powered machinery in 1904.[22]

After Customs clearance, travellers made their way along Ndia Kuu to find somewhere to stay. There were three places from which to choose: The Grand Hotel, which did not live up to its name, in MacDonald Terrace, The Cecil, almost next door, run by a Greek, or The Africa which was Indian run and owned, in Vasco da Gama Street. The alternative to all three was to bed down in the discomfort of the booking hall of the station overnight, braving the clouds of mosquitoes and the certainty of introduction to malaria.[23]

For a select few there was always the Mombasa Club. This was one of the two main institutions at which Europeans met in 1903; the other was the non-residential Sports Club, for which the coast Liwali, Sir Ali Bin Salim, had given the land. At Mombasa Club the food was good; here members 'drank cooling, if un-iced, drinks, read the ancient newspapers and feasted their eyes on the splendid collection of trophies that lined the walls.'[24]

Married couples were automatically excluded as residents however because women were only allowed on the premises at certain hours. Though they were permitted to read the newspaper here, a bell was rung at 7 pm to remind them to leave.[25]

The Grand Hotel, built in 1899, could be called the first choice for the majority. Attracted by the comforts they imagined it would offer, they were in for a shock. It was run by entire novices, an apparently inseparable trio, G. W. Anderson, his Belgian wife Maia and their German friend Rudolf Mayer. They had leased the hotel two years earlier and they claimed to outfit safaris for guests. But as letters and diaries from that period reveal they could be relied upon no more as safari outfitters than for reservations for rooms. Travellers who thought they held bookings would often be informed with a rueful smile that the hotel was full; the option was to accept a mattress laid on the floor of the billiard room after the bar had closed or a camp bed on the upstairs verandah instead.[26] Those who had the misfortune to be allocated an inner room had no windows to provide air or light and hurricane lanterns added to the heat. Torn nets ensured that there was little rest from mosquitoes and, far worse, huge water rats found their way through archways—there were no doors. Complaints to Rudolf Mayer were met with the suggestion that they might prefer to try the Hotel Cecil run by Mr Filios.[27] The Cecil, if more primitive than the Grand, was at least clean whereas The Africa was little more than a hovel and the food execrable. Not only that, the multitude of smells from insanitary earth closets, decaying fish, cats, rancid ghee, spices and mangrove poles, known as *boriti*, which were used in traditional Lamu building, drifted up towards the ribbon of blue sky above the bazaar. Pervading all other smells, however, was the stench from a nearby well that was topped up regularly with shark oil, which was used for boot-topping and for the hulls of dhows as protection against worms. The Andersons and Rudolf Mayer had stayed here themselves to begin with until all their cash was stolen from Maia Anderson's money-belt which she thought she had hidden safely in her room. Then they had been forced through lack of funds to live in a small, abandoned shed at English Point until they sorted themselves out. Before undertaking the management of The Grand, Mrs Anderson took in washing for a short time.[28]

Europeans in those days got about Mombasa in small hooded trolleys. The Administration provided them for officials, most residents owned theirs and a few could be hired. They ran on narrow gauge lines and were pushed by Africans dressed in sailor blouses and shorts. In this odd choice of uniform they sweated profusely as they carried out the task, singing and chattering as they went. Pride was taken in the smartness of turnout; ownership was identified by the choice of colour and trim just as it was among Nairobi rickshaw boys. The trolleys could carry four passengers, two in the front and two behind; a *'gharrie'* was given a shove and the African then hopped on from behind once it was moving. Along the hot white roads flanked by mango and flamboyant trees the white men and women were propelled about their business. Journeys were a little agitating to the nerves if a dog wandered over the lines as the vehicle was going fast down an incline.

Block stayed with an obliging and courteous Armenian Jew who went by the unlikely name of McJohn. His full-time job was to manage Smith MacKenzie, the European trading company, but at night he ran a small bar backing onto a couple of rooms to let near the Cecil, of which in 1904 he became manager. When Block scanned Mombasa for co-religionists, he was struck by the number of Indian and German traders in the town and he discovered that the agents for the line on which he and his friends had sailed were Jews. These two partners, Otto Markus and Rudolph Loy, had just founded The East African Trading Company.[30] Their trading ramifications stretched beyond the boundaries of the Protectorate, wherever trading could be done. It was Loy, short as he was, who on his flat feet took 26 months to lead a safari of 400 porters from Entebbe to Boma Matadi in the Congo. It was a courageous undertaking and he returned without losing a single man and brought back over 25 tons of ivory.[31]

Their firm, probably better known later as The Old East African Trading Company which they founded after the First World War, became famous for its coffee curing and exports but, above all, for the export of hides and skins. They were among the earliest employers of African women, using them to sort the beans in their Kilindini coffee works. In 1904 it was Otto Markus who discovered wild rubber and cotton growing in Uganda.[32] Their offices were by the harbour in the first imported pre-fabricated building. Their chief clerk burned incense on a tray to deter the mosquitoes and its pleasant smell drifted about Block as he introduced himself.[33] Markus, who sported an elaborate set of whiskers, towered above Loy—a dapper little man—and both wore white tropical suits and shoes. They were welcoming and sympathetic but since it was assumed that a Jew would be connected with trading, Markus was probably relieved to learn that this group intended to farm. Both Block's and Markus's motives for coming to British East Africa were rooted in opportunity and escape, but while Block was of farming stock Markus's family were well-to-do landowners who placed much emphasis on learning. During adolescence, cruel schoolboy taunting had stamped Markus with a deep desire to leave Central Europe as soon as it was within his power. After graduating from the Vienna Export Akademie (one of Europe's first business schools) he and fellow graduate Rudolph Loy decided to go to British East Africa to found a business, for which they obtained grants from the Austrian Government. Initially, however, they had been to England and had fitted in well, enjoying both apprenticeship and working in commerce.[34] Markus assisted Block and his group by writing a letter of introduction to Ainsworth and they left for Nairobi on the first train they could get.[35]

The journey up-country from the coast was regarded as an initiation test for the incoming settler and at that time took thirty-six hours. But the scramble to board and get a place at the front of the train was inseparable from the ritual of departure, even when in later years the journey took less time.

The reason was that the farther back one travelled, the dustier one became because the track was laid straight on the ground, without ballast. Consequently not only were passengers shaken about (those wearing false teeth were advised to remove them in advance), but they arrived at their destination coated in layers of red dust which found its way into hair, clothes and luggage. One settler, Daisy Pitt, so as not to arrive looking like a Red Indian in 1910, swathed herself and her children in rags, the oldest clothes she could find and which, on the final approach, could be thrown out of the train window while crossing the Athi Plains.[36]

Most Europeans automatically travelled first-class, unlike Block who could only afford a second-class ticket. The old Indian coaches had no corridor, and were referred to as 'the loose boxes' or 'horse boxes'. Each compartment slept four, the bunks lying parallel to the track so that progress was animated by a ceaseless jolting action only to be relieved by the halts made for meals. These were served in '*dak*' bungalows where the catering was under contract to a Goan, Mr J. Nazareth. Block, being more familiar with the necessities of life than the luxuries, thought the standard of food was good and happily paid one rupee for lunch and dinner and seventy-five annas for his breakfast of boiled eggs and tea.[37] But his opinion was the exception. Generally newcomers were startled by Nazareth's menu which seldom varied from watery soup, tinned salmon, meat balls and fruit and custard. More puzzling still was the nostalgia the railway meals summoned in the old hands, who appeared to find comfort in their awfulness. It was something to do with being back where they belonged.

Dinner was served by Goan stewards in white gloves as multitudes of winged insects, attracted to the lamps suspended low like billiard lights over each table, slid down the shades either into the soup or lodged themselves in the butter.

The first meal taken on the journey was the moment of introduction to the infamous tinned butter from Bombay. Likened to axle grease, it had already suffered three months' exposure to heat in transit before reaching the tables of British East Africa. Such was the disgust that nearly all letters and diaries in the early days refer to it making it easy to understand why '*Siagi ya Queenie*', as Mrs Sandbach Baker's home-made butter was called, was such a success.[38]

Dinner was usually rounded off by a snifter of brandy which was said to help ward off mosquitoes and, when the guard had eaten and was satisfied, the clanging of a bell sent passengers back into the train. Bedding was not provided but those in the know brought blankets and cushions with them for comfort, though it was quite common for people to be awakened by the smell of burning in the night as these or some item of clothing smouldered from a stray cinder.[39] The sparks from the wood-fired engines flew back, tending to blow into the carriages unless the mosquito-gauzed windows were pulled up. There was no water available for drinking or washing between stations let alone to douse the flames. When men wanted to shave in the morning the driver obligingly let down steam from his engine during the breakfast stop.[40]

In the daytime, privileged travellers could ask for a seat to be mounted on the front of the engine; this had been designed so that VIP's could view the great herds of game and the scenery. Not to be outdone, less important passengers used the carriage roof, clambering up the narrow, iron rungs intended for the lamp-lighter's use at dusk.

One driver, Sam Pike, used to halt between stations and, descending from his engine, walk back along the line and demand a whisky or beer if his passengers wished to proceed. A hidden bottle would be produced without argument. Pike was a man of few words who repeatedly got away with his mild form of blackmail because, when he did speak, they all knew he meant what he said.[41]

The discomforts meant nothing; rail travel was the essence of romance then and most people loved it. Friendships formed as gossip was exchanged, love affairs begun and properties sold. As the train slowed to chug up the steeper inclines, male passengers walked along the foot-boards, hand-over-hand, stepping across the division between coaches, to visit friends farther up the train while it was still on the move. Conversations varied from the number of trophies that could be bagged in one year to speculations about plots, crops or the raising of pigs. No scheme was too wild to dismiss without due consideration.[42]

Regular travellers up or down the line soon learned to make themselves thoroughly comfortable and took spirit lamps for making tea, picnic baskets, snuff, flasks of whisky, *kibokos* or guns in case the train stopped and gave them the opportunity to shoot some game.[43]

The railway trucks carried a bizarre variety of cargo from domestic livestock to exotic trophies; propped up against carpet bags would be rhino horns and elephant's feet; Maasai spears, *kikapus* woven from palm fronds and filled with mangoes or coconuts, leopard, lion and hyrax skins beside sacks of flour, chests of tea and the occasional grand piano.[44]

Freight was often curious in the early days but perhaps none so strange as that dispatched by one Mombasa merchant in 1906. Plague, sleeping sickness and small-pox were rampant in Port Florence and in an effort to control bubonic plague one of the Medical Officers offered a bonus for all rats' tails brought to him. His scheme was considered brilliant until the railway traffic department received a query from a consignee in Mombasa, asking the cost of sending rats' tails to the end of the line.[45]

Unusual pets were also a common sight on the trains; monkeys, young gazelle, hyrax, mongooses or sometimes tame baby leopards or young lions appeared in the carriages and frightened the Goanese '*babu*' out of his wits when he came round to punch tickets. The communication cord was seldom pulled for an emergency. It was used rather to advise the driver that there was a lion or an antelope near the line which someone wished to bag. Drivers were quite indulgent in this respect and several went so far as to blow a whistle to draw attention to interesting game as they approached it.[46]

On one occasion a couple of young blades drank so much champagne that they ordered the engine driver out of his cab and drove at a reckless pace through the next station. Travellers also sometimes brought machinery into the carriage, but if an official insisted that a plough should travel in the guard's van, its owner would go with it, refusing to pay his way on account of being forced into the discomfort of perching among the luggage.

Delays were frequent. Markus and Loy were on one train when its boiler was punctured by a charging rhino. It was not an uncommon event for passengers to have to hop out, put their shoulders to it and push the wheezing engine up an incline. On the steep climb from the coast sometimes the only solution was to send back to Mombasa for a supplementary engine.[47] Plagues of army worm—which appeared after periods of drought—impeded progress as their tiny bodies were crushed against the line, making it so slippery that the wheels lost their grip. Heavy rain sometimes washed away chunks of track; passengers then had no alternative but to walk to the nearest *dak* bungalow, where the Goanese staff were somewhat alarmed at the unscheduled prospect of soothing dozens of hungry and tired people.[48]

The arrival and departure of trains was regarded almost as a social event in 1903. At Mombasa, offices closed on those mornings when it was due to leave and at Nairobi Station the same rule applied.[49] It was essential to find out who had come to settle; new contacts could lead to all manner of developments; the shortage of women was acute. For years in the Protectorate there were between fifty and one hundred men for every twenty women. In 1913, one settler, Freddy Ward, climbed a station lamp-post to get a better look at those alighting from the boat train as a new Governor, Sir Henry Belfield, stepped on to the platform with his two daughters. At the sight of Vi Belfield, Ward remarked to his pioneer friend, Donald Seth-Smith, 'One day I'm going to marry her.' And within a few months they were man and wife.[50]

Major H. F. Ward had been attracted first to the country, like so many later wealthier settlers, on a shooting safari and in 1904 became a resident and involved himself in many pioneering schemes including the setting-up and equipping of a safari for the Crown Agents' consulting engineers who in 1909 assessed the cost of exploiting Lake Magadi for its soda. It was he who obtained samples for the English laboratories.[51] But Ward will best be remembered as the agent of Morrison Estates, the firm that just before the First World War founded Muthaiga Club and also put up the first multi-storey stone building with a cellar in the town known as Nairobi House.★ Ward was also very kind to Block on an occasion when he had nowhere to live and offered him a room in his home.[52]

After Mombasa's distinctive Arab atmosphere, Block was disappointed in Nairobi and described the whole town as 'a slushy mess'. He was, moreover, short of cash. Three hundred pounds was considered quite adequate capital with which to start and within a matter of weeks Block's colleague Hotz

★ Nairobi House was demolished in 1982 despite a considerable amount of public protest.

settled at Molo while the others dispersed round Kiambu and Ruiru on 640-acre 'farms'.

Sir Donald Stewart, the man who succeeded Eliot as Governor, emphasised that the country needed men of 'the right stamp . . . with about £500 capital to start with, to make a success of a homestead within five years.'[53] In 1908 Donald Seth-Smith, who was struggling to establish a farm at Makuyu wrote home to his father, 'if only settlers with £3,000 each would come to BEA as opposed to shooters. The place swarms with safaris.'[54] Block, however, needed a job. He probably had about £23. Fortunately he was a man of unusual resource.

A typical example of how Block improved his circumstances was the way he borrowed five pounds from his friend Max Nightingale in order to buy a couple of sows. He put them in litter but, being unable to afford sties, dug pits to keep them in. He persuaded one or two hotels to give him scraps for swill and, once the fully-grown piglets were ready for market, offered them to these hotels for bacon and ham, at a special price which ensured a quick sale. Once the loan was repaid, the profit was put to work on some similar scheme. And no matter how small the margin he usually made a profit.[55] There is no evidence that he allowed himself ever to get into debt; his deals took time to execute but were worked out with painstaking exactitude beforehand. He drove himself hard, expecting employees do the same, and was never able to take his ultimate wealth for granted. If he spied a nail in the dust he would pocket it. The only sign that he was ever nervous was a life-long habit of sucking the tip of his little finger, in moments of tension. He became used to rising at 4 am when he got his first farm and the habit drilled a lifelong pattern into him.[56]

By 1903 Wood's Hotel, besides the four rooms to let, boasted a butcher's shop and a tailor's; the dining room seated twelve and, if unpretentious, this ensured that strangers became acquainted quickly. The hotel faced a rutted track known as Station Road (which later became part of Government Road) where in 1902, in an attempt to improve its unremitting ugliness, Ainsworth had planted eucalyptus saplings right up to the bazaar at regular intervals during the heavy rains; they grew to over fifty feet but many were felled to make way for power and telegraph lines as Nairobi developed. From the verandah at the back of the hotel the view was glorious. As the sun rose over Donyo Sabuk, it illuminated mile upon mile of plains thick with herds of game grazing in peace, and Thomson's and Grant's gazelles came right up to the back door to feed.[57] Block took one of Wood's shabby rooms; the daily rate was three rupees and included meals. The room was barely furnished with an iron bedstead and lumpy mattress, an old chair and a paraffin box for a table upon which stood an enamel jug and basin for washing.[58]

Seven in the morning was the time when those still in bed learned their first phrases in Swahili as Tommy Wood, bothered by an abnormal number of Africans wanting things, could be heard repeating in a loud voice, 'Wataka Nini? Wataka Nini?' (What do you want? What do you want?) And the

Africans, whose minds run parallel with a culture of fable and myth, christened him 'Wataka Nini.'[59]

It was usual, after very short acquaintance, for the Africans to deal out names to those Europeans with whom they came in contact. These were not always complimentary but, in their aptness, displayed either wit or perception on the Africans' part for they laugh from reasons different to those of Europeans and just as often for sheer content as from spite. They called Block '*Kamundo*' at first, meaning midget, on account of his stature but, as his ability to better himself became apparent, the Kikuyu who knew him best looked upon him as a man of vision and called him '*Kamiano*', meaning a prophet, one who sees forward, even when he sleeps.[60] A. Johansen, a Norwegian who lived near Block, was known as 'Mafungo' meaning Jack-of-all-trades because he was a lay-preacher and farmer; Commander Niverson, another neighbour, was always on his dignity, insisting that his labour called him 'Bwana'. However he mispronounced the word as 'Bano' so they christened him that, as well as his farm.[61] The elephant hunter Neumann earned the strange title of *Bwana Nyama*, Swahili for meat, because he always tied it in a fly-proof muslin cloth whilst out in the bush, a precaution which puzzled the Africans completely.[62]

These names were used when sending runners to friends with a note, for the Africans were able only to identify a white person by his African name. District Commissioners quickly recognised their usefulness; local registers were drawn up, listing the Europeans with their Swahili identification alongside. The system simplified their work in locating a farmer living some twenty miles or more from an Administrative boma. There was always the fear of being mocked nonetheless. One DO confessed to his mother, 'I have . . . just discovered that I am called "Bwana Murujuru" which means smart, neat, chic, etc. I had a horror I might be called "squeaky legs" . . . while my gaiters were new, they creaked in a very noticeable fashion. Tate is called Bwana Kongoni . . . native for hartebeeste.' (This was because Tate had a long face and, like the animal, a mournful expression.) 'Capell, the D.C. at Dagoretti is known as "the man with two wives" because he has a nurse in his house for his children. . .'[63]

Employment was impossible for Europeans to find in 1903. Block was prepared to turn his hand to anything; his contacts, Tommy Wood and A. M. Jeevanjee, with whose racehorses Block's ponies were stabled, could scarcely have been bettered. But the prevailing mood in Nairobi was one of uncertainty. People were waiting, unable to commit themselves fully to investment or development while the siting of the town was still in question. Otto Markus remembered the apathy of bidders. When the first land sales had taken place a few months before the whole of what is now Government Road could have been bought for £500, yet not a single plot was sold. Everyone believed that a more favourable location would be chosen.[64]

However there are always those who disregard general attitudes. Mayence Bent was sure that the town would not be moved. She was about to open The

Hotel Stanley, named after the African explorer. The newness of the corrugated iron was all that separated its appearance from the other scores of buildings on stilts with wooden steps but apart from the fact that she had no mattresses she was ready to receive guests. Block heard of her dilemma and seized the opportunity to earn some money out of it. While he was riding about looking for work earlier that September he had noticed a great many bundles of dried grass which had been cut from either side of the railway. Believing that this would make suitable mattress filling he obtained permission from the Railway Superintendent to collect enough; he found ticking in the Indian Bazaar and, with the help of Mr R. M. da Souza, a Goanese merchant who provided Block with a tailor, worked out the dimensions. And then Block discovered that there were no mattress needles with which to assemble them. Ingenuity worthy of any pioneer overcame the problem; he sharpened and punctured two old bicycle spokes and stitched them with these instead. Mayence Bent approved the sample and ordered twenty-three more. He delivered them three weeks later and was paid 10 rupees each (the equivalent of about 14/6 in 1903).[65]

With his mattress profits Block decided to buy a farm on the 'pay-as-you-earn' system.[66] Dotting the Kiambu landscape were a number of new homesteads belonging to Europeans; mostly *rondavels*, round thatched huts built in the Kikuyu tradition; the walls were made of red mud and cow dung and cost little to construct. The roof was thatched and the floors were of beaten earth. Some were already surrounded with patches of experimental crops, others barely developed at all.

Two German farmers, Dr Ufferman and Mr Lauterbach, alerted Block to the fact that a man called Corran had put the disposal of his 640-acre farm 'Njuna' seventeen miles from Nairobi in their hands and left the country. They offered it to Block for 1,500 rupees and were willing to accept payment at his convenience. 'Njuna' was in the Upper Kiambu district; the ground was cleared but not broken.[67] Though it was not like Block to buy without seeing anything first, perhaps he feared that, by riding out to inspect the land first he might lose the favourable deal to someone quicker off the mark. He paid Ufferman a deposit of one hundred rupees and sought legal advice to clinch the verbal arrangements.

Luck rather than shrewdness played the more significant part in final negotiations. Block was too early for his appointment with Bertram Allen of Tonks and Allen, who were still the only solicitors in Nairobi, and Allen happened to be unengaged. Thus Block had the opportunity to discuss his scheme more elaborately than he had planned. After listening intently, Allen suggested, to Block's surprise, that as he had £100 lying idle, he was willing to pay for the farm whilst taking transfer in Block's name. The title deeds could be held as security by Tonks and Allen until the loan was paid off.[68] Through B. G. Allen's generosity and trust, Block acquired 'Njuna'. It was to be a profitable piece of land, part of which was sold and the rest divided into three farms; later still it was developed again and renamed Kamundu Estate.

Block purchased a few tools from a kindly Roumanian merchant, Mr J. Marcus, and with a renewed feeling of optimism loaded up one of his ponies. Mounted on one, leading the other, he rode out to see what he had bought.

J. Marcus, who should not be confused with his namesake, Otto Markus of the East African Trading Company in Mombasa, was also Jewish, but had arrived from India in 1902 and was involved in the first potato rush in Nairobi. He hired out rickshaws and provided tools for the early farmers in return for selling their grain, hides and other harvests; prospectors bought their blasting powder, safety fuses and mining spoons from him to begin with; eventually he became an estate agent and auctioneer, earning a reputation for fair dealing.[69]

When Block got to Njuna he discovered that it had more to its name than he thought. There was a hut in which was a crude home-made bed and some cooking pots and there were even a few chickens scratching about outside and some pigeons but a local mongoose took these before he had the chance of a meal from them himself. The frames of the door and windows were covered by sacking and there were also a number of paraffin boxes, the inevitable alternative for furniture.[70]

Lowly the empty paraffin boxes and tins may have been, but how the pioneer would have managed his life without them is hard to imagine. For a start, the empty tin or *debe* was vital, especially to farmers, for the transportation of water. The McQueens fetched their water from the river in them for years but even in Nairobi as late as 1908 domestic supplies of water in the Parklands area were still obtained from a standpipe where they were filled by waterboys who carted the cans back to each home, half a mile or more.[71] In fact the *debe* was invaluable for gathering anything from ghee to coffee. The four-gallon iron measure used in the modern coffee industry is derived from those early harvests when pickers were paid by the *debe*. It could be flattened and used as roofing, hammered into jelly moulds, baking or roasting tins or turned into a make-shift oven perched on three stones. Dover stoves were not imported until 1906 so that this was a real step forward after open fires. The bride of Richard Geater, one of Nairobi's earliest architects, was impressed in 1908 at how civilised everything was but in particular she marvelled at the ability of the African *mpishi*, the skill with which cooks could produce bread and three-course meals in ovens contrived from two *debes* placed side by side. Perhaps it was not so surprising for Africans seem to have a natural gift for cooking, making soufflés and sponge cakes or other European recipes with the barest of equipment and from memory, though these are alien to their own simple needs.[72]

Discarded paraffin tins also made excellent coolers. First they were punctured liberally with a hammer and nail, then filled with charcoal. A small chamber created from cedar posts and double wire netting into which more charcoal was rammed formed a cooling room. Meat was suspended from a hook into this. The charcoal packed *debe* was placed on top, water was added and filtered down to the netting 'walls' below. Sometimes this contraption was built round a tree but always out of doors so that the wind acted as the cooling agent. In this chamber, butter, ghee or a freshly killed sheep could be kept safe from ants and uncontaminated by flies or heat for a fortnight, while venison lasted three weeks.[73]

The wooden packing cases surrounding the paraffin tins were no less adaptable; the late Nellie Grant, mother of Elspeth Huxley, describes staying with Alan Tompson, a pioneer who lived at Karura in 1913, where they were used in lieu of chairs in 'a hovel where you sat on petrol boxes, your feet on dust floors inhabited by myriads of fleas, and ate the most divine things from Fortnum and Mason.'[74]

Everyone used them, not just to sit on, but as chop-boxes, occasional tables, bookshelves, dressing tables, chests of drawers and cupboards. They could be stacked whichever way was needed, providing shelving for everything. Many of the next generation were taken on safari in a paraffin box; four handles were attached turning them into the perfect litter in which to transport babies and small children.[75]

Innovation, particularly when it was brought about by frugality, tended to brand the pioneers with an unshakeable sense of economy not to say meanness. Later, when they could afford to be less hard on themselves, most of the old timers were reluctant to part with money for what women considered 'decent' furnishing. The experience of doing without had tempered their idea of necessity. Gunny sacking and paraffin boxes had been good enough for Block and, in the last five years of his life when his wife suggested that they should buy new curtains and furniture for their cottage at the Norfolk Hotel, he looked upon her request as frivolous.[76] Luxury always will be relative. After months of travelling through the bush, the notion of dining off a white tablecloth, turning on a tap and sleeping under one roof becomes that of heaven. There is nothing like deprivation to quicken a lost sense of appreciation for the simplest of pleasures.

The year that Block got his farm and the one after were abnormally dry. The farmer who lives through drought will never forget watching his crops wither to nothing when as seedlings they had been so full of promise. The lack of rain was blamed for the failure of experimental cotton, clover, rye-grass, lucerne and Egyptian clover in 1903 and 1904.[77] Maize millet, wheat, barley, lentils, fenugreek and native beans withstood the dry conditions moderately well. Luckily for Block his seed potatoes, linseed and beans fell into this category. But he had to plough and break his land before he could sow anything.

The need for a plough posed a new financial crisis. His ponies were precious to him but they were also his only saleable asset. Reluctant as he was to give up his only form of transport, he concluded that something to ride was less vital for survival than machinery to break the soil. Imported ponies were scarce and commanded a high price at the time and so there was no difficulty in finding a buyer. 'Bano' Niverson bought them for a thousand rupees—almost as much as 'Njuna' had cost, the equivalent of £75.[78]

Supplies of any sort were seventeen miles from 'Njuna'. The so-called road was only a track. All the higher country around was covered by forest, dense bush, bracken and Kikuyu grass; humus a foot deep, soaked up rain like a sponge, feeding the rivers by a process of percolation from one rainy season to the next. Soil erosion, which came later, was then unknown. Apart from a slight discoloration in the rainy seasons, the rivers such as the Nyare, ran clear for most of the year round.[79]

The walk to Nairobi took Block two days, there and back; because he had no cow, nor were there cattle, African or otherwise, nearby, he had to buy tinned milk. That had to be carried if not by himself, by Kikuyu women, on the homeward journey.[80] Unless a farmer had a horse or mule, he travelled on foot beside a bullock, resigning himself to its unhurried pace and of having to take the long way round.

It was not easy either for the early farmers to dispose of produce. On more than one occasion Block trekked into town with his ox-cart laden with cucumbers, cabbages, lettuces and garden peas to receive only 10 rupees for his trouble.[81] The days of all the pioneers were filled with the minutiae of like disappointment. The Niversons had put most of Bano under ramie, a fibre which was used to make lamp mantles and, in India, high-class underwear but they had completely overlooked the fact that to process ramie they needed a decorticator. Luckily they tried coffee next, which throve in 'Kyambu', as it was then spelled.[82]

'Kiambu *Boma*' was the administrative centre of that part of Kikuyuland but all Government *bomas* took on a uniform look, their layout being dictated by identical sectors of the administration. Each consisted of a District Commissioner, known at first as a Collector, because he collected taxes, and a number of District Officers. There was also a Police Post in the charge of a European Officer as well as one or two Goan clerks and a medical centre, which usually developed into a hospital. The paths between them were flanked by low, red flowering Christ Thorn and the Union Jack was flown every day. Wherever these posts were set up Asian traders soon followed and opened one or two '*dukas*'. Before long they multiplied to become flourishing trading centres until all the African trade for miles around was in their hands.

Block managed to get women to work for him, but the supply of labour was generally difficult for years.[84] Those members of the Kikuyu tribe who could be persuaded to work came from Fort Hall, and further afield from Ndia and Embu, living over sixty miles distant near the foot of Mt Kenya. They were far less sophisticated than those near to Nairobi and many had never seen a white man before. Timid by nature, those who were employed often ran away on the last day of the month never returning to claim their pay. Fortunately, few farmers were unscrupulous enough to take advantage of this but the Ndia were so ignorant that they were looked down upon by the rest of the Kikuyu as simpletons.[85]

The change in the Kikuyu attitude, in being prepared to leave their homes to work in 1903 for Europeans, was to earn money to pay their two rupee hut tax. The East Africa Protectorate had followed the example of Uganda where it had been introduced in 1902 at the higher rate of 3 rupees per annum.[86] This was the very first experience of tax paying for Africans. Being based on the number of huts rather than heads, the economic pressure was felt immediately among the Kikuyu and most other tribes, for the richer a man was, the more wives he had. And, since each wife had to have her own hut, her husband was taxed accordingly. But though it was quite a fair form of tax, the single man who shared a communal hut was unaffected and therefore, to even things out, the hut tax was later replaced by a poll tax imposed on all males regardless of status.

Block had to walk a total of eighty-five miles just to get his plough and six oxen to Njuna.[87] He had been lucky to find a plough to buy because until 1904 none were imported on a regular basis and the demand had been so erratic that the shortage was acute. Wealthier settlers were able to import them but farmers like Binks and McQueen had resorted to making their own. So unsatisfactory was this situation that by January 1904, the East African Agricultural and Horticultural Society decided that, if any worthwhile development was to take place, they must organise a system of importing ploughs from Australia. These could be sold to anyone for cash, but the one hundred and twenty members of the Society would benefit from paying on the instalment system.[88]

Block's Rudsak plough was borne home on the backs of Kikuyu women traditionally by means of a strap which went up round the forehead; it was adjustable so that each load sat snugly in the small of the back. To take the weight off the brow, the women stooped forward constantly so that by middle-age most of them bore a deep depression round the forehead and were pigeon-toed from having already spent half their lives in toil.[89]

Ploughing virgin soil was a tough occupation, not only physically but emotionally. As Donald Seth-Smith, Alan Tompson's farming partner at Makuyu explained in a letter home in 1908, 'it is a heartbreaking game—ploughs break, bullocks die—you teach the boys, then they leave you; when one's back is turned they sleep and it takes a week to plough two acres, so you see, to make a nice farm of a thousand acres would take a lifetime with oxen.'[90] After breaking the soil needed to lie fallow for six months before re-ploughing and harrowing took place. At best, two teams could manage to plough four acres of land in a week with a skilled driver behind them.

That first year Block grew potatoes and oats on the small section that was ready for them; he caught the rains and was so successful that the harvest brought what he decribed as 'a handsome profit', leaving him enough seed to plant another two acres of each.[85] His Rudsak dealt efficiently with the tough Kikuyu grass but teaching the Africans to work with machinery required enormous tolerance. Many of the methods of the Europeans were incomprehensible to them. Few had seen a turning wheel before and, rather than trying to understand, they regarded all contraptions as just another instance of white man's magic.[91]

Block's existence however was solitary; neighbours were too distant to drop in on one another. Essential visits only were made to Nairobi and even then a chance encounter with lion or hostile tribesmen might delay travellers.

Some pioneers owned bicycles but, unless a track was suitable, it was not necessarily a quicker means of travel. In the dry season wheeled progress could be impeded by six inches of dust. During the rains, rivers became raging torrents. Usually one could swim across these but occasionally more drastic action was required. A. B. McDonnell, who planted the first tea in the country at Limuru, was forced on several occasions to pull his bicycle to bits, swim across with each piece and put it together again on the other side. The disadvantages of the bicycle in a country so deeply cut by river valleys are evident, though some overcame them by employing a labourer to run behind and push it up the hills.[87] The founders of the sisal industry, Randall Swift and his partner Ernest Rutherfoord, managed to at least reduce the exertion of walking the forty-six miles from Makuyu to Nairobi by sharing one bicycle. They devised a relay method by which one of them would set out on foot from Punda Milia* at dawn, to be overtaken by the other on the push-bike several hours later. It was then handed over to the walker, who rode for the next ten miles, leaving it on the side of the track for his partner to pick up later. Ernest Rutherfoord once rode it to Nairobi and back, against a strong headwind, on the homeward lap with a pulley wheel weighing 30 lbs tied to the back. It was an extraordinary feat. Rutherfoord, however, who was known by the Africans as *Kiama*, meaning 'very young', took his physical condition seriously and used to carry a bag of maize on his back and one under each arm just to improve his stamina.

Block and the other potato growers dreamed of the fortune they were going to make out of 'spuds'. W. J. King went to South Africa with samples of potatoes on behalf of the Planters' and Farmers' Association and sold them at £12 a ton in the Transvaal.[88] When he returned triumphant with this news, settlers in Limuru and Kiambu planted potatoes as fast as they were able, but growing them successfully turned out to be one side of the coin; exporting them quite another. McQueen had already cornered the local market by selling all he could grow to the King's African Rifles lines.[89] Local demand was minimal because, with the exception of the sweet potato cultivated by the Kikuyu, potatoes were virtually unknown to the Africans. Young Herbert Binks, farming at Limuru, was so disillusioned after his efforts failed that he considered 'flitting to Australia'. During his first year he had tried growing peas, castor oil trees, orchids, khol rabbi, celery, cauliflower, leeks, spinach, Brotherton's early York cabbage, carrots, turnips, tomatoes, onions, ramie, coffee, plums, apples and pears. He built his own house, experimented with brick and basket making, had made his own wooden plough and, 'wonder of wonders to the natives', a tin windmill. He could not afford a servant, so he taught himself to cultivate yeast, bake bread and to carry out all other

---

* The name of their farm, so called on account of its massive zebra herds.

household chores and, after his pony dropped dead from horse-sickness on a journey to Nairobi, he walked therafter to obtain his supplies too. [90]

Not long after regular consignments of potatoes were exported, complaints from South Africa were received. The potatoes were deteriorating in transit. This put an end to that particular vision of success and, in fact, though experiments with numerous varieties continued, even by 1912 growers were unable to establish a satisfactory export market. [91]

Day after day for almost two years Block farmed by himself at Njuna but when he was old he confessed that the solitary existence, monotonous diet and failure to make real progress, insidiously weakened his resolve. [92] But it was not only that.

Joseph Chamberlain's plans which had grown out of his discussions with Theodor Herzl four months earlier in London, had come to light in Nairobi on 27 August 1903 with a vehement display by the remainder of the community against a 'threatened Jewish invasion'. Reactions were violent, ugly and, as might expected, revealed anti-semites in Nairobi where none had seemed to exist before. If the pioneer settlers could be compared to hardworking ants beforehand, by September they were behaving as if their nest had been overturned.

The paradox, so far as Block is personally concerned, is that in 1905 the Chairman of the Anti-Zionist Immigration Committee, Lord Delamere, would be the very person to dissuade him from leaving the country. [93]

Ernest Gedge, the expedition headman at Machakos, 1889 with Frederick
Jackson, James Martin and Dr Archibald Mackinnon, treaty making with the
Kikuyu Chief Kamiri on August 11th. (Royal Commonwealth Society).

Indian coolies moving camp along the line towards Nairobi during construction
of the Uganda Railway *c.* 1896. (Royal Commonwealth Society).

The Old Harbour, Mombasa 1904. (Royal Commonwealth Society).

Ndia Kuu, the main street from the old port in Mombasa *c.* 1904 showing the trolley transport and narrow gauge lines. (Royal Commonwealth Society).

Sir Charles Eliot and John Boyes, probably *c.* 1903. (Olga Rogers).

Dr Rosendo Ayres Ribeiro riding the zebra he ⟨n⟩amed. Nairobi 1907. (Dr Ayres Riberio).

Rudolph Loy and Otto Markus outside their office in Mombasa *c.* 1906. (Harry Markus).

The McQueen family at Rhino Farm, Mbagathi. (Minnie McKenzie).

Mary Walsh 'Pioneer Mary' also known as 'Bibi Kiboko'. (Iris Mistry).

Mayence Bent's Stanley Hotel before the great Fire of Victoria Street in 1905. (Jan Hemsing).

Martin Seth-Smith in a double-terai with a buffalo trophy. *c.* 1908. (Anthony Seth-Smith).

Helen Sanderson with her two daughters, Kitty and Biddy, on the way to Miss Seccombes School on Railway Hill as weekly boarders by rickshaw. *c.* 1907–1908. (Kit Taylor).

The original Norfolk Hotel built by Winearls and Ringer in 1904.

Fred Cole, skinning a carcase of a gazelle, shot f
the pot on E. Powys Cobb's farm Keringet.
Behind him can be seen the fireplaces and
chimneys of Keringet then under construction.
(Dorothy Vaughan).

Lord Delamere among his thatched huts at
Soysambu. (John Ward).

braham Block with a group of pioneering friends probably taken just before the first world war.
Ruth Rabb).

Members of the Klapprott family on the road to the Uashin Gishu. *c.* 1906. (Peter Faull).

Boer traders accompanying the Klapprott family on their safari to the Uasin Gishu. (Peter Faull).

The Klapprott team of oxen hauling the timber for their house across the Uasin Gishu Plateau. *c.* 1906. (Peter Faull).

CHAPTER 5

⌒﹋⌒

An Ante-Chamber to the Holy Land

'The missionary carried the Bible; the soldier carried the
gun; the administrator and the settler carried the coin.
Christianity, commerce, civilisation: the Bible, the coin, the
gun: Holy Trinity.'

Ngugi wa Thiongo, *Petals of Blood*

The handful of Jews already settled in the country had come not as pedlars or
traders but as artisans and farmers who were essential to the community.
Now, as anti-semitism made itself felt for the first time, suddenly all races felt
threatened. From the outset of colonisation, relations between Africans,
Indians and Europeans were jeopardised by misunderstanding through
ignorance of each other's culture. Of the three ethnic groups, the Jews were
included in the European sector but those with whom they shared it regarded
them as an alien race.[1]

When it became known in Nairobi that Chamberlain had set aside 5,000
square miles of uninhabited land in the Eastern Province of Uganda for
Jewish immigrants it was to Delamere that the settlers turned; he was still
confined to bed in his temporary home after his accident. All those wanting to
discuss the horrors of the threatened 'invasion' called at his hut on the south
side of the swamp. From here, his long red hair spread on his pillow, he
embarked on the path of spokesman and father of white settlement. His
vociferous campaigns for improvement of conditions for settlers were to
become as famous as his attacks against injustice by the Government. The
Europeans were lucky to have him; there was no-one as yet to speak up for
the Africans and Indians.[2]

The first pioneers to hear of the proposed Jewish Settlement scheme were
those resident or visiting Nairobi. It took two months for the news to filter
through to Nyeri, ninety miles away, in spite of the displays of outrage by, as
The African Standard put it, 'pulpit, public and press'.[3]

Meinertzhagen, in Nyeri, heard through 'Kongoni' Tate, the District
Commissioner, in October; 'Tate tells me that there is a plan on foot to offer

the Jews a home on the Uasin Gishu Plateau. I hope they refuse it, for it is just asking for trouble. In the first place the Jews' home is in Palestine, not in Africa. The scheme would only add to the political confusion and God knows there will be enough trouble here in 50 years when the natives get educated. Also the Jews are not good mixers—never have been; they have their own religion, customs and habits and would constitute a most indigestible element in East Africa if they came in any numbers. Why not persuade the Turks to give them Palestine? The Arabs are doing nothing with it, and the Jews with their brains and dynamic force would be a tremendous asset to Turkey.'[4]

What had actually happened was that the British Government, following the tentative negotiations with Herzl and other Jewish leaders, had sent a definite proposal on 14 August to Leonard Greenberg, Chairman of the Actions Committee of the Zionist organisation.

The Sixth Zionist Congress met at Basle on 23 August. Nearly 600 delegates and over 2,000 spectators were present when the British proposal was put to Congress, which was asked to send a Commission to East Africa to enquire into the viability of the scheme, a proposal that was greeted with squalls of protest. The Russian delegates rejected the scheme unanimously. When votes were taken after days of heated exchange, 295 were for sending the Commission, 178 against while 90 delegates abstained. But there were no funds available, and feeling ran so high that it threatened to divide the whole Zionist movement.[11]

In Nairobi Delamere lost no time in dispatching an expensive cable to *The Times*: 'Feeling here very strong against introduction of alien Jews . . . Flood of people that class sure to lead to trouble with half-tamed natives jealous of their rights . . . Englishmen here appeal public opinion, especially those who know this country, against the arbitrary proceeding and consequent swamping bright future of the country.'[6] The cable cost £20, but he was starting as he meant to go on.

Next, he had a twenty-six page pamphlet printed. It contained an indictment of the Government's methods of land alienation, the cause of so much bad feeling, and he opposed the scheme on the grounds that it was contrary to the undertaking given by the Commissioner on the subject of white settlement; Jews were parasites not agriculturalists and would tend to form a poor white class. The area in question would affect the Maasai presently occupying it; it was unsuited to small scale peasant farming and unsuitable for European settlement.[7]

Naturally, having applied through Eliot for land himself only two months ago, Delamere felt as strongly as anyone about the Zionist scheme. He had hoped for land on the Laikipia but Eliot disagreed because it was too far removed from the railway and administrative centres for successful sheep farming, which was what Delamere intended to do. Ironically, as was later proved, he had been refused one of the best areas on which to raise sheep in the country.[8]

Delamere applied next for 100,000 acres near Naivasha but this too was turned down lest the Maasai be deprived. The land he got in the end lay on the western flanks of the Rift Valley between the Molo River and Njoro, and he invested several thousand pounds in sheep-raising on it before discovering it was quite unsuitable. This was the only direct grant he ever received and his annual rent was £200 for a 99-years lease. The condition was that he had to spend £5,000 developing it within five years but throughout these negotiations Delamere's health was so fragile that, as a precaution, Eliot drew up a special paper so that if he died his land would revert to Government.

Coincidentally, three Australians, V. M. Newland and his partners, the brothers Henry and Leslie Tarlton, had also applied from Johannesburg for land at Naivasha at this time. Once it had been tentatively granted, they arrived to take it up. In Nairobi, however, the Land Officer informed them that their grant was no longer available as the Government had now decided to reserve the whole of the Naivasha area for the Maasai tribe.[9] They were offered an alternative site north of Nakuru, but finally chose a thousand-acre farm in Kiambu and a residential plot in Parklands. Lack of capital soon forced them to sell the larger property at an absurdly low price. But as a result of the fiasco Nairobi acquired its first auctioneers and estate agents and within three months they had started their safari concern.

As the Jewish question raged, Delamere's first batch of imported stock was on the water. His agent at Vale Royal had shipped 7 Ryeland rams, 10 Ryeland ewes, 2 Lincoln rams, 2 Border Leicester rams, 2 Romney Marsh rams, 3 turkey cocks, 12 turkey hens, 2 Aylesbury drakes, 10 Aylesbury ducks, 2 ganders, 10 geese, 2 cock pheasants, 6 hen pheasants, 1 Short-horn bull, 2 Short-horn cows, 1 Hereford bull, 2 Hereford cows, a pony and some pigs which arrived in the care of a Scots shepherd, Sammy McCall, towards the end of the year.[10]

Meanwhile Delamere, though delicate physically, used his active mind to cook up schemes in preparation for when he was mobile again. Ideas were culled from resident farmers and thrown into the local melting pot from which everyone could draw. He even organised an essay competition in the press, and donated prizes for the three best submitted under the heading, 'The advantages this country offers to the White Settler for Agriculture, Planting and Stock Handling'. The winner was W. S. Bent.[11]

Already the vanguard of Nairobi's tiny Jewish community had established itself. Besides J. Marcus, Block and his friends from South Africa, were Sam Meddicks, a tinsmith who was trying to keep pace with orders for water-tanks (it was desirable to have one at each corner of the house for rainwater storage), John Rifkin, Michael Harrtz—Russian blacksmiths, and Sam Jacobs who started The Dustpan, a furniture emporium which stocked everything.[12]

Wood's advertisements bore a new slogan, 'East Africa may be Jewed but you will not if you deal with T. A. Wood, Nairobi Stores.' Gatherings of protest were held at Wood's Hotel. The Railway Institute housed the largest meeting to have been attended by white men so far in Nairobi where an Anti-Zionist Immigration Committee was formed. A hat handed round to finance a 'defence fund', collected one hundred and sixty-two rupees. Though absent, Lord Delamere was proposed and made Chairman by Dr Atkinson who had come in to chair the meeting. Another neighbour of Block's, McClellan Wilson, together with Wood, the Reverend P. A. Bennett and a coloured settler, P. E. Watcham, excelled themselves as they voiced their opinions as to the threat the Jewish settlement scheme posed. Atkinson could hardly have been termed 'desirable' as a resident himself after his recent trial; yet he coolly declared that he 'knew that it had been proved that Jews rendered themselves obnoxious to the people of every country they went to, and he was quite sure that they would only turn out to be a hindrance instead of a help to British East Africa. It was the duty of the meeting to bring forward every objection to these undesirables being landed in their midst.'

Wood observed that 'the British tax-payers wanted people to settle who will give a return on the money invested. How can they expect this if they located possibly the lowest class of white men in the heart of the country?'[13]

The Reverend 'Pa' Bennett, as he was known, described the Jews as 'a people who were alien in their habits, thoughts and actions'.[14] He was certain that they would prove objectionable to everyone in the country. Poverty was the prime target for his objection; in fact Bennett was so poor that he supplemented his meagre stipend by cutting fuel for the railway six days a week on the escarpment and because he could neither afford to buy his children clothes or his wife a sewing-machine she had to make them by hand, as well as their underwear out of flour bag linings. In those days flour was imported from Australia in double bags. The outer bag was of coarse hessian, known as 'gunny', the inner bag of cotton was the part she used to make underclothes. Bennett could not afford to replace his one threadbare suit at Tommy Wood's, where bespoke suits cost less than forty rupees—about three pounds. Yet he had turned up to hold a service on a farm, with the seat of his trousers worn right through from the constant friction of the wooden seat of the little cart he drove. His host gave him a pair of trousers which were out at the knees but had a complete seat, so that, worn on top of one another, they took care of Bennett's respectability.[15]

In a despatch to Lansdowne, Eliot wrote, 'I do not see how we can afford to reject the scheme, but I deeply regret that H.M. Government do not see their way to initiate or actively patronise some plan for peopling the Protectorate with British Colonists.'[16]

When Delamere tried to enlist Eliot's support for another cable to *The Times* the Commissioner would not side with him because of the economics of the project. As he explained to Delamere he had 'no wish to hinder you from expressing your opinions but I will, if you wish, forward a statement of them to the Foreign Office, if you like to put them in some suitable form. I am not anti-semitic myself and do not share your objections to Indians and other non-English settlers but I confess . . . I view it with very mixed feelings. But you must understand the importance of the financial question. This Protectorate alone costs the Government at home £256,000 per annum. If the settlers here were British tax-payers they would be the first to protest against what they would call a monstrous waste of money. As long as we go on in this way we are always exposed to the risk that a radical Government may cut our vote in aid, and what should we do then? We should simply collapse and it is better to be supported by Jews than do that. Meanwhile the best way of practically defeating the Jewish scheme is to increase the number of British immigrants. It is almost absurd for the present settlers to talk about their rights. They are so few, and as taxpayers so unimportant, that they can hardly logically claim to have a voice in deciding the destinies of the country against the Government which expends hundreds of thousands on it every year.'

In Europe the Zionist organisation endeavoured to find funds to finance the Commission and the bitter attacks on Herzl went on. He fell ill and more delays due to his inability to attend to business followed. Then, unexpectedly, a donation of £2,000 was received from the Hon. Mrs E. A. Gordon, an English Christian sympathiser who had once been a lady-in-waiting to Queen Victoria. Unfortunately it arrived too late for Herzl to appreciate for he died on 3 July 1904.[17]

Herzl's death rather than lack of funds, delayed the Commission. Only at the end of 1904 did the President of the East African Commission Committee, Professor Warburg, announce that three men had been appointed to inspect the land on offer and would arrive at Mombasa in January 1905 to make their report.

However during the sixteen months since the scheme was first mooted, conditions in the Protectorate had altered and, in relation to these, Eliot's opinion also. His determination to obtain settlers from South Africa in particular had paid off and they were now coming in by every boat to Mombasa. Some of them settled on the Uasin Gishu Plateau, the area designated for the Jews. In *The East Africa Protectorate* Eliot took pains to explain his altered views: 'in the near future all the surrounding area will be occupied by people of British race and that being so, although I am not an anti-semite, I greatly doubt the expediency of putting in the midst of them a body of alien Israelites.'[43]

But as it turned out Eliot's opinion counted for nothing. Major A. St H. Gibbons, Professor Alfred Kaiser and M. Wilbuschwitz arrived in 1905 to be met not by Eliot but by his hard-drinking replacement, Sir Donald Stewart.[19]

CHAPTER 6

A Letter of Resignation

'East Africa is the home of the leopard, the tick, the baboon
and the amateur official.'

Ewart Scott Grogan

Though Eliot resigned over a different issue in 1904, his decision to do so did
not diminish the insecurity among settlers for the next twelve months. Their
fear that Jews would enter the country in droves put them in a sanguine
mood. Each individual whose brand of cussedness was intrinsic to the very
spirit of pioneering now developed a hardy resistance to the hand of
authority. Collective though they were as a society, each white man stood
alone, dwarfed by the hard edges of Africa with many diverse and incon-
gruous elements tugging at his life; it was all part of the rough-hewn process
of development and at the core lay the influences of 'the three As', as Cyril
Connolly once put it, of 'alcohol, altitude and adultery'.

The growth of Nairobi's riff-raff shifting community had inevitably
nurtured other tensions, not least the question of caste. In a community
dominated by males, the Englishmen who went out just after the turn of the
century were not so bigotted about the colour of skin where sex was
concerned. Before the day of the inviolable memsahib, concubinage was
recognised (if unmentioned) as one of the perks for those who went out to the
tropics alone and in this respect Nairobi was no different.

Flourishing side by side were respectability and squalor. The establishment
of various clubs and societies overshadowed the seamier life of the Nairobi
community but for all that, it existed and by 1904 prostitution had become a
grave social menace. Their shocking lodgings were behind Victoria Street
and provided not only sexual relief but a rendezvous for bad-hats and a
repository for stolen goods.

The most 'respectable' house of ill-repute was known to the men as 'The
Japanese Legation' and in the tradition of brothels was housed near the station
end of Victoria Street. It was far superior to the squalid offerings in the Indian
Bazaar and its nickname had been acquired by word-of-mouth because of the

number of Japanese girls working there who were alleged to have come from Zanzibar. In the First World War the soldiers who frequented it returned to the bush to reminisce over the girls, the food, the beer and the gramophone music.[1] So long as they conducted themselves in an orderly fashion the police sanctioned this particular brothel's existence unofficially and in return for the oversight, for years the women acted as useful informers.[2] Another well-known brothel was opened later by a Mrs Hall on the Athi River Road; she 'stocked it with Syrian girls brought down to Nairobi like a load of cattle'[3] giving their Japanese competitors a run for their money.

The question of colour affected moral, material, social and religious issues, and the British faction, so readily contemptuous of things and persons 'foreign', compounded this bias and treated those who were not Anglo-Saxon, at best, with polite condescension. Anyone suspected of having the faintest 'touch of the tarbrush' was more likely still to experience the open ugliness of bigotry.

Even after Nairobi's Anglican cathedral was completed after the First World War, the white congregation successfully demanded that the English speaking service be held before the Swahili one on the grounds that the pews would then not be soiled by their black co-religionists. But the bishops, more in keeping with the ideals of Christianity, resisted these demands for a segregated church synod with the result that it was to be the first multi-racial governing body in the land.[4]

By 1904, the chimes of new railway station clock could be heard to the utmost limits of Nairobi and the Indian *fundis* in the railway workshops could turn out furniture to order and 'anything from a needle to an anchor'. One of the most visually fascinating areas in the town was the future site of the Khoja Mosque opposite Bazaar Street where a track led down to the swamp. Bead traders operated on this corner, including The East African Trading Company, and the ground was covered with piles of fantastically coloured beads for the Maasai and Kikuyu.[5]

Olive Grey observed that it was possible now to 'pass a very pleasant time in Nairobi perhaps one day the capital' of the country. But '. . . the melancholy swish of the rain that falls constantly . . . gets on one's nerves and depresses those who live in East Africa for long.'

Because the white community was so dispersed, raceweek was the one time when everyone converged on the town, travelling sometimes hundreds of miles to attend to business, meet friends, catch up on news and views and have some much needed fun after months of isolation. Nairobi could not cope unless tents were pitched to overcome the accommodation problem. Extra trains were put on at excursion rates from Mombasa and Nakuru to encourage passengers. Everyone was determined to enjoy himself. Thus it became customary for those up-country, to confine visits to Nairobi to raceweek, though they might not necessarily attend all fixtures.

The East African Turf Club had their course on the far side of the swamp, two miles north of the township. Their rules were adapted from those of the

Calcutta Turf Club to suit local conditions in 1903.[6] Polo was not yet played but pig-sticking was already an established sport at the racecourse, where participants used 'sword-bayonets' cut down and fixed on any sort of shaft.[7] When the rains were on, fixtures had to be abandoned as great gaps and caverns appeared in the black cotton soil in which rider and horse could almost disappear. But, when the sun ruled, from the new painted stands, it was reported that 'the view . . . always enchants us . . . across the course . . . the green expanse beyond to the forest in the background and far beyond is Mt Kenia (sic); then by a half-turn across the Athi Plains and on to Mt Kilimanjaro—a prospect which cannot but please the most fastidious.'[8]

The absence of thoroughbreds to begin with was made up for by keen attendance. Everyone went to the races from the Governor down. Nearly all rode to the track and to begin with, it was generally a question of 'owners up'. 'The Kifaru Stakes' originated from an incident in 1903 when a rhinoceros had appeared during the second race and held up proceedings for half an hour. After a feeble attempt to charge the horses it became bored and trotted off.[9]

The Africans were fascinated by the races and, clad only in skins or a blanket, stood and stared at the more flamboyant spectators—the brilliant saris and turbans of the Indians.[10] The settlers usually wore a contrast of luxury and deprivation—elegance at odds with some shabby detail. Almost every white woman carried a green-lined parasol and liked to appear fashionable. But even the best of them tended to miss the mark. Of one occasion Helen Sanderson remarked, 'The leader of society wore a sky blue dress and a hat of pink roses, the effect, since she had a face like a full-blown cabbage rose herself, was very cheerful.'[11] The men, most of whom had probably not seen a white woman since the last time they were in Nairobi, were undeterred by such details. Many ordinary-looking girls who came out as nurses, governesses or maids had to be replaced with boring regularity. As Lord Cranworth remarked of the bachelor settler, he was 'ready to see beauty in the most meagre of charms'.[12]

The inception of the East African Turf Club and its four annual fixtures had far more effect on the pioneer community and on development itself than the breeding of horses. For these were the weeks around which all plans revolved and serious concerns were dealt with such as confrontations with the Governor. Agricultural or protest meetings were also held, supplies replenished and appointments kept with the doctor, dentist and lawyer. The women dealt with the more frivolous aspect and sent invitations out by runner and arrangements became frenetic as weddings, celebratory dances, moonlight picnics, hat-trimming competitions and fancy dress parties were organised to fill every available moment. It was hardly surprising that raceweek, more often than not, developed into an alcoholic binge as friends took advantage of the rare opportunity to meet.[13]

The gulf between the fashionable image of the white settlers and the view held of themselves is wide, and distorted. Largely, the reputation of the sybaritic white men and women luxuriating in a land of sunshine, parties and affaires, waited upon by servants with endless glasses of champagne has been perpetuated by one *clique* who lived in the Wanjohe Valley in the late 'twenties and 'thirties. Their 'fast' behaviour made titillating copy for the gossip columnists in London, with whispers of drugs, drink, adultery and divorce, culminating in 1941 with the murder of Lord Erroll. They reigned uncontested along the Wanjohi River in the Aberdares which became known as 'Happy Valley' and those are the people who are responsible for this image, not the pioneers. The way of life for the earliest farmers whatever their background or financial resources was as appreciably different as it was arduous. In no sense could they be referred to, as the later community very often were as 'verandah farmers'.

When, in January 1904, Delamere travelled by rail to Njoro to begin farming he could only walk again with difficulty. The train stopped at a level crossing between two stations, Njoro and Elburgon, so that he could complete the journey on a stretcher. He never went back to Cheshire to live and from now on all his money, energy and every resource he possessed was channelled into building up his farms and business enterprises in BEA.[14]

Delamere's hut stood on the lower slopes of the Mau, which rose forested, dark and ridged, behind it. Because the line ran through his land he called it Equator Ranch. His shepherd, Sammy McCall, arrived at Njoro with the first stock and was an outstanding pioneer character who never made any concession to the African climate. Come drought or rainy season he wore a bowler, Highland tweeds and a waistcoat. Usually he had a cigarette dangling from his lip and had lived all his life among sheep. It was said that he kept a letter of resignation in his top pocket, which he tendered every few months to Delamere whenever they failed to see eye to eye.[15] When he reached Equator Ranch he was not amused at being charged by a fierce cock ostrich and, starting as he meant to go on, delivered his ultimatum to Delamere without ceremony: 'Either that bir-r-rd goes the noo, my lord, or ye'll be needing a new manager.' The bird went.[16]

McCall had barely had time to settle in before he was sent off to New Zealand to buy 500 pure bred Merino ewes, four Hereford bulls and seven cows with which he returned at the end of the year. In the meantime Delamere, impatient to start sheep farming, decided to put the imported rams with native ewes which sounds simple enough but was more complicated than it seemed because the Maasai, who had the best sheep, were not interested in being paid money for their animals. They would only agree to trade with Delamere on the understanding that they received one cow in exchange for twenty-five ewes. Luckily he overcame this problem by sending to German East Africa for cattle, which were brought back to Naivasha and traded for sheep as the Maasai asked.[17]

Delamere also planted his first wheat in 1904. The next four years were concentrated on trying to overcome 'rust', a fungus which affected every crop just as he thought he had found a solution. He never lived to see its conquest for it took forty years before anyone realised that it was not simply a fungus, but had a tenacious and unexpected capacity to match every move made by the plant breeder.

Delamere's single hut soon grew into a cluster of similar buildings. Before going out to work at dawn each day he wound up his gramophone and, from this relic of civilisation, across the African bush in the mornings drifted the strains of the music hall song 'All Aboard for Margate'.[19] He put up galvanised sheeting round his encampment, to keep lion out and, as Equator Ranch developed, it filled with every sort of farming equipment, some in the latest design, the rest in every state of dilapidation.

The average house was not renowned for comfort even of those with money, but the rough way of living ensured fitness. One bachelor wrote to his mother, 'If you people at home sat on boxes and sawn tree stumps at your meals you wouldn't take so long at them and in consequence your health would improve.' Beds were usually of rough hewn wood too, consisting of frames through which holes had been bored at four-inch intervals all round and laced with narrow strips of zebra hide.[20]

Like Delamere, many men were nearly always heavily in debt not only to their suppliers but to the bank, despite the front that was put on for visitors. The lavish parties thrown for VIPs or relatives who came out were in keeping with the extravagant energy of the pioneers but things were not always as they seemed. If stores ran out it could be months before they could leave their farms to replenish them. In any case, supplies relied almost solely on the chit system. Indians allowed their white creditors to run up bills sometimes for years before presenting a statement of account. This enabled the gin to flow like water while the reputation for Kenya hospitality grew unchecked, often with predictably disastrous results.

In 1906, one old farmer who attended a dinner given in Winston Churchill's honour, having done himself rather too well before dinner, picked up the menu, peered at the 'Fleur de Lys' on the top and enquired drunkenly of his neighbour at the table.

'Is that the coat of arms of East Africa?'

'No, it is not.' replied the man.

'Well what is the coat of arms of East Africa then?'

'It's a peg rampant on a pile of chits.'[21]

The rampant peg represented the staking of land claims, the chit, the unlimited credit extended by *dukawallahs*. Once banks were opened, competition was keen and the bank overdraft became a way of life. Later on managers were faced with some strange situations when pioneer farmers overreached themselves.

In the wake of the war when, in 1921, conditions in the farming areas were as difficult as they could be. Banks were trying to reduce these long-outstanding overdrafts, and the branch manager of one in Nakuru arrived at his office one morning to find himself besieged by four hundred head of intractable cattle, driven up against the walls of the bank by Maasai herds-men. Their European owner, at a loss for another solution, had driven his one remaining asset to the bank.[22]

Delamere involved himself in every aspect of white settlement, even urging his manager at Vale Royal to campaign for him. 'Help me advertise this country in any way you can . . . If any Cheshire or Lancashire man brings me a letter from you I will see he gets a good 640 acres.' Pointing out that others were just as enthusiastic, he wrote, 'Settlers . . . say it compares with the best of New Zealand . . . A South African who has had much experience was here the other day and said he wouldn't take 20 acres in South Africa for one here.'[23]

He had a brochure printed, with contents in this vein, for distribution in England and among the two hundred settlers who responded were his brothers-in-law, the Honourable Galbraith and Berkeley Cole who arrived in 1904 and 1906 respectively. These two sons of the Earl of Enniskillen became farmers and were among a number of rich and influential aristocrats who bought land cheaply.

The conquering of difficulties also made the pioneer possessive of the country as his intimacy with it grew. As Block pointed out when giving evidence to the Land Commission in 1932, 'we did not ride or drive we had to walk every inch of the land'.[24] That closeness made the settler fiercely protective of his rights.

Galbraith Cole's spirit showed itself indominitable when he walked up-country, even though he was already a premature victim of arthritis. Upon reaching the north-eastern wall of the Rift Valley escarpment, the only way of surmounting it was to dismantle his wagons, carry them piecemeal to the top and reassemble them there before trekking over the high plateau to Laikipia where he had his first farm. As far as is known he was the second European to reach Thomson's Falls, named after the explorer in 1883. All his life Cole refused to accept the limitations imposed on him by sickness. An example of his single-minded ruthlessness was his shooting of a Maasai sheep stealer in 1911 at Keekopey, his next farm, above Lake Elmenteita; he was determined to halt stock theft when the administration could do little to curtail it.

There were not enough hotels in Nairobi in 1904, so that newcomers had little alternative but to begin life in BEA at 'Tentfontein' and often camped for months before land titles were allocated. Helen Sanderson's journal reveals conditions of life there at this time, disclosing the dilemmas of speculative visits. Neither she nor her husband, who had been with the Green Howards, the 3rd Yorkshire Regiment in South Africa, had any idea of how he would earn their keep.[25]

Captain E. L. Sanderson was appointed Nairobi's first Town Clerk in September 1904, a post he held for five years before retiring in 1910 to take up in England the headmastership of Elstree School. He proved energetic and successful in the role of Town Clerk but on his arrival in 1904 Sanderson was recuperating from an illness contracted in Johannesburg. On the voyage up he suffered a relapse and by the time he reached Nairobi he was 'ghastly white, sick with pain and hardly able to stand. There was no cab or rickshaw of any kind.'[26]

The reference to the lack of transport may surprise readers who are familiar with Nairobi history for hardly an early memoir exists in which the name, Ali Khan, does not appear. In fact this Cape-coloured transporter reached Nairobi some weeks after that journal entry. Ali Khan originated from South Africa, and arrived with a mob of horses to sell which he had picked up along the Benadir coast.[27] Henceforth he met every train and drove passengers to their destination in one of his buggies, drawn by pairs of grey mules. The first impression of him was unforgettable. He wore breeches and gaiters like many of the men, but his waxed moustache bristled beneath blue framed sun-glasses. His *kiboko*, swished over the ears of his mules; as he took brides to their weddings and coffins to the cemetery and was known by all the town-dwellers who soon accepted him as a reliable source of information. The connections he made through his Livery and Bait Stables in River Road enabled Ali Khan to enjoy a unique privilege among those who were not white. He was the only coloured man in Nairobi who was allowed to set foot in the Hotel Stanley. [28]

Besides having no transport the Sandersons could find nowhere to stay. Wood's Hotel was full, so was the Hotel Stanley but as Mayence Bent was listening to their tale of woe, Sanderson almost fainted and, just as his wife was imploring Mrs Bent to take them in, a man who had been convalescing from fever overheard the conversation and offered them his room—the best in the hotel. She observed: 'It was quite bare, the windows with no curtains, opened onto a blind alley leading to the bar. I had to go to bed in the dark. Five men were sleeping on the floor of the next room. There was no sitting room, only a small bare place where we ate very tough goat.'[29]

There were no banks then in Nairobi, so their £75 was carried in a canvas belt which they took turns to wear because it was so heavy and uncomfortable. They thought the town a hideous place but as soon as Sanderson was well enough they moved to the campsite which they found quite pretty 'all around there is grass and trees just like home . . . There are about twelve white women here and our tent is near the Ross's* tents. We have two camp beds with rugs etc., a folding canvas washstand and a little folding table . . . You hang your clothes on pegs screwed round the tent poles, you keep brushes in one trunk and . . . books in another and . . . food in a basket . . . I was having my first experience of a sleeping bag . . . unbearably uncomfortable but had to stay put until Major Ross left . . . Then the hyenas began, not far off, the most awful noise, like a devil laughing, it makes you shiver . . . between the rockiness of the camp pillows and the stuffy scratchiness of my neck (no sheets allowed) and flying ants two inches long, dropping on me and

* Major C. J. Ross, the elephant hunter.

huge beetles flopping about, I was nearly frantic when I suddenly realised how funny it was . . . It is a glorious country and we are going to live here if we possibly can . . . Building is cheap here and servants are £12 a year or less. Washing is 13/4d for one hundred articles but badly done. Potatoes are 1/4d for 60 lbs and meat is 3d a pound now—it was half that lately.'[30]

At Tentfontein among others at that time whose contributions to development would be vital were the Harries family, who eventually established the pineapple-growing industry at Thika. Allen Harries had lost all he had in South Africa when his house had burned down during the Boer War. He and his wife Olivia had been poor anyway, struggling to bring up seven children, and felt that they had nothing to lose in following their friend Russell Bowker's lead. They could not afford to investigate first so, hoping for the best, went to Nairobi to apply for land. Olivia Harries remained at Tentfontein with four of her children while her husband walked over seven hundred miles with their third son, Cecil and Louis Brummage, a relative who was helping to choose four farms.[31]

Barton-Wright instructed them how to identify the land they wanted. Providing no African was living on it, they were to put in a peg and a Government surveyor would be sent out and would intimate in which direction from this peg, Harries could have his farm. The survey fee was £28.

The Harries party set out on foot in the rainy season. They had no horses, mules nor money for porters so, having to carry everything themselves, were limited to the barest of necessities. They slept on the ground in the open, braving the lion and hyena. None of them possessed waterproof clothing and they became thoroughly fed up at being drenched. Brummage who objected to getting his feet wet resolved it by stripping off all his clothes as the first drops of rain fell, cramming everything, including his boots, under his helmet. The Kikuyu round Fort Hall, unused to clothes themselves were as fascinated as they were unprepared for the spectacle of a naked European wearing only a topi, wandering about the bush with his fully-clad friends in the rain.

The Harries's quest for suitable farm-land took them to Limuru, Makuyu, Ruiru, Nyeri, Nanyuki, Timau and over the Kinankop to inspect the lakelands of Naivasha on foot. At Gilgil they took the train to Lumbwa. From here they walked to Kericho, Sotik and Port Florence, returning to Nairobi by train. Harries chose two properties on behalf of his son-in-law, Herbert Cowie, who followed in 1906 with more relatives, the Stocker family, and picked land at Chania on the Ndarugu River where he himself wanted to live, besides 10,000 acres at Naivasha. Accordingly a peg was run in at Ndarugu Height as a marker (the name Thika was adopted later). Now began the tortuous dealings with the Land Office.[32]

Although the process was slow when viewed through the eyes of the individual who was impatient get on to his land, the fact is that by 1905 a total of 368,165 acres had been annexed for white settlement. By 1915 it had risen to 5,275,121 acres.[33]

That September the five Harries children walked with their parents alongside one of Ali Khan's wagons hired to get their belongings to Thika thirty miles away. Loaded on to it was their piano and a wood stove (believed to have been the first brought into the country). The smaller children were carried by porters during the journey. Camping on the edge of the footpath at night, after dinner, wrapped only in blankets they slept without canvas between them and the stars. Fires were kept alight until dawn to ward off predators.[34]

That same scene was repeated over and again throughout the Protectorate as small cavalcades of settlers set out from Nairobi, walking at little more than two miles an hour, beside ox-wagons piled high with domestic effects as gradually the land was pounded into submission by feet and hoofs and wagon wheels. For those children who were old enough to remember, the first trek to their farm was an unforgettable event.

The men and women were eager, fearless of the task ahead of clearing bush, sinking bore-holes and building dams. At times the landscape appeared so serene that it almost resembled parkland in Europe, and they watched in wonder as tick birds, the yellow-billed ox peckers perched on their cattle, which grazed, like the plains game, in contentment. Then, where only moments before the scene had been one of outward calm, sudden violent images erupted. Wild dogs in a pack rushed through a flock of sheep, taking bites as they went, sometimes grabbing a leg or an udder, or perhaps a lioness would bring down a zebra for her young.[35]

The Harries's put up a temporary house, water came from the Ndarugu River at the bottom of a 250 foot gorge. The countryside was absolutely wild. At night the children were kept awake by the roaring of lion, circling round their flimsy bedrooms. Yet 'Karamaini', far from being a realm of fear, seemed idyllic with a zoo on the doorstep abounding with kongoni, wildebeeste, ostrich and zebra. Freedom without limit prevailed between the knuckled outline of the Ngong Hills on the one hand and Mount Kenya's peaks a hundred miles distant on the other.[36]

This mountain is known to the Kikuyu in whose territory it lies as 'Kere Nyaga' making the theory as to how it was re-named interesting.* It is said that when Ludwig Krapf saw it from Ukamba for the first time in 1849 he asked the local tribe what it was.[37] The Akamba have no R in their alphabet and in their dialect they told him it was 'Kee Nyaa'—hence Kenya. But the Kikuyu name for it, 'Kere Nyaga', means ostrich, the male bird, being predominently black with splashes of white, is not unlike the snow-capped mountain itself.[38] It could be seen at times from Thika, its peaks sparkling in

---

* The question of pronunciation of the word Kenya is frequently questioned depending on whether the long or short 'e' is favoured by the speaker. I have been unable to obtain any satisfactory explanation for this curiosity other than the fact that during the Colonial phase it was common practice to use the long 'e'. Since Independence, possibly because it conveniently reflected the name of her first President, Kenyatta, the short 'e' has taken precedence and is officially recognised and preferred.

the sun, but at others it was almost indefineable, as delicate as a watercolour against the encroaching clouds.

The going was tough. Crops were not proven in that district until 1908. Allen Harries tried to grow wheat, coffee and potatoes and to raise cattle, ostriches and sheep at 'Karamaini Estate'. None was really successful. Disease, theft and lion played havoc with livestock; the potatoes grew but McQueen had cornered the only regular demand. Wheat would not grow. Bit by bit the Naivasha land was sold off to support the family. Courage more than anything else kept Allen and Olivia Harries going until 1910 when they managed at last to establish a small herd of native cows which produced enough milk to make butter. Every two months it was sent to Nairobi by donkey-wagon (their sole means of transport) for sale to the residents of Parklands. However, the donkey took two days each way to make the journey, exposing the butter to heat which was no good for it. Then a Kikuyu was employed for the task; he managed to carry 40 lbs of butter on his head, returning with an order of groceries on the same day. The proceeds from the butter helped but after six years there was still no proper income from the farm. They survived by living very simply and through self-sufficiency. When the children were old enough they contributed as best they could, catching ostriches for their feathers, taking out 'safari' parties and driving taxis. The two elder sons working in South Africa sent money to help too.

The pineapple farming for which they became famous happened accidentally. Mrs Harries's son-in-law, Herbert Cowie, who was living in Parklands, had imported a number of different fruits with which to experiment but the pineapples would not grow. He uprooted them in disgust and threw them over the fence. His mother-in-law who had taken an interest in his progress was appalled when she learned what he had done and reacted by harnessing the donkey and driving to Parklands to retrieve the unwanted pineapple suckers. She replanted them at Karamaini and they took root and in effect founded the pineapple growing industry at Thika.

Not until 1927 could the Harries's afford their first tractor or a lorry or to take a holiday for twenty-three years. By 1955 Karamaini was growing 360 acres of coffee, 200 acres of pineapples besides 200 acres of other fruits while the Thika canning factory, the second largest of its kind in Africa, was canning 140 tons of pineapples a day at the peak of the season. But that was fifty-one years after the Harries family with little but hopes and dreams had trekked out from 'Tentfontein' to virgin bush and forest.[39]

'Tentfontein' more-or-less surrounded Pa Bennett's house – a shack known as 'The Manse' which was bought by Kenya's silver-tongued politician, Ewart Grogan in 1904. On it he built 'Chiromo' a large house of grey stone. He hardly ever occupied it himself but it became an historic residence in that many policy-making decisions concerning development in BEA were made round the dinner table here. Lord Cranworth rented it in 1906 and then it was bought by the American millionaire Northrup McMillan in 1910 as his town house. It was here in her drawing-room that Lady McMillan broke the news to the Danish writer, Karen Blixen, that her lover, Denys Finch Hatton, had been killed when his Gypsy Moth crashed at Voi in 1931.

Grogan had been precisely the type of settler Eliot was hoping to attract when he had advertised 64,000 acres of forested land in a Johannesburg newspaper in 1903. Grogan was born a rebel and, perhaps because he was one of a family of twenty-one children, always favoured the dramatic gesture for attention. He was educated at Winchester and Jesus College, Cambridge but while reading law he was sent down for tethering a goat in his room. Next he tossed a coin to dictate his future: it came down on the side of adventure rather than art though he attended the Slade before volunteering as a trooper with Rhodes's Columns. He was wounded at the time of the 2nd Matebele Rising in 1896 and while convalescing in New Zealand, fell in love with Gertrude Watt, a descendent of the steam-engine Watt.[40] Her step-father rejected Grogan as a suitor on the grounds of lack of achievement and dismissed him as a useless fortune-hunter but would have been nearer the mark had he sensed that he was a womaniser. Grogan's defence was to walk from one end of Africa to the other to prove him wrong. Setting out in 1898, he took two and a half years to reach Cairo surveying Rhodes's intended rail and telegraph route as he went and emerged from obscurity a hero. The name Grogan was on everyone's lips for though somewhat theatrical, it had been an act of courage, romantic in purpose and rare in spirit.

The Union Jack he had carried was presented to old Queen Victoria when she received him. Braving cannibals, illness and hunger he had won his bride. After marrying Gertrude Watt, he lectured for a while in the Americas, but Cecil Rhodes, whose attention Grogan had commanded after his historic walk, was convinced that Africa was where Grogan's future lay and had urged 'Give yourself to Africa, you will never regret it.'

Rhodes was right. Grogan did not regret it. He immersed himself politically and commercially for half a century in British East Africa. But in giving himself to Africa, he also ensured that Africa gave herself to him in return; when he died at the age of 92 he had acquired over half a million acres of land there.

After the Grogans' first daughter was born in England, they left for Johannesburg where Lord Milner had nominated him as his personal representative on the Town Council. Grogan farmed too for a while but he fell ill in 1902. Whilst recuperating from an operation for an old liver complaint he was visited in hospital by a friend, a Canadian lumber merchant from Delagoa Bay whose name was Edward Lingham. He showed Grogan Eliot's advertisement offering a concession of forest in BEA. Together they went up to investigate. Eliot, who was at the height of his campaign to attract white settlers, welcomed them effusively, arranging for the Conservator of Forests to show them over that part of the Mau which was on offer. The lease ran for ninety-nine years for the equivalent in rupees of about £150 per year.

Eliot was so anxious for Grogan to settle he had painted a rosier picture than he should have done. Due to the Nandi Rebellion the area was actually closed and, in the opinion of the Conservator, the useable timber was inadequate. However Lingham, as a skilled lumberman, recognised the wealth of podocarpus, a high quality softwood, growing there; in a fast developing country it was admirably suited for building purposes. In addition there was an abundance of cedar which was ideal for roofing and furniture. Provided the demand for timber for construction anticipated by the optimists was forthcoming, these two woods alone would earn them plenty.

Grogan's cunning nature, supported by a dangerous and fertile mind, irked many a Government servant and was now brought into play. Sensing Eliot's readiness to negotiate at almost any price in his quest for white settlement, Grogan remained cool. He intimated that the project was an absurd gamble, and that he required a good deal more inducement to establish a timber industry than 64,000 acres of virgin forest, even at that price. He could not contemplate settling with what he would be required to invest without the promise of an export market for which he would also need at least 100 acres of coastline in the form of deep-water frontage at Mombasa. To Grogan and Lingham's surprise Eliot granted their requests. Grogan's psychology had paid off handsomely. For the asking, he received 140 acres of land at Mbaraki. In time, one of Grogan's boasts was that he would have nothing to do with a scheme which yielded less than £200,000 profit. With land going for so little, with enough income to allow him to bide his time while it appreciated in value, how could he possibly lose?[41] In 1904 Grogan returned from Johannesburg for good to 'that miserable scrap heap of tin' as he called Nairobi.

Until at least 1912 those arriving from England to settle were easily outnumbered by South Africans, the most volatile and influential element in the Protectorate before the First World War. Like Grogan, they were almost entirely of British descent whose farming methods, attitudes towards labour and objectives were all rooted in precedents culled from South Africa's politics.[42] Bowker, Newland, the Tarlton brothers, A. C. Hoey and his brother, A. S. Flemmer and Robert Chamberlain were among these and Grogan too was influenced by the period he had spent there.

For the greater part of his life, Grogan involved himself in similar speculation to the forest and harbour negotiations. One needed boldness of vision to risk and run up huge overdrafts and he had that quality and pulled off deals that were little short of spectacular. It was he who stocked Kenya's streams with 40,000 trout which he imported in 1906,[43] and drained the valueless Nairobi swamp for market gardening. He hired a saw-doctor, Thomas McClure, in South Africa[44] for his timber project but Grogan's reputation as the first saw-milling baron is misleading as the Morson brothers had the earliest saw-mill.

Sam and Tom Morson were gentleman farmers from Wales. They had been persuaded by Delamere that Sam, who was a saw-doctor, was the sort of man whose skills were desperately needed in BEA for he had trained with Spear and Jackson—famous saw-makers—and was also a professional wain-wright besides being something of an expert with boilers, steam-engines, wagon building and black-smithing.[45] They applied for twenty-five square miles of thickly forested acreage at Limuru, wisely choosing it not just for the timber but for its proximity to the railway line. The Uganda Railway to whom they supplied fuel and camphor wood sleepers under contract became their biggest customer.

Sam and Tom Morson also founded the British East African Wagon Works in Nairobi where Sam made and repaired cross members, wheels, axles and wheelbarrows until they were bought out in 1907 by G. W. Cearn. The workshop was in Station Road through it hardly warranted the name in 1904 for it was only an ever-widening cart-track.[46] One of the problems was that a team (sixteen oxen were inspanned at a time) needing great width to turn, did nothing to improve its shape or its surface, which fluctuated from mud to dust. Rutted by wheels of every sort it expanded sideways as traffic detoured those vehicles which had broken down or, in the case of the long rains, became bogged-down. Four-wheeled *Hamali* carts, carrying small packages from the station to the bazaar, threaded their way between two-wheeled *tongas* driven by Asians. These were a cross between a milk-float and a governess' cart, usually hauled by a pair of trotting oxen. They had holes in their nostrils through which a rope ran, serving the same purpose as reins. Their driver sat on the pole between them, not unlike a monkey on a stick, pulling on one rope while pressing the other animal forward either by tickling its back or beating it with a baton-like whip. They talked to the oxen in Hindustani, and made sounds like the popping of champagne corks as they urged their beasts forward.[47]

In the Rift Valley and the Highlands the encroachment of settler families was beginning to be felt. Eliot's dilemma was rooted in the fact that the Europeans, to whom a railway was vital, would make better economic use of it than nomads to whom it was no more than an iron snake. Hitherto the Maasai had wandered unchecked over territory stretching from the Tana River in the north to the far German border in the south, from the coast on the east to the realm of the Turkhana on the west. In 1900 they had still grazed immense herds of cattle and sheep around Gilgil and Elmenteita, which, out of all this land, was their preferred grazing ground and was now divided by the railway, making it impossible for them to continue their traditional life of hunting and grazing their flocks on lands they had earlier used uninter-rupted.[48] The urgent question therefore arose whether or not they should be given a defined reserve of their own. What Eliot feared was that if he allowed Europeans to settle where the Maasai continued to roam at will he might have to answer for a repetition of the Jameson Raid.[49]

Eliot and Lord Lansdowne had trodden warily with one another to avoid clashing over the Jewish Settlement Scheme. But the rot had set in the year before when, without consulting Eliot, Lord Lansdowne granted the East

African Syndicate five-hundred square miles of land north of the railway which was virtually the pick of the Maasai grazing lands now in question near Naivasha.[50] Major Burnham, representing the Syndicate had been prospecting, fruitlessly for minerals for a year before applying for the concession direct to Eliot in June 1903. Besides the five-hundred square miles north of the railway, Burnham had asked for two fifty-mile square blocks of agricultural land, one at Limuru, the other near Nairobi.[51].

After some bargaining Eliot made Burnham an attractive offer; but he pointed out that it still required Lansdowne's approval. He then ommitted to advise Lansdowne but promised land at Naivasha also to two South Africans, Robert Chamberlain and A. S. Flemmer.[52]

Meanwhile the Foreign Office had been contacted by the Syndicate's London agent and instructed Eliot to grant the land for which they had applied on easy terms. Eliot assumed that Flemmer and Chamberlain were equally acceptable as candidates for land in that district. He was soon to find out how mistaken he had been.

Eliot was all too familiar with the shortcomings of the Land Office in Nairobi. With only Barton-Wright, an ex-railway surveyor and an Indian assistant to cope with the paperwork, at this moment it was in arrears with surveys to the tune of 400,000 acres. Thus when Flemmer and Chamberlain first applied, Eliot had cabled Lansdowne requesting Foreign Office approval before committing himself to them. Hearing nothing he followed the cable with a dispatch. When Lansdowne did not answer this, Eliot mistook silence for approval.[37]

What had actually happened was that the Foreign Office had mislaid the Commissioner's original cable but did not admit to the loss for six months. Imprisoned between the simple human failing of not wanting to lose face and embarrassment Lansdowne and Eliot were both trapped. Neither felt he could go back on his word.

The misunderstanding worsened when the Foreign Office denied ever having received Eliot's cable which had been crucial to the possible allocation, in London, of the Maasai grazing lands. On top of this a Memorandum had been prepared by Jackson now sub-Commissioner of the Naivasha Province, who was never an admirer of Eliot's, in which he criticised Eliot's actions and ideas on the Maasai. He submitted this while on home leave contributing to the build-up of tension at the Foreign Office and openly opposing Eliot, by projecting the case that no European should be allowed to settle on any of the Maasai grazing land.

Meanwhile the Foreign Office, whatever the outcome of the Maasai issue, was not going to back down on their long-standing agreement with so powerful an interest as the East African Syndicate.[53]

Eliot had given his word to Chamberlain and Flemmer as the Commissioner and a gentleman but the Foreign Office cabled him refusing to entertain sanctioning their application. He was outraged by a policy which could deny individuals who were willing to pay for smaller blocks of land whilst giving large tracts away free to a powerful syndicate with influential directors in London. As a man of scruple, he felt unable to carry on. 'Sooner than let this be done under my administration,' he wrote, 'I will resign the government service.'

On 9 August 1904, the East African Syndicate formally leased Lake Magadi for a period of twenty years, with the option for a further twenty-one.[54] These negotiations were concluded by the man who took Eliot's place, Sir Donald Stewart, and the question of the Maasai Reserve was dealt with by him too. The decision to move the tribesmen with 45,000 head of cattle out of the Rift Valley to the Laikipia Plateau came about as the result of an agreement with Maasai elders witnessed by Stewart and signed by the *Laibon* Lenana on 4 August. It did not prove satisfactory and, as will be seen, another solution had to be found. In 1913 the poor, confused Maasai were moved yet again; it cost them dearly in lives and many head of cattle perished on the way.

Eliot had seemed a thorn in the settlers' side, but his sudden departure from the Protectorate and break with the Colonial Office was bemoaned by them at once. Nor did it take the settlers long to decide that Eliot's absence created a void that would be difficult if not impossible to fill. He may not have entertained quite as the local snobs would have liked but he was as gentle as he was brilliant. He appreciated Chinese verse and also claret, and he deplored violence. He may not have been decisive but he was flexible; and above all his heart had been wholly in the task of opening up the country.[55] Stewart in contrast was a hard-drinking bachelor believing in using force when necessary, and was not particularly concerned with diplomacy when it came to making decisions.

However the paradox was that these same difficulties acted as catalysts too, playing a vital part in the growth of private enterprise. Problems were exploited by people of initiative such as J. H. Gailey and D. O. Roberts, both engineers who, after completion of their contract with the Uganda Railway in 1901, had set themselves up as Licensed Surveyors, estate agents and retail ironmongers and could be consulted for advice. To newcomers seeking first-hand knowledge of the country, theirs was worth paying for. Soon their commercial activities had extended beyond surveying, engineering and contracting and they were appointed agents for farm machinery, harness and saddlery, handling shipping, insurance and banking as well. But by early 1905, like an adolescent child which suddenly grows too tall, Gailey and Roberts found that they were beginning to over-reach themselves.[56]

Just as farmers were buoyed up with optimism over harvests when everything seemed set fair for continued prosperity, the commercial pioneers were undermined by forces beyond their control too. Gailey and Roberts had obtained a £30,000 contract for the alignment of thirty miles of railway line running between Mazeras and Mackinnon Road which was to reduce the ruling gradient from 2% to 1.5%. They were able only to complete four or five miles before admitting defeat because it proved impossible to recruit labour and asked to be released from their contract. Luckily the crisis had forced them to recognise their limitations. Over and above the complications of engineering, the commercial intricacies of buying, shipping, costing and accountancy had proved too much for them. They needed a qualified accountant. Wisely they invited George Ramsay, another ex-railway employee, to join them. As their Chief Accountant he proved a welcome friend to many a settler enduring lean times. Ramsay was still on the board when he died in 1953.[57]

If 1904 was a year of uncertainty, it was at least rounded off with a flourish when Major C. G. R. Ringer and his partner. R. Aylmer Winearls opened the doors of the Norfolk Hotel on Christmas Day. It faced Nairobi's jail and was on the same side of the track as the native hospital.[58] Nobody seems to know how it got its name. Mervyn Cowie claims that when the foundation stone was laid, the ceremony was eclipsed because someone had to shoot an elephant just round the corner.[59] Construction began without title deeds because as usual the Land Office were unable to supply them nor did they arrive until the hotel opened for business.

The Norfolk Hotel was built to last from stone foundations to tiled roof, and Winearls and Ringer intended that, compared to theirs, the other shanties (including Nairobi Club) would be considered nothing but doss houses where, as in the mining towns in the American West, rooms could be hired for the day or night.

They succeeded, for in effect the Norfolk became the Claridge's of Nairobi. Five Europeans ran it with the help of twenty-four Africans. Its two cottages for married couples and thirty-four bedrooms were rarely empty; the dining room could seat up to one hundred people and was ideal for banquets. Insurance automatically covered all goods left in the baggage room, which, as the Norfolk established itself as the starting point for shooting safaris, was a real asset. Wealthy guests disappeared into the bush for three and four months confident that possessions left there were safe. The Norfolk also offered hot and cold baths, laundry, a barber, a billiard room, good stabling, rickshaws, carriages and baggage gharries which met every train.

Nairobi had never seen anything like it especially after the tough old goat on Mayence Bent's menu. Winearls had brought in a French chef from the Waldorf Astoria, Louis Blanc.[60]

Abandoning their former ramshackle haunts the residents of Nairobi turned up at sundown to drink in this sophisticated atmosphere where they could sit on proper chairs. One of their regular amusements was to take pot shots with their revolvers from the verandah at the street-lamp opposite next to the police-station, using the jail wall as a butt.[61]

When the police did not object it was because their commanding officer, Robert Foran was sitting with Delamere. 'D' as everyone called him, had his own special chair here and when he was in town, the word spread so that people turned up on the off-chance of meeting him. He rarely consumed alcohol on the farm but now came the time to relax. Rounds of drinks were ordered; D's strange way of summoning waiters was to tap his bald dome above his shoulder-length hair with his fingers. And the more liquor consumed, the more riotous the party.

More often than not it was here that Delamere's most outrageous escapades began; on one occasion he rode postillion, one foot on each of the two horses that pulled a wagon along Station Road. He liked also to organise Rugby matches in confined spaces—a bar or drawing room was equally suitable.

Before the Norfolk opened, the élite had little choice of rendezvous, and now, understandably, it became their favourite place until a more exclusive alternative presented itself. Then, in the tradition of the wealthy they moved on, joining Muthaiga Club when it opened on New Year's Eve in 1913. Meanwhile the Norfolk was dubbed 'The House of Lords' where, it was claimed, more land transactions took place at its bar than anywhere else in the Protectorate.[62]

CHAPTER 7

No Colours nor Crest

There's a legion that never was listed,
That carries no colours nor crest,
But split in a thousand detachments
Is breaking the road for the rest.
Rudyard Kipling, *The Lost Legion*

In 1905 the land boom was in full spate; new faces appeared everywhere. Ewart Grogan called them 'sunshine days'.[1] Along Station Road new buildings sprang up like mushrooms.

Towards the end of the year the whole of Victoria Street was burned in a disastrous fire which gutted the Hotel Stanley. The conflagration was never properly estimated but was thought to have cost anything between 100,000–300,000 rupees.[2] Mayence Bent rented an unfinished two-storey building in Station Road, covered its roof-timbers in tarpaulins borrowed from the railways and carried on. The second Hotel Stanley was born.

By now the National Bank of India had established a small branch in the Treasury Office, the first in a row of shanties next to the Magistrates' Court. On its books was a mixture of clerks, merchants, railway employees, settlers, artisans, army officers, one solicitor and a windmill expert.[3] Also the MacKinnon brothers had opened a general provision and wine store, Charles Heyer had started a gunsmith's shop and Tommy Wood's store had expanded. Rumour had it that whenever his wife wanted corsets for herself, she ordered six sets, selling five in the shop to pay for one.

Many Britishers who had served in the Boer War ended up in Nairobi, having returned to Britain before defecting to Africa again. England had become too tame, its conventionality anathema to them. To be one's own master in Africa was heady and they yearned for the magic of open spaces, where aloes blossomed red in clumps among the rocks and there was joy in the sound of the spurfowl going up and down the chromatic scale after the rain. The longing was like an undulating fever for which there was no real cure. Also there was the question of personal identity. As Block put it when as an old man he was asked by Alfred Johansen who had known him since 1904, why, when he had made his fortune, he did not sell out and return to Europe. Block replied, 'Why should I retire to England? In this country I am somebody; in England I would only be a number on a door.'[4]

In Europe too they missed the thundering of rain on the corrugated iron roof. As they sheltered from the wet even the walls of their primitive homes spelled adventure. These were adorned with ever-growing collections of animal horns, hooves, reptile skins, ostrich eggs, lion claws, the pelts of colobus monkey, lion or leopard. Porcupine quills served as pen-holders. To each relic was attached a unique tale. These occurrences, the babies delivered at home without help, the paucity of medical facilities, were part of daily existence in the bush. And without them, life could be compared to a shadowy pastel, the sharp edges smudged for the sake of ease. Europe was more secure and comfortable but undeniably less exciting.

Even so, having left convention behind, the pioneers transplanted their rituals and traditions on to African soil as soon as they could. Caledonian and St George's dinners were now held and soon such events were as fixed on the social calendar of Nairobi as the Old Etonian dinner held on 4 June at the Norfolk Hotel. The pioneer settlers were a mass of contradictions; some were quite capable of sinking into a queer, suburban life upon reaching Nairobi becoming smug and censorious in outlook.

Nevertheless, some women, like Mrs Boedeker for example, never became completely at ease with their surroundings. She was often left alone if Dr Boedeker was called out and in 1906, when he was on safari in Sotik, she was living in the *dak* bungalow generally reserved for railway travellers, at Nakuru which consisted then of five wood-and-iron bungalows. A friend called to see her one morning when one of her three small children had blood-poisoning; she had no nurse to relieve her and no means of communicating with her husband and was also coping with a cook who was drunk constantly. The night before three lion had been rolling about under the *dak* bungalow and this had been the limit. Dressed as immaculately as ever, after greeting her visitor she broke down completely and confessed that she became paralysed with fear when Dr Boedeker was away and was seldom able to sleep out of terror.[5]

But on the whole the lure of the safari and the wide open spaces compensated for daily problems. 'The worst of it,' wrote Helen Sanderson, was that 'you hunger for a long safari or sport, it bites you badly. Sometimes in the morning, when the boys smash your crockery and clean your silver with gravel and knife powder and steal rupees and tea and sugar and again at night when you imagine a native rising and hyenas, you think how heavenly and safe it must be at home. But when I go about with Ted, I feel the most fortunate creature in existence; it is gloriously interesting.'[6]

Africa attracted a high percentage of Scotsman. Perhaps the leanness of existence appealed to their frugality or possibly it lay in the magnificence of the land itself. At Njoro, Elmenteita and Naivasha when the early morning mist rolled back it revealed mountain, lake and forest. In the higher areas beyond the Mau and on the Kinankop, icy streams trickled between peat and bracken. There was a feeling of remoteness, a chill not unlike the Scottish Highlands. Notable among the pioneering Scots in BEA besides the McQueen family and Mrs Boedeker were Jimmy Smith, Nairobi's first miller, who loved practical jokes and brought about a coal rush, McClure, Grogan's saw-doctor, and the shepherd Sammy McCall whose brother-in-law, James MacKay, also came out to work for Delamere in 1911. MacKay proved an invaluable member of the farming community. He founded and finally became President of the BEA Farmer's Association and also contributed half the capital so that Delamere could start his flour-milling enterprise, Unga Ltd, in 1908. Its first manager, Alec White, came from a milling family over three centuries old in Scotland who came out with the machinery to set it up. MacKay eventually became President[7] and when he left the country in 1963, after half a century of devotion to its development in agriculture, he returned 'home' with an OBE, broken-hearted at leaving Kenya for good.

It was through Scotsmen that Elliot's Bakery was started and like so many firms in Nairobi began from adversity and a chance remark. Mrs M. S. Elliot went to South Africa as a bride before the Boer War, where her daughter was born during the siege of Ladysmith. The war ended, her husband joined the Uganda Railway in 1903 and in Nairobi was reputed to be something of a drunkard. To earn some money of her own, Mrs Elliot made a few extra haggis at Hogmanay and from a casual encouraging remark from a resident Scot, her destiny changed. He begged her to make more Highland specialities and she was soon producing flapjacks, scones, shortbread and griddlecakes. This was in a kitchen so small that it was more like a cupboard than a room in a shanty of the railway quarters. When she could no longer cope with lack of space, she moved to Duke Street and opened Elliot's Tea Room. Custom increased; a professional baker was brought out from Scotland. To this day, though it no longer belongs to the family, Elliot's is one of Nairobi's largest bakeries.[8]

Delamere's shepherd, McCall, had by 1905 moved to Soysambu, Delamere's second farm, with most of his cattle and sheep from Equator Ranch. They had fared badly at Njoro and it was hoped that Soysambu would prove better for stock raising. Flocks were being built up carefully by crossbreeding as it emerged that not only were hybrids resistant to disease but yielded a fleece of outstanding quality. Delamere was experimenting at Njoro with pig-farming, ostriches and the growing of lucerne and clover for pasture.

It was on one of Delamere's rare visits to Nairobi in the middle of that year that he ran into Block as he was talking to Otto Markus at the Travellers' Club. Block looked so miserable that Delamere was prompted to ask the reason and he replied bluntly that he was throwing in his hand and returning to South Africa. In Block's words, this is how Delamere dissuaded him. 'His Lordship was the essence of understanding and strongly expressed his

concern emphasising how important it was that I stay. The country could ill
afford to lose young settlers at this stage . . . he was most persuasive that I
reconsider. He even went so far as to help . . . this I gladly accepted in the
form of a few oxen to draw the double furrow plough and money to enable
better living conditions. He immediately dictated a letter . . . for the manager
of his . . . farm, instructing him to deliver to Limuru Station, twelve of his
best oxen and a couple of dairy cows. He also asked Marcus to give me
monthly 100 rupees and to debit his account . . . With his warm encouragement and material aid, I enthusiastically set to work . . . within six.months I
had about forty or fifty acres cleared and ploughed . . . as soon as the next
rains came, I planted up peas, potatoes, beans and oats . . . I was the first
farmer to experiment with flax which proved most successful. Unfortunately
the market price for such commodities . . . was so low that I was forced to
harvest by hand in order to make a sizeable profit. But . . . with the help of a
few boys, I was able to re-build my house and make a much more habitable
abode.'

He struggled on, converting Njuna slowly from bush into smallholding
and ever afterwards maintained that it was only through Delamere's help that
he managed to make a go of things. After enlarging the house and replacing
the leaky roof of *Mkuti* or palm thatch, with threshed flax Block went to work
as a labourer on a neighbouring farm for 90 rupees a month including midday
meal. The hours were long; only by getting up at 4 am could he organise his
labour before walking to his job. He returned as the fire-flies emerged,
prepared supper for himself and spent what was left of the evening juggling
his accounts by the light of an oil lamp until bedtime. By this means, day after
day for two years, he slowly repaid his debt to Delamere.[9]

Legend has it that shortly after Delamere prevented his departure, Block
overheard two strangers discussing a plot they would buy in Nairobi if only
they had the money. Apparently the owner had refused to negotiate with
them because they could only raise half of the asking price. Block lost no time
in discovering the whereabouts of both seller and plot.[10] In 1905 it was a
featureless site and it is possible that before attempting to buy it Block
consulted Tommy Wood, who, as a friend and Municipal Councillor, would
have been aware of its potential for development in relation to the layout of
the town. After Sixth Avenue became the main thoroughfare, this plot was
one of the prime sites facing onto it, half-way between the New Stanley Hotel
and Nairobi's General Post Office.*[11]

Block had no money either but the opportunity was too good to ignore.
The pawnbroker would take his gold watch and chain if only the seller could
be talked into accepting a deposit for the land. This was agreed, on condition
that the balance was received within a specified number of days. Block

---

* Identifiable later as Gillies Petrol Station standing on Delamere Avenue, renamed Kenyatta
Avenue after Independence. The rear half of the plot which he sold immediately ran right up to
where the Nairobi City Hall stands today and for many years was the site of Brunner's Hotel,
demolished in 1983.

pawned the watch, made a downpayment on the land and went to look for the two fellows who, without realising, had alerted him to the opportunity. He introduced himself somewhat prematurely as the new owner and explained that he was prepared to sell the rear half. The price he asked was exactly what he knew they could afford. This adroit piece of dealing took twenty-three years before it paid off, when in 1927, he exchanged the Norfolk Hotel for £500 and this plot.[12]

In 1905, scarcely before the Norfolk had a chance to prove itself, Winearls and Ringer advertised it as 'a fashionable rendezvous of the Highlands'. Their confidence was nothing if not prophetic. The names in the guest book have been compared to a condensed *Burke's Peerage*, *Almanach de Gotha* and *Social Register*.

One of its first tourists was the elderly widow of an Indian Civil Servant. Winearls was fearful of what might befall her after sundown once the drinkers assembled and hit on an idea of ensuring her safety. After she retired to bed, he secured her door with six-inch nails.[13] This drastic measure indicates that the pranks played by some guests called for precaution towards others. Apart from any other consideration, the manager clearly had little or no control over them. Once, after a private dinner party when he reminded guests that it was past closing time and could not serve any more drinks, they locked him in the meat safe with some sheep carcases and continued the party.

Before the electricity supply was connected in 1908 oil lanterns were enclosed in glass cases and stuck on the ends of poles. One stood between the hotel and the Nairobi River, the other on top of Ainsworth's hill, and there was an occasion when 'D's' tom-foolery had more far reaching results than he and his friend, Freddy Ward, had bargained for. Ward, who was living at the Norfolk, suggested at midnight that it was time to hail a rickshaw to take Lord Delamere home to his rented Parklands house on the outer edge on the Limuru Road, opposite the entrance to City Park today. Ward went with 'D' and returned later. As usual Delamere could not resist taking a few pot-shots at the lamps. The police, familiar enough with his trick, ignored the noise but Ainsworth was awakened by a rain of bullets; not only had 'D' misfired but the sound had magnified as the bullets hit the tin roof. Ainsworth thought he was being attacked and sent a runner to the police-station telling those on duty that there was a native rising.[14]

The trouble was that his fear had some foundation. There had been a bad scare in Nairobi the July before when the railway hooter had been sounded off at intervals during the day after a number of volleys had been fired the night before. At the sound of this alarm all white people were supposed to flee for their lives—no-one knew quite where. A small company of Maasai in full war-paint, with lion head-dresses and spears had been encountered by the Sandersons running towards them at speed, which rather brought it home. When they asked their cook if he knew anything, he had replied in broken English, 'I met one Maasai bibi, she say Maasai come morning, still dark, finish all *mzungus*', meaning white men. Exhausted by fear, they had retired very late to bed. Sanderson slept soundly but his wife, Helen, experienced the longest night of her life. The bush was full of noises at night but the silence in between was worse. The comfort of dawn's light had been bliss.[15]

Though it had been false alarm, Ainsworth's explanation for his reaction shows how easily misunderstanding could bring about a critical situation. Some troops from the west coast had come to Nairobi and the Maasai at once believed that they were to be wiped out and had better attack first. Ainsworth was alerted as soon as the warriors began removing their women from the bazaar. Day and night he had had runners waiting to bring in news from the *manyattas*, as well as at his house ready to fetch outlying settlers to safety.[16] That scare had been genuine. Naturally Ainsworth did not take kindly to Delamere's pranks at midnight. No amount of castigation had any effect and in 1909 he was caught red-handed firing dozens of shots at the lamps outside the Provincial Commissioner's house. By then the administration had grown less tolerant and dined out for weeks on the fact that 'D' was fined £5.[17]

Throughout 1904 and 1905 the Nandi, albeit fifty miles beyond Njoro, caused trouble continually. Trains were not allowed to go through the disturbed area at night for fear that passengers might be harmed. They had to break their journey, sleep at Nakuru to go on up-country the following day.[18]

The Nandi resented the arrival of the white men and the hut tax. They harrassed the administration with theft and war was only narrowly averted twice. Peaceful negotiating had proven useless and, when nine askaris guarding Railway property were killed, Stewart took a harder line than his predecessors. He gave them one month to not only bring forward some of their tribesmen who had speared the askaris to death but to agree to pay the tax.[19] He warned them that it was their last chance and that the army would be sent to deal with them if they did not submit to his wishes. During the month of grace, an African clerk was sent to collect hut tax from a Nandi chief whose response was to murder the man, sever his head and return it with the message 'This is the hut tax of the Nandi.'[20]

Sir Donald Stewart ordered six columns into the Nandi country immediately. Meinertzhagen, just returned from home leave, was one of the eighty European officers in charge; the force was made up of men from the Kings African Rifles from Uganda, Nyasaland and Nairobi. The truculent Nandi continued to resist them until 1906.

Hut tax was resented deeply by most Africans. They felt that they were being made to pay for improvements with which they would rather do without, such as roads, police and streetlighting. If, at this early stage relations between Africans and Europeans were already being jeopardised by misinterpretation through ignorance, yet another source of friction was emerging. The Foreign Office was suddenly bursting with ideas for settlement. The Jewish and a Finnish Scheme notwithstanding, they also recommended that Indian settlement should be encouraged. Whitehouse and Johnston had been in favour of Indian settlement, and the latter had predicted that they would be more welcome to Africans than the European 'who is apt to be too autocratic and unobliging in his methods of trading.'[21] Now the white settlers, already nervous for the sanctity of their claim to land in the Highland region, were alarmed at the thought of being outnumbered by orientals. The Indian question gave rise to serious disagreement soon enough but in the meantime Stewart appointed a Committee, under Lord Delamere, to inquire into the Protectorate's land problems in relation to Indian settlement. Stewart died before this could be submitted but he did receive the Zionist Commission during his brief term of office.

When Stewart had taken over from Eliot, he had been given the direction that, should 'the Jewish Scheme go on, the colonists would be granted not more than limited powers of self government and would be subject to the general laws of the Protectorate'. Accordingly Stewart had received the three men in January 1905. They called on him in Nakuru while awaiting their porters and baggage before inspecting 'the Promised Land'. They walked up to the Uasin Gishu plateau from Nakuru via Ravine, splitting up near Sergoit in order to make independent surveys of as much of the land as possible before leaving in March.[22]

Considering the controversy surrounding it, it is not surprising that the visitation gave rise to several tall stories propagated by a few settlers determined to have the last laugh. One apochryphal tale circulating for many years was that Messrs Wilbuschwitz, Gibbons and Kaiser had taken to their heels after only three days.[23] Their conclusion as to the untenable nature of the land had been reached after spending the first night terrorised by a herd of elephant outside their tents and by an encounter the following day with a party of *moran*, Maasai warriors in full war paint, who threatened them. They had suffered blistered feet as they crossed part of the five thousand square miles of veldt making up the Uasin Gishu plateau. They had been apprehensive when Nandi warriors attacked the rear of the caravan, wounding a headman and making off with a number of loads and a rifle. Possibly they were concerned to learn from a Boer farmer that cattle were rustled by the Nandi fairly often. But nothing diverted them from their task. They took a month to walk over the district and were reasonably qualified to make their report.

The Commission was led by Major A. St Hill Gibbons of the Foreign office, an ex-soldier who had seen long service in British Central Africa. Wilbushwitz was a Russian engineer who had worked in Palestine in conditions not unlike those in BEA and Professor Alfred Kaiser, an experienced traveller, had explored other parts of Africa in 1896 and 1897. Wilbuschwitz's diary refers to discussions with Marcus, who had founded the Nairobi Zionist Association in November 1904, and meetings with Block, Sulsky, Hotz and London by name.[24]

The Uasin Gishu Plateau was bounded on the east by the Elgeyo escarpment, on the west by the Nandi escarpment, on the north by the Trans Nzoia River and on the south by the precipitous wall of the great Rift Valley.

European settlement hardly existed here yet but the Commission met those who lived there, three brothers, Bon, Dirk and Piet van Breda who had obtained a grant of 10,000 acres near the Elgeyo reserve.[25] The three brothers told the Commission how cattle theft by the Nandi had dogged their lives since they first went there in 1903.[26]

There were also two other families of Boers living in the region who were squatting illegally on Nandi property called Garvie and Steyn. They were only discovered by Meinertzhagen when they asked for a guard from Nandi Fort to protect them. But the officer was so disgusted by the squalor in which they lived that he reported them to the authorities in the hope of evicting them.[27]

Bon van Breda had been the first white man to build a grass hut and live on this remote plateau. Before the Boer War had ended he had escaped over the Portuguese African border, made for Lourenço Marques and then turned up at Mombasa. He had worked on contract to the Uganda Railway at Nakuru and, during a shooting trip, wandered across the plateau empty of anything but game, liked it, settled and sent for his two brothers to join him. Piet was a surveyor. None of this area had been surveyed before the Zionist Commission attempted it and their reports were remarkable pieces of work, providing a thorough survey of the Uasin Gishu Plateau.[28]

It had been agreed that, no matter where people settled in the Protectorate, between 5,000–10,000 acres was required by each family to make a living out of cattle or sheep breeding. This being so, Wilbuschwitz, who was primarily concerned with the population potential of the area, rejected it on the grounds that the territory on offer, a mere 5,000 square miles, could only support 500 families at most. One cheerful note in his otherwise disheartening report was his discovery of the Sosiani rapids, which he came across when he was lost for five days in the Kipkarren Basin. His assessment of their potential was proved later when, as the Selby Falls, those rapids became the source of Eldoret's electric power.[29]

Kaiser had concentrated on the agricultural aspect for his report. His rejection was based mainly on financial and Jewish national grounds. He felt that the Jews were unable to colonise a country unless they could select the persons carrying out their scheme of immigration . . . only then could they become a pastoral people once more. He pointed out that economic conditions on the plateau were so unfavourable that a portion of the immigrants would be bound to leave again; thus there could never be a colonising association which would work successfully. The immigration would cost millions rendering the usefulness of the scheme totally out of proportion to the labour expended. Ideally a more promising country should be sought, less remote from communication with the rest of the world.[30]

Again they were right. The Afrikaaners who eventually dominated settlement there were never happier than when farthest from civilisation. The Boer character was the antithesis to that of the Jews. The great Van Rensberg trek of 1908 was to be the biggest influx. They were unambitious when it came to development and their ideals for self-sufficiency, based on a religious creed peculiar to their folk–culture, filled their lives to the exclusion of all else. Freedom and solitude were prime motivators in their choice of the Uasin Gishu; the last things to concern them were developing markets or the existence of neighbours for they loved the wild. They shot game for the pot, salted and dried the meat for biltong and were seldom happier than wandering across the veldt with a gun, a dog at their heels. Their children ran barefoot, uneducated and were as little concerned with progress as the game itself.

This emphatically does not imply that Boers did not contribute to development. Quaint they may have been but they were a solid, homemaking, family–rearing people of big and powerful physique. If unenterprising they were ideally suited to African conditions, possessing a natural virility, a strength which absorbed hardship. They undertook much of the monotonous labour from transport riding and ploughing to general farm superintendence on behalf of absentee landowners. Their skill with oxen alone contributed sterling progress in the opening up of the transport network.

Being less convinced of its unsuitability than Wilbushwitz and Kaiser, Gibbons felt that experimental pilot schemes should be tried before the concept was rejected. His proposal was that an agricultural expert be sent out with a staff of ten intelligent farmers accompanied by 100 peasants to inhabit ten chosen districts. One farmer should be put in charge of every ten peasants, each allotted a small piece of land with which to experiment. By the second year they would have a very good idea of the possibilities for a larger scheme.[31]

Kaiser and Wilbush submitted their reports to Gibbons who, as head of the Commission, prepared a supplement to the reports in which he scathingly attacked the views of his colleagues. But on balance their assessments were actually more realistic and accurate than his own. Subsequently the area was settled by some 3,000 Europeans on only 600 farms.[32]

In July 1905, the 7th Zionist Congress met in Basle at which the Commission recommended to that 'the profferred land was not sufficient in extent or the resources for colonization on a large scale'. Congress thanked the British Government sincerely for its offer . . . 'but shall not engage itself further with the proposal'.[33] With this resolution the Jewish East African project came to an end and the search for a Jewish homeland shifted from Africa to Australia.

In conclusion, though the result was abortive, neither Chamberlain's ideas nor Herzl's scheme had been wasted. Whilst it created schisms in the Zionist ranks to begin with, there is little doubt that it eased the path for Balfour's landmark pledge in 1917. As Charles Miller wrote in *The Lunatic Express*, the long-run effect of the proposed scheme was to consolidate the identity of the Jews as a nation. The very fact that Herzl and other Zionist leaders had dealt with the British Government at its highest levels gained the movement an elevated status, not to mention stimulating sympathy in Balfour and Lloyd George. And it must be admitted that at the same time it had drawn a certain amount of much needed attention to the potentialities of the Protectorate itself so that more and more prospective white settlers wanted to see it for themselves.[34]

In October 1905, when Sir Donald Stewart had been Commissioner for barely, a year, he developed pneumonia, while duck-shooting, a condition not helped by heavy drinking. He was buried in a dreary cemetery on a plain at a church he could not bear the sight of.

Oxen and wagon of the Klapprott
family travelling to the Uasin
Gishu. (Peter Faull).

A rare photograph of the Laibon Lenana taken by Herman Klapprott in 1910 during the Maasai move from Laikipia to Loita. (Peter Faull).

Jack Riddell riding Black Bess, the mare on which he raced Winston Churchill in his car from Thika to the Norfolk Hotel and beat him in 1907. (Olga Rogers).

◀ Samuel Block, Abraham Block's father. (Block fam

he Duke of Connaught's party being helped
ross a river during their 1909 safari. (Olga
ogers).

President Theodore Roosevelt on a visit to the
American Mission at Kijabe with its head, Mr
Hurlburt, during the 1909 Roosevelt safari.

Bror and Karen von Blixen talking to Ake Bursell (centre) the manager of their coffee
farm at Ngong shortly after their marriage at Mombasa, January 1914. (Elizabeth
Gregory).

German East African Campaign. A mule being transported across a river near Ruwu Top, April 1917. (Imperial war museum).

German East African Campaign. A stretch of road between Dakawa and Duthumi, April 1917 (a distance of ten miles). The water for many miles was rarely below one's knees and frequently waist deep from April to June. (Imperial War Museum).

Captain Ewart Grogan – in Meinertzhagen's Intelligence team
1915. (Richard Meinertzhagen).

The wedding of Donald Sharpe and Violet Donkin at Northrup and Lucy McMillan's house 'Chiromo' *c.* 1917 when it was turned into a nursing home for wounded officers during the First World War. Centre back can be seen the white haired 'uncle Charles Bulpett; far right Northrup McMillan. Seated 3rd from the right is Lucy McMillan. Spencer Tryon is seated first left and standing a little to the right of the groom is Catchpole, then Commissioner of the Police. (Diana Cadot).

A Harley-Davidson party setting out for a picnic to the Blue Posts Hotel. Thika. *c.* 1919. Photograph by Eisdell Cooper. (Norah Shipley).

After the Great War it became fashionable to picnic on the Chania Falls at Thika, motor cycles made it within easy reach despite the rough roads. Photograph Eisdell Cooper. (Norah Shipley).

Jack Riddell's camp for the safari of their Royal Highnesses the Duke and Duchess of Connaught 1909. Left to right: Capt. T. Rivers-Bulkely, Princess Patricia, Capt. Brackenridge, the Duke of Connaught, Capt. Riddell, The Duchess, Mr Phillip Percival, Prince Arthur of Connaught, Miss Pelly. (Olga Rogers).

The Norfolk Hotel 1927, the year it was acquired by Abraham Block. Photograph D. E. Fleming. (Doria Block).

Ali Khan with his mules in Bazaar Street. Photograph D. E. Fleming. (Doria Block).

CHAPTER 8

Perplexing Disarray

'One would scarcely believe that a centre so new should be
able to develop so many divergent and conflicting interests . . . The white man versus the black; the Indian
versus both . . . the official class against the unofficial, the
coast against the highlands . . . all these different points of
view, naturally arising, honestly adopted, tenaciously held
and not yet reconciled into any harmonious general conception, confront the visitor in perplexing disarray.'

Winston Churchill, *My African Journey*

Stewart's successor, Sir James Hayes-Sadler or 'Old Flannelfoot' as he
became known, was appointed by the Colonial Office, to which the
Administration of the Protectorate had been formally transferred from the
Foreign Office, in April 1905.[1]

Meanwhile preparations were under way for the punative expedition by
the Nandi Field Force and an incident in which Meinertzhagen was involved
moved the sabre-rattling into real conflict. The force assembled under
Colonel E. G. Harrison at Nandi Fort put an end to fighting the following
year but this was precipitated by the slaying of the Chief *Laibon*, who was said
to have been behind the trouble with the Nandi in the first place.[2] Meinertzhagen's diaries reveal that in his impatience to bring the *Laibon* to heel he
intended to capture or kill the trouble-maker anyway. Unable to take the
Laibon by surprise, Meinertzhagen suggested a meeting near Kaidparak Hill,
some twenty-four miles from the Fort. Just as the two were walking towards
one another at the appointed hour, an arrow pierced the officer's sleeve and,
although the *Laibon* was holding out tufts of grass, in the manner of the white
flag of truce, Meinertzhagen apparently did not understand the gesture and he
and an African officer shot him simultaneously.[3] Leaving several others dead,
the party left for the Fort under a flight of poisoned arrows. Almost three
months passed before the Nandi accepted surrender terms. They were then
fined 2,000 head of cattle as a punishment for their insurrection which were
sold by auction in Londiani; their disposal in 1906 ended the only serious

military expedition ever carried out in BEA against one tribe (apart from the Mau Mau Emergency).[4]

Meinertzhagen's behaviour gave rise to much divided opinion when rumours began to circulate that he had trapped the *Laibon* in order to kill him in cold blood. The Colonial Office removed him and he did not return to Kenya until the First World War.

Abraham Block never forgot that Londiani cattle sale. Probably this was because of his own participation, for he pinned the time that he started cattle trading to the end of the Nandi Rebellion in 1906.

Around Christmas 1905 his father, Samuel Block had joined him in Kiambu with Lily, Abraham's sister, after eight years of separation. Within two years they arranged for Block's mother and sister Freda to come to Kenya as well.[5]

On the voyage from Cape Town, Lily went ashore with her bicycle at Lourenço Marques to explore but was arrested for cycling about the city without a licence. She had no money to pay the fine so the policeman who detained her suggested that, as there were no roads where she was going, she could leave her bicycle with him as security and collect it on her way back to South Africa in a few weeks. She never saw it again. Lily Block's 'holiday' extended over the next fifty years in BEA.[6]

During those years, Lily Block became responsible for the management of a number of farms for her brother as he bought, divided and sold properties. The same pattern was always repeated. They cleared the land on each new farm, or improved it by making bridges and roads or experimenting with crops and then it would be sold. The family worked from five in the morning until dark, mostly in the *shamba*. Their meals were cooked on an open fire, water was carried into the house. Sewing, washing and ironing were done in the evenings. When trips had to be made to Nairobi, Lily walked there and back in one day. The only other European they saw was a policeman who rode his mule round the district visiting them once every four weeks.[7]

Despite the deprivations, however, Lily confessed that the rhythm of Africa had caught her. She worked side by side with the Kikuyu and came to know them as well as her brother. Then, quite often Chief Koinange engaged in long conversation with her. They made a quaint sight, the long-skirted girl with a wild mass of hair and the man, intent on Kikuyu politics, wearing a scarlet blanket, talking and talking in his language.[8]

Block was also made a blood brother of the tribe by Chief Kinyanjui just as Delamere and Galbraith Cole became blood brothers of the Maasai in the Rift Valley.[9] Obviously the closeness which this honour implied contributed to harmonious relations at a basic level. It was considered bad form by the Administration not to be able to address the Africans in Swahili, yet for the African to attempt to speak to the European in English was judged downright insolent. In any case, most Africans in outlying districts could only speak their tribal dialect.

Block's children, even at the end of his life, were unaware of how well he spoke Kikuyu. This and his private knowledge of the tribe stemmed from a quality within his own nature, the secrecy of the gambler who does not mind whether his hand is under or over-valued so long as its exact nature remains a mystery. An African will seldom give a direct answer to a direct question. And Block recognised the tortuous workings of their minds and went along with it, learning more through quiet observation than by pressing them.

Like the Africans themselves, he knew every twist of the track and each tree between Kiambu and Limuru; he attended the *Chira*, a Kikuyu Council of elders, understood its complex social structure, knew where the circumcision rites were performed and where the Dorobo and Maasai grazed their cattle simply because he had traded with them for years.[10]

Block's first transaction of any significance involved two friends who put up the capital. One was Ben Garland, an experimental maize farmer, and the other Fred Raper, who later founded Nairobi's best saddlers, Raper and Pringle. Block's contribution was to purchase cattle in Uganda and drive them to Nakuru for sale. Travelling by train, boat and on foot he lugged the equivalent of £200 in rupees with him to Fort Portal.[11]

Until April 1907, the authorised coinage of the Protectorate was based on the silver rupee, a coin stamped specially for it but linked with the Indian currency by inheritance and tradition. All the early accounts were kept in rupees, annas and pice. Then the Government decided that this was too complex for the Africans to master, so they withdrew the anna and pice, replacing them with cents with a hole in the middle, one hundred to the rupee.* This cent was minted purely for the convenience of the Africans so they could be threaded on a string, for it was many years before they adopted the European practice of wearing trousers. Actually, the Government under-estimated the African. He had already learned to count perfectly well in annas and pice but with the new currency he became so confused that he had no idea of how much money he had unless he put the cents into threes and called them two pice.[12] There were many Maasai stockmen who never learned to read or write but bought native cattle and sheep on behalf of Europeans and were entrusted on these trading safaris with hundreds of pounds, certainly more than any one of them could envisage earning in a lifetime. They returned after months of absence with every cent accounted for.[13]

Block's negotiations to buy two hundred Ankole cattle were swift but the return safari overland took three months. He lost count of the days as, every morning, his only goal was to reach the next water-hole for the animals.

* Withdrawn in 1928. Banking and commerce were handicapped by the lack of any currency notes and for years to come the transport of silver rupees and copper coins was arduous and precarious. Africans buried their money for safety but it was found that it corroded and the coins defaced so easily in the damp earth that eventually a replacement had to be found. In 1920 the rupee was finally withdrawn but the cent though holeless, is still used today. All the same, cumbersome though it was for them, the banks delivered cash from Nairobi to the door of account holders as far afield as Kiambu. It was brought to the door of residents by a runner, who carried it in a bag tied to a stick. Robberies of money were unknown until 1918 when for the first time, one of them was stopped in Karura forest and relieved of his load.

Only after counting them at night could he sleep. When he wakened, before him lay another day of herding, checking numbers, urging the long-horned cattle forward towards the next river, towards Nakuru. By the time he reached the Rongai Valley twenty miles from there, he had forgotten which month it was. Nor did he realise that he had camped on Florida Farm where Delamere had just started growing maize.

One morning, as the mist lifted over the green-grey thorn scrub, a Somali arrived at Block's tent on a mule. He brought a note from Lady Delamere whose boy had informed her that there was someone camping on the river and as it was Christmas Eve she was inviting him to join them in celebration. After twelve weeks on the road Block felt too dishevelled to dine with the Delameres and on these grounds declined with thanks.[14]

Two hours later a yellow and black buggy—the Delamere colours—arrived with Florence Delamere herself. She insisted Block join their party and pointed out that all her guests would be wearing khaki like himself or pyjamas. That Christmas dinner was the first decent food Block had eaten for weeks.[15]

At Equator Ranch, urban visitors came in for a number of shocks. There were no proper doors or windows and when the oxen or cows were driven into the boma at night for safety, if curiosity got the better of them, they were inclined to stick a head through the gunny sacking 'window'.[16] As usual plumbing was non existent and the 'long drop' was so distant from the house that men 'visited Africa' when they needed to pass water. Once when Delamere had a group of English peers coming to stay he was suddenly conscious that his sanitary arrangements were not quite in keeping with those in Europe. To redress the situation he had a dozen porcelain chamber pots sent up to Njoro from The Dustpan in Nairobi. When these were unpacked he said to his Somali major domo, 'each Bwana must have one of those . . . do you understand?' All was understood. When he and his VIPs were summoned to dine, on the table at each setting stood a flower-adorned chamber pot from which rose the steam from their soup.[17]

The Delameres' dwelling had graduated now to something larger though the floor of the one room was still of beaten earth. It was dominated by a huge stone fireplace in one corner, an enormous four-poster bed in another and a mahogany dining table with eight matching chairs which had been shipped out from Vale Royal. Their one concession to luxury was a Goan cook. Dinner generally consisted of Thomson's gazelle chops and blancmange or tinned peaches. Christmas fare was limited by what was available though Lady Delamere was breeding turkeys at this time.[18] Plum puddings, generally dispatched by loving relatives from home in November, seldom made the tables in Africa for which they were destined before the middle of January, sometimes arriving as late as Easter.[19]

After dinner each evening six or more Maasai arrived besmeared in sheepfat, to crouch on their haunches about the fire and, as one of Delamere's friends put it, 'talk about those things they wanted Delamere to hear'.[20]

Block went on to Nakuru with his cattle in the New Year, to meet Raper and Garland. After the transaction was complete each walked away from the sale with three thousand rupees in his pocket.[21]

Many important stock sales took place at Nakuru though Naivasha had been intended as the centre of farming development. This shift of emphasis probably had something to do with convenience for Lord Delamere for in 1908 he built the Nakuru Hotel to solve the lack of anywhere to stay and in the late twenties Block acquired it briefly in a land deal. But he realised that the hotel would never do well and sold it.[22] Even in its best years, Nakuru generated an air of disappointment though it did supersede Naivasha in importance.

Nakuru came to life when farmers trekked in from miles around to buy and sell stock. Once business was over, as in Nairobi with race-week, the celebrating began.

Arnold Paice, an assistant farmer to Tom Chillingworth from Naivasha, remembers Delamere selling over a thousand head of cattle just after the hotel opened. One hundred and fifty farmers turned up and 'never before have so many white men been seen together in this colony.' Afterwards, Delamere organised a dinner party for as many as cared to attend with champagne thrown in. Towards the end of the meal, suddenly 'D' noticed a farmer wearing a red tie and, as he was not wearing one himself, he promptly rushed at the man, pulled the tie off with a shout of accusation, 'Take it off, he's a socialist!' The victim was rather annoyed and seeing another guest with a tie nearby retaliated by tearing it off. All hell was let loose. By the time they had finished all those who arrived wearing ties ended up without. And, as Paice put it 'a lively time ensued. They also played . . . games like boys . . . at school, lying in a heap on top of one another on the floor, etc.'[23] Block's partner, 'Fatty' Garland, was quite capable leading the rest although he weighed over twenty stone and was also a heavy drinker. The Africans called him '*Tumbo*', stomach.

Block and Garland earned themselves a reputation for supplying very good steers but on one occasion were both caught for breaking East Coast Fever quarantine regulations.[34] The herds in the north were infected with pleuro-pneumonia so that all movement southwards of cattle was stopped. An attempt was also made by the Government to check the spread of ECF, as East Coast Fever was commonly known, by labelling regions 'clean' or 'dirty'. Although there was no ECF on the Northern Frontier, in order to reach settled areas such as Naivasha or Kedong to be sold, stock had no alternative but to pass through a dirty belt. Consequently all who traded cattle became a risk. A quarantine camp was established at Naivasha to enable the authorities to prove that ECF was endemic. Nairobi was encompassed by a twenty-seven mile long barbed wire fence and could only be entered at the quarantine gates and it became illegal to move cattle from a dirty to a clean region; this raised a whole new set of problems for traders, farmers and administration alike.[24]

ECF was the deadliest and most devious of all threats to cattle. It was not realised then that a diseased cow could take up to thirty days to die. Wherever it went, the ravening ticks were affected as they swarmed, carrying the poison for a year, contaminating fresh ground where they fell, so that healthy animals picked up the disease when the same insects sucked their blood. No-one understood either that the game that so impressed each newcomer with its abundance was also partly responsible. The rich loam upon which the best agricultural farms were founded happened also to attract huge herds of zebra and gazelle which innocently helped to create this endless cycle of disaster. The worst of it was that one animal that was sick with ECF could infect an entire herd. Delamere lost nearly all his stock from this disease at Njoro. Dipping, which at least helped slow down infection, was not practised until just before the First World War.[25]

Traders such as Block and Garland were immediately hit by the problem. In their haste to get their cattle to where their market lay, they often took the law into their own hands, taking short cuts across clean areas having travelled through a dirty belt on the way. One of the worst offenders in this respect was the Boma Trading Company founded by Jack Riddell after Winston Churchill's visit in 1907. But whenever the police attempted to catch them out and arrived on his door-step, they were disarmed with a smile and a drink and the matter was usually dropped.[26] Block and Garland were not so lucky and shared a brief spell in Naivasha gaol.[27]

'Fatty' Garland was among the group of farmers in the Nakuru area who were breaking the soil to grow maize in the Rift Valley north of Menengai. They gradually realised that, where the land starts to fall from the 6,000 feet level of Nakuru to the 3,500 feet of the Baringo Basin the altitude, fertility and rain were perfect for its cultivation. In fact, maize was to grow so successfully that they became pioneers of monoculture as well as settlement and in 1919 experienced a glut of maize.[28] Garland farmed with G. L. Cundy who later became involved in mule-train transport and met his death when one of his wagons skidded on slippery mud in the rainy season and crushed him against a bank on the road to Eldoret.[29] To begin they bought land at Olpunyatta, a grassy area, devoid of human life, trampled for generations by game and occasionally grazed by the stock of the Tugen and Njemps tribes. Others who grew maize in that same long flat valley of Solai were the Stanning, Eames and Baillie brothers, Frank Watkins, Nancy Rutherfurd, Rex Allen, G. Reynolds and W. J. Dawson who eventually lost all he had made through growing experimental geraniums. Another group grew maize in the Florida Farm area between the Rongai and the lower Molo Rivers, including Sammy McCall, Alick Gray, Will Evans, A. F. Duder, and A. Armstrong.[30] They were all successful though Florida Farm yielded record crops and was developed into the biggest maize proposition of all. In its prime, it produced 70,000 bags of maize in a single season. The average yield per acre in South Africa is less than three bags. Delamere's farm had produced thirty to the acre.[31]

It may come as a surprise to those who take for granted that *posho* as the staple diet of the African, that maize is not a native East African crop. It was still being imported from South Africa in 1903. Probably it reached the White Highlands with the first Europeans; Africans did not take to growing it for themselves with any enthusiasm until 1913. From then on they were so keen on its cultivation that growers in the Rongai district had to look for overseas markets for their harvests, which, in a roundabout way, was how the Kenya Farmers' Association was formed. Faced with the problem of surplus maize during the First World War, they formed the Maize Growers Association in an attempt to find an outlet for it.[32]

Ostrich farming was so much in vogue in 1907 that Clifford and Harold Hill, among others, came up from South Africa with the express intention of farming them in BEA. The fashion for nodding plumes on women's hats in the gay 'nineties and the Edwardian era had made modest fortunes for South African farmers. At Machakos and Ulu, following the example of the Hill brothers, F. O'B Wilson, Philip Percival, Archie Lambert and Sir Alfred Pease tried seriously to raise ostriches but the chief obstacle was lion. In 1906 birds had to be stockaded for protection. In the Rift Valley they were being reared by Paice and Chillingworth, Archie Buchan-Sydeserff, Delamere and Leslie Tarlton, whose ability to herd up to a hundred cocks at a time drew admiration from everyone, for it was a savage sport.

Enthusiasm was high at first, particularly as so little outlay was needed beyond the licence of 10 rupees a year and the patience to catch them. Ostrich egg hunting was tricky but the income just from selling eggs was worthwhile. Farmers often went into the blue for a month or longer with a tent and a dozen Africans to help obtain either eggs or newly-hatched chicks. It entailed rising before dawn so as to scale a vantage point from where it was hoped that the male bird could be spotted as it handed over guardianship of the nest to its mate. The hen sits out the day shift, the pair taking turns on twenty or more eggs. Having located the nest, one person approached on the plain whilst another, on higher ground, guided him verbally until the hen was driven off and robbed.

Next came the monstrous task of getting the clutch to an incubator (each egg averages five and a quarter pounds in weight). Farmers kept eggs constantly warm in sacking wrapped round hot-water bottles, replacing these as they cooled, or sometimes made their own incubators. Delamere imported his along with a pedigree ostrich cock from Somaliland to run with the hens that were caught on his farm.[33]

Jackals and hyenas often stole eggs before they were hatched even in captivity but if they survived, the chicks, for a while, were simpler to tend than the eggs. They were inquisitive creatures with coats more like hedgehog spines than feathers. *Totos*, young African boys, were employed to appease their insatiable appetites. It was a day-long job chopping greenstuff and breaking up shell and bone for them. Clipping began at eight months when birds were usually kept quiet by slipping a sock over their heads as a blindfold. The young feathers were not worth much and only after repeated clipping were they valuable. The ostriches were tame and friendly enough for eighteen months but the real trouble began when they matured at the age of three. African herders quickly learned that the only way to avoid violent kicks from their charges was to prod them along with a long piece of thorn tree in self-defence. Herders led a risky life, often suffering a broken thigh from a fierce male bird's kick.[34]

One Naivasha farmer owned a cock bird that had achieved notoriety by rushing up and knocking down anyone it noticed on sight, then mounting guard over its victim making it impossible to summon help or drive the bird off. Young Arnold Paice thought that this had its advantages. '. . . where you get one of these ferocious birds, you won't get any niggers trespassing . . . they don't knock you with their wings but strike at you with their great feet and can rip a man open with these formidable appendages.'[35]

Ostriches lent the air of the circus to the Nakuru stock sales where Delamere sold them, seventy-five at a time. Surrounded by pigs, cows, sheep, ducks, mules and ponies, occasionally a bird charged a barbed-wire fence with such ferocity that it cut its own throat or occasionally eluded the auctioneer's hammer altogether. The changing whim in millinery and the advent of the motor car eventually made it pointless to farm ostriches and most farmers gave up after five years and changed over to cattle. Those who continued found that, besides all the other problems, the feathers were being stolen. A handful, which could easily be hidden under a stockman's coat or blanket, could buy the thief an ox or make a splendid Nandi headdress. Theft of feathers was so prevalent by 1910 that the Naivasha Farmers' Association passed a resolution through a meeting of the Colonists Association designed to make it a punishable offence by law.

Once the Colonial Office took control of the territory, Sir James Hayes-Sadler, as Governor, was instructed to set up a Legislative Council.[36] It held its first meeting in the tin-roofed railway institute on 17 August 1907 and consisted quite simply of eight members—five official and three unofficial.[37] The Colonists' Association, under Grogan's presidency during 1907, was followed in 1910 by the Convention of Associations, founded largely through Delamere and Robert Chamberlain's energies in Nairobi at the Carlton Lounge.[38] As will be seen, it became the organ of general settler opinion, an 'unofficial parliament', accepted and listened to by the government.

In 1907, Winston Churchill, Under-Secretary of State for the Colonies, paid a visit. Settler opinion when he left was that, although he had made himself agreeable, his speeches were 'all rot', giving no guarantee of anything in the way of reform. What could any visitor know about the everyday life of a settler farmer? Could he envisage, for example, how, in order to get imported sheep to his farm, it could be necessary to throw each animal, one by one over a swollen river, re-crossing it not once, but three times in order to reach home?[39]

Churchill's ambition, common to most visiting men, was to bag a lion. Jack Riddell, who had served with him in the 16th Lancers of India, took charge of his safari. They camped on the Thika River where the Fort Hall Road crosses it which today is utterly devoid of wild life. Only seventy-five years ago it was a glorious hunting ground, teeming with buffaloes, lions, rhinos and moist-eyed elands, their silken dewlaps flapping as they jogged among the other plains game, the leaping impalas and Grant gazelles.

Round their camp fire at night while Churchill was Riddell's captive audience he talked of opening up trade with Abyssinia, and founding a firm to do it. Riddell explained that it could lead to an important new market for Lancashire cotton goods. So far, the scheme had not got off the ground because he needed arms for his caravans to travel 800 miles overland but this infringed various local regulations, therefore permission had been refused. Riddell convinced Churchill that the scheme was viable because he offered to support the founding of the Boma Trading Company.[40]

Before leaving camp, they took a bet as to who could cover the thirty miles back to the Norfolk Hotel fastest, Riddell on his black horse or Churchill in the car he had brought out from England. It had no windshield and every few miles it boiled, so that Churchill had to stop and fill it up with water. Riddell arrived just ahead of him.[41]

The chief reason for Churchill's visit was to smooth out difficulties concerning the Land Laws and when he went to meet Delamere, with whom he did a bit of pig-sticking, the luncheon held in his honour at Soysambu was the social event of the year.

Churchill, unlike his superior Lord Elgin, was far from certain that the exclusion of British Indian subjects from the Highlands could be regarded as a valid policy and felt impelled to say so. Sir James Hayes-Sadler was well disposed towards the Indian Community, and this immediately contributed to the growing opposition towards Indians shown by some of the European settlers.[42]

The Indian Community had in April 1906 subscribed 20,000 rupees to enable them to present their cases over the right to acquire land in the highlands to the Governments of the Protectorate, of India and of the United Kingdom. But in view of the composition of the Land Committee and the climate of opinion at that time, it is hardly surprising that their report firmly supported the view that the highlands should be reserved purely for Europeans.[43] Lord Elgin, Secretary of State for the Colonies, was sympathetic and his dispatch, approving and setting down these opinions, subsequently became known as the Elgin Pledge. After Churchill's visit, Elgin actually modified his earlier statements in March 1908, maintaining that, as a matter for administrative convenience, land in the Highlands should be granted to Europeans only, but that there should be no restriction to the subsequent legal transfer of land simply upon racial grounds.

Churchill, the first of a series of political dignitaries who stayed for a few weeks in the Protectorate, marvelled at its beauty and the opportunities offered, only to leave, pass judgements and write a book. But a sense of poetry pervades his impressions in *My African Journey*. 'To appreciate all these charms the traveller should come from the north . . . before the autumn rains have revived the soil . . . when every tree, be it a thorn tree—is an heirloom and every drop of water is a jewel.'[44]

Such lyricism did not wash with the toughened residents who remained sceptical. They had been promised improvements, yet Land Titles still took up to two years to acquire and the muddles over plots flourished as land was promised and then withdrawn; there were still no maps of outlying districts. Permission to cut timber, *shauries* over labour now that there was more demand for it and the increasing harassment of stock theft, all involved waiting for an authority of some sort, be it the Land Officer, the Police, the District Commissioner or some subordinate officer. If authority was required from the Colonial Office, vital decisions were taken without any understanding of the problem on the spot.

Much was made of visiting dignitaries, however. The scramble for invitations to Government House and various receptions for Theodore Roosevelt and his son Kermit as well as the Duke and Duchess of Connaught was uninhibited. In March 1906, Nairobi was 'gorgeous with arches and bunting', Maasai and Kikuyu warriors lined the street as the Duke unveiled a statue of Queen Victoria in the gardens which A. M. Jeevanjee had given to the town. The organisers became a bit panicky on the day that the party was due at Nairobi station, when they learned that the Duke's daughter, Princess Patricia and her lady-in-waiting, Miss Evelyn Pelly were with him. It was decided that the young women could not be faced with a great many undressed Africans, for the Maasai wore nothing but a 'shuka', a shift of *americani* tied over one shoulder. Someone had the bright idea of buying-up every red blanket available and dressing them in these. The effect was excellent and would have taken care of any embarrassing moments had not a shower of rain begun just as the Royal party was taking their leave for Government House, when every Maasai automatically twisted his blanket over his head to keep it dry.[45] The cream of Nairobi society were to be presented at the unveiling of Queen Victoria's statue in Jeevanjee Gardens. The Duke and Duchess sat with the Governor, on a high, specially constructed dais bedecked in red, white and blue bunting. After the speeches the chosen few climbed a steep ladder and walked along the narrow platform to halt, 'no closer than 6 inches' before their royal highnesses. Despite all the practising that had gone on, only Helen Sanderson and Gertrude Grogan managed to 'bob' correctly. Most of the women were 'as funny as any farce; they grabbed at the royal hands and Princess Patricia and Miss Pelly were in fits . . .'[46]

Elaborate precautions had been taken to see that Africans who were to appear before the Connaught party were clad decently, but one Maasai gentleman escaped the net and appeared at a garden party, held by the Master of the Masara Hounds, Jim Elkington, without his blanket or any other item that could pass for clothing. The Duke, urbane to the last, remarked, 'The Elkington livery I presume.'[47]

With Churchill's blessing Jack Riddell asked Freddy Ward and W. G. Sewell to join him in starting the Boma Trading Company. Sewell was a wealthy Bostonian and had been educated at Harvard. Like Northrup McMillan, he came out to hunt but had stayed on and developed land. After meeting in London to arrange the finances the three made a reconnaissance safari from Djibouti and they opened up the trade route from Nairobi to the Abyssinian border and even beyond. As gentleman buccaneers it was a moot point as to whether they narrowly avoided breaking the law in their dealings over ivory, beeswax, ponies, donkeys and cattle or simply never got caught.[48]

The arrangement to go ahead and trade with Abyssinia was that in return the Boma Trading Company would map out routes and place these at the disposal of the Colonial Office. Three further conditions were also laid down: the white traders were to respect Emperor Menelik's authority; reports had to be submitted regularly; and a deposit of £1,000 was to be made against good behaviour.[49]

Within two years the company found itself strangled in infancy by a network of quarantine restrictions, but while it lasted, this was a romantic enterprise—'it had an Elizabethan air' Elspeth Huxley wrote.[50] After the initial expedition, it employed the services of Count Hornyold and two brothers, Alec and Frederick Roy, sons of a ship owner both of whom became deeply involved in the Protectorate's commercial world. Alec answered a London newspaper advertisement and came out as Riddell's accountant and confidential secretary. Before long he found himself acting as chief outfitter for safaris for the Boma Trading Company and coping with any task that came his way. Fred, his brother who had lost an eye from the kick of a horse, followed soon afterwards.[51]

As Riddell, Ward and Sewell pioneered the route, they purchased Abyssinian ponies which were much valued in BEA and still in short supply. The safari itself was fraught with difficulties. Water-holes were rare and law and order non-existent. Ward became so ill with Somali dysentry that he almost died. He pulled through with doses of ipecacuanha and champagne but nevertheless had to return to Nairobi. Sewell alone completed the route. Riddell brought one hundred ponies back by ship. Each fetched £30 on the Nairobi market and had only cost £2 originally so that they imagined they were set for business.[52]

Between 1907 and 1909, Fred Roy and Count Gandolfi Hornyold based themselves at Marsabit and travelled continuously for the Company. They traded via Meru, under Mount Kenya, which was the last place where supplies could be bought before entering Marsabit to cross the desert to Moyale. It was a tough assignment but had it not been for them or John Boyes and other individual traders the colonists would have been faced with the almost insoluble problem of how to obtain native sheep.[53]

Whereas the Maasai were not interested in selling them the Rendile and Samburu were willing to trade them for cloth. In 1907 *americani* cost the equivalent of 2d a yard; Roy and Hornyold measured three to six 'arms', as the lengths were called, from elbow to fingertip in exchange for one sheep or goat. An average day's dealing might involve 35 heifers and two cows being traded for 1,500 goats and sheep but was just as likely to involve the exchange of 395 lbs of beans and flour, 5 pots of honey and tobacco for 10 goats. The goats were bought in Samburu for the equivalent of 8d each which according to Fred Roy's calculations was profitable enough, working out at 6/8d for 3½ cwt of beans and flour traded at Tirranong. However if Boyes's caravan arrived in the vicinity it could hinder business seriously particularly if he had many fat cows when trade with Roy stopped immediately.[54]

The Norfolk Stores, run by John Boyes, openly competed with Riddell for Boyes had tried to inveigle the Boma Trading Company into employing him. Riddell and he had an unholy row after he was turned down and Boyes stomped off to the Polo ground where the settlers sometimes raced their horses, won £400 in wagers and set off for Abyssinia.[55] A year later an impressive train of camels, laden with some of the finest ivory and followed by a long string of donkeys and horses came jogging along Station Road. They were all in first class condition and were heading for the Norfolk Hotel. Boyes, astride a white stallion, led the caravan and waved to passers-by, urging anyone who felt like it to meet him for a drink. Those who knew both men believed that the motive for this cavalcade was rooted in the Yorkshire-man's determination to irritate Riddell and beat him at his own game.[56]

The Boma Trading Company even smuggled down Abyssinian ponies against Menelik's wishes, thus breaking one of their fundamental trading provisos. As Elspeth Huxley puts it, they 'became bootleggers in cattle'.[57] The key was to get the herds to their destination secretly. Block and Garland used Will Judd's farm; the Boma Trading Company used land belonging to the Kedong Valley Syndicate, of which Riddell was a member. The Boran cattle from the north were exchanged here for Maasai sheep which were then sold quite openly.

No-one was more delighted than Boyes when the Boma Trading Company came unstuck because of quarantine regulations. All movement south-wards was stopped. Nothing could convince the Veterinary Department that ECF was endemic. They even accused the Boers of bringing it with stock from South Africa. Eventually cattle were sent to Kibigori for six months and if they survived were then branded with the initials AMT, a sign which increased their value considerably on account of their immunity. With these creatures, transport was restored.[58]

Until 1920 the labour problem dogged every settler's existence. Arnold Paice was understanding of the African, as this extract from a letter shows, 'before we came to this country, the various races, Maasai, Kikuyu, Wakamba etc., were always raiding and at war with one another, conditions of life at times must have been harder . . . yet it . . . seemed extraordinary the way in which . . . the native seems to take for granted that the white man is master. Why should they come and work for us at rupees four per month? . . . I shouldn't if I were a nigger. Why should they stand being hammered by a white man when they would fight like anything if another nigger struck them?'[59]

Paice was also sympathetic of other difficulties that Africans faced. 'These natives have perils and hardships to undergo, though not a severe climate, in the heavy rains, it is not an uncommon thing for natives caught in the open plains to succumb with cold and wet. At intervals all along the road crossing the Kinankop Plateau I have seen human skulls lying—the skulls are the only parts the hyenas and jackals leave. But what *we* consider hardships, the natives don't. How they can sleep (even with a fire going) in a hut just made of branches through very cold nights we often get, beats me . . . their idea of a bed, just rough split pieces of cedarwood laid on the floor. A piece of calico about a yard square by way of a blanket, we should soon peg out but they are as happy as kings if they get plenty to eat and not too many hammerings . . .'[60]

At hearings of a labour commission in 1907, several European witnesses freely admitted the application of the *kiboko* to keep labour in line. Fred Roy's excuse for beating one of his men who had stolen half a left-over rice pudding, was that he denied the fact. The culprit had stolen before and had been promised the *kiboko* if anything went astray again because 'the African nigger has a great propensity for theft of any article whether useful to him or not.' Roy also made his porters work on Sundays because they were ignorant of the meaning of the Sabbath and did not consider his actions immoderate. 'My men cannot stand the *kiboko*, I gave a man fifty the other day and he howled from first to last. I have not kibokoed many as I generally plug 'em or take a shot for good luck at their rear end.'[61] The concept of 'discipline' varied enormously, depending entirely on the individual. One settler 'supervised' his labourers by firing a rifle in the direction of anyone whom he thought to be slacking.[62] A Boer farmer near Nanyuki chased one of his stockmen in his car and, when the man fell, drove over him, fully aware that despite the terror it would cause, he would not maim the man because the car chassis cleared his body by several inches.[63]

Paice devised a cruelly bizarre means of 'teaching them a lesson' after discovering that one of the herd boys had not been doing his job properly. The man would not 'slack' again Paice wrote to his mother, first explaining how the Maasai enlarged their ear lobes for ornamental purposes and described the alternative uses to which the resulting loops of flesh may be put. '. . . They are able to insert such articles as jam jars . . . They start . . . quite young by making a small hole . . . shoving a bit of stick or bamboo through . . . by degrees every few months they insert bigger and bigger things. I consider it horribly disfiguring especially when there is no ornament in the ear, as the lobe hangs loose to the neck. The Kikuyu treat their ears in just the same way. I have found it a very satisfactory way of shackling them . . . once

I came across a herd boy who had . . . gone to sleep . . . when I met him, he was wandering about looking for cattle he should have been herding . . . by way of punishment as I was mounted . . . I took the crupper of the pony and fastened it through the ear and on the D of the saddle. Then I shoved my heels in my pony and set off at a canter . . . the nigger had to canter too . . . it would have been painful to have his ear pulled off or rather broken . . . I led him quite a nice little chase until we had found his cattle . . . On another occasion we tied a lot of trespassers together by the ears and made them carry timber from the forest. I do not consider their ears beautiful but they are certainly handy at times.'[64]

No country was opened up by meek individuals. Pioneering called for energy, resourcefulness, resolution and forcefulness, but in the instance described below, Grogan carried his ideas too far. One of his biographers describes him as 'one of Africa's fairest employers' a statement which certainly casts doubts on the majority. What happened was this:

On 14 March 1907, in full view of a European and native gathering, Grogan conducted a public flogging of his three Kikuyu rickshaw boys because he felt they had insulted his sister, Dorothy Hunter and her friend, Miss MacDonald.[65]

As President of the Colonists' Association Grogan received complaints of Africans behaving disrespectfully towards European women. These had become so frequent that, in Grogan's opinion, it was unsafe for white women to leave their homes without a male escort.[66]

The question of native dress also arose when Nairobi was impounded to enforce the quarantine regulations. The Municipal Committee decided that it was time that Africans covered their nakedness in the name of decency. Thus, askaris were posted at the quarantine gates to ensure that men were prevented from coming into Nairobi unless they were properly clad. The Africans regarded this as a colossal joke; crowds collected at the gates and the bold in spirit rushed them with jeers of derision for a bit of sport. The position deteriorated; rules for these misdemeanors were passed authorising small fines for which explanation was useless—indecent exposure did not exist in the mind of the African. The worse cases were checked, but one fellow called Karanja who rode his employer's bicycle to fetch the post, used to borrow it, passing through the gates with clothes on and unnoticed by the guards among throngs of Kikuyu women going to market. Once inside the fence, Karanja undressed completely, mounted the bicycle and proceeded in to town where '. . . the uproar when he entered the main street . . . emptied the shops and brought people hurrying from side-lanes where they met this amazing sight.'[67]

Many of the settlers with wives and daughters were shocked and offended. Grogan was bombarded with complaints. He accused the Government of lethargy and urged them to do something before rape or murder was committed. 'You will never keep these savages under control with a handful of askaris. Build up a proper European Police Force, introduce a scale of punishments that the negroes will fear. Get off your bottoms, act before it is too late.' Nothing was done.[68]

Then on 13 March his rickshaw boys, worse for drink, gave Grogan's sister Dorothy Hunter a terrible fright. She had come to live in Nairobi the year before after marrying Wilfred C. Hunter, an associate of the Chartered Institute of Secretaries. Neither she nor the friend she was with had noticed that the boys were drunk when she ordered the rickshaw to be brought. The ride was conducted at great speed and as the men raised and lowered its shafts in a see-saw action the women screamed out in fear of over-turning. When the vehicle was finally halted, Dorothy Hunter and Miss MacDonald, very much shaken by the experience, walked home. They recounted the experience to Grogan whose reaction was to go after the offenders immediately but he was unable to find them.

In his frustration, Grogan went to his neighbour, the estate agent, Sydney Fichat, who also happened to be Vice-President of the Colonists' Association. After discussing the matter, Fichat advised Grogan to sleep on his mood and warned against taking the law into his own hands. Grogan's outrage was no less in the morning. On 14 March, ignoring Fichat's council, he was determined to administer the punishment of his rickshaw boys himself.[69]

That morning Russell Bowker was having breakfast at his Nairobi house, 'Tharfield', near the racecourse with his wife and daughter, Margaret and a guest, Captain Thord Gray. Bowker had asked for their horses to be saddled up preparatory to leaving for town on business, when a runner appeared with a pencilled note. It was from Grogan and asked Bowker to help deal with three rickshaw boys who had insulted his sister. Bowker and Gray left at once.[70] Bowker's walrus moustache and bulky figure was imposing enough but the hat he always wore added a certain ferocity. On it was mounted the mask of a leopard. Many settlers wore a modest band of leopard pelt round the crown of a hat but this was an entire head, showing bared fangs, narrowed yellow eyes and ears flattened in the most dangerous of snarls.[71]

Meanwhile Grogan had manacled the rickshaw boys and, with a crowd of more than fifty Europeans at his heels, marched them to the Magistrate's Court. In spite of protests by the magistrate, Mr E. R. Logan and a police officer, who, when faced with too large a rabble to handle alone, had disappeared to get reinforcements, the flogging was carried out. Each offender was given twenty-five strokes. Grogan beat one, Bowker another and Gray took on the third.[72] On being released the Africans were taken to the Native Hospital for treatment. Their lacerated backs were photographed and prints were sent to Members of Parliament in London.[73] A diary mentioning the incident states that Grogan almost killed one of the men.

If Grogan, Bowker and Gray had any regrets for their actions at all it was for an oversight: the stupidity of administering the beatings within the court-house boundaries.

Afterwards, Grogan had gone to a meeting at Tommy Wood's and

Bowker, who had arranged to leave for a shooting expedition that afternoon, joined his wife, daughter and son-in-law for a short safari on the Thika and Chania Rivers to bag hippo. A warrant for Bowker's arrest arrived whilst the party were camped there. He was escorted back to Nairobi under armed guard.[74]

The trial was farcical when, in due course, they were brought before an inexperienced magistrate. They should have been tried by jury. (Grogan later appealed on these grounds and his appeal was upheld.) The original charge of assault was reduced to 'creating an unlawful assembly' according to Indian Penal Law. Since it took five people to constitute 'an unlawful assembly' the two reporters who were taking notes for the local papers were included in the charge. They qualified only because they were standing within the fence at the time.[75]

Tiller, editor of the *East African Standard*, supported Grogan's use of physical punishment. It was justified because . . . 'It does not matter whether the assault was committed on a native or a European. We have never heard of any man who . . . appealed to the law to punish his wife's insulter . . . Blood beats and in a tropical climate the Caucasian is apt to be intemperate.' Tiller made sure that his readers understood the implication that the accused also happened to be one of those who was most critical of the Administration. He described the verdict as, 'the most wilful error of judgement'.[76]

Grogan was sentenced to one month's imprisonment with a fine of 500 rupees. Gray and Bowker were each fined half that amount and fourteen days imprisonment. By midday the three of them were shut up in the native jail opposite the Norfolk Hotel. Grogan, ironically, was then a visiting Justice of Nairobi Jail. He had made an inspection just a few weeks before and denounced conditions as 'an absolute disgrace.'[77]

The verdict of the trial aroused wide indignation as bush telegraph brought those settlers within easy distance of Nairobi pouring in on horseback or bullock-wagon—anything so long as they could have their say. They began to dismantle the walls of the jail by unscrewing the panels of iron from it. Things looked bad when an askari tried to intervene and Margaret Bowker, who was a keen participant, drew her revolver from her belt and threatened him. After two or three panels had been removed, those outside could see the squalor within where Bowker sat on an upturned box in a filthy cell, smoking his pipe and treating the matter as a joke. When a *suferia* of boiled beans was served to the captives by a chained gang of Africans, the spectators were no longer amused. They became threatening and it looked as if shots would be fired.[78]

Next a deputation of settlers marched up to Government House demanding speech with Frederick Jackson, then acting Commissioner. ('Flannelfoot' was on leave.) After a good deal of unpleasant talk, the following night the prisoners were transferred to a bungalow on the Hill. Conditions were so appalling in the native jail, had they been left there it was feared that blood might have been shed.[79]

Life, under 'house arrest', could not be described as hard. The men were not allowed to smoke and lights were put out at 8 o'clock but the Nairobi community smuggled in home-made cakes and also brought a gramophone up to serenade the prisoners from just beyond the fixed bayonets of their askaris.

Grogan seems to have been quite unrepentent during his internment. On one occasion he kicked the sweeper over the verandah rail for daring to enter the bungalow with his shoes on, for showing no respect because they were prisoners. The sweeper's face went into the bucket of dirty water he was carrying and as he fell from the blow the dignified askari was almost knocked over too.[80]

Some three months later Grogan and Gray appealed and the judge reversed the magistrate's decision and disallowed a fresh trial because they had already suffered the term of imprisonment to which they were sentenced.

The flogging case gravely damaged the reputation of settlers in Britain. Grogan was quite unlike most of his contemporaries, which is why such cases were rare. Less fortunately those that occurred left an ineradicable stain of cruelty on the characters involved and did nothing to cement harmonious relations. However the ill wind did blow some good. Before Grogan was released, Churchill informed the house that the Government had decided to reorganise the Police force of the Protectorate by recruiting a rank and file of Europeans and, moreover, a new prison would be erected.[81]

Before this horrible incident, the Colonists' Association, to which the behaviour of the Africans remained a 'genuine and continuous concern', had appointed Grogan, Gray and one other member as a committee to formulate a defence scheme for the European community. Grogan had resigned presidency in April 1907 but was re-elected two months later. There had been some dissension in the Association as to his share in the flogging. The commercial sector complained bitterly that the fear of native aggression was hampering immigration and preventing trade. In a reassuring vein, Jackson, published a Government Notice informing the Europeans that a state of unrest among the native population did not exist and 'there is not the slightest ground for such supposition.'

Delamere replaced Grogan as President of the Colonists' Association in October. Around this time the Land Office granted them a plot for their headquarters and now they pressed for the Legislative Council to increase its unofficial members from three to five, to be elected by the male white population of the Protectorate. Delamere had been looking for 'complete self-government' but Churchill felt that it would be a long time before it could even be contemplated. The most he was prepared to promise was a future goal of 'elective non-official representation.'

Ideas for combined action moved slowly to begin with and Delamere became increasingly impatient for self-government. No count was kept of the number of times he resigned from different bodies in BEA to get his own way. In a circle that was formerly wide but was narrowing, the point was that until now threat alone had often been effective enough for him to achieve his ends.

CHAPTER 9

Trek-Fever

'The earth is a beehive; we all enter by the same door but live in different cells.'

Bantu proverb

The long rains were imminent when, in March 1908, the settlers became so heated over the labour question that they confronted the Governor in person in his new residence on the Hill.

In Africa the arrival of rain after a long spell of dry weather is naturally looked upon as a blessing rather than a curse. Several inches may fall each day but it never seems to be quite enough. There are two wet seasons and two harvests in Kenya. The long rains continue from March until May and the short rains can generally be depended upon the fall after the third week in October. These as a rule are heralded by storms and last until November.[1] The outcome of so much depended on the success or failure of them.

As the sullen clouds build up there is pleasure in the sight of them for the ground is thirsty by the time they are due. The long hot days leading up to them frayed the settlers' nerves and seemed to affect the Europeans psychologically. They became jumpy and notoriously touchy. While it may be coincidental, a preponderance of their more impetuous actions took place during these waiting months of February, March and early April. As the settlers recognised this edginess in themselves, they began to refer to this phase as 'the Ides of March'.[2]

As combined labour and land problems gathered momentum and seriously affected the country's development in 1908, it became more evident than ever that it was impossible for those living thousands of miles away, however capable on home ground, to keep in touch with the Protectorate's requirements.

The settlers urged that labour be recruited with the help of the DOs, who were constantly and suitably in touch with Chiefs and elders who in turn would persuade those who followed them to co-operate. But the Colonial

Office was acutely conscious of the need to avoid anything which could be interpreted as 'forced labour'.

But the simple fact was that, no matter how it was attained, the farmers needed a regular labour supply. The Africans, far from anxious to work anyway, let alone regularly, were mainly content with their level of subsistence, and, when they did work, once they had earned enough to pay their hut tax were content to leave. Farmers lost crops for lack of reliable manpower; indeed such were these frustrations during 1907, that a number of them abandoned the idea of settlement altogether. Desperate settlers began engaging professional recruiters. These received a commission for each labourer who signed on and were not fastidious as to the means by which they coerced other Africans to work. Officials tried to prevent this method of approach. One went even further, advising the Kikuyu against working on European farms.[3]

The cry for a statement of policy on labour became insistent until the Governor agreed to meet the settlers at the Railway Institute in Nairobi. One morning towards the end of the dry season they gathered to air their grievances.

At this meeting Delamere asked that all Government officers should be directed to encourage the native, assisting those who required labour. 'I feel so strongly about this matter that I cannot speak about it.'[4] As a stock farmer he made clear that he was not as affected as those who needed long-term labour on contract to grow coffee and sisal. The Maasai he employed worked because they liked him and were able to steal the odd cow or two occasionally. He also had a few squatters to work for him as well.

Hayes-Sadler did not produce the labour policy he had promised. Charles Miller writes that 'this man may have been the least articulate civil servant ever to hold a high post in the British Empire'.[5] Those shortcomings seem to be summed up in his closing comment to the disappointed gathering, 'I can say nothing at the moment.'

The settlers left the meeting feeling cheated. Many had travelled far. As they lunched together and exchanged opinions, no doubt interspersed with a pink gin or two, they became very worked up. Before the meal was over they had decided to march on Government House and demand an explanation. The three unofficial councillors of Legislative Council, Arthur Baillie, Russell Bowker and Delamere led the gaitered and holstered column. They were determined to get some definition of a labour policy out of Hayes-Sadler.

Their frustration was aggravated immediately when he failed to appear. They refused to budge. When Hayes-Sadler did emerge it was to be addressed, as he later wrote to the Secretary of State, 'in an excited and offensive manner' by Delamere. 'They were all dissatisfied with this morning's meeting . . . I had treated lightly their representations . . . I had only dealt with unimportant points . . . I had given no satisfactory answers to the points which were of extreme importance to settlers.'

Hayes-Sadler had announced that he could not deal with such important matters offhand and would give them an answer the following day. Delamere was outraged. Unable to contain himself any longer he shouted, 'Tomorrow, tomorrow, it is always tomorrow, we are sick of tomorrows; we are not schoolboys, we demand an immediate answer on the spot and nothing else.' Cries of 'Resign' made the Governor wish them a curt good-evening as he retreated behind the safety of his doors.

Further calls for his resignation were heard as the crowd withdrew and then regrouped within the grounds a hundred yards away where, after a quick exchange of opinions and a few cheers of self-congratulation, they dispersed.[6]

Helen Sanderson records that Nairobi was convulsed all week. 'Over two hundred men went up to see the Governor, who refused to alter the labour Ordinances, which were ruining the settlers. He then gave way next morning, sacked Lord Delamere and Arthur Baillie . . . little Mrs Baille is in such a state of fury. The Club is positively dangerous these days. Poor Lord D is dreadfully upset; he has done so much for the country and loves it so (he was coming to dinner last night but didn't as is his vague custom). In such a little place as this where we all know each other socially most amusing things happen. One of the secretaries most concerned, is deeply in love with one of the ladies and was nearly off his head about it all lest she would never speak to him again. On Thursday, I spent the afternoon, first with one friend, then another, both of whom were choking with indignation over their respective sides of it.'[7]

Hayes-Sadler had wasted no time in sending a dispatch to the Secretary of State. In divulging the incident he put it down to 'the spirit of political unrest, impatient of any form of government but its own, which has been so marked a feature of the uplands.' He admitted, 'But there is no question that of late there has been a serious falling off of labour.' This was attributed to the increase of hunting safaris because shooting parties were willing to pay twice the usual rate to porters; the stopping of the practices of certain chiefs who were sending out men by methods 'little short of forced labour' and other factors. Delamere's attitude, the Governor added, had been 'truculent and aggressive.'[8]

When 'D' and Baillie were officially suspended from the Legislative Council, Delamere broke down and wept. Their banishment actually only lasted six months because their suspension aroused such indignation in Nairobi that the Governor realised that the only redress was to re-instate them both. Though the crisis passed, the dearth of skilled labour continued for many years.[9]

1908 probably saw the peak of settlement when on 11 July 250 Boers arrived at Mombasa. Their leader, Jansen Van Rensberg, had chartered the *s.s. Windhoek* to bring in twenty-seven Boer families including his own. The same day, on special trains, they went up-country. A handful got off at Athi River and the rest went up to Nakuru where they set up a camp five miles from the one-street shanty town. From here a party of horsemen went on a reconnaissance safari over the Uasin Gishu Plateau, so as to blaze a trail for the rest who filled in their time by training oxen. These had been bought at a special sale organised by the District Commissioner at Nakuru.[10]

The Governor had promised van Rensberg in 1907 that each family he brought up to settle would be given a farm proportionate to the extent of his assets. The Boers imported complete farms, unloading houses, seventy-two horses, forty-two wagons and a variety of stock and were destined to create their own small township, Eldoret.

When the Jewish Scheme was under question, there had also been great agitation over a rumour that the arrival of 300 Boer families was imminent. Its object was to establish a self-governing colony by those who were ruined by the Boer War, the so called 'irreconcilables' faced with the possibility of starvation unless they moved on. The Boer leaders in South Africa, far from supporting this exodus, had been as unhappy as the British Government and did all in their power to prevent the project, but too many had already sold their land in the Transvaal and Orange River Colony to stop it. Thirty families had already set forth.[11]

In Nairobi in 1904, the rumour that three hundred Boer families were due to arrive was pruned to size by the *East African Standard*. They were heading for German East Africa. With some gloating the Nairobi press reported that the Boers were given a frigid reception and the panic subsided.[12] Two years later, when eight Boers came over the border escorted by the Game Ranger, Blaney Percival, they had been greeted by jeers in the headlines. One editor wrote that they should be forced to take the Oath of Allegiance. They were accused of introducing ECF.[13] Regardless of the obstruction and prejudice from the established community, John de Waal, Abraham Joubert and A. F. Arnoldi, went to look at the Uasin Gishu and as a result of staying with the van Breda brothers, settled. De Waal was the first man to grow wheat on the Plateau. In 1907 Fred Loxton, Arnoldi and his wife and two daughters were the first white women to live there.[14] When War broke out in 1914, A. F. Arnoldi raised Arnoldi's Scouts and was mentioned in dispatches after losing his life in 1916 while fighting for the British in German East Africa.[15]

In 1908 these Boers with their hand-made reins and shoes, their bone and olive-wood harrows, were derided as old-fashioned. With their mystical desire for trekking (known as Trek-fever) they were also God-fearing individuals. They had a quiet ability to persevere and establish their worth and got on well with the Africans. They taught them to make wagons and wheels and bought unbroken oxen from them which were sold at Londiani after training. Thus the transport network was opened up across the Protectorate.

In August the voortrekkers left Nakuru, travelling in two columns, each wagon pulled by sixteen oxen. When rocks hindered progress they stopped and heaved them out of the way. Some men walked, others rode while the women and children were jolted along in the huge Cape wagons from the back of which swung carcases of game, strung on the iron hoops that held up the canvas. Each night they cut their meat from these and made bread and stews over the fires within the protective circle of their wagons. While the women cooked, the men made a boma with thorn scrub for the outspanned oxen so that lion could not get them. They took their time, resting after each difficult episode and doing their laundry and tending their children. Ovens were made out of river banks and ant-hills; they scooped a hole out of the earth and put in enough hot ashes to heat their huge cast-iron pans.

At Ravine the land rises from 6,000 feet to 9,100 feet across nineteen miles where in places the clumps of bamboo grew so densely it was difficult for a man to pass. As Elspeth Huxley has written, only the Afrikaaners could have done it.[16]

Six miles from Ravine they built a bridge to cross a river and when they met the forest beyond, the men hacked away seven miles of trees, widening a passage for the wagons. After felling, the trees had to be sawn in pieces and towed away by oxen. When the way was clear enough for the first column to move, they moved on. But the leading column churned up the ground for the rear party which took four days to get through because the men who went back to help first had to construct a make-shift causeway from bamboo canes placed over the soggy ground. A more treacherous phase confronted them. The great wagons had to be driven up an escarpment along a narrow, slippery track, so steep that it looked impossible to surmount.

African forests are rich tapestries of sound from birds, treefrogs and crickets. The Boers also encountered the rare bongo antelope, elands, buffaloes, rhinos and elephants. One forest was named after Fred Loxton; when he had travelled to the plateau the year before, he was trying to press the rear oxen past a tree when his foot caught and he slipped under Arnoldi's wagon. The front wheel went over his chest and he would have been crushed entirely by the rear wheel as the wagon slipped back, but Arnoldi managed to drag him clear.[17]

At last the Van Rensberg trek reached Timboroa where they gazed on the veldt their community dominated for the next thirty years. Sticking and straining, under the cracking of whips, the teams made their way to the Sosiani River towards Kipkabus. When they came to the notorious Sugar Vlei swamp, each wagon needed three teams of oxen to pull it out. The only human victim of this incredible safari was a two-year-old girl who got pneumonia and was buried under a cedar tree at Timboroa.[18] At Sergoit on 22 October the columns fragmented into families which chose land as it took their fancy. A crude survey had been done by Piet van Breda; the condition of lease was that a sum equal to forty times the rent must be spent on development within five years. Once fulfilled, their leases were granted and on these terms, one hundred and four farms were taken up, varying in size between 900 and up to 5,000 acres. Depending on acreage, the annual rental was from 3 to 18 cents of a rupee. Hurriedly they located springs and broke the ground, living at first from the wagons or in tents. They sowed South

African wheat, maize, beans and vegetables that month but unfortunately they had missed the crucial rains. They lost all their young plants. [19]

Supplies had to come from Londiani to begin with and the journey took fourteen days each way by ox-cart or, if conditions were bad, six weeks. Generally the Boers preferred to go in convoy, for to attempt the journey alone was to court disaster. Sometimes as many as 72 oxen were required to shift a wagon if it became bogged down at Burnt Forest. Despite the unsympathetic attitudes towards the Boers at first, the other settlers soon began to appreciate how skilled they were with oxen.

Upon 'Farm 64' the town Eldoret developed gradually on the Sosiani River. By coincidence Eldoret happened also to lie 64 miles from railhead at Londiani and was often called 'Sixty Four' instead. In the accustomed manner, Indian traders shortly followed the Boers to open *dukas* there and ease supply problems. Though the Afrikaaners were virtually self-sufficient they needed ammunition to shoot game otherwise they were without hide, meat and fat and every scrap, from every zebra and kongoni carcase, was used for some aspect of their simple life. [20]

Ironically the game, the appeal of the simple life on a short term basis, was just beginning to turn BEA into a Mecca for the wealthy tourist. The fashion was for wide open spaces rather than cities and hunting offered the rich and blasé a brand new thrill. It represented a challenge to sportsman, and was recognised as the perfect anodyne for those crossed in love. Then there were the unmentioned advantages. If getting away from it all meant leaving the wife at Home those men with a mistress could safely take her on safari and the discretion of the white hunter escorting them could almost be guaranteed. [21]

The benign climate and the reputation as a sportsman's paradise was even more appealing once regular train services guaranteed comfortable accessibility to the Norfolk Hotel, their jumping-off place. To the settlers, the fashion for big-game hunting was heavensent. Shooting safaris brought enormous sums of money into the country and when clients were satisfied, often led to investment. Supplementary employment was provided for many Europeans; the safari was the bedrock upon which the success of Kenya's modern tourist industry is founded although today shooting, except with a camera, is forbidden.

Abraham Block's connections with the safari world were tenuous and hardly the sort which pointed to his family's enormous involvement with the industry in years to come. One was his friendship with David Tulipmann, a young Jewish accountant who worked for the most prestigious of the safari outfitters, Newland and Tarlton who happened in a roundabout way to bring about Block's marriage. [22] The other was through a brief partnership in farming with a white hunter, W. C. Judd, who was one of the string on Newland and Tarltons' books and took Theodore Roosevelt out in 1909. The hunters were a freelance breed, working for others or themselves depending on circumstances. [23]

'Billy' or 'Will' Judd was a veteran of the Boer War, the Matabele rebellion and the Jameson Raid and had worked in Australia, America, Rhodesia and Portuguese East Africa before coming to Nairobi in 1902.[24] He had done a good deal of elephant hunting in the Lado Enclave about which he wrote the occasional article for *The Field*. He was one of Northrup McMillan's first hunters, who when Judd had acted as a guide to some visiting peers, paid him so well that he took up hunting professionally. He and his wife Hilda had a small stock farm at Kabete.[25] Judd owned a trading store in the Nandi country and with Block bought land together near Naivasha and on the Uasin Gishu where they grew experimental barley at Hoey's Bridge. It was probably managed by one of the many Boers who looked after farms for absentee owners here, for neither of them lived in the Uasin Gishu themselves.[26] Judd and Block must have made a comic pair on those rare occasions when they were seen in tandem (both worked independently and were usually on the move) for their physical difference was marked. Judd was six feet tall and weighed over 200 lbs and it was said that he could carry a mule on his back. He lost his life tragically when he was shot by his own son with the bullet intended for an elephant which had seized Judd.[27]

There was always a stir of excitement in Nairobi when the old porter safaris left. They could form a mile-long string as eighty to a hundred of them, bearing head-loads, left for the bush with a small knot of white men, the clients and hunters, bringing up the rear.

Originally the term 'white' hunter referred to a sportsman whose colour of skin singled him out from the Africans, the amateur who stalked and shot game by his own prowess. It may be apocryphal but there is a plausible story that the term originated through Alan Black, who, even in 1907, was much respected as a 'white hunter'.

Scion of a distinguished line of clipper captains, Black took French leave from school to join in the Boer War, and by the age of seventeen, in 1903, had investigated settling in Nairobi. Delamere needed two hunters to shoot game for his porters (possibly when he was immobilised from his fall on the Athi Plains) and employed Alan Black whose skill at shooting with a bow and arrow was as great as that with a gun. But the second hunter was a Somali who also acted as *Neapara* or headman in camp. To differentiate between the two, on account of Black's surname, the Somali was referred to as 'the black hunter' while Black was always called 'the white hunter' and from this circumstance, the term caught on and stuck.[28]

At any rate for the first time in Africa's history the role of white hunter was created, romanticised and then glamorized. More often than not, full-time professional hunters emerged gradually out of the ordinary pioneer farmer who shot well and was attempting to earn extra income. Full-time did not mean a year-long occupation but being fully committed to clients during the hunting season. A man had to be courageous and had to know the terrain as if born on it. He must speak Swahili, understand the African, know the uncertain nature of the bush and the game: but he also had to have the manners of a society club man and the tact of a diplomat—that meant second sight as to every need of his client.

Those listed on Newland and Tarltons' books possessed these virtues in individual ways, building up world-wide reputations with men who stalked and shot game through their own prowess, their names just as likely to be mentioned over a stockbroker's desk in Wall Street as over luncheon at White's in London. Newland and Tarlton's early lists included the great in the hunting fraternity, many of whom have been immortalised in books about BEA. The earliest of these were G. H. Cuninghame, Fritz Schindelar, George Outram, Jack Lucy, Alan Black, Jack Riddell, Bill Judd, Leslie Tarlton, followed closely by Pat Ayre, Philip Percival, G. H. Anderson, Al Klein, Denys Finch Hatton, Bror von Blixen and many more.[29]

When a safari was due to depart, the area beyond the Norfolk Hotel's white picket fence, which was never was very quiet, became a place of phenomenal activity. Here the retinues of cooks and porters assembled to be joined by pack animals, syces, askaris and gun-bearers on the day of departure. A great accumulation of chop-boxes, medicine chests, folding baths, mosquito nets, tents, salt for preserving skins and ammunition piled up hourly with all the necessities for perhaps four months in the bush. After every item had been checked, they were dealt out to the porters in 60 lb head-loads.

Thirty porters per hunter were required on a shooting expedition and for every two clients, between 80 and 100 porters. Stipulations for comfort depended on a client's idea of luxury and varied from armchairs and cases of champagne to Goanese cooks who were expected to provide eight course dinners. Theodore Roosevelt's safari in 1909 was a vast affair consisting of 500 porters not counting gunbearers, trackers, personal servants, cooks, skinners and tent boys.[30]

Strange people came out to hunt game and some used strange methods. W. D. Boyce, a Chicago newspaper-owner, thought that a balloon was the surest and safest way of photographing game. He arrived with two photographers, an enormous balloonograph and several journalists one of whom was his chief leaderwriter. The last stayed behind at the Norfolk to file the material, sent back by those covering the safari, to Boyce's chain of newspapers in the USA.

True to American form, Boyce wanted his departure for the Rift Valley to go off in style. He tried to hire the KAR band to lead a procession from the Norfolk to the station but any hope of recruiting it had been sabotaged by his reference to Nairobi as 'this military backwash'. He meant 'backwater' but they were not amused. Boyce had to make do with porters blowing horns and banging the food boxes with sticks. The Stars and Stripes were borne aloft and as Binks recalls, 'They made a grand show as they crossed the plain. At least the front portion did, but the dust they raised obliterated most of the rear section . . . they left for up-country bedecked with hundreds of replicas of the American emblem.'[81]

W. D. Boyce's balloonograph expedition was a flop. The animals either crouched down or made for cover the minute this peculiar flying object presented itself. One day, the leader writer, bored with waiting at the Norfolk Hotel for material from Boyce, passed the time by compiling a letter to a friend, describing in great but fictitious detail all the animals he had seen and shot and the adventures he had had whilst in the African wilds. In fact he had hardly been off the verandah.

These were the disastrous results. The recipient sent it to a rival group of newspapers who published it in large print on their front page. Boyce's own group, who had received nothing, demanded to know what was happening. Boyce was livid but, since he had failed to get material to his employee, was at a loss as to how to get his own back other than sacking his leader writer. He took his vengeance by reporting the man to the Game Ranger for killing game without a licence and sent a copy of the original letter as support of his accusation.[32]

Another unusual safari was that of Buffalo Jones with his outfit of cowboys who, mounted on cow-ponies, roped everything even the larger species of game. The ponies were terrible to ride, not unlike a small Clydesdale with a walk and trot that shook the rider unmercifully except when they cantered. Of the animals that were roped the hartebeeste was found to be the most dangerous and one of these gored and killed a cow-pony. As for the cowboys, they were up to every short of prank when they returned to refit in Nairobi. One day, G. H. Goldfinch, a whipper-in with the Masara Hounds, was relaxing in the Norfolk Hotel bar with a glass of beer. A stout fellow, he was reading the newspaper and smoking his pipe at a table next to the window overlooking the verandah. Suddenly with no more than a whistle over his head, one of the cowboys had lassoed him and the next thing he knew was that he was sitting outside on the murram.[33]

Newland and Tarlton safaris were always the smartest and most memorable of hunting departures with their porters all turned out in navy blue jerseys bearing the scarlet initials 'NT' on the front. Each man was issued with a blanket, an obligatory pair of brand new boots, a three-pound bag for his daily posho ration which was tied round his waist, a water bottle and a length of rope for securing his headload. One *suferia* was allocated between four porters. Boots however were still so much of a novelty with Africans that they remained slung round the neck on the march, regarded as prestigeous items rather than protective covering and saved for parading round town.

It took at least a fortnight to recruit porters, and when uniforms were supplied, usually khaki shirts and shorts were run up for them at incredible speed in the bazaar on the whirring sewing machines of the Indian tailors at Alibhai and Ahmed or Ahmed Brothers. The latter gained their expertise early on, becoming supremely efficient in meeting vast orders at short notice. In 1928 they outfitted the Prince of Wales's safari which entitled them afterwards to carry the Royal feathers over their door with much pride.[34] Pay was good, at twenty rupees per day for porters, too good those without labour grumbled. Sometimes three or four men were taken on just to carry the whisky supply.

Askaris with muskets were part of the safari entourage, their place at the front and rear of the column to keep porters from deserting, and were responsible for keeping an eye on the general behaviour of the men.[35]

As each safari went out, residents lined the route to watch the white men, clients and hunters, riding slightly apart from their black retinue—a spectacle which oozed privilege and money. In the very early days they were accompanied by one of the quainter personalities, the safari jester. Though no particular tribe was favoured for the role of highly paid clown he was employed solely to keep the men happy. His act had to be good enough to sustain spirits when they flagged, when the going was tough or as they tired at the end of the day's march. There were no set rules but in the tradition of clowns so long as the effect was comic, the more bizarre his dress the better. He often attached a set of horns or an amusing hat and would run up and down the line of porters, full of puns, grimaces and gestures, poking fun, making lewd jokes and best of all, mimicking his employers.[36]

Inevitably Nairobi seemed empty after a safari had pulled out but it was only a lull for the Norfolk generally buzzed with some form of activity. There were always a few 'pushing' and 'pulling' boys hanging around waiting for rickshaw passengers and the train from up-country also used to stop there.

Travellers from the Highlands to Nairobi were supposed to buy their tickets at the point of departure but once they realised that these were only collected at the station, they seldom bothered. By disembarking at the Norfolk they found that they did not require one. Much to the annoyance of the many who had benefitted, this racket came to an abrupt end one day after senior Railway Official overheard two passengers discussing their free rides.[37]

The citizens of Nairobi by this time were a thorough mixture of all races and, as Grogan observed, no country required a more delicately adjusted combination of dash, tact and perseverence. Those who did not frequent the Norfolk were almost certainly hovering round the Hotel Stanley, which more than ever resembled a Wild West outfit. Mayence Bent now employed a receptionist called 'Biddy', who came from Southern Ireland, booked people in and led them upstairs to their 'room' like a dormitory with six beds in each. Kit and blankets were thrown on to a bed to reserve it but it was quite common to return and find it occupied by a drunk. At these times, Biddy would be summoned; she advanced on the bed, pulled the clothes off and, with the complainants' help, rolled the intruder on to the floor which generally started a fight.[38]

Fires were frequent until Nairobi had electricity and they remained a risk because the early buildings of wood and iron went up like tinder-boxes. Most of the early victims of these fires courageously picked themselves up and began again, but some did not have the heart. George McDonell, who had

come out with his wife and parents in 1903 fell in love with the country and he
and his wife decided to settle. They bought a house and sent for all their
antique furniture from England. One night when they were warming a bottle
for their baby over a paraffin stove, it toppled and set light to the house. They
lost everything and were so deeply affected by the experience that they left for
good.[39] It was A. B. McDonell, George's brother, who introduced and grew
tea in Limuru. He worked for the Morson brothers to begin with, dragging
logs with an ox-wagon from the forest to the mill for them. Then in 1918
when an army friend from India came out for a holiday, bringing tea seed as a
gift, McDonell planted 20 acres of Limuru land.[40]

After the great fire of Victoria Street private subscriptions towards a
fire-brigade began coming in Nairobi had to make do with a volunteer force
until 1920. A fête, the brainchild of the man who started a society journal, *The
Globetrotter*, David Garrick Longworth was held on the verandah of the
Norfolk Hotel to raise funds.[41]

The Globetrotter made irresistible reading for the local snobs. Pandering
mainly to the importance of the Norfolk Hotel guests, it noted what they had
'bagged' while on safari as well as arrivals and departures. Disasters such as
the time when the chef, Louis Blanc, was sacked after a drama on its own
doorstep, were ignored. The prim little Frenchman, having built up his
reputation during four years of nervous strain in the hotel kitchens, suddenly
went beserk in 1908 after a furious row with one of the Somali servants which
culminated in Louis Blanc chasing him round the kitchen and stabbing him in
the head mutilating his face seriously.[42]

The rickshaw with its accompanying jingle from the anklet of bells worn
by the pushing and pulling boys was the cheapest and most efficient way of
getting around Nairobi and continued to be so for years but the motor car had
made its debut already. Barton-Wright's small red vehicle with three wheels
(the single one being at the rear), which was steered by a tiller was one of the
earliest in Nairobi. The town was still so small that newcomers needing the
Land officer were given a description of the car and told to call up a rickshaw
boy who would take the visitor straight to him.[43]

Nairobi remained village-like in character for years and, being the hub of
officialdom, class distinction made itself clearly felt. Within the Aminis-
tration, where colour, religion and social standing were always under
consideration, these differences were almost impossible to ignore. The
first-class officials lived on the Hill and would not have dreamed of taking
afternoon tea with those of less importance who were scattered among the
Parklands residents.

Village-like too was the way in which everyone had a say in controversial
matters. One famous street incident occurred in 1908 over the founding of
Unga Ltd.

Ever since Delamere had learned that approximately £10,000 worth of
flour was being imported from India annually, he had dreamed of milling it
locally. Now after five years of waiting for fulfilment it was over the site for

Unga mill that he had one of his most famous rows with Montgomery of the Land Office. It had actually donated the land for the site of this important development on condition that Delamere invest £2,000 worth of machinery as his contribution. However once 'D' learned that this machinery was to cost double, by his reckoning if the land was to be commensurate with his own investment, the plot ought also to be twice the original size. Jack Riddell, who was also a contributor to the scheme, went to put this proposition to Montgomery on Delamere's behalf.[44]

Before Riddell had the chance to speak Montgomery announced that the plot allocated for the mill was being used instead by 'a man out from home' for a public park and they could no longer have it. Riddell was nonplussed but pointed out that those involved had accepted the offer in good faith without title deeds. The steam-powered flour mills had arrived and Alec White was engaged already as manager. Montgomery was unmoved.

Delamere came to Nairobi and, accompanied by Hornyold and Johnnie Van de Weyer, who were also financially involved, went to confront Montgomery in his office. 'You think more of the pattern on a native woman's dress than of a bloody flour mill,' Delamare cried. Montgomery was highly offended and retorted, 'If you are going to be rude to me, go out.'

'Out,' Delamere spluttered. 'I'm not coming into your bloody office again,' and left.

Once in the main street, he summoned anyone he could see. Pulling rupees out of his pocket he shouted at some Kikuyu, 'Go and get me wood—I'll burn the bloody place down.' And he would have, but for the persuasions of his three companions who calmed him down so they could settle the matter properly. They got their extension of land though the site was in a slightly different position and the mill was completed in 1909 and faced the Indian bazaar at the Sadler—now Koinange—Street end.

When Hayes-Sadler was posted to the West Indies few settlers were sorry. On 18 June 1909 the Nairobi press welcomed Sir Percy Girouard's appointment; he would arrive in October. Rumour had it that he had no tact, but the Administration believed this to be an indispensible quality when it came to dealing with the settler community. In fact, Girouard contributed much towards Kenya's future prosperity and had two things in common with Sir Charles Eliot. He was the first Governor since Eliot's departure to take up the cudgels on behalf of the settlers and he also resigned in his fervent belief that what the Government was doing was wrong.

CHAPTER 10

❧

The White Man's Burden

'We negroes are in racial unity with you whites—different yet the same. A crocodile is hatched from an egg—and a flying bird from an egg.'

The Emperor Mushidi[1]

Girouard arrived in September 1909, having won golden opinions as successor to Lord Lugard as High Commissioner in Northern Nigeria. Born in Montreal, this French Canadian had a penchant for railway building. It was largely due to this interest that the Thika line was constructed.[2]

The new Governor's outlook was influenced by his experiences in Nigeria and South Africa, where, while reconstructing the railways under Milner, he married into Transvaal society. Before long the Colonial Office was faced for the first time with the powerful combination of united opinion of the settlers and their Governor, all of whom intended to press hard for self-government.

Girouard's briefing was to report on the whole East African situation. He was shocked at the contrast with Nigerian conditions but within two months he produced a masterly survey in which he disclosed that in general there was an 'utter absence of any defined policy' to native administration, the form of land tenure or with regard to the Indians. Girouard believed that their presence was essential as subordinate government staff even though Europeans and Africans were apprehensive over them. The new Governor objected to the settlement of concessions in London without adequate consultation with local authorities and became a defender of the small settler. He recognised that while Europeanisation had been hasty it was now an accomplished fact and that 'a broader view of the situation' was now demanded.[3] Girouard was determined to redress the harm done by his predecessors and he made himself available for discussion on all matters, in contrast to Hayes-Sadler.

Throughout 1908 there had been suggestions that the Maasai required an alternative reserve to the Laikipia but Hayes-Sadler had been transferred just as the relocation of the northern Maasai had been thought viable. It also seemed that Sir Donald Stewart's premonition that the settlers would cast envious eyes on the valuable Laikipia grazing grounds had not been far-fetched after all. For the moment, however, the Laikipia Plateau remained strictly out of bounds unless the Maasai themselves expressed the wish to make alternative arrangements.

In the event this is precisely what happened. At the end of 1908, Lenana had been gravely perturbed at their growing division since the split in Eliot's time in 1904 and expressed his wish to the Government that the northern and southern Maasai be reunited once more. The *Laibon* met the Governor for discussions and the outcome was that the Maasai should return south with their herds. They were now allocated some 9,200 square miles on the Loita Plains—twice the size of the Laikipia Reserve—and those European settlers who had to forfeit land in consequence were promised three acres of Laikipia for every two acres they had surrendered.[4]

As had happened so frequently in the Protectorate's brief history, just when continuity was needed most for crucial manoeuvres Hayes-Sadler had been transferred and it was Girouard who secured the formal agreement with Lenana. The complete operation was accomplished in 1913 but not before an unbelievably tortuous saga had played itself out during which Lenana had died at Ngong before seeing his ideals fulfilled.

Within the first week of Girouard's arrival, he discovered just how the official and settler factions felt about one another on a pre-breakfast run. He was intensely aware of physical fitness, conscious perhaps that his wife, who dressed like a fashion-plate, was half his age.[5] One morning, in shorts and pullover, Girouard met a young man taking similar exercise and greeted him with a courteous 'Good Morning'. There was no response. Either he had not heard or was being extremely rude. Giving him the benefit of the doubt Girouard repeated himself. There was still no reply. Rather annoyed he now raised his voice, 'Excuse me, young man, I said "Good Morning" to you.' The man in question was a newly-appointed assistant in the Secretariat who had not yet met the Governor and did not recognise him. Looking coldly at him he retorted, 'Oh, go to hell, you bloody settler.'[6]

The settlers thought Girouard 'rather a peculiar person, under middle-height, strong, ugly but by no means displeasing in countenance. Rather a gruff manner and way of speaking. Shakes hands in a funny way. He gives you his hand, gives you a good look out of one of his eyes which you cannot make out, and that is that . . . not a word does he utter. Tate is terrified of him.'[7] Girouard was undoubtedly rather forbidding before one got to know him, especially as, 'his two eyes look two different ways and a most alarming monocle is stuck in one . . . everyone looks at the wrong one and he doesn't like it.'[8]

Girouard's obvious ability and willingness to co-operate at every level of the community soon overcame any initial misgivings. Randall Swift, the Irish sisal planter from Punda Milia, and his partner Ernest Rutherfoord were among the first to benefit from Girouard's particular style of co-operation. Swift met the new Governor by chance in Nairobi and introduced himself.

But the minute Girouard recognised Swift's name he remarked. 'It is you people who have brought out that tractor which has been breaking my bridges.' Swift explained that so as to extend cultivation for their sisal they had obtained permission from Hayes-Sadler to import a Cooper's Steam Digging and Traction Engine. They had been assured by him that the existing bridges would be strengthened to take its weight but he had pointed out that once this concession had been made they must make their own way as best they could between bridges. This was fine but there was no means of crossing either the Thika or Chania rivers and they had had to construct rafts to get over them. The traction engine had been brought in for their own use but proved such an asset that they were contracting out to other farmers. Now those bridges Hayes-Sadler had promised to strengthen were so shaky that the risk each time they were used was considerable.

After Girouard had heard Swift's side of the story, he had the bridges reinforced. He also intervened on their behalf when the railway had charged highly for transport. When their first sisal decorticator was railed from Mombasa, Swift had challenged the cost on the grounds that in their catalogue was a cheaper rate for 'machinery manipulating country produce'. But the authorities argued that since sisal machinery was not itemised it did not qualify. This meant paying a difference of £100. Ironically the railway manager promised in future to charge the lower rate. As soon as Girouard learned about it he arranged for the £100 to be returned.

Swift and Rutherfoord were originally from Mortlake where they had been brewers. Before they had decided to grow sisal, they had met with little but disaster from their efforts at Punda Milia. The clearing of their first 100 acres of bush and stumps with single furrow ploughs had been agonisingly slow. They planted 100 acres of cotton but it ripened just as the short rains began and it was ruined. They tried groundnuts and maize, both crops were destroyed by game after which, in despair, they sought advice from the Department of Agriculture. What they were told there was daunting, 'at Punda Milia you are rather too high to do any good with fibres . . . you are rather too low to grow wheat or barley . . . maize or beans would grow well with you but . . . you are too far from the market . . . stock . . . should do well but there are so many diseases in this country that I would not recommend that. In fact Punda Milia is one of those betwixt and between places and I am glad I did not advise you take up land there.'[9]

Swift and Rutherfoord ignored the comment about fibre and decided to try sisal. Ainsworth had been chiefly responsible for its reaching the Highlands but until the drought of 1907 it had made little impact as a plant with potential. Without rain, everything else that was green had perished except for the sisal plants. Sisal was growing over the border in German East Africa and had been introduced in 1893 when 1,000 plants had been imported from Florida. Only sixty-two had survived the journey but these were carefully tended, new plants had been propagated from them at Kikogwe and thereafter the sisal industry in German East Africa* had progressed at a remarkable rate.[10] The tale of how Swift and Rutherfoord founded the industry in BEA at Punda Milia exemplifies that determination which was so much part of pioneer farming. They set out for Taveta, some two hundred miles distant, with two ox-wagons. But when they got there the District Commissioner informed them that they could not enter German East Africa to buy sisal as export of plants was suspended.

Russell Bowker had so alarmed the Germans by ordering 200,000 plants that they had stopped all export temporarily. Later a prohibitive export tax was imposed of £4 per 100 bulbils.[11]

Stunned at the news after their tortuous safari, they hit on the following plan. Their head herdsman was instructed to drive their oxen towards the German border so as to arrive at the boundary by 5 pm. The animals were to be abandoned here and the herdsmen were to return and report that the oxen had strayed. On this pretext, Swift and Rutherfoord and their men went out for the next few evenings looking for the oxen and under the cloak of darkness they slipped over the border and helped themselves to sackloads of bulbils until they had enough for their needs.[12]

From then on there was a big demand for bulbils and soon the crop was well established for conditions were perfect for its cultivation on their six thousand acres at Punda Milia. In the same area, two brothers Donald and Martin Seth-Smith, Mervyn Ridley, his brother-in-law Lord Cranworth, Lady Cranworth and Alan Tompson also went into partnership to form Sisal Ltd at Makuyu. Despite the war, by 1917 with A. F. Pape the American settler's concession at Voi and Powys Cobb's estate at Kilifi, there were over 10,000 acres already under sisal in BEA.[13]

Girouard's interest in railways and communications made him quick to perceive that what was lacking was a transport network connecting the fertile country lying between Nairobi and Mount Kenya, where coffee and sisal plantations were slowly being cultivated within bicycling distance from the main line. But although only fifty miles lay between the farthest of these estates and Nairobi Station, the sole means of getting produce to it was by ox-wagon along a track of dust and potholes that was almost impassable during the rains. Beyond Makuyu, hundreds of miles of fecund Kikuyu soil lay unexploited.

Although in 1909 the annual revenue of the Protectorate had reached £250,000, expenditure amounted to half a million pounds. The annual grant-in-aid of £130,000 at the time helped but was barely felt in a drowning economy. Agriculture would ultimately make up for the deficits, but without labour, transport and now schools, hospitals and veterinary services on a larger scale to support the existing community, development in the Protectorate was stranded by its inability to move efficiently in any direction.

* Renamed Tanganyika by the British after they took possession after the First World War and today known as Tanzania.

Four-fifths of the total annual revenue was taken up in the maintenance of the police, the Public Works Department and army. What was left over was destined to repay the grant-in-aid. This meant that any annual revenue increases went automatically to the British Treasury. It was hopeless, a treadmill of disaster from which, without a vast infusion of capital it was impossible to escape. The railway needed maintenance and further development yet rolling stock had deteriorated so badly that the outward movement of produce was reduced to a crawl. Overseas shipments from Mombasa were hobbled by the absence of a deep-water pier at Kilindini. Ten years had lapsed without branch lines being built to Kikuyuland or northern Kavirondo. Yet Eliot had pointed out in his time that it was absolutely vital to provide feeders for the railway's traffic.[14]

Girouard had kept a brilliant psychological card up his sleeve. When the line to Mount Kenya was turned down, he suggested a modest alternative, 'a tramway' of narrow gauge, forty miles in length which would serve the sparsley inhabited but promising area as far as Thika.[15] The cost was negligible compared with the original project and was agreed upon. Girouard built it for £2,500 a mile and if he cheated a bit, by matching the gauge to the Protectorate's main line, what did it matter? The effects he achieved more than compensated for his white lie. In 1912, when it went into operation, it became the first branch line of the Uganda Railway★ and was well timed to ensure the steady flow of sisal and coffee exports.[16] After that on Mondays and Fridays a 'special' train was put on for farmers. Mr Good, its permanent guard, obligingly cashed cheques for his passengers who hailed the train by simply stepping on to the line at a point nearest to their land. New farms multiplied around Thika once prospective farmers realised that the 'tramway' would provide the transport which the area had lacked and land rose in value from ten shillings to three pounds an acre. In due course, as Girouard had hoped, the line took in Kikuyuland and when it reached Nanyuki in 1930 proved itself one of the busiest and most profitable of branch lines.

Girouard managed an even more important step towards solvency after complex negotiations with the Treasury to ease the grant-in-aid payments. Known as 'the half-and-half' arrangement, it meant that only half each annual increase was set aside for the repayment instalments, whilst the balance was used for the country's own needs. Within three years the manoeuvre had turned the tide in favour of the Protectorate and the Treasury made its last grant-in-aid in 1912, a triumph for Girouard. His efforts with the budget, the harmony for which he had largely been responsible, which in turn had contributed towards mounting productivity, enabled the Governor to secure the Protectorate's very first loan. Modest the £250,000 may have

★ The Magadi Soda Company line was under construction during 1912 and the rails reached Magadi Lake on 24 May 1913. It was expected to open at the end of that year but failed, was taken over by the Uganda Railway and progress was then interrupted by the outbreak of war. Ultimately it opened section by section between January and August 1915.

been but it enabled him to complete of the Thika tramway and begin construction on the vital deep-water berth at Kilindini.

The fact that Girouard and Delamere got on well undoubtedly helped to promote the fact that more constructive days had dawned between settler and official. As Lady Delamere remarked, 'It is a great encouragement to think that at last we have a man at the head of affairs who is really interested in the country and wants to make it prosper.'[17]

Electricity had come into domestic use in Nairobi in 1908 and in 1909, as the wheels of Delamere's flour mill began to turn, it became the first industrial user of power.[18] During 1907 and 1908 as poles and transformers had been erected all over the town, the shining new insulators proved too great an attraction for young marksmen and the official opening of the Ruiru power station had to be postponed indefinitely because so many insulators had been vandalised—even beyond Nairobi.[19]

The Nairobi Electricity Supply* was set up by Charles Udall, and its first dam was on the Ruiru River. Ruiru dam worked three turbo-generators which provided a capacity of 500 b.h.p.; it was a great moment for progress when the switch was pulled to illuminate the Nairobi's streets for the first time in 1910.[20]

The Nairobi population numbered 350 Europeans, 2,100 Asians and about 2,500 Africans in Girouard's time and 'had everything in the way of trades and professions from jewellers to blacksmiths'.[21]

While electric power brought a sense of real achievement, nevertheless Africa continued to hold its own. Man was still thwarted by the wild where he least expected it. A hippopotamus managed to get into one of the wooden flumes carrying water to the generators; being unable to turn round it had become jammed, causing the town's lights to flicker and dim for several hours before the source of the trouble was located.[22] (In 1920 a stork managed to inflict total blackout for twelve hours before it was found the next day, seared to an overhead cable.)[23]

Meanwhile, Girouard's diplomacy embraced all sectors of the community though he did question A. M. Jeevanjee's appointment as a Legislative Councillor.[24] Among the Administration, he did all he could to uphold the authority of tribal heads and, through their persuasions, coax the Africans to work without loss of dignity. He held a great meeting of Chiefs dressed in war paint, so as to present each with a gold-topped malacca cane in order to impress upon them the importance of their office. The exercise proved effective for the Chiefs felt highly honoured though one of them, no doubt hoping to impress the Governor in his European dress, appeared in khaki shorts and a trench coat, was sent away. But when Girouard instructed his ADC to tell him 'to come back dressed as a Chief, not like my *syce*'—a groom, the man was not offended.[25] The Africans liked and respected

---

* The Nairobi Electricity Supply became the East African Power and Lighting Company in 1926, having been sold in London.

Girouard who somehow managed with tact, to convey through his District Officers via the Chiefs, that it was the Government's wish that the young men should find employment which made a considerable improvement to the dearth of labour and the shaky economy.

In order to beat the problem of rust in wheat, Delamere engaged a botanist, George Wyndham Evans, to experiment in the laboratory he had built at Njoro specially to breed a rust-free strain. Evans had been trained in India as an optician, joined the railway and, after its completion, started to farm in partnership with P. E. Watcham, another ex-railwayman, near Nairobi. But by his mid-thirties Evans was engrossed in plant breeding. By the end of 1911, at Equator Ranch alone, 2,000 plants were growing in roughly rigged up cages with over 200 varieties and innumerable hybrids in five other experimental centres. One after the other they were rejected until, in 1912, a pair of sturdy hybrids after three consecutive seasons of rust free infection, emerged. From Delamere's crude Njoro laboratory the wheat industry was built. Evans named the wheat better suited to growing at high altitudes 'Equator', the one for lower areas was named Kenya Governor.[26] After nine years, in 1912, Delamere's vast wheatfield of 1,750 acres produced a harvest which filled two trains. This extraordinary achievement was also the largest crop he ever grew and yielded six and a half bags per acre. The triumph seduced the men into believing they had beaten rust for ever. Delamere imported seven Australian Sunshine Harvesters and then their success proved no more substantial than a mirage. For forty more years whatever progress was made in BEA 'rust' matched it with sinister regularity and undermined wheat farmers continually.[27] As Huxley wrote, 'The problem itself was without precedent, for nowhere else in the world are three forms of rust, each with several physiologic strains, known to attack wheat in the same district and sometimes in the same season.'[28]

Among those growing coffee in Kiambu, perhaps the earliest planter was J. R. Wood and although he only had 500 trees of his own (it was usual to plant 600 trees to the acre) he also managed Lady Delamere's. Two Frenchmen, Felix and Favre, whose homosexual relationship raised a great many eyebrows around Kiambu, cultivated coffee at St Benoist and by the time their first hundred trees bore, they already had their own nursery of 9,000 foot-high plants and double the number of seedlings. McClellan Wilson on the Riara River became outstanding among these early Kiambu growers.[29]

Coffee growing is a long job. Shining young plants from the nursery are set in geometric order in the wet ground, care taken not to bend each tap-root or the bush dies. Shading from the sun is vital. After four to five years, providing the plants withstood black-jack, rats, cut-worm and wood-lice, among other pests, they came into bearing.

At Kitisuru, on the other side of Nairobi, A. T. Mabert had been successful with seed cultivated at St Austin's Mission by the French Fathers. It was he who sold part of his land to a Syndicate formed by Douglas Cooper, Alan Tompson, Major Gailey and Col. E. G. Harrison and in 1906 they were followed by Guy Lushington and C. R. Watson and in 1910, by Gooch and Taylor. Charles Taylor played a significant part in the development of the coffee industry. He settled in 1909 with Grogan's encouragement and bought a modest 35 acres of Lower Kabete land with five year old coffee on it, from A. T. Mabert. The next year he acquired 600 more in partnership with Capt. E. D. A. Gooch from an early grower, Douglas Cooper.[30] Much of this, as a flourishing coffee estate farm, was bought eventually by Block and Raoul Massader, a man who became his partner for a while after the Second World War. Today this area on the outskirts of Nairobi is the suburb of Kitisuru.

When the coffee farmer was not working in the *shamba*, he was conjuring up improvements in the production of the harvest. Machinery was usually something of a Heath Robinson affair. Tom Deacon, the pioneer who had won his Donyo Sabuk land in a bet for example, had no engine so his first crop was pulped by jacking-up his Model T Ford Ford at the rear to run his pulper. Because such problems were not allowed to stand in the way, gradually the plantations emerged shining green and brilliant in contrast to the uncultivated grey-green land surrounding them. The planters were plagued by jackals and monkeys at Kitisuru where the latter were so partial to the berries that the only remedy was to shoot or poison them.[31]

Coffee blossoms at the beginning of the rains. The bushes become radiant with chalk-like flowers, reminiscent of bridal wear, and their slightly bitter scent is not unlike blackthorn.

In 1907 exports were valued at £270, a small sum, but within two years Kenya coffee began to make a name for itself, though the dearth of labour affected the harvesting and development of the industry. Farmers could not break new land because men could not be found to clear the bush. The white men felt resentful because, as Delamere put it in 1908, 'It was wrong for young men to loaf about in red paint watching their womenfolk work while coffee was literally blackening on the trees for lack of hands or pick it.'[32]

A determined few hired Kikuyu women instead. When the branches became weighed down with crimson 'cherries', the little families of Africans shouted and sang as they picked and were paid by the *debe* and made a lot of money. Each group of workers was presided over by a *neopara* wearing a red blanket and a fez. He brandished a small wand as *debe* after *debe* was filled with the scarlet harvest, loaded on to ox-wagons and taken to the factory.

In time, the attitude of the African men changed and the young bushes were needed and pruned by wild looking, near-naked males whose limbs shone with red ochre and mutton fat. They plaited their hair with string and plastered it into a plaque with the same shining mud. The lobes of their ears were stretched to accommodate cigarette tins, holding their month's wages or little snuff gourds, in the absence of any other form of pocket.[33]

By 1909, a Coffee Planters' Union was formed. As the coffee driers turned, the beans rumbled like shale tossed by waves on the beach before being dispatched in sacks by ox-wagon to Nairobi, ready for shipment to London. Between the years of 1909 and 1911 the production of coffee almost doubled, rising from 422 to 800 tons, and the price paid for it soared correspondingly from £45 to £80 a ton. As the value of the harvests improved, thousands of pounds were spent by planters in providing their workers with stone cottages, improved sanitation and piped water supplies in place of their stark thatched huts. Close by, farm schools and dispensaries were built and were generally appreciated but modern housing was unpopular. Innovation was looked on with caution by the Africans who are deeply suspicious of change. Over the years affection trust and understanding was forged into friendship between employer and employee. The farm wife was called *Mama* (pronounced mahma) by the Africans, who turned to her to help solve their problems.

By 1913 the value of coffee exports had vaulted to £18,000 and within fifteen years Kenya's coffee crop reached 10,000 tons and was worth more than £1,000,000 annually.[34] But even though by this time the whole area from Marura to Kiambu township was under coffee, the harsh blows of disease continued to shake confidence over and again, coming as they did from so unexpected a quarter. In 1912 the coffee on certain farms was attacked by himileia. It was considered so terrible that the only remedy, based on practice in Ceylon, was to burn the entire plantation.[35] It was then that Africa's sense of sarcasm seemed more cruel, more unreasonable than any amount of European logic could justify. The white men, unlike the African, whose passivity appears to be absolute, felt alienated. The loss of a harvest, left a feeling of depressing solitude.

The sad story of the flax boom of the early twenties illustrates the point that Africa was full of horrid surprises. After the First World War flax was thought to be the crop by which the soldier settlers of 1919 would make their fortune. An earlier settler, W. J. Dawson, had farmed it near Nakuru in 1916 and it was fetching 300–400 pounds a ton on the London market by 1919.[36] The BEA Disabled Officers' Company put every resource into flax on 25,000 acres of land at Kericho and so did many others.[37] In 1920 the price soared to 500 pounds a ton, the following year it went up again. Then, without warning, the British Government decided to import Russian flax from the Baltic. By this agreement they successfully ruined the Kenya market as the price dropped by over £400 per ton without warning. One man was reduced to selling his harvest for as little as £28. The Allison family were among the many flax growers to face bankruptcy and so were 'Samaki' Lindstrom and his wife Ingrid (more famous today as Karen Blixen's dependable friend than as a farmer), who had emigrated from Denmark especially to grow flax at Njoro.

Dawson's Achille's heel turned out to be geraniums rather than flax for he had sold his estate when the market price was at its highest. With the proceeds he bought machinery with it to build a distillery for essential oils and planted a 1,100 acres of geraniums. They looked wonderful for six weeks. Rot then set in and within a month the entire crop had perished and with it his investment.[38]

In 1910, Girouard reported on the revision of the Crown Lands Ordinance, and in it opposed the writing in of rent revision after thirty-three years. He also pointed out that before then settlers 'would very probably get self-government.' Suddenly Nairobi seemed full of optimism.[39] By the end of that year thirty farms had been allocated to European settlers in Western Kenya and Arnold Paice was the first white farmer to take up land. Now with the possibility of rail facilities (the land was thought to be ideal for wheat), he obtained a plot south of the Equator on the outskirts of what became Nanyuki township. In September he left Chillingworth to farm for himself on the Nanyuki river, walking across the Aberdares with his entire worldly goods—thirteen chickens and four dogs.

Nyeri, thirty miles away, was but a boma, occupied by five Europeans. There was a post office and European-run shop but Paice hardly expected to find that there was also a golf course. However he discovered that McClure, the District Commissioner, and a forester who was posted at Nyeri had made one. The Commissioner told him that he 'ran his Kikuyu mowing machine over it'. In other words, hundreds of Kikuyu were used to pluck the grass with their fingers. Paice was speechless that, when farmers had no labour, these officials had obtained as much man-power as they needed through Chief Mbogo to enhance their hours of leisure.

Paice, was very much on his own at Nanyuki but the Honourable Berkeley Cole shortly followed to live at Solio, his 20,000 acre farm on the slopes of Mount Kenya. Paice's 3,083 acre farm Rotherwick was modest in comparison but was nevertheless 11 miles in circumference—quite enough to tend alone. He shot zebra for meat for his dogs and himself. From their skins he made raw-hide rope, invaluable for securing roof thatching for his mud hut, for reins and stringing beds. He made a kiln for himself and after three years of experimenting with the local clay aided by a *toto*, had fired enough good bricks with which to build a proper house. Today there are more remains of pioneer brick dwellings round Nanyuki than in any other farming area, evidence of Paice's gifts to the newly married. Each couple was given a load of bricks as a wedding present to start building their first home. The big shooting safaris stopped at Rotherwick to buy eggs, butter, milk, potatoes, fresh vegetables and anything else Paice could supply.[40]

The difficulties of transport in that area dominated the lives of those who farmed there for twenty years or more until the branch-line reached Nanyuki. In 1910 the route connecting Nyeri to Meru and the Northern Frontier was only a track without bridges. Before the advent of a road suitable for motor vehicles, all provisions had to be carted in ox-wagons in three-ton loads from the Thika railhead—after 1912.

When Paice needed to get the pigs he had reared to Uplands bacon curing factory at Kijabe, they had to be walked via Nyeri, over the Aberdares, across the Kinankop, the long narrow headland overlooking the Rift Valley, and down to Naivasha which was his nearest station, seventy miles away. The four-foot path regarded as a road connecting Nyeri and Naivasha had a gradient of 1 in 3 in places. Unfortunately each pig, sold on its weight, lost at least 12 lbs between leaving the farm and delivery.[41] However there was no alternative and by 1911, despite such problems, Uplands had progressed from limited supplies of bacon and ham to offering bath chaps, pure leaf lard and pork sausages.[42]

Even after the First World War, trading involved crossing the Aberdares. May Roberts and her husband Alick went via Kipipiri rather than the Kinankop route. May was a daughter of the pioneer Captain Thomas Edward Aggett, who had seven children. They came by charter ship from the Cape to farm on the Loita Plains in 1910 and brought with them their transport wagons and animals to Mombasa. Aggett's sons, George, Ted and Boyce, ran successful transport businesses with ox-wagons plying between Narok, Gilgil and Thomson's Falls, along with a number of trading stores and farming enterprises. In 1918, May married Alick Roberts and trekked by ox-wagon from Naivasha to Nanyuki to take up a Soldier Settlement Farm. In the post-War depression, when she only had two dresses to her name, she knew there was valuable trading to be done with ghee, prized by the Indians for cooking, if only she could devise a means of getting it to Gilgil. The ubiquitous *debe* provided the solution.

She skimmed the cream, made it into butter and boiled it on an open fire to rid it of impurities. Once she had eight gallons her husband rode with two *debes* slung on his pony's withers, over the Aberdares to Gilgil, a seventy-mile journey, braving the rhinos, buffaloes and elephants in the Aberdares and beyond in the cedar forests of Kipipiri. The Indians at Gilgil were keen to exchange ghee for sugar, flour, *americani*, soap and tea. Alick Roberts returned with provisions in sacks and the transaction kept his family going when, after one year at Nanyuki, the Roberts family had run out of cash. May Roberts milked her own cows and once Nyeri grew beyond trading post status, the ghee was taken there instead. She also made her own washing soap in long yellow bars out of Magadi soda, animal fat and carbolic. Bottle-brushes were fashioned out of wart-hog bristles entwined with wire. She was one of the few women to qualify for a Soldier Settlement Farm because she had trained as a nurse in South Africa and came to Nairobi as a hospital matron at the outbreak of the First World War.

May Roberts was one of the band of wonderfully practical women in BEA who appear to have thriven on hardship. Iris Mistry recalls how hard life was for her parents. Her father did not rid himself of an overdraft until she and her sister were educated—after the Second World War. Their house was built from red pencil cedar and, like everything else they had, made with his own hands. Even in the 'twenties journeys were undertaken by ox-wagon and doctors were still an unthought-of luxury. Paraffin removed jiggers and was also rubbed on chests for colds as an external measure while onion juice was drunk as a remedy. Treacle and sulphur were taken, one spoonful a day, for boils. Thorns, which festered with alarming speed were extracted by home-made poultices, of mashed carbolic soap and sugar, which drew even the deepest of thorns effortlessly. The Maasai on May Roberts's farm were shocked by her inclusion of sugar because it cost money while their traditional poultices were free and just as effective. They caught flies, crushed them and then applied the resulting paste to a leaf used in the same way as a piece of lint.[43]

The wives of the European farmers set up schools where the African *totos* had their very first lessons in reading and writing. They also ran clinics and became doctor, nurse, judge, arbitrator and advisor to their servants and were expected to deal with cuts, broken limbs, bruises, burns and deliveries of babies (sometimes their own), which, if an African woman had been circumcised, was notoriously difficult. The experiences which many of the European women faced as they dealt with these things was quite unique for the times into which they had been born. Even in the mid-twenties, after aeroplanes had made an appearance, the elements and topography of Africa always seemed to be in control.

A high percentage were totally ignorant even of how babies arrived. Rose Cartwright, the wife of a farmer at Naivasha, went into labour with her first child during the rainy season in 1924; her husband, Algy, went to fetch a woman who had been a nurse and, by African standards, lived quite close, only six miles away. But the rains had reduced the track to a river of red mud and prevented his return until the following day. By then his daughter, Tobina, had arrived though she was still connected to her mother by the umbilical cord. Rose Cartwright knew nothing about confinement. When her husband had gone for help, in the hope of finding a book to guide her, she looked through their shelves and found, '*Mothercraft*'. The introduction read, 'Put the cot behind a screen . . .' There was not a word on the subject of birth itself. Alone and unable to do anything useful she opened a bottle of champagne and sipped it between the pains until her four-pound baby was born.[44]

In 1910 anyone living in the Kiambu district was twenty miles from the nearest hospital. Dorcas Aubrey, the niece of Isabella Beaton and married to an early coffee planter at Ruiru, like everyone relied on ox-transport which was unbearably slow. When she received word that a Kikuyu was dying on the path below her house she found that he had had a fight with another African and his intestines were spilling from a gaping hole in his abdomen. He could not be moved until his guts had been replaced. Unless she could think of some means of saving him herself he would certainly die. She removed a string from her violin and threaded it through a sacking needle to sew the man up where he lay on the path. A litter was made from branches of trees to carry him up to her house, where she nursed him back to health.[45] Innovation such as this went on in every homestead.

In November 1910, Girouard attended the inaugural dinner of the Convention of Associations. Its Chairman, Grogan, had very definite views with regard to the Indian question to convey to the Foreign Office especially on the subject of immigration. Though the problem was referred to somewhat abstrusely as 'the Indian Question', the word 'question' hardly came into it. The issue had been smouldering away steadily between the two races ever since 1902. Asiatic immigration was felt to be 'detrimental to the European settler in particular and to the native inhabitant generally'.[46]

Throughout Kenya's history Indian political ambitions on the one hand and European demands for restrictions of Indian immigration (which was unlimited) on the other, cropped up at intervals but before 1914 Indian claims for political representation were ineluctable.[47] White men expressed their ideas on the subject of Indian residents in the basest of terms. There can hardly be any *question* about the energetic effort that was applied to keeping the White Highlands white.

Meanwhile, Lord Cranworth denied that the question was racial, it was a matter of character. 'If the Indian in the Protectorate were represented by the type dear to tourists, we would welcome him with open arms. It is not because his skin is black that he is unpopular; it is because he is a foul liar, a drunkard and a thief.'[48] Lady Delamere claimed that 'to be in measureable distance of an Indian coolie is very disagreeable'.[49] And indeed the weightier charge, that the Indians were so unhygienic that they constituted a health hazard, was nearer the truth. Plague, venereal disease and other contagious ailments were attributed to them, the result, as Cranworth pointed out 'of living conditions under which no English farmer would dream of keeping his pigs.'[50]

Lord Cranworth's fears were justified when, in Narobi in 1911, 1912 and 1913 there were outbreaks of bubonic plague. The medical authorities were very shaken but ought not to have been surprised for they were aware that the bazaar was overcrowded without adequate sanitation. It was no longer possible to order its destruction by fire as they had in 1902. Dr Spurrier, a Medical Officer reported that 'damp, dark, unventilated . . . dwellings on filth-soaked and rubbish bestrewn ground, housed hundreds of people of most uncleanly habits who loved to have things so and were so left.' Another had declared that the bazaar was a collection of tin-huts used indiscriminately as dwelling-houses, shops, stores, laundries, wash-houses, opium dens, bakeries, brothels, butchers' shops, etc., and that conditions of life there were 'miserable and filthy in the extreme.' As more permanent buildings were erected, the question of shifting the bazaar had been ruled out because of the cost. In 1906 it was estimated by Arthur Tannahill, a valuer and member of the Municipal Committee, that the exercise would cost £83,000.[51]

Such squalor naturally counted against the Indians yet even in 1905 Ainsworth had reported that until that time European capital and enterprise were almost entirely absent and that '. . . fully 80% of the capital and business energy of the country is Indian.' What the Europeans were determined to do, although they would not have been able to manage without the Indian commercially, was to see that he had no say in the country's politics. In 1906 the Indians had held a mass meeting of protest. The resulting commission was not to obtain equal rights with the Colonials in British colonies in Africa but, as A. M. Jeevanjee put it, 'only to secure fair treatment of the Indian subjects of the King-Emperor.'[52]

Churchill, who was one of Jeevanjee's staunchest supporters, responded by asking, 'Is it possible for any Government with a scrap of respect for honest dealing, man to man, to embark upon a policy of deliberately squeezing out the native of India from regions in which he has established himself under every security of public faith?' In 1908, Hayes-Sadler had recommended that Jeevanjee be nominated to represent his community on the Council, and Churchill through the Colonial Office endorsed it and felt that there could be no reason for 'excluding this large and meritorious class.' He had urged the Governor to 'Begin early to instil good principles in the East African Protectorate.'[53] But if the Europeans could not actually block Jeevanjee's entry into the Council, they certainly felt no need to encourage him. And Jeevanjee, no doubt sensitive to the feeling of disapproval (quite different from that which he had encountered on the race-course where he mixed socially with the very same people), decided that one Indian member, in a Council 'otherwise European and largely hostile, served no useful purpose.'[54] He withdrew and was not replaced. It was twelve years before another Indian was nominated.

As Chairman of the Convention of Associations Grogan argued the case against Indian immigration from two standpoints. The first was that the Government had no authority to promote it: the second, that it was to the disadvantage of both the European and the African communities and therefore the Protectorate as a whole. 'The mandate is granted to the British and to nobody else. The Government is dishonouring its trust by allowing the Indians to swamp the country in this way.'[55]

Grogan's influence as a public speaker is well known; when he was accused of prejudice, he denied it with fervour and claimed that he had none whatsoever against the Indian race but there was plenty of evidence to the contrary. Though Grogan originally bought the Nairobi swamp in partnership with an Indian, he was anti-Asian, anti-semitic, the type of man who regarded those who were not British as undesirable aliens.

In 1906, he and Sharif Jaffer had purchased the 120 acre swamp stretching between Ainsworth's Bridge and Racecourse Road for a nominal sum on a 99 years lease. to the majority it appeared to be useless papyrus but Grogan had named it 'Gertrude Swamp' after his wife, and had commissioned a surveyor to canalise it.[56] By 1908 much of it had been let indiscriminately, allotment by allotment, to Indians for market gardening. Where it had been a malarial hazard before, their presence, as Cranworth had predicted, turned it into a foetid bed of squalor where among the hovels of tin and the human ordure with which they fertilised their *shambas*, their scores of children ran barefoot. Not surprisingly there were outbreaks of dysentery, the source of which was believed to be from the vegetables grown in the swamp and bilharzia became an added danger. Also recommendations for drainage were not put into effect in Nairobi for many years, and this did not help cut down the occurrence of disease either. By 1913, the bazaar, still on its old site, was worse than ever and the Government appointed a sanitation expert, Professor Simpson, to advise on town planning. His solution was complete removal of the bazaar to the north side of the swamp, but then War broke out and, after it, the adoption of a new policy repudiating racial segregation, invalidated his findings.[57]

In 1910 Grogan bought out his Indian partner's share in the swamp for £3,000, but kept it until 1948. The Nairobi Municipal Council* tried to buy it in 1929 but when Grogan asked £60,000 the notion of such a sum was laughed off as preposterous. Convoluted negotiations continued for the next ten years, when the Council had the nerve to rate the property at £300,000, taxing him on that figure while attempting to press him into selling it for the original price he had asked. Now it was Grogan's turn to jeer. After a great deal of dithering, during which a number of individual plots were sold off to Indians, the bulk of Gertrude Swamp was bought in 1948 by the Heptullah brothers with the remaining 50 years' lease, for £180,000.[58]

Grogan's powers of oratory and his constant cry that the Indians were upsetting the balance of the community by driving a wedge between the complementary interests of the Europeans and Africans, failed to convince the British Government. The struggle between the Europeans and the Indians continued but the outcome was delayed by the 1914–18 war. However immigration was allowed, the power of the Indians soared and culminated in their gaining representation on Legislative Council eventually in 1924.

In 1910 Delamere and his wife left Njoro to live at Soysambu. This farm took its name in Maasai from a ledge of brindled rocks forming the terrace behind their hut. Here Delamere became engaged in a new but unremitting battle against theft and disease affecting his sheep and cattle. Instead of 'rust' he became familiar with the death blows of heartwater, pleuro-pneumonia, rinderpest, red-water and streptotricosis which had hitherto been dealt with by Sammy McCall.[59] By 1909, largely through McCall's care the flocks, which included some pure-bred merinos and Corriedales though mainly cross-breds, numbered 15,000. The shepherd began to find the size of Delamere's flocks unmanageable but he had also examined the potential of the market for mutton and wanted to open his own butchery at Lower Molo.[60] In 1910 McCall could stand the unwieldy numbers of sheep that roamed Soysambu no longer and the letter of resignation which had lain folded for five years in his pocket was now handed in. McCall, simple shepherd though he was, was also extremely shrewd; he left Delamere's employ with enough capital to start a farm of his own and a butchery.

* Nairobi Council became Nairobi Municipal Council after the First World War in 1919. In 1950 Nairobi became the first Charter City of the Commonwealth; thereafter the Municipal Council became Nairobi City Council.

eventually he became Chairman of the KFA. By the time he died in 1930—a year before Delamere, McCall was numbered among the well-to-do men of the Colony.[61]

Delamere, though deeply in debt, continued to blaze the trail for many new industries. Besides Unga Ltd, from which he never drew a dividend during his lifetime, he opened a plant for the disintegration of wattle bark at Njoro and founded Nyama Ltd, from the Swahili word for meat, with branches in Nakuru, Nairobi and Mombasa. Delamere nurtured ideas of supplying the Protectorate with meat and developing an export trade akin to that of New Zealand in frozen lamb and mutton. Since trains only ran twice a week to the coast, cold storage was vital for the Mombasa branch and involved Delamere in further capital outlay. He had spent £40,000 during his first six years in converting Equator Ranch, Florida Farm and Soysambu into farmland and hardly knew where to find the money but the machinery was imported. After the plant was built, he secured a contract to supply ships with the only fresh, grade-mutton north of Durban. At one stage the Mombasa cold-store was receiving five hundred wethers a week. Qualified butchers were hired from England as the company grew, providing an outlet for the experimental sheep-breeders in the country and enabled them to just show a working profit. Thus export trade in meat was developed, a stock-breeders' co-operative was organised and in time merged with the Kenya Meat Commission.[62]

In 1911 there were over four hundred Europeans living on the Uasin Gishu Plateau when a second group of South Africans destined for Eldoret arrived under the leadership of C. J. Cloete. He brought fifty-nine more colonists from Durban plus eight hundred sheep, one hundred horses and one hundred and twenty-one head of cattle; these Boers swelled the number of European residents in the Protectorate to over three thousand.[63]

By now the Government was insisting that whoever applied for land must have a minimum of £500 worth of assets. To establish this, it became necessary for chattels to be paraded before District Commissioners. When newcomers fell short, kindly residents lent a team of oxen or a wagon to increase their worth. On one occasion when the District Commissioner of Eldoret had seen the same team and wagon paraded before him more than half a dozen times, he suggested with a repressed smile that perhaps they should break for a while to give the oxen a rest. One farmer so feared that his land would be confiscated near Eldoret that he went so far as to mock-up a windmill and house on an ox-cart;[64] this was intended to hoodwink the Land Agent into believing that his improvements were adequate when he had done nothing at all.[65]

Despite the regulations against absentee landlords and the use of 'dummy' claimants M. P. K. Sorrensen observes in his *Origins of European Settlement in Kenya* that distribution of land was so uneven that, 'By the end of 1912 Delamere, the two Coles, Grogan and the East African Syndicate and East Africa Estates, held one fifth of the alienated land in the Protectorate. In the

Rift valley, at the same time, half the alienated land was held by two syndicates and four individuals. These figures which read like those recorded by Epps and Reeves for Australia and New Zealand, indicate that the much-dreaded land accumulation has come about in the East Africa Protectorate.[66]

The Cole case and the Maasai moves are inextricably part of the history of 1911. In March 1911 Galbraith Cole was losing sheep from theft every night. It was not easy for a stockman to forgive theft of animals which have been bred and raised against the odds of a bewildering array of disease. Stock theft had been on the increase in the Naivasha district for some time but Cole's complaints to authority made no difference; it was impossible to curtail it with such great distances between police posts and farms. Keekopey, where Cole lived at Elmenteita was isolated. He had also set traps which the robbers eluded and still he lost his sheep. By April, exasperated beyond reason, he took the law into his own hands when he caught three thieves in the act of skinning one of his sheep. He captured two of them, and shot the third as the man tried to escape.[67] But for his arthritis, Cole might, like any other man, have been tempted to destroy the evidence and bury the corpse. But he had been too crippled and there were also two, albeit scared, black witnesses. By early May, Galbraith Cole was up on a charge of 'murder or culpable homicide'.[68] Speculation as to the outcome was rife for there was great curiosity as to the nature of the defence. The general opinion was that no white jury would convict the son of an aristocrat (indeed stock theft was so bad that they might offer a vote of thanks), although, if Cole shot to kill, hanging was the penalty at that time. Nevertheless disbelief prevailed: 'how could they hang the son of the Earl of Enniskillen for blotting out a miserable sheep-stealing nigger?'[69]

Cole was tried in September. He refused to perjure himself by saying that the man's death had been accidental, but he was acquitted by the jury on the grounds of justifiable homicide rather than murder.

The case attracted much publicity in England; Cole was related to Delamere and that could not be discounted in the verdict. By coincidence a parallel case had occurred in Rhodesia, and for a time it looked as though the suspension of the jury system in both BEA and Rhodesia was inevitable. The outcry in the press therefore was doubled; two miscarriages of justice, both in favour of white men against black, had taken place. The Secretary of State intervened.[70] Galbraith Cole was charged with 'inciting racial enmity' under a provision in the Indian Penal Code. The Governor, taking advantage of a rare ordinance, without discounting the idea of impressing people at Home, ordered Cole's deportation.

Delamere was in England at the time, having been summoned when his wife had suffered a nervous breakdown. Her collapse was put down to the strain of running Soysambu in his absence as times spent away from the farm became more frequent and left her to shoulder the responsibility.[71]

Delamere did all he could in London to get Cole's deportation rescinded but it was impossible. He was a man who was much loved by those who knew him and his fellow Europeans were appalled at the turn events had taken. While the case was remembered it did not stain him.

Alex Davis made a strong protest in *The Leader* after the deportation, against what he considered 'a disgraceful and gratuitous punishment, not strict justice', but, as he put it, the Cole family accepted it philosophically. Conflicting stories state that Galbraith Cole went to Zanzibar and South Africa. Wherever he spent his exile, in 1914 after the war broke out, with the help of friends and wearing a beard, he was sneaked back to his farm, disguised as a Somali, whose customs he knew well. When the Governor, Sir Henry Belfield discovered his return he gave Cole permission to remain. [72]

By 1929 Galbraith Cole was reduced by arthritis to skeletal proportions and was confined mainly to his chair and so bent that he could move only by dragging himself along on two sticks and unable to turn his head left or right. [73] When he died his wife, Eleanor whom he had married a little over ten years before, had him buried overlooking the lake he loved, on the farm for which he had been prepared to risk his life. As was the custom then, the spot was marked with an obelisk.

The paradox of the Cole case, so far as Delamere was concerned, was that in his heart, he was in sympathy with the Maasai. He dealt with theft at Soysambu by means of small fines and never called in the police.

It is a strange coincidence that two of the Protectorate's best Governors, Eliot and Girouard, both resigned from office before finishing their term, that their departures were connected with issues and affairs involving the Maasai and that both of them were also finally undermined by a telegram and the bungling of policy. As Charles Miller observed of the Maasai in *The Lunatic Express* 'in the eviction of the tribe from its second home, one finds it difficult not to detect the Caucasian hand of the colonists'. [74]

The Maasai were nomads and, as such, the shifting of the tribe from one place to another was perhaps more acceptable to their gypsy-like nature than it would have been to the Kikuyu or Nandi. Nevertheless, it is astonishing that so proud a warrior race showed no resistance, remaining passive and malleable during these upheavals which extended over a decade. Words were not minced by the official history in *The Blue Book*, which stated fully that 'the suggestion to move the Maasai was undoubtedly made in the interests of the European settlers.' [75]

As has already been mentioned, the fecund grazing on the Laikipia had so swelled the Maasai herds that they had outgrown the area. Gradually they had seeped over the boundaries allotted to them and, though both Stewart and Hayes-Sadler had extended the Reserve, this had not solved the problem. As time went on, Lenana also realised he was losing his grip as *Laibon* over the northern Maasai, and the complications of the division of the tribe were not helped by the fact that in 1908 the Maasai were forbidden to use the half-mile wide road promised by the Government. It was to have linked the Southern and Northern reserves but had become infected by pleuro-pneumonia and rinderpest, a foul disease which erodes the flesh of the live animal. It was closed by the authorities and quarantined to prevent the spread of disease. But vital as that restriction was, not only did it cut the two factions of the tribe off completely, in doing this the Government had effectively broken its promise.

By now the European farmers openly recognised that in choosing land for stock formerly occupied by the Maasai, they could not go wrong. These age-old pastoralists instinctively understood the nature of the land. Sabukia was a poor land on which to raise stock and so was Delamere's Equator Ranch, Njoro. Seth-Smith took some cows with a few oxen up from Makuyu to break the land at Sabukia. His cattle died; no one could find a reason. Once the oxen lost condition they were moved back to Makuyu. It was only when these were found licking desperately at some blue clay, a sample of which taken for analysis, that the nature of the Sabukia soil was properly understood.[76] Both Njoro and Sabukia were deficient in cobalt as was the northern side of Lake Naivasha. Another settler family, the Hop-crafts, were advised by a Maasai not to take land there if they wanted to raise cattle.[77] Delamere discovered later that that part of his Njoro farm which was no good for his animals was known to the Maasai as *angata natai emmi* because the deficiency was such here that even rhinos could not suckle their young. They named it 'the plain of the female rhinocerous without any milk.' The disease in such areas became known as Nakuruitis.[78]

As Paice observed, the Laikipia Reserve 'is a splendid tract of grazing country, the Maasai would not be there if it weren't . . . I have written to the Vet officer in Nairobi to see if there is any chance in the near future of being allowed to take my cattle into Laikipia . . . there are other native sheep to be got elsewhere, but the Maasai Laikipia sheep beat all others hollow.'[79]

In 1909 the idea was mooted for the removal of the northern Maasai to a single, extended Southern Reserve, south of the railway. Lenana had agreed that the northern Maasai should remove themselves thither. But Legalishu, spokesman for the northern Maasai, remained non-commital.

To reunite the Maasai as Lenana wished, it had seemed obvious to reach beyond the existing Southern Reserve to include the huge uninhabited stretch of grazing country which amounted to a million and a half acres west of it. The three practical advantages behind this concept were that administration would be simplified, disease minimised and the tribe reunited. Water, always a prime consideration in Africa, was a problem though there were two permanent rivers running through. McGregor Ross, head of the Public Works Department, devised a scheme and for as little as £5,280 an irrigation scheme could overcome that.

Early in 1910 Lenana pressed Girouard to execute the move for he feared that he could no longer hold his tribe together for his influence as *Laibon* was weakened by the tribe's physical division. A mass meeting was held at Ngong and all the Chiefs were in favour of the move but for the dissenting voice of Legalishu. He objected that the Southern Reserve was too small. Girouard suggested that Legalishu, Lenana and another chief send deputies to examine

it. Afterwards, Legalishu held to his original objection. Weight was now
added to his argument when the northern Maasai now also changed their
minds.

For nine months the Maasai had lived in indecision.[78] Behaviour of the
colonists, including much evidence contained in private diaries, letters and
official papers of the period confirms the suggestion that the white men had
set their hearts on gaining access to the Laikipia. Of this they made no secret
nor of their opposition to anything which might forestall them. Yet on the
face of things cleverly they managed to seem philanthropic. An extract from a
letter written by Paice in February 1911 hints at the chaos and rumour which
the situation generated. 'For years the authorities have been intending to shift
the Maasai out of the Laikipia into the Southern Reserve. Naturally . . .
Government wants to let the white settlers take it up . . . time after time the
Maasai have just been going to trek when something has happened to stop it.
The last . . . was gastro-enteritis (a deadly complaint in young stock)
amongst their cattle . . . now the Government has forbidden any fresh cattle
being taken into the district so as to get it completely free from disease, before
the Maasai move . . . into the Southern Province . . . but I have heard this
from the DC so often. I am beginning to doubt if they will ever move the
Maasai from Laikipia. The Maasai are very sick about it and don't want to
go.'[79]

Stock officers were needed urgently to supervise the Maasai move. A
number of Europeans were taken on in a temporary capacity by the Veterinary Department to assist what was to be a massive exodus by any standards.
After completion in 1912, these stock officers had supervised the shifting of
200,000 cattle, over one million sheep and their owners and families,
amounted to 10,000 people.[80]

Farmers with a good knowledge of stock, the language and the terrain,
were glad to be recruited by the Veterinary Department. The job came a
godsend to those who had fallen on difficult times, like Herman Klapprott.
He was a South African farmer who had lived in Kiambu since 1907, had a
wife and seven children to support and had lost his entire herd of cattle from
ECF. The blow was softened when he was taken on as a Maasai stock
inspector. His faith, curiously enough, was unaltered by his loss of cattle and
this experience with the Maasi led him into the research of cattle disease at
Kabete, after he obtained a farm on the Kinankop when the move was over.
He lived and travelled among the Maasai for months, obtaining rare photographs of them and one of Lenana himself, dressed in a hyrax cloak and
looking frail and ancient just before he died in March 1911 at Ngong.[81] It was
said that his dying wish was that his people should be reunited.

This seems to have affected Legalishu's next decision. For, at a meeting
held to appoint Lenana's successor, Legalishu informed Government representatives that his people wished after all to move to the Southern Reserve.
It also seems that Legalishu's change of heart was brought about because the
Government, since the return of the Maasai to the Northern Reserve,

expected them to pay rent in cattle for it. Another meeting between Girouard and the Maasai at Legalishu's request was held in Nairobi. The Governor made clear once more that they were free to stay on Laikipia but they chose to move.[82]

On 4 April the second Maasai Agreement was signed and was approved in May by the Secretary of State. The northern Maasai undertook to abandon Laikipia for an enlarged Southern Reserve.

While all Nairobi was agog over the Galbraith Cole shooting, that June, the Maasai move began. Despite increased staff to handle the vast numbers of the northerners' stock, arrangements proved inadequate. Some routes proved waterless, others devoid of pasture, then the rains came, making them impassable. Cows and sheep died in droves and once rinderpest broke out the stock officers despaired of keeping a semblance of order. By mid August the situation had so deteriorated that Ainsworth was called back from the Lake Province to take charge. He feared that the move could become a rout unless he acted swiftly. All those Maasai who could be were turned back. The move would be completed in relays.[83] Only 10% were thought to have reached the Southern Reserve. The settlers talked of many Maasai women and children dying of cold on the Mau and 80% of those who lived, returned to Laikipia.[84] In the middle of September thirty Maasai elders descended upon the Magistrate's office at Nakuru to complain of the loss of life and a doctor was sent up to investigate.[85]

A cable arrived from Lewis Harcourt, by now Colonial Secretary, suspending the move on the strength of insufficient grazing on the Loita plains; it must be postponed until the northern section reaffirmed its 'full and free assent' to be transferred.[85]

Girouard cabled Edmondson, the Veterinary Officer at Nakuru, asking his opinion of conditions.[86] He replied that the move was going well despite the cold weather and some cattle deaths—the Maasai were not suffering too much hardship, as had been alleged in the House of Commons. Wise after the event, the conclusion now was that the Maasai should never have been moved anyway. The doctor reported that between 2% and 4% of the Maasai population had perished.[87]

Legalishu reversed his wishes and yet again the Laikipia was declared a Maasai Reserve until the end of time. In fact that was to be little more than nine months.

Eliot had the integrity to recognise European interests were paramount. Eighty years later the instability of the African independent countries lies just as much in the hands of a few élite whose interests are paramount too. Usurpation passes for authority and its only stability comes from the people themselves, whose break with tradition has never been completely made.

Girouard was taken aback when Lewis Harcourt, the Secretary of State, decided that no one was to be compensated with Laikipia land in connection with the Maasai move. It had been taken for granted that Laikipia would become available once the Maasai had vacated it. Girouard received a cable from the Colonial Office on 5 October and, in reply to Harcourt two days later, informed him that no rights had been granted or promised to Europeans in connection with the Northern Reserve. This was incorrect as he had already committed himself in a Land Office letter dated 4 April 1910. Somehow the copy of that letter never reached the Colonial Office files. Besides this, Girouard appears to have forgotten sending the cable which had been worded ambiguously. What he really meant was that no *specific* areas on Laikipia had been allocated to Europeans.[88] It was this confusion that lay behind the misunderstanding and subsequent row between Harcourt and Girouard in 1912, before he resigned and accepted the highly paid position of managing director of Armstrong-Vickers.[89]

Girouard went on home leave early in 1912 and then Harcourt accused him of disobeying his instructions and acting without consulting the Colonial Office. Thus one of the best Governors the Protectorate ever had never returned to it. He was succeeded towards the end of that year by Sir Henry Belfield.

Legalishu countered with a move that the white man could not have imagined of the black in 1912. Through a Nairobi lawyer, he obtained a temporary injunction restraining the Government from carrying out its eviction order. The Maasai case took its place in the queue for legal attention. A year passed before it was dismissed. Legalishu appealed and in December 1913 the case was thrown out. As Charles Miller puts it in *The Lunatic Express*, 'on a point almost as delicate as it was astonishing. The verdict held that the East African Protectorate was, juridically a foreign country in its relations with Britain, that all agreements with the Maasai and Colonial office were therefore treaties between two nations, and not "cognisable" in the courts as such.' There was little alternative but to accept the verdict, though had funds not been exhausted, the Maasai could have appealed to the Privy Council.[90] And while the legal wrangling had been taking place the northern Maasai, no doubt wearied by the chopping and changing of direction over the past two years, had trickled quietly into the Southern Reserve on their own initiative. Twenty years later the Land Commission described them as 'the most wealthy tribe in all Africa both in the matter of land and the stock which they are able to keep on it'.[91]

During Belfield's term, the Colonial Office could do nothing but yield to the promises made to the white men by Girouard two years before and thus convinced the settlers that the man on the spot would always win. But the affair had yet another and more important result. It had evolved into something of a *cause célèbre* in England. For the first time humanitarian attention was focussed on the Protectorate and for a while happenings were carefully watched.[92]

Three officials certainly harboured misgivings with regard to the second Maasai move: Ainsworth was ever after suspicious that outside pressure had been brought to bear on Lenana, and McGregor Ross believed that Lenana's deathbed wish was probably no more than 'a convenient report'. Even

Frederick Jackson, who had favoured the move, confessed that it had been 'a sorry show'. Edmondson the veterinary officer, who openly disliked Delamere as 'a land grabber', was of the opinion that the entire gambit had been arranged to suit Delamere and others who had land in the southern Guaso Nyero.[93] The rumour circulated among those in Nairobi, when Legalishu went to court, that Ainsworth had put him up to it. Some dismissed him as a nigger-lover. Gossip provoked Delamere into writing to the Chief Secretary of the Protectorate, 'I hope this is untrue as I believe in his wrong-headed way Mr Ainsworth has the interests of the country at heart. But he has always denied the rights and benefits of civilisation to which he should be a prop . . . and it is possible that he has taken up this attitude with regard to the Masai movement.'[94]

Sir Percy Girouard was an outstanding Governor, contributing to the Protectorate's quick advancement on many levels. In his three years of office he had initiated the delegation of authority to native chiefs and during his regime the first Native Authority act was drawn up but was passed in 1912 after his resignation. This increased the legal powers of the chiefs and head men considerably, which sounds simple enough but it had not been a straightforward matter of grafting English ideas on to an already existing organisation of native government. The tribes in the Protectorate were not even coherent units. The division of the Maasai has been explained but the Kikuyu were no less complex, being made up of hundreds of clans to say nothing of the Luo and Wakamba or the coast people. Girouard's Ordinance of 1912 was designed to create a rudimentary system whereby natives, so long as they remained in their Reserves, should be governed to some extent through their Chiefs and elders by methods they recognised, with the proviso that 'such native custom and law is not repugnant to morality'. It also contained a provision that able-bodied males in the Reserves might be called upon by the Government to work without wages for not more than six days a quarter on watercourses or other schemes undertaken for the benefit of the entire community.

Girouard's fiscal reforms, the goodwill his ability generated and the increasing flow of wealthy safaris and new farmers mean that BEA was set fair for prosperity two years before the outbreak of the First World War. When Belfield arrived to govern the land which was gaining recognition as 'the winter home for aristocrats', the white man's dream was just turning into a sound investment.

CHAPTER 11

Sunshine Days

Not for delectations sweet;
Not the cushion and the slipper, nor the peaceful and the studious;
Not the riches safe and palling, not for us the tame enjoyment,
      Pioneers! O Pioneers!
Do the feasters gluttonous feast?
Do the corpulent sleepers sleep? Have they locked and bolted doors?
Still be ours the diet hard, and the blanket on the ground,
      Pioneers! O Pioneers!

                                Walt Whitman

By the time that Girouard went on leave in May 1912, British East Africa was changing its general appearance; up-country land had been cleared of ant-hills, and ploughed stretches had replaced rocks and bush that had lent it the character of a wilderness for centuries. Delamere's Equator Ranch was made up now of geometric shapes where wheat, maize, potatoes and barley grew within one hundred and fifty miles of fencing; two thousand acres were under wattle. Nairobi's tin shacks were giving way to stone buildings.

Taking advantage of the improved economy, a drive took place in 1912 to encourage commercial firms to come to BEA. Living expenses for the salesman class of settler were £5 per month though to live comfortably £10 was required. Offices could be rented for £2 a month and telephones cost £8 per annum. It was pointed out that there was power and lighting even if it was a little uncertain during the dry season.[1]

Towards Molo by now, instead of thatched huts there were houses with shingled tiles surrounded by large lawns and gardens, brilliant with exotic shrubs. Sheds had given way to brick stables and cattle had cut paths across the rolling plains where before there had only been game tracks. In the harvesting seasons, oxen bearing grain to the homesteads were lead by men dwarfed by the maize. On the wealthier farms where the strings of wagons were long they move closely behind one another and from a distance appeared to have come to a standstill. Because the best oxen were trained by

Boers, Captain C. B. Clutterbuck employed them to school his teams at Njoro.

Clutterbuck was an ex-Burma man and pioneer race-horse trainer, near Njoro Station. His daughter, Beryl Markham the aviatrix who flew solo from England to America in the 'thirties, grew up here at 'Clut's mill'. The African's christened her father 'Clutabuki', chanting 'Clutabuki, kata kuni,' to rhyme with the sawing of wood and the sound of the train as it chugged up to Njoro. His racing stud had been built up since 1905 when Delamere began importing bloodstock. It was then that the first races for country-breds were initiated. With the money Clutterbuck made grinding posho and flour, he bought two old railway engines, fitted them with pulleys and started a sawmill. He sold thousands of tons lumber to the Uganda Railway but nevertheless Clutterbuck was bankrupt by 1921. In the meantime he had trained and bred numerous winners for The Produce Stakes and the Kenya Derby.[2] And his daughter Beryl later was no less successful.

He was closely followed by Spencer Tryon at Molo, but Clutterbuck was considered the best by all who raced. McMillan, Greswolde Williams, the Cole brothers and Delamere all took their horses to him. They formed the backbone of the racing crowd with Captain Gooch, B. F. Webb, C. A. Neave, Robert Stordy the vet, A. S. Flemmer who acted as starter, Jim Elkington, Master of the Masara Hounds[3] and Powys Cobb, who imported the famous stallion '*Talisman*', the sire of many winning Kenya-bred horses.[4]

Racing was still run by The East African Turf Club on the course two miles north of the swamp at Nairobi and in 1911 Nakuru had held its first races. There were already a number of professional jockeys, though it was still generally a question of 'owners up' for those who could make the weight. No amateur stood much chance against Henry Tarlton. He wore four-inch long spurs. After bloodstock was introduced there were still a few races for Somali ponies but a shortage of mounts and money was the bane of the Turf Club's existence for years.[5] Dress was motley, flags and bunting fluttered around the grandstand whilst the KAR, who supported the Turf Club by turning up at every meeting, paraded for the spectators in their regimental drag, drawn by four bay horses which cantered round the race-course accompanied by much horn-blowing. The Police, not to be outdone, fitted up a wagon which was pulled by sixteen mules as four-in-hand horses, and upon which all available Police Officers sat. Following in the wake of the KAR drag, an officer blew lustily on an elephant tusk which had been converted into an Arab horn and added to the general merriment.[6] Besides racing and hunting with the Masara Hounds there was plenty of other sport. Polo was played (Mervyn Ridley and his own private ground at Makuyu) and cockfighting was held in an abandoned railway shed beyond Nairobi. Pig-sticking, lion-hunting with dogs, duck-shooting and fishing were also popular. Clubs burgeoned suddenly like mushrooms and the keen travelled far to these to participate in golf, tennis or cricket matches which were becoming regular week-end occupations. The Railway Club at Kisumu boasted two tennis courts as well as a golf-course laid down through Ainsworth's persuasions, though later it had to be moved. Originally it went around the Indian quarters and when one afternoon the rather stout wife of one of the babus got hit by a ball on her backside as she was bending over in her yard, such a fuss was made that the course was shifted.[7]

In Nairobi a live theatre was being contemplated and three more stone buildings were under construction besides the New Stanley—Whiteway Building, the District Commissioner's Office and, up on the Hill, the new Nairobi Club. Plans for a more exclusive club were already afoot between Freddy Ward and J. A. Morrison who had come out on a hunting safari. Whisky cost 4 rupees a bottle and all was right with the world despite outbreaks of bubonic plague in the bazaar.[8]

Government Road (formerly Station Road) was the scene of fresh enterprise, there was even a bioscope. A pair of quaint zebra-cross donkeys belonging to A. H. Wardle who had opened his chemists could often be seen hitched up near Nairobi House and his buggy became as familiar a sight as that of Dr Ribeiro jogging along the bazaar on his zebra. Pioneer Mary had started Fairview Dairy nearby where she served cream teas and sold dairy produce from the thoroughbred cattle she had imported in 1906. W. D. Young was kept busy with family portraits at the Dempster Photographic Studio and towards the station, Sammy Jacobs had added a butchery to his well-stocked emporium *The Dustpan*. Opposite Nairobi House, Emile Jardine's wine an spirits shop and became the gathering point for the aristocrats after they had finished shopping. Usually they dropped in at midday in the hope of meeting friends and sampling Jardine's newest delivery of champagnes. Freddy Ward was running an estate agency and Newland and Tarlton's safaris were so much in demand that they had acquired a junior partner, Claude Tritton, to run their London office in Pall Mall.

Although amateur theatricals were the mainstay of prewar entertainment, celluloid had made its debut thanks to J. Garvie. If films were little more than flickering shadows thrown across a screen, many paid to sit on wooden forms at Garvie's Rooms to watch them. When the quality was very bad, the performance was interspersed by jeers as disapproving members of the Travellers' Club nearby threw empty bottles and more vulgar things on to the tin roof of the little theatre.[9]

During race-weeks now, with a few motor cars chugging along the dusty streets, Nairobi took on the look of a Mack Sennett comedy. Horses still predominated in 1912 however and a new hitching post for them was established outside a second bank, the newly opened Standard Bank of South Africa.[10] A vehicle that was much in evidence, besides Lord Cranworth's 15 hp Napier was Northrup McMillan's Ford in which he was chaufferred by Scott, one of his two black American drivers. He was so huge that the bodywork of the Ford had to be cut out at one side to accommodate him. Every time he clambered into the vehicle from the rear it was feared that it would tip up.[11]

Mayence Bent had married Fred Tate. On 20 November 1909 an announcement was published in *The Leader* and read, 'The marriage of Miss Mayence Woodbury with Mr Fred Tate was celebrated on the 9th inst. at the Catholic Cathedral at Zanzibar.' If it was not a printer's error it should have read 'Mrs Mayence Bent'. But it looks as if she had lived with Bent as his common-law wife which is probably why she and Fred Tate slipped away to Zanzibar for their wedding.[12]

Could this have been the union in which lay the origins of the once impertinent but now threadbare jibe, 'Are you married, or do you live in Kenya?' Though the Happy Valley crowd certainly perpetuated the question before the Second World War, it was said to have stemmed from a vaudeville act at the Alhambra, though nobody could remember who had performed it. Supporting this likelihood is the fact that Fred Tate's brother and sisters were connected with the London theatre.[13] Equally, the saying may have grown out of a scandal concerning the famous Miss Marie Lloyd in 1913 when she was deported for travelling on the Uganda Railway as Mrs Dillon when she was not Bernard Dillon's wife. Dillon was a jockey and when they crossed the Atlantic together under the same circumstances, they incurred the censure of the US Department of Immigration in New York. They were detained on Ellis Island and an order for their deportation was issued on the grounds of moral turpitude but at the last moment Washington agreed that they could stay for £600 bail and on condition that they did not cohabit.

Mayence and Fred Tate were ambitious and needed something larger than the Hotel Stanley. Even with thirty bedrooms, not counting its annexe in Khambatta Building, it only met half the demand of which they were capable. Their sights were set on something more appropriate to their Thurston billiard table and Bechstein piano. Fred Tate decided to bid for one of two plots of identical size that came up for public auction in 1912. One faced Hardinge Street, the other, Sixth Avenue and the Tates had agreed that they could afford to spend £350. Since each plot was identical in size and formed a corner, it was immaterial which they bought. Tate came back from the auction with both.[14]

The view from the site along Sixth Avenue towards the Hill was interrupted now by an important-looking clock-tower that emerged from *The East African Standard*,* which had moved from Mombasa to Nairobi in 1910. The undeveloped plot beyond it was the one for which Block had pawned his gold watch and chain. Farther along still was the Post Office where a varying array of flags indicated the movement of mails. To those waiting for letters in 1912, a blue flag meant that the ship had left Aden for Mombasa with post; a red flag meant that overseas mail had arrived and a white flag or arc-lamp displayed at night told people that mail was ready for distribution.[15]

---

* In a lecture in August 1955, C. W. Anderson, explained that his father changed the name of the *African Standard* to the *East African Standard*. Apparently the European editor, Tiller, fell out with A. M. Jeevanjee, the paper's original owner; in order to disassociate themselves entirely from the former organisation it was renamed at this point.

It was a shock to Mayence Tate when her husband confessed that he had spent double the amount they had agreed but they need not have worried. The New Stanley opened in 1913 and in three years, thanks to the war, had done so well out of the hundreds of soldiers brought in to fight the campaign, that they were able to retire. In 1947, ten years after Fred Tate died, Block's eldest son purchased the New Stanley from Mayence Tate on his father's behalf.[16] People remember Block standing on the steps of the New Stanley, after he became its owner, a familiar figure wearing a suit and a worn Trilby, his hands clasped behind his back.[17] Alternatively he could he found sitting in his favourite chair at the Norfolk in the foyer, puffing away at an expensive cigar (he bought only the best once he could afford them; they were his one concession to luxury). As the receptionist dealt with guests' accounts on the day of their departure, Block would lift his hand towards her, so that she could pass him the bill for scrutiny. It was then handed back. Unless it was at fault not a word passed between them.[18] 'Keep the back doors locked,' he always instructed his managers, 'whatever comes in here comes through the front doors; whatever leaves, goes out by them also.'[19]

In the interim Block's sons acquired more land on the hotel's frontage and by the time they had finished developing it in 1974, though it had long been the centre of Nairobi, the New Stanley with its world famous 'Thorntree' meeting point, was valued at almost half a million pounds.[20]

In 1912 the Tates commissioned the architects Robertson, Gow and Davidson for the design.[21] As the builder dug its foundations on the outspan where oxen and horses had been tethered, their owners used an empty, grassy plot opposite belonging to Grogan—nearer still to John Rifkin's forge behind Nairobi House.* Later Grogan developed this site for Torr's Hotel which acquired its name when Joe Torr, former baker to Northrup McMillan leased it.[22] Torr's Hotel rivalled the New Stanley for popularity from the Second World War for years.

Dan Noble, the former post master, bought the old Hotel Stanley because, after his retirement he loved Nairobi so that he could not bear to leave. Noble's claim to fame was that he found the largest nugget in the Kakamega Gold Rush of the late 'twenties.** The Tates dealings with him ended in acrimony when Noble contested their rights to transfer the Stanley's name to the new building. After a court case, which the Tate's lost, they were forced to call their establishment the 'New Stanley' in order to confirm the fact they no longer had anything to do with the original hotel.[23]

By now Delamere's biggest challenge was the laying of a pipeline to water 40,000 acres. Besides his huge fencing scheme at Soysambu to divide as much land as possible into paddocks, he was building dips, wool-sheds, stables and drafting-yards but lion interfered with the laying of the pipeline and caused Delamere's labourers to strike.[24]

---

* At the back of where Woolworths' stands today.
** The Elbon Nugget so named by reversing Noble's surname.

In a serious drive to reduce lions on Soysambu, Delamere invited Paul J. Rainey, an American, who intended to experiment in a radically new way—to hunt them with dogs. The assorted pack consisted mainly of Airedale mongrels, and everyone was fascinated by this idea, including Delamere. Binks was taken on as Rainey's chief photographer during this exercise, recording some dramatic moments at Soysambu with his camera. These included those leading up to the death of the Austrian hunter, Fritz Schindelar, at Naivasha.[25]

Schindelar was much sought after by the titled from Europe for his talent for bagging record heads for his clients. He was a wanderer who had arrived out of nowhere in 1906 and when not on safari, usually stayed at the Norfolk Hotel. He loved to gamble and would sit on the verandah at a table upon which were piled hundreds of gold sovereigns. His mysterious past made him as attractive to women as his looks, for little was known about him except that he had served in a crack regiment of Hungarian hussars. He was a first-class horseman, an ace shot and, because of his style it was impossible to believe his claim of having worked as a hall porter, luggage master and head waiter. However, at the Norfolk Hotel, to the amusement of staff who had a great affection for him, he did duty as a waiter himself occasionally. Arriving back from the bush with hair matted, clothes torn and skin covered in grime from the final march back to civilisation, he appeared two hours later shaved, moustache beautifully waxed, immaculate and ready to serve his friends' orders on a tray or dance with the prettiest girl available.[26]

Schindelar was as intrigued as anyone with Rainey's use of dogs to hunt lions and went to his farm at Naivasha, which the American had bought in order to train his dogs. Rainey took the trained pack to Soysambu for a fortnight where each evening kills were put out. Delamere and his cronies who had come out to participate were up at 4 am to inspect the spoor and there were some exciting moments and plenty of lion were accounted for though a number of dogs were also killed.

Schindelar was with Rainey and Binks at Naivasha in January 1914 when the dogs bayed-up a particularly savage lion in thick bush by the lake. Unexpectedly it charged the Austrian, clawing at his pony's rump and sending Schindelar flying. Even so, he managed to fire one shot at point blank range. But he missed and the lion sprang on to Schindelar's stomach in one bound. He was buried in the Nairobi cemetery.[27]

Delamere's pipeline was so successful that he developed a passion for laying on water. Though it cost £25,000 by the time he had finished, he had thirty miles of pipeline and fifteen sets of tanks serving Soysambu alone. His cattle and sheep fared well in 1913 and the year leading up to the war saw steady improvements on all fronts. Profits on wool began to pay back his overdraft but in the middle of 1913 he himself fell ill. He tried to run Soysambu from his bed but his health worsened until, at the beginning of 1914, he was forced to return to England and enter a nursing home. His courageous wife who had rallied (though not completely) from her breakdown, attempted to run the estate alone. Her loyal support had a bad effect on her health. She was only thirty-six yet the strain on her heart had so weakened her that at times she could barely walk a few hundred yards.[28]

Meanwhile Lily Block had a suitor. She had not realised that Simon Haller's frequent visits to Limuru to talk to her father had anything to do with his attraction towards her. She had taken it for granted that their joint involvement in the building of Nairobi's first Synagogue brought them together. But as the number of meetings intensified, Haller began to court her openly. They became engaged and married early in 1913.[29]

Simon Haller had come to the Protectorate directly as a result of the likelihood of Jewish Settlement. He had been living Durban after leaving Russia before his passport was withdrawn at the age of sixteen to enforce military service which, for the Jews, was extremely harsh. In South Africa, before proper refrigeration, meat was taken aboard passenger liners at night and this was how he port-crawled his way to Durban.[30] In Nairobi in 1905, when the Uasin Gishu was turned down by the Zionists, he took a job as a tin-smith with the farrier, John Rifkin and they made some of the earliest tin baths and water-tanks in Nairobi.[31] Michael Harrtz, another Russian tin-smith, settled under the same circumstances. Haller saved enough money to buy a farm at Kiambu where he grew potatoes, beans and oats and was so convinced of the great future to be had for young people in BEA in 1911 that he persuaded relatives in Poltava to allow four nephews to join him.

Eddie, Archie, Charlie and David Ruben joined 'Uncle Haller' at Kiambu in 1912 just after he became engaged to Lily Block. The young Ukrainian boys spoke no English, but learned it at school in Nairobi and when not at their lessons, helped their uncle on his farm. After the war Eddie Ruben started a small transport company with eight mules and two wagons bought from John Rifkin. From such modest beginnings he founded what became a huge organisation, the limited company, Express Transport.[32]

Probably Lily and Simon Haller married at the DC's office as the Nairobi Synagogue did not open until October 1913. A high percentage of European weddings took place at Mombasa rather than up-country in the early days, though when couples were married at Nairobi, wedding processions tended to be a funny combination of finery and practicality. Guests formed a quaint procession as they travelled to the wedding breakfast (usually a private house) riding bicycles or mules, by rickshaw and bullock or pony carts in a manner that lent itself to much gaiety and ragging. The wedding to which Kenya people refer most in pioneering days was that which joined two well-known settler names, the Venn Fey and Nightingale families. Captain Venn Fey's twenty-three year old daughter, Nell, was carried by sedan chair from the South Kinankop to Kijabe Mission to marry young Max Nightingale in December 1908. They had fallen in love while he was surveying 'Njabini' where the Venn Fay family settled in 1905.[33]

Other weddings in Kenya were less grand. They tended to be small, rather impersonal functions, motivated more by propriety than celebration. Witnesses were often strangers, whether the ceremony was performed in Mombasa Cathedral or at the DC's office in MacKinnon Square. Many brides-to-be sailed out to marry at Mombasa after months of separation when their fiancé had gone ahead, sometimes as much as three years earlier to establish some future security before settling down. A few bachelors found suitable girls locally but the prettiest were snapped up within weeks of their arrival if they were single. The usual pattern was to marry someone they had met whilst on leave. Afterwards the journey to the Protectorate often took the place of a proper honeymoon.

Girls who were betrothed were usually married within hours of coming ashore at Mombasa. An exception was made if some suitable woman friend or relative could meet and accompany her to Nairobi by train. A chaperone was essential to avoid scandal when travelling on the same train as her future husband.

Wedding gowns were chosen without the least notion of how humid Mombasa could be, particularly in the first two months of the year. The wedding of Mabel Lavinia Hunt, who sailed from Southampton to marry her fiance, Alex Davis, editor of *The Leader*, in February 1909, typifies matrimonial procedure there in those days. At Mombasa, Alex Davis was rowed out mid-stream to the German ship to greet her and help her ashore.[34]

They were married after luncheon by the DC and a local solicitor witnessed the formalities. Their rickshaw was decorated with heavily scented frangipani flowers which was pretty and festive but their clothes could hardly have been more stifling. The couple were both encased in white. Mabel Hunt's mushroom topee with a lace-edged veil befitting a bride, hung to her shoulders and hid her coiled blonde hair. This was her greatest pride and when loosened was waist-length. Alex Davis wore a twill suit, a gold watch and chain, white helmet and shoes.[35] Hundreds of couples went through that same routine and in 1919 when the *Garth Castle* came in with the Soldier Settlers, there were so many brides on board that couples were married three at a time.

Several women took one look at Mabel Davis's outfits and suggested that she order more suitable clothes from Ahmed's in the bazaar, where cotton twill was stocked for everyday skirts and shirts in sensible khaki and could be made up quickly to her exact measurements. Like Mrs Boedeker, Mabel Davis dressed in the height of Bond Street fashion. She was in for a number of shocks when she arrived at her new home. It was a three-roomed building of grey stone, in Crooked Lane, Parklands behind Ainsworth Bridge. As usual the kitchen of wood-and-iron was some distance from the house. A *debe*, planted sideways on three stones, passed for an oven. Food supplies were kept in a gauze cage on four legs, each of which was standing in a tin of paraffin so as to discourage ants. Bathwater was heated out of doors on an open fire. When it was needed it was carried in to a tin bath. Alex Davis was well-established in business by 1909 and therefore was able to run two rickshaws, one for himself and one for his wife.

Soon enough Mabel Davis was aware that compared with other people whose turnouts were smartly upholstered and whose boys wore uniforms to match, hers were shabby. After much coaxing, her husband agreed that she could get their rickshaws re-covered. The pushing and pulling boys were measured up by a *dhersie* in the bazaar. Mabel Davis chose a hard-wearing grey fabric, patterned with small black crosses and was particularly delighted with the effect that her new turn-out created when she rode into town. It was only when Davis came home enraged and accused her of making him the laughing stock of the town, that she realised her *faux pas*; the fabric she had chosen was that used at Nairobi jail for the uniforms of convicts.

Mabel Davis's first few months in Africa were not happy. After three weeks in Nairobi, she fell unaccountably sick and Dr Henderson, a close friend, was sent for as she was too ill even to talk. She was suspected by Henderson of having ignored his advice and eaten the cress that grew wild in the Nairobi river. Two Africans carried her to the far side of Nairobi on a stretcher to the hospital. Henderson walked alongside, shielding his patient from the sun with a parasol. At the hospital he strapped her down to a water bed. She had such a high temperature that Dr Henderson knew she was in danger of losing her beautiful hair. To try and prevent this, her head was packed in ice but unfortunately the precaution was useless and during the next two months while she was bed-ridden, she lost most of it.[36]

Perhaps Dr Roland Wilks Burkitt's cold water treatment would have proved better for her. The splenetic Irish doctor had opened his consulting rooms in 1911 and the surgery stood between the post office and Block's plot, just off Sixth Avenue. Here, when time allowed, he also engaged in bouts of horse selling. He was a friend of Denys Finch Hatton, who by now was cattle trading and looking at mining prospects and land with a view to settling. Burkitt used one of Finch Hatton's blue bowler hats, in which to rattle a stick, so as to make the ponies trot out well and show off their paces to likely buyers.

One morning early in 1912, Freddy Ward was tipped off by Grogan that an ex-Grenadier, Archie Morrison, was due in on the train that day and was being taken on safari by a hunter, Jack Lucy. Morrison, Grogan pointed out, was a wealthy man who might do much to help the development of the country if Ward could influence him. Ward took Grogan's advice. Not only did he meet J. A. Morrison at the station but invited him to stay with him at Chiromo. Ward was living here as a member of the syndicate that leased it and included Delamere, Atkinson and the Sewells.[37]

Morrison was the grandson of a City Merchant of London and was extremely rich. Before starting out on his last safari, during breakfast he announced to Ward that he wanted to develop an office block, a modern residential suburb with a Country Club and a nine-hole golf course. Consequently, Ward took an option on all the land available in Nairobi for building purposes against Morrison's return. When the time came for inspection, Ali Khan drove them round in a barouche and Morrison chose Muthaiga as the best for his purposes. This had originally belonged to the Sandbach Bakers.[38] The name Muthaiga is a corruption of two Kikuyu words—'Muthiaka' their name for the Greenheart tree which flourished there and 'Muthika'—its bark, much used in Kukuyu medicine.[39]

Since Archie Morrison was leaving for Europe within two days, a meeting was hastily arranged at the Standard Bank with its first manager, J. J. Toogood. The 'bank' was one room in which stood a desk and chair for Toogood, a couple of chairs for clients and a safe. After Morrison outlined his plans, without mentioning any figure, he wrote out a cheque. With the promise to return in five weeks time, he handed it to Toogood and left with Ward. The manager was staggered when he realised that Morrison had made the cheque in Ward's favour to open the account for £60,000. Ward set up Morrison Estates but Archie Morrison never came back though his company founded Nairobi House and Muthaiga Club, which opened officially at the end of 1913.[40] During construction, Donald Seth-Smith undertook the reporting of progress by letter to Morrison; to do this, he periodically rode his mule the thirty-five miles from Makuyu, with his servant hurrying along behind on foot, carrying Seth-Smith's dinner-jacket in a suitcase balanced on his head.[41]

Arrangements were made for Muthaiga Club to open with a New Year's Eve dinner. But the difficulty was to get enough members to make a party. The Club was not at first popular and was criticised for being before its time and far too far from the town centre. Only fourteen members could be persuaded to dine on 31 December 1913, for a celebratory banquet with all the trimmings—hats, crackers and a band.[42]

Two people, a little girl and a woman, both of whom became writers, were forming their ties at this time with the country which brought them both fame. One was Elspeth Grant, whose parents, Nellie and Joss set out from the Norfolk Hotel on April Fools' Day in 1913, to make for Chania Bridge with an ox-cart filled with their possessions. Their daughter, Elspeth Huxley, immortalised their early lives here in her book, *The Flame Trees of Thika*.[43]

The second was the Danish woman, Karen Christenze—or Isak—Dinesen. She was engaged to Baron Bror von Blixen who planned to grow coffee at Ngong. She was twenty-eight years old and her head was filled with dreams of becoming a wealthy Baroness. Her fiancé had promised her that 'gold meant coffee'. Bror von Blixen bought 4,500 acres near Nairobi from Mr Sjogren of the Swedo-African Coffee Company and about the same amount of land near Eldoret. Arrangements were then put in hand for Karen Dinesen to join him towards the end of 1913. Her experiences culminated in the writing of *Out of Africa*, a classic in which her prose was forged with pain, joy and disaster. Her wedding was planned for January 1914; the date depended finally on sailings to Mombasa.[44]

Block too had marriage on his mind. Over the winter of 1913–14 he met a young Jewish girl in Palestine, Sarah Tulipmann, the sister of a Nairobi accountant David Tulipmann. Their wedding, which took place on 23 June

1914, was a large bourgeois affair at Sarah's home near Tel Aviv. After the reception and a tearful parting, Sarah and Abraham Block, accompanied by his father-in-law, left for Jaffa and thence by train to Natanya, where they spent a week before sailing to Port Said and Mombasa.[45]

Unlike most people Sarah hated the train journey up-country and, far from being enchanted by Africa, was apprehensive of all that was new to her. There was nothing romantic in the alien and she felt menaced by insect and animal alike. Thoughts of the dust-loving scorpion and the bite of the centipede haunted her and the strange sounds and smells posed no less a threat. In her misery home-sickness possessed all her waking hours.

Sarah Block's parents had been certain that Block was a wealthy landowner and, in terms of acreage, he was, to those unfamiliar with African conditions. She had always trusted their judgement implicitly and at the age of twenty-one had never been separated from her family before. Not unnaturally she was troubled by the fact that she was expected to use paraffin boxes for book-shelves and cupboards. She claimed all her life that, had it not been the fact that war was declared in Nairobi less than ten days after her arrival, she would have returned to Palestine as soon as she had secured a passage for herself.[46]

While Block had been away, Lady Delamere, who had been so kind to him, had died in May 1914. Apparently, because she was too frail to remain at Soysambu, she was persuaded by friends who were concerned over her health to stay with them in Nairobi. Two days after Delamere returned from his bout of sickness in England she was dead.[47]

On 4 August 1914 the Protectorate was caught with its defences down. The fact that a few weeks before an Austrian Archduke had been assassinated had not impinged on Nairobi. At the time the main concern in Legislative Council was the question whether or not there should be a close season on duck shooting on Lake Naivasha. A messenger interrupted this debate and handed a cable to the Speaker. This was how the news arrived that England was at war with Germany and the fact sank in that British East Africa and German East Africa were no longer neighbours but enemies. At first, many believed the oft-repeated phrase, 'over by Christmas', and the mood was patriotic and jolly rather than grim.

CHAPTER 12

❧

War

Hooray, hooray! We're off to GEA.
Hooray, hooray! The squareheads we will slay.
And so we sing this happy song
Upon this happy day
As we go marching to Tabora.[1]

When the Great War started those in British East Africa could not envisage what it would mean. Disbelief was the first reaction. Sir Henry Belfield, the new Governor, rang Alex Davis in the early hours to report the declaration of war in Europe. Davis left at once for *The Leader*, to up-date the latest edition and organise the printing of official leaflets which were distributed in town several hours later.[2]

Delamere learned the news on Elmenteita Station. On the morning of 4 August. He happened to have gone there to make arrangements about a truck for some cattle to be dispatched. His immediate reaction was to walk up and down the small platform cursing violently on account of the interruption that war would cause to progress.[3]

Rumour was rife as martial law was proclaimed. The sale of ammunition was halted and a handful of German nationals placed under arrest. As the shock waves reverberated from Mombasa to Lake Victoria, settlers began to descend on Nairobi in droves. The monocled Belfield issued an appeal to all European to give their services in defence of the Protectorate but already hundreds had volunteered.[4]

Thus on 4 August Nairobi was in turmoil. With no organised reserve or defence force it was hardly reassuring that one battalion of the King's African Rifles in Nairobi was the sole military force. People armed with shotguns, revolvers and knives rushed to the Norfolk and later regathered at Nairobi House. Rudolf Mayer of the *East African Standard* was one of the first to be interned. He had lived for many years in South Africa before coming to the Protectorate, but none-the-less was a German subject.[5] Under the direct supervision of the military authorities, his printing works were used for the production of maps and confidential documents relating to the campaign. In 1916, Meinertzhagen used him for Intelligence at Moshi.[6]

On the eve of hostilities, His Majesty's armed forces in Kenya and Uganda numbered some 1,900 askaris commanded by five dozen European officers. They consisted of the Third King's African Rifles and the fourth KAR (Uganda) and four companies of the first battalion from Nyasaland. The second battalion had recently been disbanded. Of the seventeen companies, six were engaged in operations on the Juba River and the rest were on garrison duty in the north, preparing to mount an expedition against the Turkana. The Royal Artillery amounted to Maxim guns carried on a Model T Ford. Two of these weapons had jammed for Lugard in 1891 and had 'continued to malfunction faithfully ever since.'[7]

Under their one-eyed General, the enemy was slightly better prepared. In Dar-es-Salaam they had 2,540 askaris and 2,154 German soldiers, many of whom had arrived on the same ship as Sarah and Abraham Block in July.[8] There were also forty-five Germans in their Police Force and 2,154 African constables though these were not trained to military tactics.

General Paul von Lettow Vorbeck had been in command since January.[9] During his voyage to Dar-es-Salaam on the s.s. *Admiral*, he made friends with Karen Dinesen who was coming out to be married to Baron von Blixen in Mombasa and he asked her to find ten good horses, preferably Abyssinian, for him to buy in BEA. In all innocence she had promised to do so. Baroness Blixen looked for horses for Lettow Vorbeck but the declaration of war put a stop to their dispatch. The English became suspicious of the new Danish member of the community and, in the light of events, thought her pro-German. The women avoided her while the war was on.

Lettow Vorbeck's forces were backed up by forty modern field pieces, seventy machine-guns and what the British feared was an airforce. Actually it was one bi-plane which had been imported as an exhibit to celebrate Germany's Central Railway to Lake Tanganyika; it had crashed on its first flight, but this did not prevent warnings of air-raids in Nairobi, where the scare persisted for several weeks.[10] Throughout the campaign the British forces were likened to 'a lepidopterist on the hunt, with holes in his net, for a butterfly which kept turning into a wild bee'.[11]

In Nairobi, enlistment fever took over. Recruiting offices opened and the assortment of men taken on was extraordinary. Descriptions of their tatty uniforms, their red and white pennants affixed to bamboo, make this aspect of the campaign sound more like a fancy dress party than a gathering for war. Far from being a lark, however, the East African campaign was grim. Two years passed before Tabora fell (to Belgian not British troops) and Lettow Vorbeck led the British forces such a dance that German East Africa did not become British territory until 1918.[12] It ended as a *danse macabre* with the loss of almost 50,000 African, Indian and English lives: animal mortality was even higher. By 1916 it was reckoned that already sixty thousand horses and mules and twice as many oxen had perished.

In August 1914, the three KAR battalions were rushed from outposts and deployed along the German border. An armoured train patrolled the railway line along the vulnerable section of the Rift where the Germans held the southern boundary. Three hundred miles of track between Nairobi and Mombasa needed to be defended. Just by destroying a few bridges, the enemy could cut off the highlands completely from the coast and all new supplies. Askaris were posted along it but for several days no trains ran until all the culverts and bridges were sand-bagged and strengthened.[13]

German raiders frequently managed to breach the line and on one occasion the bridge was captured at Athi River only twenty miles from Nairobi and two trains were destroyed in the night by sending their locomotives in opposite directions. The debris from the smash was strewn along the banks of the river for months.[14]

The white population numbered about seven thousand, half of them able-bodied men. As the news of war percolated up-country, farmers saddled their horses and rode to Nairobi. Personal considerations were set aside in the urgent need to meet the threat of attack.[15]

War was then looked upon as a glorious adventure. The younger men were the more impatient to join up, and within a few months 85% belonged to a unit of some sort. Regiments of mounted rifles and infantry were raised and a number of scout corps formed to operate along the frontier to give intelligence of German movements. Eventually some sort of military cohesion shaped these into the East African Mounted Rifles from Wessell's Scouts, Bowker's Horse, Arnoldi's Scouts and Wilson's Scouts. The most aristocratic squadron of the EAMR was made up of settlers and was referred to as 'Monica's Own' after the Governor's pretty younger daughter. To begin with these bizarre groups of men, dressed in a medly of clothing with mules, donkeys and race-horses for mounts, were part of the first line of defence.[16]

The main recruiting office was in Nairobi House. At the station, sandwich men with enlisting placards marched up and down on the platform. Within a fortnight the town was swarming with regiments of volunteer cavalry raised by ex-army officers.[17] As usual the sequence of normal events was turned on its head. Just as the settlers had preceded the railway, BEA earned the distinction of having the only army which fought first and trained afterwards.[18]

Berkeley Cole took 800 Somali-horsemen under his command. The Boers from the Uasin Gishu formed a mounted unit, The Plateau South Africans. Only fourteen years before they had fought the British in the Boer War. Other squadrons were the East African Transport Corps, an ox-transport unit headed by Europeans over African drivers. The East African Regiment was an infantry unit consisting of settlers with a few commercial men thrown in. Doctors and nurses joined the East African Medical Corps. The East African Pioneer Corps was predominantly African with European officers who worked with the East African Supply Corps handling the distribution of foodstuffs and supplies. The East African Motor Transport Corps was made up of Europeans who had to be trained to drive.[19] Finally there was the Carrier Corps* with whom thousands of porters perished as they bore vital supplies to the front where there were no suitable roads for transport. When pack-mules and oxen began to die in droves, it was the Carrier Corps who replaced them.

Delamere's intimate knowledge of the Maasai, whose loyalty and co-operation were essential now, was invaluable. With a group of Maasai volunteers he went into the bush to patrol the Kajiado border.[20] Meanwhile queues of young men appeared before Dave Genower, the recruiting officer. Lance Corporals were signed on at 5 rupees (about 6/8d) per day which compared favourably with the pay of British troops who only got 1/3d. Registration numbers started low but later were jumped up by a thousand. It was believed that the reason for this was that, in the event of capture, it would convince the enemy that the British side were stronger than they actually were. Genower also needed people to look after those who had been detained on account of their nationality. Among those enlisted in the East African Prison Guard was Eddie Ruben who, at sixteen, was too young even though he had volunteered. The detention barracks was behind Nairobi Club and the other internees besides Mayer were Dr and Mrs Konrad Schauer from the Kijabe Hill Health Resort whom Mervyn Ray, a Naivasha sheep farmer, had arrested and brought in and Markus and Loy who were Austrians and therefore now regarded as enemies.[21] As Markus was Austro-Hungarian consul he had Diplomatic Immunity and was sent home to Austria, whereas Loy was interned in India with most of the others in 1916 and was not released until 1921.[22] After the POWs were shipped to India, Ruben joined the Loyal North Lancashire Regiment and under colonial conditions of service, by the age of seventeen had his own batman, free lime juice and a half bottle of whisky per day and excellent pay.[23]

The Nairobi Racecourse was hurriedly changed into a transport depot and became the headquarters of the Carrier Corps. Recruits without accommodation slept in the jockey's weighing room overnight and in the morning, khaki tunics, shorts, spine-pads and large sun helmets, as issued to British troops serving in the tropics, were allocated.

'Training' started as soon as they had been kitted out but was really a question of priorities in the dilemma of who knew what to teach whom. In the Transport Corps, for example, young men were shown a herd of oxen, told to inspan them and make up teams with a gang of Africans on one side and a line of wagons on the other. The Nandi with whom they were expected to work, though pastoral, had never worked oxen before, nor could they speak Swahili. To make them understand what was wanted was not easy. The oxen were a mixed lot and some had never been yoked let alone trained. Luckily the South Africans helped out. They referred to the English as 'the

---

* The area known as Kariokor in Nairobi today takes its name from this unit and came about in the First World War.

bloody *ruineks*', a term left over from the Boer War because the British complexion reddened so fiercely under the African sun.[24]

The first real fight took place on 4 September at Taveta, a post which had been regarded as untenable by the British earlier and abandoned. A small German force took it over and advanced through the waterless scrub towards the railway but a mounted Nubian company of the KAR intercepted and forced it to retreat.[25]

With this the EAMR left for the front but beforehand paraded in front of Sir Henry Belfield in full dress. Elspeth Huxley observed that when the Governor and Commander-in-Chief inspected the regiment it was, 'hard to know whether he or his troops excelled in unconventionality of military dress.' He took the salute in a Norfolk shooting jacket, a pair of cycling breeches and a white helmet. With three cheers for the Governor the troops set off for the station singing to the tune 'Marching through Georgia'. They entrained for Kajiado and marched for the border. Base camp was set up at Bissel and scouting parties were sent into the bush towards German territory. As yet no proper transport had been organised and no supplies of food, they shot game, preparing it as best they could, thanks to those old hands who had thought to bring billy cans and suferias with them.[26]

Since the Colonial Office and not the War Office was still responsible for the defence of the Protectorate, Sir Henry Belfield appealed to them for assistance. In response, a request was made to India to provide forces to capture Dar-es-Salaam by sea and reinforce those on land in East Africa. But long before help could be sent, *Astrea* and *Pegasus* had opened fire on Dar-es-Salaam and Dr Heinrich Schnee responded by hoisting a white flag. A truce was made with the Germans with the proviso that they refrain from hostile acts during the war. A similar encounter followed at Tanga on 17 August; another truce was made on the understanding that the German police in the town should not number more than fifty. When the British Government refused to ratify either agreement, Schnee concluded that it would be wiser in future to allow his Commander-in-Chief to conduct the war in East Africa as he saw fit.[27]

General Paul von Lettow Vorbeck began his campaign by moving his headquarters into the Kilimanjaro area and entrenched himself on Longido Mountain. Both armies were faced with impenetrable bush conditions but Lettow Vorbeck's strength lay in the fact that the British had to protect their railway. This meant that they had to cross the parched country separating the two forces and he knew that they had no hope of patrolling or protecting the entire line, nor could they intercept all the attacks launched against it. His main objective, therefore, was to keep the German force intact so that they represented a constant threat to the British.

The first Indian reinforcements reached Mombasa by September when the Punjabis and Kapurthalas joined the EAMR on the border. Though there were heavy demands made upon India in various theatres of war, preparations were made also for a second, larger force to attack Dar-es-Salaam.

However, due to Lettow Vorbeck's activities further north, these were modified. Tanga was attacked instead on 4 November, the purpose being to see that the outlet of the Usumbura railway fell into British hands whilst a land force advanced at the same time on the western slopes of Kilimanjaro from the rear. Both manoeuvres failed. On 2 November two columns attempted to dislodge the Germans by advancing on Longido Mountain from either side while Bowker's Horse attempted to cut off retreat from behind.[28] Captain F. O'B. Wilson, whose scouts won acclaim for their courage and efficiency, rolled boulders on to the German camp only to discover that they were attacking their own transport corps men on their way up, so dense was the bush.[29] The curious thing is that by the end of 1916 the EAMR might have been a phantom army. It had dwindled to a major, a sergeant and two troopers but it never disbanded. When the war was over there were no records or lists of any sort as proof of its existence and when F. O'B. Wilson received his DSO in London, he had no proper uniform either and had to make one up at Gieves. He arrived for the ceremony looking like a cross between a Mountie and a Cossack. The only recognition of the EAMR that survives is a list of names carved on the cavalry war memorial in Hyde Park among the Lancers and Hussars.[30]

There were hundreds involved in the first 'scraps' with the enemy at Ngito and Longido and on 6 November the list of deaths and casualties reached Nairobi. Those left behind realised now that the war was no lark. Alex Davis wrote of the consternation, the anger, the hot unreasonable anger after news was received from Longido with the names of the first to fall, among whom were Ronald Tompson, whose brother Alan was later killed in France, F. Sandbach Baker, Alton Forrester, Lionel, Leslie Tarlton's eighteen year old son, Drummond, Smith and 'others unknown'. Thereafter too the collection of mail, which had been a pleasure, was now a task filled with dread as news trickled through of those killed in France.[31]

War dominated all thought and conversation, but those settlers not directly involved did their best to go about their normal routine. Many were women but they all did their bit, even newcomers like Elspeth Huxley's mother, Nellie Grant. In April with the guidance of Charles Taylor, the Kitisuru coffee farmer, she had planted out 33,000 coffee seedlings. By December when her husband Joss rejoined his regiment in England, she alone was responsible for their welfare. She knew nothing about coffee but her future depended on the survival of those fragile plants.[32] Like hundreds of other women she made the best of things. The luckiest soldiers were those whose wives kept the farms going but where there were none the *neaparas* or native headmen coped as best they could.

Some women opened their houses to men recovering from wounds and illness, others like Nancy Rutherfurd, who drove a Red Cross ambulance pulled by oxen, nursed the wounded out in the bush.[33] Lady McMillan and her black companion, Louise Decker, the daughter of a slave in America, ran Chiromo as a nursing home for officers and arranged fund-raising fêtes just like the women in Europe. Lady McMillan organised the Woman's War Work League to make bandages, sheets and curtains out of *americani* for the camp hospitals which had no comforts of any sort. Later as the numbers of wounded filled the tents of Nairobi's military hospital they took turns at visiting.[34] The spinster, Cara Buxton, quite used to farming alone at Lumbwa, now rode hundreds of miles through the bush by herself to oversee the farms of absent men, her saddlebags weighed down with cents to pay out their labour each month. Her mission resembled the painting of the Forth Bridge for no sooner had she completed her rounds than it was time to set out again, so great were the distances she covered.[35] The experience brought these women new responsibility and they found that their activity on the farms became an extension of their whole being. Never again would they sit by and watch the men run their farms. May Stocker, who eventually ran a 4,000-acre farm with two hundred labour to organise and control, far from regretting her involvement, relished the fact that she lived a life that ordinarily only a man would lead.[36]

Delamere patrolled the Kajiado border until January 1915. His bases amounted to a chain of trading stores at which the Maasai scouts reported their information. At first it was forwarded to Nairobi either by runner or carrier pigeon. Then Bror von Blixen was commissioned by Head of Intelligence, Captain Woosenam, to arrange communications between Nairobi and Delamere. Nils Fjastad, Ture Rundgren and two other Swedes formed Blixen's team, riding Harley-Davidson motor-cycles on the worst roads. In the bush runners were used.

Before Delamere had returned in May he had been warned in London not to forget to treat himself as a convalescent. By November he was spending anything up to twelve hours a day in the saddle. At night he had not even the comfort of a fire for warmth or to ward off animals lest it gave away his whereabouts. He lived off maize meal and chocolate and was continually on the move. He fell sick first with dysentery, malaria followed.[37] Huge doses of quinine were taken to keep it at bay and how it did not develop into blackwater fever is a miracle.

With her husband's involvement, Karen Blixen found herself unexpectedly in charge of an ox-wagon expedition to Kajiado. At his request she had employed a young South African, one of Herman Klapprott's sons from Kiambu, to go with the wagons to Delamere. Klapprott was arrested on suspicion of being German when he failed to produce the correct papers of identification and Baroness Blixen took over the convoy. Unfortunately the incident added ballast to the impression that she was pro-German. It was on this occasion that she courageously beat off two lionesses with her stock-whip.

Not long afterwards, Delamere was running to get to an observation post in the midday sun and collapsed. Malaria got the upper hand. He returned to Soysambu by ox-cart with the added complication of a strained heart. His manager was so alarmed at the look of him that he called in the dreaded Dr

Burkitt, who pumped alternate doses of arsenic and distilled water into a vein in Delamere's arm. It was hardly a reassuring exercise. Burkitt got the manager to stand on a chair pouring two quarts of the mixture, cup by cup into Delamere's arm as he pumped it in the old-fashioned manner. Every so often Burkitt warned, 'Don't let in a drop of air, or ye'll kill the man!' Delamere was moved to the Scott Sanatorium in Nairobi, where once more, he conducted affairs from his bed.[38]

Early in 1915, while the soldiers in Europe froze in the trenches, at Voi they sweltered and eked out their paraffin ration. General Phillips, based there for three months, had three of his Indian soldiers taken by lion in the Tsavo River. His unit forced the Germans back from Tsavo via Kasigau but it cost him dearly in lives. Out of nine hundred and twenty soldiers, all but one hundred and seventy men were casualties, including himself. Paraffin for lamps was so short that General Phillips buried a *debe* of it in case of emergency: it lies there to this day.[39] Block's use of his paraffin ration in the early part of the campaign was fairly unique. And, where thousands of horses and mules fell prey to horse-sickness and Tsetse fly, was a simple enough precaution but an effective one. Paraffin was dished out only in the evenings but rather than use it for his lamp, Block soaked rags in it so as to rub his pony down night and morning which acted as a repellent to Tsetse fly, prevented it from being bitten, and as a result was one of the last men to remain mounted in his unit.[40]

At the beginning of 1915 appeals had gone out for more volunteers. The terms were limited to two months training and two months active service. These new recruits had a more arduous time in a sense than the first batch because they were equipped with new uniforms and saddlery. There were double the number of horses to men, so they rode one animal and led another to get replenishments to Bissel, twenty miles beyond Kajiado. The friction of the stiff leather against the men's limbs was so damaging that without exception, they needed two days' sick leave when they arrived.[41]

At Bissel, Colonel Swinton-Home put them through riding school—a rectangle, the size of three tennis courts hacked out of the bush. He reckoned that the quality of their riding equalled their variety of dress. His end-of-course speech was without hope, 'Gentlemen, I have now to pass you out of riding school but I don't want you to imagine you can ride. Some of you won't learn to ride before the end of the war.' He was right, but largely because there were no horses left by then.[42]

As soon as war had been declared, home prices rose. When Paice sent to the *duka* on the morning of 5 August for mealie meal and provisions, the Indian sent back a note informing him that he was raising prices 5% and wanted cash from now on. By the time Paice reached the store after lunch, costs had gone up by another 5%. By 19 August at Naivasha, storekeepers were charging as much as 50% more on every item, including petrol. Instructions were issued by the Governor that no-one was to sell items over 15% above ordinary prices but even as early as this the shortage of wheat flour meant that bakers were mixing mealie maize with wheat flour to make bread. By November all mules had been commandeered for service, so that anyone trying to run a farm was severely handicapped. Mobility was also cut to frustrating proportions. Police checked the Naivasha farms to ensure that animals had not been withheld.[43]

At the beginning of June 1915 Block was summoned from Taveta to Nairobi, where his daughter Rita was born.[44] Nairobi swarmed with Indian officers and troops. Decorated with tabs of every hue, filled with their own importance, they dominated the New Stanley Hotel, the Norfolk and the clubs, grumbling over the absence of pukka golf, polo, sahibs, bearers and everything else that was back in India. Before long most of them were suffering from acute bacillary dysentery. There were so many cases that at the Carrier Corps Hospital where Burkitt presided the pharmacy ran out of ingredients for its cure—Epsom salts and castor oil. In looking for a suitable alternative, Burkitt thought to try out rhubarb powder and the effect was miraculous. The death rate dropped to almost negligible figures and every case that was treated early enough at the Carrier Corps Hospital made a rapid recovery.[45]

With the arrival of these Indian troops there was much dissatisfaction over the question of volunteers. On 7 September those who were not out fighting gathered at the Theatre Royal in Nairobi from all over the country in the largest meeting to date. They were convinced that the Government was unequal to the first real emergency that it had been called upon to handle. Their trump card was well-worn but still powerful enough to have an effect. If they were expected to volunteer, they reasoned, then they must have some say in the running of the country. The old cry went up, 'No taxation without representation.'[46]

They had the Governor where they wanted him. How could Belfield impose such a measure as conscription* unless he had the settlers goodwill? Then Grogan stepped onto the platform. His talent for timing and public speaking roused his audience to cheering pitch. In a recruiting speech in which he started off by calling those who had not joined up 'rabbits' he urged all who were men to take up arms. (He himself worked for Intelligence.) The response was a triumph. Belfield was asked to prepare for conscription without delay and a War Council was formed by the Government the next day. When the settlers asked if they might elect representatives, Belfield disarmed them by consenting. Ill wind though the war was, in this situation, settlers were granted electoral privileges for the first time. The War Council was only advisory but Belfield bowed to its significance and on no important issue did he by-pass it. In terms of diplomacy, this was tact personified and altered the whole attitude of the European towards the Government. Resources were to be catalogued and inventories taken of crops, cattle and

---

* In fact British East Africa was the first country in the Empire to legalise conscription; it was passed into the law in March 1916.

buildings. Certificates were to be issued to those in the indispensable class and the rest were required to enlist. [47]

From 1915 to 1916 the campaign in East Africa resolved itself into a pattern of guerrilla warfare. There were confused stories of defeats and counter-defeats at Voi, of Smuts's brilliant dash in GEA and of the arrival of British troops. [48] Those based at Bissel staved off boredom in off-duty hours with football and boxing matches while Spencer Tryon, believing that the best thing for the inside of a man was the outside of a horse, tried to improve the standard of riding of anyone interested in off-duty hours. [49]

As the Germans continued to raid into British territory, there was a period when neither side gained much which was broken only by two significant actions brought about not on land, but by the naval forces. Before August 1914, the Germans only had one tug, the *Muansa*, a forty-ton vessel, on Lake Victoria whereas the British had nine small steamers, which maintained a passenger and goods service between the terminal of the Uganda Railway at Kisumu and the principal ports on the lake. Two weeks after the declaration of war, the British learned that the *Muansa* was being armed. It was then they decided to mount the only available gun, a saluting piece at Kisumu, on board the s.s. *William MacKinnon*. By January, five of these nine ships were organised into a naval flotilla and throughout 1915 bombarded a number of posts on the enemy shore. Its most important action was a large-scale raid carried out on Bukoba in June when the British occupied the wireless station, destroying it and the fort before re-embarking. If nothing else, it helped to sustain the morale of the British at a time when successes were few and far between against the Germans on land in the Kilimanjaro area.

The next encouraging news for the British, after the Bukoba raid, came from the Indian Ocean when, on 11 July, the German cruiser, *Konigsberg* was badly damaged in the Rufiji River. This blow to the enemy was a real morale booster, for since September 1914 when the Germans had sunk the *Pegasus*, the *Konigsberg* had eluded them. Even so, before the Germans abandoned and blew up the *Konigsberg* themselves, they managed to salvage ten 4.1-in guns and two 3.5-in guns. With these, the crew made for Lettow Vorbeck and, despite the unsuitability of the guns for rapid movement, proved of great value to the German forces in the subsequent campaigns.

That November, the East Africa Force came into existence, embracing all troops, African, Indian and British already in East and Central Africa together with further companies to be raised from South Africa. Military preparations for the big advance on the enemy had now been made. An extension of the railway had been pushed forward from Voi towards Taveta and the road from Longido to Nairobi had been put in order, enabling the troops to skirt the western slopes of Kilimanjaro more easily. [50] Since neither Botha nor Smuts was available, owing to political problems in the Cape, the honour of commanding the troops fell to General Sir Horace Smith-Dorrien, a man who had won his reputation in the Boer War. He had invited Delamere (now in England because of a strained heart), to join his staff. The doctors however had advised Delamere that he must not in future remain in BEA for longer than three months at a time, and Delamere had to refuse. Then the General himself became severely ill by the time he reached the Cape and was replaced by Lieutenant-General Smuts.[51]

Smuts landed at Mombasa on 19 February. His immediate plan was to defeat Lettow Vorbeck's forces in the Kilimanjaro area before the rains arrived. The South African battalions had mixed feelings about Smuts's appointment; the English South Africans did not share the enthusiasm of the Boers and the remaining force knew little of his capabilities as a military man though he was well known for his political achievements. Smuts needed to secure an important victory if he was to win the confidence of the 114,000 men now placed under him.[52]

Assisted by the Dutch General, Van Deventer, he re-shuffled the officers and mobilised the country. The Generals and other high officers from India were sacked as soon as Smuts found that they had made no contribution towards victory. He decided that his main force must attack Taveta to advance round the eastern slopes of Kilimanjaro. Meanwhile a large outflanking force tried to push forward from Longido round the western side effectively cutting off the Germans' retreat.

The advance of the main force met heavy resistance but by March the Germans were on the retreat. In May, Brigadier-General E. Northey, who succeeded Belfield as Governor after the war, advanced into German territory with his forces on the Rhodesia and Nyasaland front to occupy the German frontier posts. Meanwhile Smuts's offensive had started from Longido. Taveta was captured by March and Moshi fell next. The enemy was forced to withdraw as the Second Division, under Van Deventer's command, stretched out like one of the prehensile limbs of a gigantic octopus, reached one hundred-and-fifty miles south of Moshi in an attempt to cut Lettow Vorbeck off; but he rallied his forces at Kahe to withdraw again across the Pangani River and as he backed off to Kondoa-Irangi, 140 miles south of Moshi, Van Deventer followed. But the British could not move fast enough: Smuts was finally sabotaged by the land.

Francis Brett Young, the author of *Marching on Tanga*, believed that exercise to cut Lettow Vorbeck off was unique, that so great a military movement had never been attempted before through the heart of tropical Africa.[53]

When Van Deventer eventually captured Kondoa-Irangi, Lettow Vorbeck, like a Bishop in a game of chess, moved back to Dodoma. The rains then began and were torrential, so that by the time they had taken Kondoa-Irangi, Van Deventer was no longer able to keep in touch with the transport.

Orders came through to advance from Soko Nassai on 23 May 1916. Among local officers under Hoskins were Frank Greswolde Williams, Berkeley Cole, Denys Finch Hatton, 'Tich' Miles, Lord Cranworth and Northrup McMillan, whose enormous size proved such a disability that he had to return to Nairobi. At his own expense he sat up two nursing homes and contributed much else to the War effort for which he was knighted.

At moonrise the columns moved forward in the dark and within three months not only freed the Tanga line of a stubborn enemy but had swept through the heart of savage country and struck again at the central Railway in pursuit of Lettow Vorbeck. The men endured the hardships with great patience. They lacked food and water yet marched day after day beneath a vertical sun and sometimes they marched at night as well. As they tramped the bruised scrub sent up its particular aroma which came from the dusty leaves and tiny purple flowers crushed by the army as they advanced at three miles an hour. For those who travelled near the ambulance carts its scent mingled with iodine and blood. Block recalled that his unit marched without provisions, for sixteen successive days.[54] Moving at a painfully slow rate, the EATC hacked its tortuous way through mile after mile of bush and in its wake left a stinking and bloated trail of dead and dying oxen. Most had been stricken with tsetse fly infection. Of the country through which the men passed, the official historian wrote that, 'The very air seemed to throb with fever and men withered away like parched flowers.'[55]

Just like the coolies who built the railway eighteen years before, the Indian battalions were ill-matched with the African terrain during the war. Jiggers, gangrene, dysentery, lions, rhinos and thirst depleted their energies as before; but now the difference was that they were expected to lead, to cut roads and show Africans what to do. Yet they knew no native language and nothing of the customs of those beside whom they marched and fought.

Meinertzhagen, by now at Intelligence HQ at Old Moshi, had been appalled at their behaviour when they had attempted to take Tanga. Some of the sepoys killed during that early battle were found in rows, with bayonets stuck in their backs indicating that very little resistance had been offered; 800 men were lost, either killed or wounded.

Meinertzhagen's organisation of the Intelligence Service expanded and increased in efficiency and proved of the utmost value. The official history claims that the advance through the unknown and ill-mapped country in the Kilimanjaro area through which the troops were now proceeding would have been impossible without his intelligence group.[56] He had hundreds of agents working for him and during the coming months raised 2,500 African scouts with the help of seven British Officers, among whom were Grogan, Jack Riddell and Freddie Guest, who in peacetime ran his dental practice in Nairobi House. Meinertzhagen badly needed extra horses at one point and for replacements everyone looked to Captain Edmondson of the East African Forces Remount Depot at Nakuru.

Edmondson had some 15,000 horses and 12,000 mules under his care at first, but as the demands for these intensified it was his conviction that part of Lettow Vorbeck's strategy was to lead the British through as much fly-infested country as possible. He was more than likely right, for the tsetse fly needed riverine forest, dappled sunlight with shade and water in which to breed and the Pangani and Rovuma supplied perfect conditions. The only way to prevent the horses from becoming infected was to stay out of the area in which tsetse flourished and as the British strove to cut off the Germans this was impossible.

Those animals to give the best service in the campaign were 'salted' and came from Abyssinia. If horses had survived sickness there for two to three years they were reckoned immune. Two Greek horse-traders, Cardovalis and Salibrakis, were reputed to supply the best 'salted' animals which they drove down in mobs to sell at Nairobi. So many were needed when war broke out, however, that Colonel R. J. Stordy, the vet, and Edmondson went to negotiate with Emperor Menelik for regular supplies of Abyssinian ponies for the troops. Menelik co-operated and some of the first Abyssinian mounts were paid for by the British in ammunition for Grasse rifles. The next batches were paid for with Maria Theresa dollars on delivery to the gate of the race-course at Nakuru which had been turned into a remount depot.

At the end of 1915 there was such a shortage of horses for the campaign that someone had the bright idea of supplementing these with Walers from Australia. Though everyone wanted one to begin with, they proved very expensive at £30 a head. Compared to the small, wiry country-bred animals they had plenty of bone so that it was assumed that they were more powerful. But their looks were deceptive. The troops quickly discovered that these had no immunity to horse-sickness, lymphangitis or tsetse and most did not even survive six weeks in the bush.[57]

Those with the Animal Transport Corps now had to deal with the prodigious number of dying mules whose average working life was no more than six weeks. When they became so thin that they could barely carry a load, they were shot. If they died in camp, the carcases had to be burned. In daylight these were dragged some distance from camp and when those in charge went to light the fire, they invariably found that all the rumps had been cut off for steaks. The men were desperately short of food. At times the African porters had to carry on in the most appalling conditions, night or day, wet or fine, food or no food and 44,000 died on active service mostly from dysentery, malaria and exposure.[58]

During the first years of the war the production powers of German East Africa suffered very little, but their troops stationed in the Kilimanjaro area made heavy demands on supplies while external trade stood still. Then, as the British began their positive advance in 1916, the enemy's administrative system began to crumble away. The retreating army left stocks of rubber, sisal, cotton and coffee which fell into British hands as they advanced. With the news that the Germans were still in Same with Hannyngton and the Second Brigade at their heels, the British had reached the moment at which Smuts had expected the Germans to retire altogether. How wrong he was. Nor had Lettow Vorbeck any intention of being drawn into decisive battle. As Hannyngton's heliograph flashed the German's departure from Same it was clear that Smuts's strategy had failed. Now a race between the enemy sides began.[59]

The Carrier Corps were by now suffering badly; without their essential services, the army could not move a yard. The whys and wherefores of the white men's campaign were not their concern, no matter how much the officers appreciated these lowly but vital men. Alfred Johansen worked alongside them and felt that if any particular unit could be said to have won the war against the Germans in German East Africa, it was this one, who with a minimum of food and clothing were called to do the well nigh impossible and were at the beck and call of every unit. Wherever other forms of transport failed, the porters were sent for especially now that the animals were seriously depleted.

The wretched oxen had become thinner and thinner and were having to be driven until they dropped. As for the army itself, those strenuous marches had brought out a lot of malaria. At first the sick were evacuated successfully and the field ambulances gave the worst cases a lift on the mule wagons. But the mosquito nets carried by the men were not used by those on picket at night, for instance, when they needed them more than those sleeping in the tents. The number of new cases at this point was formidable; the mule-wagons were overcrowded with malarial soldiers. Doctors checked their quinine stock. If regular prophylactic doses were to be issued, they would have to tap their reserves and this risk was too great to take. The army was striving against time and communications and the sick had to be left to fend for themselves.[60]

Nevertheless, Tanga fell in July followed by Dar-es-Salaam at the beginning of September, a victory which was extremely important to the British as not only was it the terminus of the Central Railway but the seat of civil government. Smuts still hoped for a final decisive engagement with Lettow Vorbeck. He was now hemmed in from all sides and had less than 2,000 white troops and some 14,000 Africans left. Smut's other advantage was that when the Belgians captured Tabora, they acquired German rolling stock, some of which was handed over to the British in return for spare parts which were needed desperately to get it moving once more.[61]

Another frontal attack was planned but after heavy fighting Lettow Vorbeck once more extricated his forces and throughout 1917 the Germans were still playing hide and seek with the British. In the New Year they crossed the Rufiji but the campaign of which Smuts had dreamed was still to be fought when in January 1917 he handed over command to General Hoskins, his Chief of Staff.

All those stationed in Dar-es-Salaam or Morogoro seem to have suffered from malaria in varying degrees and, just after Dar-es-Salaam had fallen to the British and Block had heard of the birth of his first son, Jack, on 28 September he came down with a particularly bad bout.[62] The Cape-coloured men died like flies from it but the Swahilis seemed to fight it off with a spiritual resistance that the South Africans lacked. There were so many cases that a transit camp at Iringa for those returning from or going on leave now gradually filled with black and white men recuperating from it. At Dodoma Hospital, which was manned very efficiently by the Royal Army Medical Corps, the malarial cure was a very light diet interspersed with doses of Epsom Salts and liquid quinine, which was administered after each meal. The taste of the sticky syrup tainted the mouth and remained on the tongue constantly after a fortnight of treatment. For men in the field there were daily doses of thirty grains of quinine but they did not prevent many contracting it.[63] Block's malaria developed into blackwater fever and he believed that only his will to live pulled him through a sickness which then had a 90% mortality rate.[64]

Men could be riddled with malaria for years, suffering its chills and fevers and nightmares periodically, and it might go no further. But once the urine has turned black, (hence its name) the chances were minimal. Fewer women suffered from the disease and it is now thought that the reason for this was because they tended to take small but regular doses of quinine whereas men did not bother usually until malaria threatened and then consumed massive quantities. The quinine affected the kidneys and damaged them fatally. In support of this modern theory about over-dosage is the fact that once Atabrine took the place of quinine in 1943, blackwater disappeared.[65]

When Block was well enough to travel he was transferred by Red Cross ship from Dar-es-Salaam to Mombasa. The voyage, though only two days, was horrific. European patients were allocated to the top deck whilst hundreds of sick Africans lay on the lower deck packed against one another like tinned anchovies. All were suffering from dysentery and malaria and, being unaccustomed to sea travel as well, vomited copiously throughout the journey.[66]

At Mombasa there was no organisation, probably because the number of sick requiring attention was so great. Block lay on a stretcher for two hours without shade or water before being carried to Mombasa hospital. Next he contracted dysentery and attributed the devoted nursing of Lady Duff for the sole reason that he survived. After a month he was sent to the Military Hospital in Nairobi on a Red Cross train.[67] It was largely thanks to Dr Burkitt and Tom Bell, who worked for Michael Harrtz, that Block was moved up-country in 1917. Mrs Harrtz and Sarah Block were by now close friends and after Burkitt had discovered Block's whereabouts Tom Bell organised his transfer. Sarah was shocked at the sight of 'Pops' as she now called him as he was carried along the platform on a stretcher; she had not known he was so ill nor realised that blackwater could make a man look so frail, so emaciated.[68]

The Military Hospital then was under canvas, the tents pitched on the outer slopes of the Hill beyond Nairobi Cemetery. So numerous were the sick and wounded that it stretched back towards the Athi Plains as far as the site of the Belleview Cinema today.

When lessons were over in the afternoon, the boys and girls from Nairobi

School on the Hill, among whom were the younger McQueen children, toured the beds with trays of sweets and cigarettes for the troops. Each time a soldier died, the Last Post was sounded. One child can remember sobbing whenever the strains of the mournful tune drifted up to the classrooms of the 'big' school where the smell of chalk dust mingled with the scent of frangi-pani flowers in the school garden.

It was known originally as 'the little school' and was opened by the Uganda Railway for day pupils but in April 1907 the Government had taken it over. By now boys and girls could board. It was run by A. J. Turner and his wife. Throughout the war, whenever a Red train was due the Turners marched the entire school to the station to sing for the soldiers as they were off-loaded. On these occasions the pupils dressed up almost as if for a party. The girls wore white *broderie anglais* frocks with thick blue sashes tied below the waist in a bow.[69]

Ainsworth's house* was turned into hospital for the wounded. Dr Victor Gurner Logan van Someren, who had arrived in 1912 as a Medical Officer, worked from here and became Government Dental Officer, a post which he held until it was abolished in 1928. For years he presented a quaint sight when his duties took him up-country and his red plush dental chair, treadle drill and other instruments of dental torture entered the bomas of Fort Hall or Nyeri on an ox-wagon with a dusty plume in its wake.[70]

The war had its odder moments. There were the carrier pigeons which were supposed to save time when Delamere was ordering supplies for the border. The poor things were attacked by hawks, two arriving completely plucked on one occasion. In the end, all of them died on active service and were replaced by heliograph stations.[71]

Then there was the Indian station-master at Voi who telegraphed railway headquarters in Nairobi in a panic with the message, '300 Germans approaching railway line. Send rifle and 300 rounds ammunition. Urgent.' The censors had their fun too. When a soldier wrote home that he had shot three lions before breakfast, the censor, knowing it to be quite false, added a 3, making it 33.[72]

For some, like Mohamed Ahmed who founded Ahmed's of Nairobi, the war was a turning point on the road to success. Mohamed Ahmed was the black sheep of his family and, at the age of ten, had been kicked out of India by his father for stealing from his mother's purse. Ahmed's father had one contact in Mombasa through whom his son might obtain work and this man sent the child to Nairobi to work for Nathoo, the tent-maker. For 50 rupees a year and all found, he helped to look after Nathoo's many children. He lived in a tiny room at the back of the shop in the bazaar and also learned to make tents. When he was fourteen he took a job as an apprentice with Beimer of Hutchings and Beimer, who taught him to make mattresses.

---

* Ainsworth's house was demolished but today the Ford Foundation Lecture Hall in the National Museum complex, stands on the original site. Van Someren's red plush dental chair can be seen at the Museum.

When the War began, Mohamed Ahmed learned that a unit stationed at Voi needed tents and in the hope of obtaining this work, he went by train to Voi to tender for the contract. However the unit had moved twenty-five miles away, so he walked through the bush to find them. The officer in charge was so impressed with the young Indian's courage and determination, for Asians were not renowned in BEA for such behaviour, that he gave Ahmed the contract. The order was duly delivered but by a slip-up in military administration Ahmed was paid twice. Not quite knowing what to do about this he consulted J. J. Toogood at the Standard Bank for advice. As Toogood knew the Commandant personally he undertook to sort the matter out. Ahmed's honesty more than paid off when the Commandant insisted that he keep the extra money and awarded him another contract, enabling him to set up his own business in the bazaar. He became one of the chief suppliers to the military and was already on his feet financially by the time the war ended.[73]

Early in 1917 a demand by the military for three hundred more Europeans virtually stripped the Protectorate of almost all its remaining farmers, managers and commercial men. Delamere was appalled. What concerned him most now was the country's prospects after the war. 'I know of no country,' he protested, 'where it has been thought a wise policy to leave farms lying without occupants, especially at a time when the supply of foodstuffs and raw materials is one of the gravest problems.'

In 1916 he had struggled without help at Soysambu looking after 1,800 cattle and 23,000 sheep. They had to be sheared, dosed, marked and counted and then he was unable to ship the wool. From June he tried supplying the army with meat but his sheep were dying from the tick-borne disease, heartwater, at such a rate that he was forced instead to slaughter game for the troops. At one point he dispatched 1,200 carcases of Thomson's gazelle in a fortnight. In 1917 the mortality rate of lambs from heartwater reached 25% and it was discovered that it could only be prevented by dipping.

How, in 1917, Delamere weakened as he was, found the time or energy is extraordinary. (That lambing season, 9,000 ewes were expected to give birth and this was followed by three months of calving.) He managed also to tour the country with the Economic Commission which Belfield had appointed in March to take stock of the Protectorate's assets so that suggestions for a post-war economic policy could be formulated.[74]

Lettow Vorbeck had ruthlessly cut his forces to the minimum. Employing great ingenuity with food, medical supplies and clothing, he managed to keep his main force on its feet. Soap was made from quillaia bark. Quinine, just as vital to the Germans as to the British, was acquired by boiling Peruvian or cinchona bark, of which he had adequate supplies. This repellent liquid was known as 'Lettow's Schnapps'. After Tabora was overrun and the Germans were cut off from the mint, they used brass and copper currency made from cartridge cases. Bandages were also fashioned from bark and bread was made out of any grain they could lay their hands on and mixed with boiled rice. They even experimented with shoe-making after capturing hundreds of

British saddles. Boots were patched up with leather from these.[75] With such tactics and the elusiveness of the Scarlet Pimpernel, Lettow Vorbeck continued to foil his enemies until after peace was declared.

Hoskins ordered the expansion of the KAR, increasing the army from thirteen to twenty-two battalions. These seven regiments nevertheless faced deplorable conditions. With a force of 24,000 men by May he felt that he was in a superior position and was preparing to bring the campaign to an end. The Germans were lumped together at the south-east corner of the colony and so long as the armies pressed forward north, east and west, could no longer escape. But, like his predecessors, Hoskins had underestimated Lettow Vorbeck's stamina. He had no intention of quitting yet and had already cast his eye over Portuguese Territory south of the Rovuma. Having rebuilt the army, Hoskins had to content himself with that for success. As suddenly as he had taken over from Smuts, he was relieved as Commander-in-Chief by Van Deventer. He was to be the sixth General to try to beat the one-eyed German General.[76]

From June, under Van Deventer, the twofold advance from Kilwa and Lindi pushed boldly on but casualties were heavy. Aircraft were brought in to bomb and to observe enemy movement, but Lettow Vorbeck's nerve held as British persistence pushed Lettow Vorbeck's advance guard over the Rovuma and on to Purtuguese soil. A final advance from north, east and west was made on New Year's Day 1918 but the pursuit continued southward. The final battle of the campaign lasted four days and was not fought until October. Out of 4,000 infantry in this engagement, 2,700 sustained injuries and the British were forced to withdraw. Then on 11 November 1918, Lettow Vorbeck, with the remnants of his Schutztruppe, reached Northern Rhodesia. They did not actually hear of the Armistice or of Germany's defeat until two days later, when they captured a dispatch rider who was carrying instructions for the arrangement of an immediate ceasefire.[77]

As a personal mark of respect from one gallant soldier to another, General Van Deventer allowed all Europeans in the Schutztruppe to retain their weapons, in recognition of the incredible fight they had put up. It cannot have been easy for Lettow Vorbeck to order his men to march to their captors. On his return to Germany he was regarded as a national hero. Although he was not a victor, he had achieved his main object. With a relatively small fighting force his presence had occupied a great many Indian, South African, Belgian and British troops for more than forty-eight months.[78]

In 1919, through the peace conference, German East Africa became British Territory and was renamed Tanganyika. It had been paid for with what now seems an utterly pointless loss of 50,000[79] lives the greater part of which were African.

CHAPTER 13

❦

Pioneers! O Pioneers!

The African Race is an Indiarubber ball. The harder you
dash it to the ground the higher it will rise.

Bantu proverb

The armistice can be seen, in retrospect, as a turning point in British East
African Colonial history. After the victory bonfires, balls and parades came
the stark period of assessment and readjustment.

The Africans, having observed white people at war with one another,
could no longer sustain the awe with which they had regarded them before.
For them, the war was a bitter experience. They were called upon to pay high
taxes, to provide stock for slaughter and to act as porters to support the
troops. Though the number of white deaths was negligible by comparison,
the high proportion of settlers who had engaged in the war felt no less bitter.
As they shed their uniforms and returned home they were faced with
properties and businesses that were neglected, and in many cases only just
short of ruin.

Farmers had the worst tasks. They found machinery that had rusted,
buildings that were derelict, the loss of fencing and animals and, where there
had been cultivation four years before, much had reverted to bush. Almost
everyone had to begin again from scratch but where there had been capital
before, now there was none.

Yet in the wake of war, peace brings hope. The settlers picked up the
threads of their lives once more and if anything their commitment was even
stronger than before they had fought for their country of adoption. Furthermore that commitment had vested in them the certainty that self-
government was near. As the pioneers toiled over their weed-filled *shambas*
and attempted to breed up new herds, the Protectorate was emerging from its
pioneer phase into a new era in which more clearly defined political directives
were required.

The difficulties facing the new Governor, Sir Edward Northey, were
immense when he arrived in February 1919. Elspeth Huxley believes that the

situation with which he coped has never been fully appreciated to this day. Yet through his phenomenal reconstruction he put the Colony on a sound financial footing and during his office made a number of significant steps of lasting importance. Things could hardly have been worse for the rains had failed that year and a severe famine laid waste the land, the worst since 1898. Many died of starvation in the Reserves. All grazing was demolished by game as well as domestic livestock. Zebras frequently wandered into the grounds of Government House looking for pasture and lions followed them. Then came the Spanish influenza which killed hundreds.[1]

Without these complications, conditions were difficult enough compared to those before the war. One of the worst blows to affect the economy was delivered in March 1917 when Britain had listed coffee as a prohibited import.

Between 1909 and 1911 the annual production of high-grade Kenya Coffee beans had risen from 422 tons to almost double. Just before 1914 the annual export figure stood at £18,000.[2] In prohibiting its import Britain, as the mother country, was effectively strangling her own child. Coffee began to pile up and now thousands of tons were lying in inadequate stores.

Coffee was not the only crop to lie on the shelf during the war; flax, sisal and wool as well as other locally unconsumable crops were affected by similar decisions. Between 1914 and 1918 the ratio of shipping for BEA had been exceedingly low. An appeal had been made for more in 1917 but the Imperial Controller decided that Kenya cargo was to be confined to maize, ground-nuts, copra, hides and wattle-bark. The War Council pointed out that, apart from hides, none was available for export. Not unreasonably they asked that coffee, sisal and flax, all vital crops for the life and development of BEA, should be allowed instead.[3]

Flax, as has already been seen, was a disaster story in itself. But sisal had matured faster in Kenya than the Central American variety and in 1914 fetched £20 per ton or more on the London market. And with 7,200 acres under cultivation in 1914 the political unrest in the Caribbean worked in favour of the Protectorate and both demand and price increased. In the next decade overseas markets paid £500,000 annually for Kenya's export crops.[4]

In response to the request that these important crops should be considered, in 1917 the Imperial Controller granted a concession of 500 tons per steamer bound for the United Kingdom.

Import problems were just as acute as those of export. No implements or spare parts were obtainable for machinery needed to process the three most vital exports, sisal, coffee and flax. There were no new ploughs, tractors or vehicles.[5] The few who made money out of the thousands of soldiers brought in to fight were the shop-keepers and hoteliers. The Norfolk Hotel was a favourite spot for officers and reaped a rich harvest from the money spent by the War Office and the troops. And the New Stanley did so well that the Tates retired to London until 1932 leaving Albert Waterman and his wife to manage it.[6]

But those to prosper from war were in the minority. When Markus and Loy, for example, returned in 1923 they had to begin all over again and, worse, had to compete against their own creation, their old business now trading as the African Mercantile Company. It took them years but they re-established themselves as The Old East African Trading Company which in 1949, Markus sold to the East Asiatic Company of Copenhagen, a powerful trading consortium with worldwide connections.[7] Like most old timers they loved to talk about their early foot safaris and the characters they had known such as Paul Clarke who had a grand piano carried from the coast to Lake Victoria. There it was loaded onto a sailing craft of sorts but overturned as it reached the far shore of the lake. Undeterred in his purpose, Clarke and the crew took refuge on the piano and, sitting on it, rowed themselves to safety.[8]

Another unsettling fact in 1918 was that the settlers had only had an Acting Governor, Sir Charles Bowering, in residence. The very nature of his temporary position did not instil confidence when it was most needed. Problems were further generated by drastic shortages of all basic commodities needed to redress the affects of the last four years.[9] Fifteen years of hard work were wiped out in a third of the time it had taken to build up the foundations of a decent living. With still only one tiny pier at Kilindini to serve the entire country and Uganda, the Civil Service understaffed and poorly paid, the local market negligible, drought and famine were added to already unstable conditions. Each individual had a different story to tell of straitened circumstances. Odin Sunde the Norwegian who was running a saw-mill on Mount Elgon, was so poor that he and his family lived of posho and when they ran out of money altogether his wife tore her sheets in strips to give to each man a *shuka* in lieu wages.[10]

The Convention of Associations had suspended all activity during the war, but the pressure for elective representation in Legislative Council was kept up and by 1916 The Colonial Office had accepted the claim in principle. A report in May 1917 recommended that there should be ten European elected members with Asian interests represented by two Indians to be nominated by the Governor. Africans should be represented by the Chief Native Commissioner and Arabs by the Resident Magistrate in Mombasa.[11]

Shortly after the arrival of General Northey the Government launched a scheme to settle ex-soldiers in BEA, an idea which had been discussed by the War Council as early as 1915. The War Council had recognised that the unsettling effect that the campaign would have on the indigenous population could affect the white man's prestige in the eyes of the black man. Safety, they believed, lay in a hefty influx of white faces.

On 24 February 1919 an Electoral Representation Bill was introduced into the Legislative Council. Only European males of unmixed descent should be allowed to vote, with the single proviso that they must have resided for a complete and continuous year in the territory. The Bill reflected the settlers' own points of view towards the development of a self-governing colony of

Europeans.[12] In April, at a second reading, it was proposed that this be extended to include every British subject possessing reasonable educational qualifications but was defeated by thirteen votes to three. A further amendment aimed at securing the vote for European women was passed, swayed by Northey's casting vote after the Council had divided evenly on the issue. He appointed Delamere and Tommy Wood to the Executive Council to represent the settler and commercial factions respectively and in January 1920 the first election was held.[13]

But although the East Africa Protectorate became Kenya Colony and Protectorate in 1920, any notion harboured by the Europeans of self-government were soon erased.* The 1917 proposals of the Legislative Council Committee had set off a storm of protest, primarily from the Indians who were to be denied the franchise. Until the war the Indians had been quiescent. After it they were no longer prepared to accept discrimination. They struck out boldly in opposition and this resulted in fierce controversy in 1923.[14]

By mid-1919 the Soldier Settlement Scheme was under way, and the selection boards were swamped with applications. By May there were two thousand clamouring to take part. The Nairobi ballot for plots took place in June at the Theatre Royal in Sixth Avenue.

At the Colonial Office a few weeks later the process was repeated in London. In November 1919 the *Garth Castle* sailed from England bringing to Mombasa 1,500 new settlers. They regarded themselves as *Mayflower* people and mainly settled in the Laikipia and Trans Nzoia districts, the Kipkarren block of the Nandi Reserve and around Nanyuki.

In February 1920 the stabilisation of the exchange brought hundreds of individuals, among them Lord Delamere and Karen Blixen, to the verge of bankruptcy.

During the war, world currencies ran amok; some, like the dollar, soared; others like the rouble and Mark were swamped; gold disappeared from circulation and the value of the silver rose so that the silver rupee increased in value too. In Nairobi, legally it stood at 1. 4d but it rose in exchange to 2. 6d. The commercial men were delighted. They costed and sold their goods at 1. 4d, receiving 15 rupees to the £1 sterling after buying at the overseas rate of exchange, 2. 6d—namely 8 rupees to the £1. The Government also framed their taxes at 1. 4d but collected them at 2 shillings. The banks housed rupees at their official value and sold them in exchange at 50% above par. During 1919 the exchange flickered at about 2. 4d. This Alice in Wonderland situation could not last. Farmers and storekeepers almost came to blows.

Delamere as usual had his say: 'It seems to me impossible,' he wrote, 'that any government can destroy old-established contracts made at the rate fixed in the currency Order-in Council.' The subject filled conversation and

---

* The white settlers gained elective representation in 1923 but responsible Government was firmly repudiated by the Colonial Office. In 1924 the first representative for African interests was appointed to Legislative Council by a European Missionary.

column as all kinds of wild remedies were offered. The bankers, as creditors, stood to gain enormously on paper, though in the long run they could not collect their interest if producers were forced into insolvency. Ultimately a decision was sought from the Colonial Office and the men to decide were 4,000 miles from the scene of those their decision would most affect, though Northey, Cranworth, Grogan and Berkeley Cole all tried to prevent what happened.[15] A committee in London decided to make a direct cut, pegging the exchange at 2 shillings and abolishing the rupee.

The unhappy man with a mortgage was in the position where he had borrowed at 1. 4d and had to pay back at 2s. Those who had bought property on terms for £2,000 now owed £3,000. The sellers felt clever now that the buyer's 50% loss was their gain. Anyone with an overdraft of £5,000 went to bed one night knowing what they owed. By breakfast the next morning, they were in debt to the bank to the tune of £7,500.[16] Block heaved a sigh of relief and thanked God that he had no overdraft.[17] As an electrifying outburst of protest was made against those who had done this, the new coins were minted.[18]

Had the rupee been allowed to stabilise itself as it did in India, things might have been different. As it was the changeover from rupee to shilling in 1921 was a crippling blow to the Europeans and also meant that many Africans were left holding useless rupees too. The new shilling was minted larger in order to establish in the African mind that it was equivalent in value to the rupee while cents remained at 100 to the coin. But the African was so flummoxed by this alteration that for the next twenty years many argued the point over whether payment was to be made in new or old cents.[19]

The currency exchange plunged Delamere, among others, into a disastrous situation. His personal liabilities were increased by £20,000 but not only that, he was faced with borrowing an extra £1,600 per annum in order to pay interest on a sum he had never borrowed. In the last ten years of his life, though he married again in 1928, Delamere suffered failing health and the effects of the world recession after the stockmarket crash. Moreover locusts ravaged his pastures and maize before he died. After his funeral in 1931 at Soysambu, his mourners felt that part of an era was buried with him and, undoubtedly they were right for there never was anyone quite like him in the Colony again.[20]

Over the next decade, the clash between the Europeans and the Indians reached its high point. The Indians claimed a common electoral roll and the right to inhabit the Highlands. At one mass meeting Delamere invited Burkitt to speak at the Theatre Royal in favour of the exclusivity of the Highlands on medical terms. Burkitt's summing up comment was as predictably unique as all his views. 'Why even in such a matter of urination the differences in the races is profound. The European male stands to urinate but the female sits while with the Indian it is the other way round.' The meeting dissolved into unrestrained laughter.[21]

Northey was faced with reducing a deficit of £412,000 after devaluation. In

1920 £5,000,000 was raised at 6%, much of which was devoted to the construction of still uneconomic branch railways in the Highlands. These had been planned in a phase of excessive optimism, based on higher prices realised for exports just before the war. Northey's tried to swell the revenue by raising customs duties. The awful thing was that in 1921 this crippling burden of overdrafts and debt fell more heavily on people like Delamere, who had risked most.[22]

As prices collapsed, many of the ex-soldier settlers were ruined and only through stringent control of expenditure was total bankruptcy of the Colony staved off.

It took Block months to recuperate from blackwater but little by little he reorganised and developed the small dairy at Parklands Sarah had begun. With the responsibility of two children and, by the time the war had ended, another on the way, it would provide a more reliable livelihood than stock-trading. He bought a small herd of cows and kept them on forty acres of land which he had purchased with a small house on it from Judd at Kabete. After Jack, their first son, was born Sarah and Abraham Block's union went from strength to strength.[23]

In 1919 before the Blocks moved to Kabete, Spanish 'flu hit Nairobi. A number of European children died in this epidemic and Burkitt, who now owned a Rugby car, took to running patients about to reduce a high temperature. He drove Russell Bowker about completely naked under a blanket on one occasion. On another, he brought a female patient's fever down so quickly in the car that he had to take off most of his own clothes to put them on her, lest she catch cold.[24] So many Africans died of famine or 'flu that the Nairobi Council organised carts to go about all day to pick up and remove the dead. Meru District was also very badly hit, and hyenas became accustomed to entering huts to scavenge dead bodies. They grew bolder and, when the epidemic was over, finding no corpses, took bites out of the living.[25]

As far as the Kikuyu were concerned, the age-old suspicion of death, of handling bodies which the early pioneers had met with in 1900 persisted still. Eva Noon, who was running the Salisbury Hotel on the Lower Kabete Road in Parklands, found a body lying in the garden one morning. But by the time the cart came to collect the corpse that afternoon, it had already four bodies in it which had been found on the way. The wagon broke down in the driveway and the Noons could get no-one among the hotel staff to help them shift it. Only with the utmost difficulty did they persuade their personal servants to help push the cart on to some waste land for the night.[26]

Eva Noon had overcome adversity with the same resilience as Mayence Tate. She had come out as Eva Begbie to join her husband with her two children in 1912. But at Mombasa she was told by Harry Noon that her husband had died a few days earlier. Noon befriended Mrs Begbie and they married in 1913. She took a job at the Salisbury Hotel which she managed and later bought. Later still they moved out to Ngong to a property they had acquired called 'The Homestead' which had been the first house to be occupied by the Blixens in 1914. It was set in 134 acres of forested land with a stream running through it and the Noons developed it into Westwood Park Hotel. By the Second World War, they had built Nyali Beach Hotel at Mombasa and in 1972 Block Hotels acquired shares in her company. Jack and 'Tubby' Block negotiated the takeover. Eva Noon had known them first as two little boys when they attended Miss Shelton's school at Parklands.

The young Block family lived for three years at Kabete and Sarah gave birth to her second son 'Tubby' just before Christmas there in 1919. With two labourers to help with the cows, Abraham delivered milk around Nairobi in old whisky bottles, for which he paid 2 cents each, delivering the milk from door to door in his mule-cart at 20 cents a bottle. Much later still he went into patnership with McMillan's ex-aide and manager, Destro in the Villa Franca Dairy along the Ngong Road.

When his children began to attend nursery school in Parklands Block began to work for Rosenblum, a general store opened specifically to trade with Africans in 1907. Eventually Block became manager of this firm and when, in 1925, the premises perished in one of Nairobi's frequent fires, he was able to buy out the company but kept its original name. In 1928, when the Roy brothers were selling out, Block was in a position to buy and registered the new firm as Rosenblum Bullows and Roy. In the slump of the early 'thirties, Block sold his company to the United Africa Company but remained with them and as manager was responsible for purchasing Gailey & Roberts on United Africa's behalf, a transaction that was so successful that in 1930 it also landed him the Caterpillar franchise for the company, whereupon he formed another business of his own, African Representatives Ltd. This small firm distributed Lever Brothers products and, modest though its beginnings were, was the forerunner to what today is East African Industries, one of the largest manufacturing company in modern Kenya.[27]

Over the years Block's way of life improved but he was never pretentious, though perhaps to make up for Sarah's original disappointment in him, they moved quite often to better houses in better areas. Jack's 21st birthday party was celebrated at the nearby home of the Aga Khan. The event seemed to set the tone for the future of Block's sons, who mingled with and entertained princes, writers, film stars, conservationists, industrialists, politicians and painters most of whom are outstanding men and women of their time. Almost imperceptibly at first, Tubby and Jack took over the hotel organisation to complete in a spectacular way that which had been begun so humbly.

In 1950 Block Hotels became a public company. Nine years later, after the New Stanley Hotel had been modernised and now formed the heart of the city of Nairobi, it rose nine storeys high. Gleaming under its newest coat of white paint and with a capacity of 284 beds, it had cost half a million pounds to re-build. Mayence Tate (who lived to be 98) was invited by the Blocks to attend the opening of the new New Stanley; they flew her out from London for it.[28]

Just as the final touches were being put to it, Block stood on the pavement outside Woolworths opposite and stared. He had been persuaded to go abroad when it was demolished, as he had reached that point in life where change was unbearable to him and he would not allow plans to go ahead unimpeded. After some time he remarked without emotion to a daughter-in-law, 'Look at that white elephant my sons have built.'[29] To him, waste was anathema. Once when, after the Second World War, the manager of his poultry farm at Naivasha asked if he might buy new roofing materials old Abraham asked what was wrong with the papyrus growing at the edge of the lake.[30]

Not unnaturally in the Colony of Kenya, Block became a sort of barometer of the financial climate to be tapped occasionally for advice. His judgement was respected and his moves watched closely. One of the secrets of his success was that he was a good employer and believed in looking after his staff well. He also had a particularly good rapport with his African employees; but his sons like all those born in the country, were even better, having grown up among the Africans.

Like all the second and third generations of white Kenyans, they communicated with the Africans and understood them far better than their parents ever could. It was natural when, from the day they were born, they were cradled first in the arms of an *ayah* and later ate *posho* with them, squatting in their huts and learning the language from babyhood, automatically accepting their different beliefs and ways. They played games with the *totos* and became friends with their families. Abraham Block's children are the most outstanding example of many such Kenyans.

In 1923 a deputation of settlers called on Lord Peel, Secretary of State for India, in England. Apparently weary of discussing seemingly irreconcilable claims of Europeans and Indians, he told them, 'I think the best solution of this trouble is to buy you all out.' One of the deputation looked at him blankly for a moment and replied: 'You can't do that, sir—it is our home.'[31]

That remark sums up the whole philosophy of white settlement. This was their strength and this was their tragedy; they became displaced by Independence. Kenya, they were told, was not their home—yet they had no other, nor any other loyalty or love for a country or its people and animals in the same way. Alfred Johansen was six years old when he arrived in Kiambu in 1905 with his lay-preaching, farmer father from Norway. In 1963 on 11 December he wrote what so many in the same predicament felt on the eve of Independence. 'Tonight the Colonial era comes to an end and from tomorrow those of us who have elected to stay will be living in an African country under African rule. I shall be a foreigner in the land of my adoption and my son will be a foreigner in the land of his birth, a vital change in which neither of us has had any say.'[32]

It is quite understandable that today Kenya has no use for a statue of Lord Delamere, but where is the harm in recognising what the thousands of white pioneers achieved? Everything that is Kenya's today, the good and the bad aspects, grew out of those early struggles. It was done because white pioneers loved the country and wanted to live there. Their genuine committal may be summed up in a sentence written by Karen Blixen in a private letter to her mother after the 1919 drought. 'I have a feeling that wherever I may be in the future, I will be wondering whether there is rain at Ngong.'[33]

It is not too great an exaggeration to say that most of the pioneers held that same sentiment for their adopted land.

CHRONOLOGY

1824–6 Capt. (RN) W. F. Owen's Protectorate over Mombasa which the British Government would not recognise.

1840: Seyyid Said, Sultan of Oman and Zanzibar, moved his court from Muscat to Zanzibar which became the centre of his East African Dominion.

1841: The first official representative of Britain, Captain James Atkins Hamerton, appointed British Consul, Zanzibar.

1869: The Suez Canal opens.

1870: The first steamships arrive from Europe.

1873: Barghash Said, Sultan of Zanzibar, signs treaty with Britain prohibiting sea-borne slave trade.

1877: Sir William MacKinnon asked by Barghash to form a company to exploit the mainland of East Africa but he could not get Foreign Office support.

1885: The British East African Association formed by Sir William MacKinnon to operate in the British area.

1886: Anglo–German agreement in London signed in October defining British and German spheres of influence in East Africa.

1888: The British East Africa Association becomes the Imperial British East African Company. Royal Charter awarded in September.

1889: John Ainsworth joined IBEA and posted in February 1892 to Machakos.

1890: Anglo–German agreement signed; Germany recognised Uganda as being within the British sphere and forfeited all claims to Witu and Zanzibar. Captain Lugard sets up trading post at Dagoretti for the IBEA Company. General Act of Brussels Conference, which came into operation in 1892, laid down rules for development of East Africa and suppression of slavery.

1892–3: Preliminary survey of feasibility of building the Uganda Railway.

1893: Sir Gerald Portal takes over IBEA Company interests in Uganda on behalf of the Foreign Office.

1894: British Protectorate declared over Uganda encompassing Nyanza and Rift Valley provinces, the border of which lay at Kedong. Andrew and David Dick begin trading up to Uganda. Sir Arthur Hardinge appointed Consul-General, Zanzibar and Acting Commissioner of the mainland. The missionaries, Mr and Mrs J. A. Stuart Watt, arrive at Fort Smith as the first white settlers in the highlands and settle near

Machakos in 1895. The Utopian Freeland settlers do not proceed beyond Lamu on their journey to Mount Kenya.

1895: Mazrui Arab revolt on the coast. June 15, the IBEA Company relinquishes its interests and the British East Africa Protectorate declared. The Marquess of Salisbury, Prime Minister and Secretary of State for Foreign Affairs. First rail tracks laid at Makupa, Mombasa. The Kedong Massacre. Boustead and Ridley's caravan arrives from the coast at Machakos.

1896: Sclater's cart-road built from Mombasa to Lake Victoria.

Sir Arthur Hardinge appointed first Commissioner and Consul General to the British East Africa Protectorate. British Government approves £3 million loan to build the Uganda Railway from Mombasa to Lake Victoria. Dr and Mrs Boedeker, Mr and Mrs James McQueen and Mr and Mrs James Wallace walk from Mombasa to Fort Smith. Mr and Mrs John Walsh set up Boustead and Ridley's trading post opposite that of Smith MacKenzie's at Fort Smith.

1897: Land regulations. Uganda Mutiny. November, Sultan of Zanzibar abolishes legal status of slavery in Zanzibar. Feltham arrives with two Cape wagons and eighty oxen from South Africa at Fort Smith for Smith MacKenzie. Cavendish safari arrives at Ravine from Somaliland in August from the north. Delamere and Atkinson arrive at Ravine from Somaliland in November.

1898: John Boyes lands Mombasa. An application by two transport riders from South Africa for 5,000 acres of land refused near Elmenteita.

1899: Railhead reaches Nairobi and railway headquarters established there.

1900: Lord Lansdowne, Secretary of State for Foreign Affairs, appointed November. Nandi uprising.

1901: Uganda Railway reaches Port Florence, Lake Victoria 20 December. Replacing Sir Arthur Hardinge, Sir Charles Eliot appointed HM Commissioner.

1902: Uganda boundary redefined and British E. A. Protectorate becomes the governing power of all upland areas lying between the Indian Ocean and Lake Victoria. King's African Rifles formed. Mr Joseph Chamberlain inspects Uganda Railway. Crown Lands Ordinance. White Settlement Committee formed in Nairobi. Village Headman Ordinance and Native Porters and Labour Regulations.

1903: Lord and Lady Delamere arrive to settle; he formed the Planters' and Farmers' Association, which became the Colonists' Association in 1905. Hut tax introduced. Finnish and Jewish Settlement Schemes proposed. Eliot's drive to attract white settlement especially from South Africa.

1904: Land Commission. Uganda Railway completed. First Maasai agreement signed. Eliot resigns. Sir Donald Stewart appointed Commissioner and ceases to have responsibility for Zanzibar. First Maasai move.

1905: British East Africa Protectorate comes under British Colonial Office. Earl of Elgin and Kincardine (Liberal) appointed Secretary of State for the Colonies December. Nandi rebellion. Uasin Gishu declined by Zionists for Jewish Settlement. Stewart dies; Sir James Hayes-Sadler appointed and made Governor the following year.

1906: Elgin's first pledge on White Highlands. Master and Servants Ordinance.

1907: Capital moved from Mombasa to Nairobi. Mr Winston Churchill, Under-Secretary-of-State, arrives on an official visit. Legislative Council inaugurated. Land Board appointed. Legal Status of slavery abolished in the Sultan's coastal strip.

1908: The Van Rensburg trek. Earl of Crewe appointed Secretary of State for Colonies, May.

1909: Sir Percy Girouard appointed Governor. African Poll Tax levied.

1910: Master and Servants Ordinance amended. Convention of Associations formed. Resident Natives Ordinance to regulate squatters. Rt Hon. Lewis Harcourt appointed Secretary of State for the Colonies in November.

1912: Native Labour Commission appointed. Native Authority Ordinance introduced to regulate African administration. Second Maasai move. Sir Henry Belfield created Governor. Treasury Grant-in-Aid abolished. Europen Poll Tax instituted. Thika 'Tramway' opened.

1913: Second Maasai agreement signed. Maasai concentrated south of the railway in one large reserve of 15,000 sq. miles.

1914: August 4, First World War declared. British forces in BEA Protectorate in state of war with German East Africa.

1915: Land Ordinance passed giving 999-year leases on land occupied by European settlers. Registration of Natives Ordinance passed to provide registration certificates for all Africans employed outside African areas. Rt Hon. A. Bonar Law appointed Secretary of State for Colonies, May. Magadi Soda Co. line opened.

1916: Three settlers included in the War Council which was formed to co-ordinate war effort against German East Africa. Rt Hon. Walter Long appointed Secretary State for the Colonies, December.

1917: Sir Charles Bowring appointed Acting Governor of BEA Protectorate. Economic Commission and Land Settlement Commission appointed. Formation of East African Woman's League with suffragette programme.

1918: First World War ends. Drought, famine, rinderpest and Spanish Influenza epidemic.

1919: Major-General Sir Edward Northey appointed Governor. War Council dissolved. Viscount Milner appointed Secretary of State for the Colonies, January. Europeans, males and females, granted franchise. Ainsworth outlines policy on African labour. Soldier Settlement Scheme implemented. Two Europeans nominated to Exco.

1920: First communal European elections held January. BEA Protectorate becomes Kenya Crown Colony, July. The EA rupee stabilised at 2 shillings. Income Tax proposed but rejected by European community (eventually introduced 1936).

SOURCE NOTES

Chapter 1

N.B. Unless otherwise stated interviews were carried out by the author.
1. Miller, *The Lunatic Express*, p. 368 and Dr Boedeker's unpublished essay, 'Nairobi'.
2. The diary of Morgan S. Williams, April–June 1900 (unpublished).
3. The diary of Lady Francis Scott 1919–1937, 'Pioneers, Polo & Politics' (unpublished).
4. Kipling, *The Lost Legion*
5. The diary of Lady Francis Scott, 1922.
6. Buxton, *Adventures of a Norfolk Lady*, pp. 4, 5.
7. The Letters of Cara Buxton. November 6, 1913 (unpublished).
8. Mitchell, *African Afterthoughts*, p. 62.
9. Dinesen, *Shadows on the Grass*, p. 62.
10. Miller, *The Lunatic Express*, p. 33.
11. Interview with Kitch Morson by Doria Block, Naivasha, 1978.
12. Johansen, 'The Kenya I Knew 1904–1963' (unpublished).
13. The diary of Mary Sanderson, 1904 (unpublished).
14. Joelson, *Rhodesia and East Africa*, 1958: Cranworth, 'When I look back', p. 26.
15. Ibid., p. 22.

General references in this chapter come from Mervyn Hill, *Permanent Way*; Ronald Hardy, *The Iron Snake*; Winston Churchill, *My African Journey*.

Chapter 2

1. McCrindell, Margery. 'The Diary of a Doctor's Wife', *Sunday Nation*, 5 May 1963.
2. Ibid.
3. Interview with Jimmy McQueen, Mombasa, September 1978.
4. 'The Diary of a Doctor's Wife'.
5. Purves, *British East Africa & Uganda*, pp. 57–61.
6. Ibid.

7. 'The Diary of a Doctor's Wife'.
8. A lecture about 1909 delivered by Mrs Philip Percival to the East African Women's League.
9. 'The Diary of a Doctor's Wife'.
10. Boedeker, 'The Building of the Railway', A lecture delivered at the McMillan Memorial Library, Nairobi. Pub. *East African Standard* 2 May 1935.
11. Ibid.
12. 'The Building of the Railway'.
13. Ibid.
14. 'The Diary of a Doctor's Wife'.
15. Thomson, *Through Masai Land*, p. 39.
16. Interview with Minnie McKenzie (née McQueen) by Doria Block, Nairobi, 1979.
17. Ainsworth diaries, October 1896. Unpublished. Mss Afr. S. 377. B.P.C. 2501. Rhodes House Library, Oxford.
18. The gravestone of Jean McQueen, Forest Road Cemetery, Nairobi.
19. Miller, *The Lunatic Express*, p. 174.
20. Cook, 'An Eye-witness Account of Kenya and Uganda', published in *The Uganda Herald*, a series of four articles, 1946.
21. Ibid.
22. The diary of Helen Sanderson, 1904–1908 (unpublished).
23. *The Globetrotter*, 1906.
24. Miller, *The Lunatic Express*, p. 296.
25. *The Handbook of British East Africa*, 1912, p. 160.
26. General: Miller, *The Lunatic Express*; Hill, *The Permanent Way*.
27. 'The Building of the Railway'.
28. Ibid.
29. Miller, *The Lunatic Express*, pp. 316–47.
30. Foran, *The Kima Killer*—The tragedy of Ryall.
31. Foran, *Kill or Be Killed*, p. 72.
32. 'An Eye-witness account of Kenya and Uganda'.
33. Boedeker, 'Early Days in East Africa', a lecture delivered at the McMillan Memorial Library, Nairobi. Pub. *East African Standard*, 1935 (otherwise undated).
34. Ibid.
35. Huxley, *No Easy Way*, pp. 16–17.
36. Interview with Minnie McKenzie.
37. Interview with Mrs Arthur Rainbow, Nairobi, 1979.
38. Huxley, *No Easy Way*, pp. 16–17.
39. Hill, *Magadi*, pp. 11–12.
40. Interview with Kitch Morson by Doria Block, Naivasha, 1978.
41. Interview with Hazel Taylor, Nairobi, 1978.
42. Ainsworth diaries 1896.
43. Bromhead, *What's What in the Kenya Highlands*.
44. Interview with the late James Walker by Doria Block, Nairobi, 1978.
45. Boedeker, 'A Historical Review presented to the Land Office'. Published *East African Standard*, 1932 (otherwise undated).
46. 'Early Days in East Africa'.
47. Ibid.

48. McCrindell, 'My God Said Livingstone: The story of East Africa's Early medicine', *Sunday Nation*, 14 April 1963.
49. 'Early Days in East Africa'.
50. Ibid.
51. Ibid.
52. Ibid.
53. A lecture about 1909 delivered by Mrs Philip Percival.
54. 'The Diary of a Doctor's Wife'.
55. 'Early Days in East Africa'.
56. Interview with Minnie McKenzie.
57. Interview with Anthony Seth-Smith by Doria Block, Nairobi, 1979 and Block correspondence 29 February 1980.
58. General: Blixen, *Out of Africa*; Trzebinski, *Silence Will Speak*.
59. 'Diary of a Doctor's Wife'.
60. Matson correspondence 16 May 1980.
61. Joelson, *Rhodesia and East Africa*, p. 380: Schluter, 'Coffee in East Africa'.
62. Stuart Watt papers and Ainsworth diaries 1896 (unpublished).
63. *A Handbook of British East Africa*, 1912, p. 104.
64. Huxley, *White Man's Country*, Vol. 1, p. 5.
65. 'Diary of a Doctor's Wife'.
66. 'An Eye-witness Account of Kenya and Uganda'.
67. 'Diary of a Doctor's Wife'.
68. 'Early Days in East Africa'.
69. 'My God Said Livingstone'.
70. 'Early Days in East Africa'.
71. Hemsing, *Then and Now*: Nairobi's Norfolk Hotel, pp. 45–6.
72. Foran, *The Kenya Police*, p. 33.
73. Pease, *The Book of the Lion*, p. 50.
74. Early Days in East Africa'.
75. Huxley, *White Man's Country*, Vol. 1, pp. 5–42.
76. Ibid.
77. Huxley, *White Man's Country*, Vol. 1, pp. 5–42.
78. Ibid., p. 17.
79. Ibid., Vol. 1, p. 29.
80. Ibid., p. 31.
81. Ibid., Vol. 1, p. 32.
82. Ibid., p. 24.
83. Ibid., Vol. 1, p. 36.
84. Ibid., p. 47.
85. Letter from Johnston to Sclater, 6 March 1900. F.O. A7/6.
86. Huxley, *White Man's Country*, Vol. 1, p. 50.
87. Jackson, *Early Days in East Africa*, p. 71.
88. Huxley, *White Man's Country*, Vol. 1, p. 54.
89. Jackson, *Early Days in East Africa*, p. 66.
90. Ibid., p. 68.
91. Miller, *The Lunatic Express*, p. 113.
92. Jackson, *Early Days in East Africa*, pp. 68–9.
93. Mortimer, Margery. *The Story of the Katharine Bibby Hospital*.
94. Jackson, *Early Days in East Africa*, pp. 66–9.

95. Ibid.
96. Ainsworth diaries, 22 September 1897.
97. Correspondence with P. M. Dick, Chairman of Narok Muoroto, 21 April 1980.
98. Moxon. *Agricultural Innovation in Kenya*; also Boedeker lectures and Ainsworth diaries.
99. Matson, *Nandi Resistence to British Rule*, p. 110.
100. Ainsworth diaries, September and October 1898.
101. Njonjo, *Kenya Past and Present* No. 7: Josiah Njonjo recalls, p. 12.
102. Matson, *Andrew Dick*. Published *Kenya Weekly News* (undated).
103. Cathcart-Wilson, *Uganda & East Africa*.
104. Ainsworth's diaries of 1895.
105. Matson, *Andrew Dick*.
106. Ainsworth's diaries of 1895.
107. Miller, *Lunatic Express*, p. 382.
108. Ainsworth diaries, November 1897.
109. Ingham, *A History of East Africa*, Vol. 2, p. 36.
110. Correspondence between Norman Leys and McGregor Ross, 1904.
111. Edmondson correspondence 27 February 1980.
112. Bowker family papers and interview with Roy Mayer, 1979.
113. Fox, *White Mischief*, p. 34.
114. Diary of Helen Sanderson, September 1904 (unpublished).
115. Block family data.

Chapter 3

1. Lady Whitehouse's diary, 1897 (unpublished).
2. Miller, *The Lunatic Express*, p. 363.
3. Foran, *Cuckoo in Kenya*, p. 66.
4. Maxwell, Marcuswell, *Stalking Big Game with a Camera*.
5. Lady Whitehouse's diary, 1897.
6. Ibid.
7. Preston, *Genesis of a Colony*.
8. Miller, *The Lunatic Express*, p. 366.
9. Meinertzhagen, *Kenya Diary 1902–1906*. 18 January 1903.
10. The diary of Helen Sanderson 1904–1908 (unpublished).
11. Moxon, *Agricultural Innovation in Kenya*, p. 150.
12. Blencowe, *Kenya Recollections of a Sailor*, 1906 (unpublished). Rhodes House, Oxford. EAEPS 6/16.
13. Preston, *Oriental Nairobi*, p. 57.
14. From an interview with the late Sir Derek Erskine by Doria Block, Nairobi, 1975.
15. Preston, *Oriental Nairobi*, p. 58.
16. Longworth, *The Globe Trotter*, 1906, and from an interview with Dr Gerald Anderson, Nairobi, 1977.
17. Ingham, *A Hitory of East Africa*, p. 211.
18. Playne, *East Africa (British) 1908–1909*, Its History, People, Commerce, Industries & Resources, p. 120.
19. *Kenya Weekly News*, 23 February 1953. Uasin Gishu Supplement, p. 11.

20. Interview with Brian Yonge by Doria Block, Nairobi, 1977.
21. Jackson, *Early Days in East Africa*, pp. 66–70.
22. Hunter and Mannix, *African Bush Adventures*, p. 130.
23. Interview with Jim McQueen, Mombasa, 1978.
24. Meinertzhagen, *Kenya Diary 1902–1906*, p. 60.
25. Malcomson, *Pioneers*, Pub. *East African Standard*, 1954, an interview with Jim McQueen, Mombasa, 1978.
26. Miller, *The Lunatic Express*, p. 367.
27. Ribeiro papers (unpublished).
28. Johansen, *The Kenya I knew 1904–1963* (unpublished).
29. Ribeiro papers.
30. Huxley, *White Man's Country*, Vol. 1, p. 87.
31. Ribeiro papers.
32. Diary of Helen Sanderson, 1904–1908 (unpublished).
33. *Kenya Weekly News*, 18 May 1955. Rhiwerfa Farm, Corbett.
34. Interview with Dr Gerald Anderson, Nairobi, 1977.
35. Hemsing, *Old Nairobi and the New Stanley Hotel*, p. 8.
36. Playne, *East Africa (British) 1908–1909*, p. 266.
37. From a recording of the recollections of Abraham Block made by Doria Block, Nairobi 1955.
38. From an interview with Brian Burrows, Taita Hills, 1978.
39. Block family data.
40. Nicoll, 'Mrs Haller—Woman of Faith' in the series 'Pioneers of Kenya', *East African Standard* (undated).
41. From a recording of the recollections of Abraham Block made by Doria Block, Nairobi, 1955.
42. Hemsing, *Old Nairobi and the New Stanley Hotel*, p. 14.
43. Interviews with the late Eddie Ruben, Nairobi, 1978 and 1979.
44. Pakenham, *The Boer War*, p. 569.
45. Interview with Tony Dyer, Nanyuki, 1978.
46. Interview with Brian Burrows, 1978, and the late Eddie Ruben, 1978 and 1979.
47. Weisbord, *African Zion*, p. 5.
48. Ibid.
49. From a recording of the recollections of Abraham Block (unpublished).
50. Weisbord, *African Zion*, p. 5.
51. Carlebach, *The Jews of Nairobi*, p. 21.
52. From the recollections of Abraham Block.
53. Carlebach, *Jews of Nairobi*, p. 21.
54. From a recording of the recollections of Abraham Block (unpublished).
55. Hemsing, *Old Nairobi and the New Stanley Hotel*, pp. 9, 17.
56. Interview with Kit Taylor, Ringmore, 1978.
57. Cranworth, *Profit & Sport in East Africa*.
58. Diary of H. K. Binks, 1902 (unpublished).
59. Hemsing, *Old Nairobi and the New Stanley Hotel*, p. 11.
60. Correspondence with A. T. Matson, Feb./March 1980.
61. Markus biography (unpublished), p. 34.
62. Meinertzhagen, *Kenya Diary 1902–1906*, p. 9.
63. Markus biography, p. 34.
64. Correspondence with Hamilton, Harrison and Matthews, 1980.

65. Meinertzhagen, *Kenya Diary 1902–1906*, p. 9.
66. Huxley, *White Man's Country*, Vol. 1, p. 89.
67. Hill, *Dual Policy*, p. 113.
68. Huxley, White Man's Country, Vol. 1, p. 89.
69. Correspondence with the late Dicky Edmondson, 13 June 1979.
70. Meinertzhagen diaries (unpublished) 30 August 1902 and October 1902.
71. Correspondence with the late Dicky Edmondson, 13 June 1979.
72. Ibid., 18 March 1980.
73. Ibid., 13 June 1979.
74. Jackson to Hill. 4/8/03 F.O. 3/720.
75. Roy letters (unpublished), 18 October 1907 written from Neumann's Boma.
76. Foran, *Kenya Police Report* and *Cuckoo in Kenya*, p. 145.
77. Johansen, *The Kenya I knew 1904–1963* (unpublished), p. 77.
78. Interview with Mr A. Finne by Doria Block, Nairobi, 1979.
79. Hunter and Mannix, *African Bush Adventures*, pp. 111–27.
80. Ibid.
81. Ibid.
82. John Boyes Scrapbook (unpublished).
83. Destro family papers.
84. Blixen, *Out of Africa*, p. 204.
85. E.A.W.L. *They Made it Their Home*, Muthaiga.
86. Huxley, *No Easy Way*, p. 5.
87. Meinertzhagen, *Kenya Diary 1902–1906*, Preface p. vii.
88. Ibid., pp. 9, 10.
89. Ibid.
90. Jackson to Hill, 25 May 1903, F.O./02/720.

Chapter 4

1. Huxley, *No Easy Way*, p. 4.
2. Moxon, *Agricultural Innovation in Kenya*, p. 153.
3. Huxley, *No Easy Way*, p. 6.
4. Diary of H. K. Binks, 1903 (unpublished).
5. Huxley, *No Easy Way*, pp. 4, 5.
6. Ibid., p. 7.
7. Interview with Harries family by Doria Block, Thika, 1979.
8. Huxley, *White Man's Country*, Vol. 1, p. 84.
9. Ingham, *A History of East Africa*, pp. 212, 213.
10. Foran, *A Cuckoo in Kenya*, p. 90.
11. Interview with Wilfrid Hopcraft by Doria Block, Naivasha, 1979.
12. Eliot, John Augustus, letters home 1901–27 (unpublished) Rhodes House, Oxford. Mss. Afr. S. 1179.
13. Diary of Helen Sanderson 1904–1908 (unpublished).
14. Longworth, *The Globetrotter*, 6 July 1906.
15. Diary of H. K. Binks, 1903.
16. Correspondence with Dr Richard Waller, 6 July 1979.
17. Letter from Harry Johnston to Clement Hill, F.O.3/70.
18. Huxley, *White Man's Country*, Vol. 1, p. 92.
19. Foran, *A Cuckoo in Kenya*, p. 45.

20. From a recording made by Freddy Ward about his arrival in BEA in 1904.
21. From a recording of the recollections of Abraham Block made by Doria Block, Nairobi 1955.
22. Rodwell, *Coast Causerie*, E.N.U. No. 317, Mombasa.
23. Morton, *Diary of a Railway Employee*, 1903 (unpublished).
24. Cranworth, *Kenya Chronicles*.
25. Interview with Dr Gerald Anderson, Nairobi, 1977.
26. Markus biography (unpublished).
27. From a recording of recollections made by Freddy Ward.
28. Interview with Dr Gerald Anderson.
29. Younghusband, *Glimpses of East Africa*, 1910.
30. From a recording of the recollections of Abraham Block (unpublished).
31. Markus biography (unpublished).
32. From correspondence with Eve Pollecoff, 1983.
33. Rodwell, *Coast Causerie*.
34. From correspondence with Eve Pollecoff, 1983.
35. From a recording of the recollections of Abraham Block (unpublished).
36. Interview with Mary Mitford Barberton, Nairobi, 1978.
37. From a recording of the recollections of Abraham Block (unpublished).
38. From a recording of recollections made by Freddy Ward.
39. Ibid.
40. O'Neill, *A Train Journey in 1917* (unpublished).
41. Foran, *A Cuckoo in Kenya*, p. 67.
42. Davis, *The Uganda Railway* (unpublished).
43. Ibid.
44. From a recording of recollections made by Freddy Ward.
45. Blencowe, 'Recollections of a Sailor' (unpublished), Rhodes House, Oxford, E.A.E.P.S. 6/1.
46. Davis, *The Uganda Railway* (unpublished).
47. Markus biography (unpublished).
48. Taylor, *A Train Journey in 1904* (unpublished).
49. From a recording of recollections made by Freddy Ward and O'Neill, *A Train Journey in 1917*, (unpublished).
50. Interview with Anthony Seth-Smith by Doria Block, Nairobi, 1979.
51. Hill, *Magadi*, p. 31.
52. From a recording of recollections made by Freddy Ward.
53. Hill, *Planters' Progress*.
54. Seth-Smith, Letters 1908 (unpublished).
55. Interview with Mr and Mrs James Maxwell Nightingale, Njoro, 1978.
56. From a recording of the recollections of Abraham Block (unpublished).
57. From a recording of recollections by Freddy Ward.
58. From a recording of the recollections of Abraham Block (unpublished).
59. From a recording of recollections made by Freddy Ward.
60. Block family data.
61. Johansen, *The Kenya I Knew 1904–1963*, p. 19 (unpublished).
62. Meinertzhagen, *Kenya Diary 1904–1906*, p. 171.
63. Eliot papers, Rhodes House, Oxford. Mss. AFRS 1179 (1).
64. Markus biography (unpublished).
65. From a recording of the recollections of Abraham Block (unpublished).

66. Ibid.
67. Kenya Land Commission evidence, 17 November 1932, pp. 631–7.
68. From a recording of the recollections of Abraham Block (unpublished).
69. Playne, *East Africa (British)*, p. 181.
70. From a recording of the recollections of Abraham Block (unpublished).
71. Divers sources: interviews with Jim McQueen, Iris Mistry, Desmond O'Hagen, Brian Jenkins, Tony Dyer and the late Mrs Geater.
72. Interview with the late Mrs Geater, Nairobi, 1978.
73. Interview with Iris Mistry, Langata, 1978.
74. Huxley, Nellie—Letters from Africa, p. 39.
75. Interview with Rose and Tony Dyer, Nanyuki, 1978.
76. Interview with the late Sarah Block, 1977.
77. *East African Quarterly Review*, Jan-March, 1904.
78. From a recording of the recollections of Abraham Block (unpublished).
79. Johansen, *The Kenya I Knew*, 1904–1963, p. 26 (unpublished).
80. Kenya Land Commission Evidence, 17 November 1932, pp. 631–7.
81. From a recording of the recollections of Abraham Block (unpublished).
82. Johansen, *The Kenya I Knew*, 1904–1906, p. 26 (unpublished).
83. Johansen, *The Kenya I Knew*, 1904–1963, p. 9 (unpublished).
84. Seth-Smith letters; 13 April and 4 May 1908.
85. From a recording of the recollections of Abraham Block (unpublished).
86. Interview with Mrs McDonnell by Doria Block, Limuru, 1979.
87. Swift, *The Story of Punda Milia*.
88. Huxley, *No Easy Way*, p. 6.
89. Interview with Jim McQueen, Mombasa, 1978.
90. Diary of H. K. Binks, 1903–1905 (unpublished).
91. Huxley, *No Easy Way*, p. 6.
92. From a recording of the recollections of Abraham Block (unpublished).
93. Carlebach, *Jews of Nairobi*, p. 16.

Chapter 5

1. Carlebach, *The Jews of Nairobi, 1903–1962*, p. 14.
2. Huxley, *White Man's Country*, Vol. 1, p. 69.
3. *The African Standard*, 12 September 1903.
4. Meinertzhagen, *Kenya Diary 1902–1906*, p. 117.
5. Miller, *The Lunatic Express*, pp. 246, 247.
6. Carlebach, *The Jews of Nairobi, 1903–1962*, p. 16.
7. Huxley, *White Man's Country*, Vol. 1, pp. 99, 119.
8. Delamere, The Grant of Land to the Zionist Congress and Land Settlement in British East Africa, 1903.
9. Huxley, *White Man's Country*, Vol. 1, pp. 98, 104.
10. Foran, *A Cuckoo in Kenya*.
11. Huxley, *White Man's Country*, Vol. 1, p. 99.
12. *The African Standard*, 29 August 1903.
13. Carlebach, *The Jews of Nairobi 1903–1962*.
14. Binks, *African Rainbow*, p. 61.
15. Carlebach, *The Jews of Nairobi 1903–1962*, pp. 17, 18.
16. Huxley, *White Man's Country*, Vol. 1, p. 123.

17. Matson, *The Zionist Scheme*, pp. 9, 10.
18. Eliot, *The East Africa Protectorate*, pp. 178, 179.
19. Carlebach, *The Jews of Nairobi 1903–1962*, p. 19.

Chapter 6

1. Foran, *A Cuckoo in Kenya*, p. 81 and Edmondson correspondence 1979.
2. Foran, *The Kenya Police 1887–1960*, p. 22.
3. Block correspondence 31 February 1980 and from an interview with Kitch Morson by Doria Block, Naivasha, 1979.
4. Lonsdale, *Coping with Contradictions*: The Development of the Colonial State in Kenya 1895–1914. Cambridge, 1979.
5. From an interview with the late Eddie Ruben, Nairobi, 1978.
6. Interview with the late Sir Derek Erskine by Doria Block in Nairobi (undated).
7. Huxley. *White Man's Country*, Vol. 1, p. 252.
8. 'East African Journal Extracts 1904–1908', *Kenya Weekly News* 31 December 1954.
9. Meinertzhagen, *Kenya Diary, 1902–1906*, p. 77 (23/1/03).
10. Foran, *A Cuckoo in Kenya*, p. 314.
11. Diary of Helen Sanderson, August 1904 (unpublished).
12. Miller, *The Lunatic Express*, p. 505.
13. Hemsing, *Then and Now: Nairobi's Norfolk Hotel*, p. 14.
14. Huxley, *White Man's Country*, Vol. 1, p. 92.
15. Interview with Jock Rutherfurd by Doria Block in Nairobi, 1978.
16. Huxley, *No Easy Way*, pp. 35, 36.
17. Huxley, *White Man's Country*, Vol. 1, p. 138.
18. Huxley, *No Easy Way*, p. 26.
19. Huxley, *White Man's Country*, Vol. 1, p. 148.
20. Letters of Arnold Paice to his mother, 1908 (unpublished).
21. Swift and Rutherfoord. 'The White Farmer in Central Africa'.
22. *The First Hundred Years of the Standard Bank*, pp. 299, 300.
23. Miller, *The Lunatic Express*, p. 425.
24. *The Kenya Land Commission Evidence*, 17 November 1932, pp. 631–7.
25. The diary of Helen Sanderson, 1904–1908 (unpublished).
26. Ibid.
27. Smart, *Nairobi: A Jubilee History, 1900–1950*, p. 26.
28. Divers sources: Interview with Sonny Bumpus; articles by Miss O. O'Neill, Ethel Younghusband and Alexander Davis and a taperecording of M. S. Thakur by William K. Purdy.
29. The diary of Helen Sanderson, 1904–1908 (unpublished).
30. Ibid.
31. Harries, 'The Story of my Farm—Karamaini Estate, Thika', *Kenya Weekly News*, 1955.
32. Interview with the Harries family by Doria Block in Nairobi, 1978 and an interview with May Stocker by Betty Kiggan, South Africa, 1979.
33. Sorrenson, *Origins of European Settlement*: Appendix 1. Land Alienation in the E. A. Protectorate 1903–15.
34. Harries, 'The Story of my farm'.
35. Roets papers (unpublished).

36. Harries, 'The Story of my farm'.
37. Miller, *The Lunatic Express*, p. 84.
38. Johansen, *The Kenya I Knew 1904–1963*, p. 47 (unpublished).
39. Holmes. 'The Harries Clan', *The East African Standard*, 7 January 1955.
40. Farrant, *The Legendary Grogan*, p. 19.
41. Divers sources: Wymer, *The Man From the Cape*; Murray-Brown, *Kenyatta*; Mortimer, Royal Commonwealth Society Obituary.
42. Sorrenson, *Origins of European Settlement in Kenya*, p. 66.
43. Longworth, *The Globetrotter*, February 1906.
44. McClure correspondence, 1978.
45. Interview with Kitch Morson by Doria Block, Naivasha, 1978.
46. Johansen, *The Kenya I Knew, 1904–1963*, pp. 36, 37.
47. Ibid. and interview with Brian Jenkins, Nanyuki, 1979.
48. Alport, *Hope in Africa*, p. 36.
49. William, Morgan S., 1900 diary (unpublished).
50. Huxley, *White Man's Country*, Vol. 1, pp. 126, 129, 132.
51. Sorrenson, *Origins of European Settlement in Kenya*, pp. 71, 72.
52. Huxley, *White Man's Country*, Vol. 1, pp. 129–32.
53. Huxley, *White Man's Country*, Vol. 1, pp. 129, 132.
54. Hill, *Magadi*, p. 18.
55. Alport, *Hope in Africa*, p. 36.
56. Hill, 'The Story of Gailey & Roberts', *Kenya Weekly News*, 2 April 1954.
57. Isaac, 'Rambles in Nairobi c. 1904', *Kenya Weekly News*, 18 June 1954.
58. Hemsing, *Then and Now, Nairobi's Norfolk Hotel*, pp. 16–17.
59. Cowie, 'Lions in Nairobi', *Kenya Weekly News*, 31 December 1954.
60. Hemsing, *Then and Now: Nairobi's Norfolk Hotel*, p. 10.
61. Foran, *A Cuckoo in Kenya*, p. 129.
62. Smart, *Nairobi: A Jubilee History, 1900–1950*, p. 28.

Chapter 7

1. Davis, *On the Nakuru Hotel* (unpublished).
2. Smart, *Nairobi: A Jubilee History, 1900–1950*, p. 22.
3. Hemsing, *Then and Now, Nairobi's Norfolk Hotel*, p. 195.
4. Johansen, *The Kenya I Knew, 1904–1963*, p. 48 (unpublished).
5. Diary of Helen Sanderson, 1904–1905 (unpublished).
6. Ibid.
7. Huxley, *No Easy Way*, pp. 35, 36.
8. Bicknell correspondence 1979 and interview with the late Mrs Gertrude Alexander, 1977.
9. From a recording of the recollections of Abraham Block made by Doria Block, Nairobi, 1955.
10. Interview with Brian Burrows, Taita Hills, 1978.
11. Hemsing, *Then and Now, Nairobi's Norfolk Hotel*, p. 68.
12. Block family data.
13. From a recording of recollections made by Freddy Ward from his arrival in BEA in 1904.
14. Memoirs of Richard Gethin (unpublished).
15. Diary of Helen Sanderson, July 1904.

16. Ibid.
17. Elliot, Mss. Afr. S 1179 (1). Rhodes House, Oxford.
18. Huxley, *White Man's Country*, Vol. 1, p. 156.
19. Ingham, *A History of East Africa*, p. 216.
20. Huxley, *White Man's Country*, Vol. 1, p. 156.
21. Johnston to Salisbury 26 October 1900, F O 2/300.
22. Matson, *The Zionist Offer*.
23. Huxley, *White Man's Country*, Vol. 1, pp. 124, 125.
24. Carlebach, *The Jews of Nairobi, 1903–1960*, p. 2 and Matson, *The Zionist Offer*.
25. Carlebach, *The Jews of Nairobi, 1903–1960*, pp. 20–2.
26. Huxley, *No Easy Way*, p. 57.
27. Meinertzhagen, *Kenya Diary, 1902–1906*, p. 185.
28. Huxley, *No Easy Way*, pp. 56, 57.
29. Matson, *The Zionist Offer*.
30. Carlebach, *The Jews of Nairobi, 1903–1960*, p. 22.
31. Ibid.
32. Ibid., pp. 21, 22.
33. Miller, *The Lunatic Express*, p. 432.
34. Dairy of Helen Sanderson 1905.

Chapter 8

1. Miller, *Lunatic Express*, p. 434.
2. Meinertzhagen, *Kenya Diary, 1902–1906*, p. 239.
3. From a recording of the recollections of Abraham Block made by Doria Block, Nairobi, 1955.
4. Huxley, *White Man's Country*, Vol. 1, p. 157.
5. From a recording of the recollections of Abraham Block (unpublished).
6. Nicoll, *Mrs Haller, Woman of Faith*. *East African Standard* in the series 'Pioneers of Kenya' (undated).
7. Nicoll, *Mrs Haller, Woman of Faith*.
8. Interview with the late Eddie Ruben, Nairobi, 1979.
9. Kenya Land Commission Evidence, 17 November 1932, pp. 631–7.
10. Kenya Land Commission Evidence, 17 November 1932, pp. 631–7.
11. From the recollections of Abraham Block.
12. Davis, *The Currency Question* and Johansen, *The Kenya I Knew, 1904–1963* (unpublished).
13. Arnold Paice letters.
14. From a recording of the recollections of Abraham Block (unpublished).
15. Interview with Kitch Morson by Doria Block, Naivasha, 1978.
16. Huxley, *White Man's Country*, Vol. 1, p. 147.
17. Interview with Kitch Morson.
18. Huxley, *White Man's Country*, Vol. 1, p. 148.
19. Arnold Paice letters.
20. Interview with Kitch Morson.
21. From a recording of the recollections of Abraham Block (unpublished).
22. Block family data.
23. Arnold Paice letters, May 1908.
24. Huxley, *White Man's Country*, Vol. 1, p. 243.

25. Ibid., p. 146, 145.
26. Luck correspondence, 8 March 1980.
27. Naivasha Farmers' Association papers and interview with Brian Burrows, Taita Hills, 1978.
28. Huxley, *No Easy Way*, p. 3.
29. Interview with Alban and Mary Mitford-Barberton, Nairobi, 1978.
30. Huxley, *No Easy Way*, p. 3.
31. Huxley, *White Man's Country*, Vol. 1, p. 164.
32. Huxley, *No Easy Way*, p. 54.
33. Huxley, *White Man's Country*, Vol. 1, pp. 164, 166.
34. Divers sources: Paice letters 1907–1908; Buchan Sydeserff, 'Ostrich Farming in East Africa', *The Looking Glass*, 1960; East African Woman's League, 'Machakos—Ulu Scrapbook'.
35. Arnold Paice letters 1907–1908.
36. Sorrenson, *Origins of European Settlement in Kenya*, p. 86.
37. Ingham, *A History of East Africa*, p. 220.
38. Naivasha District Farmers' Association papers.
39. Paice letters 1907.
40. Huxley, *No Easy Way*, p. 21.
41. Olga Rogers correspondence, 29 May 1979.
42. Ingham, *A History of East Africa*, pp. 212, 216, 217.
43. Ibid.
44. Churchill, *My African Journey*, p. 1.
45. From a recording of recollections made by Freddy Ward about life in Nairobi from 1904.
46. Diary of Helen Sanderson, 1907.
47. From a recording of recollections made by Freddy Ward about life in Nairobi from 1904.
48. Huxley, *No Easy Way*, p. 19.
49. Ibid., p. 21.
50. Huxley, *White Man's Country*, Vol. 1, p. 244.
51. Block correspondence, 26 May 1979.
52. Riddell, 'The Duke's Safari', *Blackwoods Magazine* No. 1533, July 1943.
53. Huxley, *White Man's Country*, Vol. 1, p. 242.
54. Fred Roy's letters, 5 September 1907.
55. 'Elgon's Diary', *East African Standard*. Undated cutting taken from John Boyes's scrapbook.
56. Hunter and Mannix, *African Bush Adventures*, p. 113.
57. Huxley, *White Man's Country*, Vol. 1, p. 245.
58. Isaac, 'Rambles Round Nairobi in 1904', *Kenya Weekly News*, 18 June 1954.
59. Arnold Paice letters, 1910.
60. Ibid.
61. Fred Roy's letters, 1907.
62. Miller, *The Lunatic Express*, p. 473.
63. Arnold Paice letters, 1910.
64. Ibid.
65. Farrant, *The Legendary Grogan*, pp. 61, 116.
66. Wymer, *The Man from the Cape*, pp. 156–60.
67. Isaac, 'Rambles Round Nairobi in 1904'.

68. Wymer, *The Man from the Cape*, p. 157.
69. Farrant, *The Legendary Grogan*, p. 117.
70. Bowker, *The Grogan and Bowker Flogging Case* (unpublished).
71. In possession of Mrs Connie Bowker-Douglass, interviewed at Mudeford, 1981 and 1982.
72. Bowker, *The Grogan and Bowker Flogging Case*.
73. Ross, *Kenya From Within*, p. 170.
74. Bowker, *The Grogan and Bowker Flogging Case*.
75. Wymer, *The Man from the Cape*, p. 160.
76. Farrant, *The Legendary Grogan*, p. 121.
77. Wymer, *The Man from the Cape*, p. 160.
78. Bowker, *The Grogan and Bowker Flogging Case*.
79. Ross, *Kenya from Within*, pp. 170, 171.
80. Bowker, *The Grogan and Bowker Flogging Case*.
81. Ross, *Kenya from Within*, p. 170.

Chapter 9

1. Barker and Benfield, *The Lands and People of East Africa*, p. 14.
2. Anderson, Newsletter No. 12, April 1955. E. A. Society of Pioneers.
3. Miller, *The Lunatic Express*, p. 471.
4. Huxley, *White Man's Country*, Vol. 1, p. 228.
5. Miller, *The Lunatic Express*, p. 471.
6. Huxley, *White Man's Country*, Vol. 1, p. 228.
7. The diary of Helen Sanderson, 30 March 1908.
8. Huxley, *White Man's Country*, Vol. 1, p. 229.
9. Ibid., p. 236.
10. Huxley, *No Easy Way*, pp. 56–61.
11. The African Standard, 30 July 1904.
12. Ibid.
13. *The Globetrotter*, 14 February 1906.
14. Steyn papers (unpublished).
15. Arnoldi papers (unpublished).
16. Huxley, *No Easy Way*, p. 61.
17. Arnoldi and Wessell's account of the Van Rensberg trek (unpublished).
18. Steyn papers (unpublished).
19. Supplement on Eldoret: *Kenya Weekly News*, 6 November 1953.
20. From a recording of recollections by Freddy Ward about life in Nairobi from 1904.
21. Riddell, 'The Duke's safari', *Blackwoods Magazine* No. 1533, July 1943.
22. Interview with the late Sarah Block, Nairobi, 1977.
23. Interview with the late Donald Kerr by Doria Block, Nairobi, 1979.
24. Host, 'Professional Hunters of East Africa', *East African Annual 1951–1952*, pp. 70–5.
25. Playne, *East Africa, (British) Its History, People, Commerce, Industries and Resources*, p. 179 (also footnote).
26. Arnoldi papers (unpublished).
27. Host, 'Professional Hunters of East Africa'.
28. Interview with the late Donald Kerr, by Doria Block, Nairobi, 1979.

29. Host, 'Professional Hunters of East Africa'.
30. From a recording of recollections by Freddy Ward.
31. From the *Diary* of H. K. Binks and Hemsing, *Then and Now, Nairobi's Norfolk Hotel*, pp. 48, 49.
32. From a recording of recollections by Freddy Ward.
33. From the unpublished memoirs of Richard Gethin, p. 20.
34. Interview with Taj Ahmed, Nairobi, 1979.
35. Host, 'Professional Hunters of East Africa'.
36. Interview with the late Donald Kerr by Doria Block, Nairobi, 1979.
37. From the unpublished memoirs of Richard Gethin, p. 20.
38. Ibid.
39. Block correspondence 8 March 1980.
40. Interview with Mrs Evelyn Mitchell, by Doria Block, Limuru, 1979.
41. Smart, *Nairobi: A Jubilee History, 1900–1950*, p. 22.
42. McCrindell, 'The Norfolk Hotel'. *Sunday Nation*, 31 March 1963.
43. From the unpublished memoirs of Richard Gethin, p. 26.
44. Huxley, *No Easy Way*, pp. 19, 20.

Chapter 10

1. Crawford, *Thinking Black*.
2. Bennett, *Settlers and Politics in Kenya*, p. 282.
3. Girouard to Crewe, 13 November 1909. CO 533/63.
4. Sorrenson, *Origins of European Settlement in Kenya*, p. 112.
5. Elliot papers, Rhodes House, Oxford. Mss AFRS 1179 (1).
6. Huxley, *White Man's Country*, Vol. 1, p. 282.
7. Elliot papers.
8. Diary of Helen Sanderson, October 1909 (unpublished).
9. Swift, 'The Story of Punda Milia', *Kenya Weekly News*, 3 August 1956.
10. Huxley, *No Easy Way*, p. 10.
11. O'Shea, *Farming and Planting in BEA*, pp. 31, 32.
12. Interview with Anthony Seth-Smith by Doria Block, Nairobi, 1979; interview with Paddy Merrit, Nairobi, 1980.
13. O'Shea, *Farming and Planting in BEA*, p. 31.
14. Miller, *The Lunatic Express*, p. 500.
15. Huxley, *White Man's Country*, p. 239.
16. Interview with the Harries family by Doria Block, Nairobi, 1979.
17. Miller, *The Lunatic Express*, pp. 503, 500.
18. Huxley, *No Easy Way*, p. 21.
19. Smart, *Nairobi: A Jubilee History, 1900–1950*, p. 31.
20. From a recording of a broadcast on early Nairobi made by Alan Bobbe; interview with Charles Udall by Doria Block, Nairobi, 1978.
21. Seth-Smith letters, 1908 (unpublished).
22. Huxley, *No Easy Way*, p. 29.
23. Recording of a broadcast by Alan Bobbe.
24. Girouard to Crewe, September 1909: Crewe to Girouard, October 1909: CO 533/62.
25. Swift, 'The Story of Punda Milia', *Kenya Weekly News*, 3 August 1956.
26. Huxley, *White Man's Country*, Vol. 1, p. 171.

27. Huxley, *No Easy Way*, p. 26.
28. Huxley, *White Man's Country*, Vol. 1, p. 74.
29. E.A.W.L. 'Kiambu Scrapbook'.
30. E.A.W.L., 'They Made It Their Home, Kitisuru'.
31. Taylor, 'Life on a Coffee Farm' (transcript of broadcast).
32. Huxley, *White Man's Country*, Vol. 1, p. 215.
33. Taylor, 'Life on a Coffee Farm'.
34. Miller, *The Lunatic Express*, p. 519.
35. E.A.W.L., 'Kiambu Scrapbook'.
36. Huxley, *No Easy Way*, pp. 43, 44.
37. Interview with Elsie Goodram, Malindi, 1978.
38. Huxley, *No Easy Way*, pp. 43, 44.
39. Bennett, *Settlers and Politics in Kenya*, p. 282.
40. Letters of Arnold Paice, August 1910 (unpublished).
41. Ibid.
42. Huxley, *No Easy Way*, p. 39.
43. Interview with Iris Mistry, Nairobi, 1978.
44. Interview with Rose Cartwright, Nairobi, 1979.
45. Interview with Kit Taylor, Devon, 1980.
46. Bennett, *Settlers and Politics*, p. 266.
47. Huxley, *White Man's Country*, Vol. 1, p. 110.
48. Bennett, *Settlers and Politics*, p. 280.
49. Miller, *The Lunatic Express*, pp. 480, 481.
50. Bennett, *Settlers and Politics*, p. 280.
51. Smart, *Nairobi: A Jubilee History, 1900–1950*, p. 32.
52. Miller, *The Lunatic Express*, p. 482.
53. Bennett, *Settlers and Politics*, p. 282.
54. Miller, *The Lunatic Express*, p. 490.
55. Wymer, *The Man from the Cape*, p. 168.
56. Farrant, *The Legendary Grogan*, pp. 112, 215.
57. Smart, *Nairobi: A Jubilee History, 1900–1950*, p. 32.
58. Farrant, *The Legendary Grogan*, pp. 112, 113.
59. Huxley, *White Man's Country*, Vol. 1, p. 142.
60. Huxley, *No Easy Way*, pp. 35, 36.
61. Huxley, *White Man's Country*, Vol. 1, p. 298.
62. Ibid.
63. Miller, *The Lunatic Express*, p. 505.
64. E.A.W.L., 'Eldoret Scrapbook'.
65. From a recording of recollections by Freddy Ward about life in Nairobi from 1904.
66. Sorrenson, Origins of European Settlement, p. 146.
67. Huxley, *White Man's Country*, Vol. 1, p. 281.
68. Alex Davis ms on the Cole case (unpublished).
69. Letters of Arnold Paice, May 1911 (unpublished).
70. Huxley, *White Man's Country*, Vol. 1, p. 282.
71. Alex Davis ms on the Cole case (unpublished).
72. Huxley, *White Man's Country*, Vol. 1, p. 280.
73. Ibid.
74. Miller, *The Lunatic Express*, p. 497.

75. Chilver and Smith, *A General History of East Africa*, p. 34.
76. Interview with Anthony Seth-Smith.
77. Interview with Wilfred Hopcraft, by Doria Block, Naivasha, 1979.
78. Huxley, *White Man's Country*, Vol. 1, p. 138.
79. Letters of Arnold Paice, February 1911.
78. Chilver and Smith, *A History of East Africa*, Vol. 2, p. 34.
79. Letters of Arnold Paice. February 1911.
80. Huxley, *White Man's Country*, Vol. 1, p. 268.
81. Klapprott, Woodsmoke (unpublished memoirs).
82. Miller, *The Lunatic Express*, p. 496.
83. Ibid.
84. Seth-Smith letters, 1911.
85. Leys correspondence, 6 November 1911.
86. Ibid.
87. Correspondence with the late Dicky Edmondson, 1980.
88. Public Records Office. LAND (9795), C/O 533.
89. Huxley, *White Man's Country*, Vol. 1, p. 241.
90. Miller, The Lunatic Express, p. 497.
91. Huxley, *White Man's Country*, Vol. 1, p. 269.
92. Miller, *The Lunatic Express*, p. 497.
93. Correspondence with the late Dicky Edmondson, 1980.
94. Miller, *The Lunatic Express*, p. 497.

Chapter 11

1. Smart, *Nairobi: A Jubilee History*, 1900–1950, p. 28.
2. E.A.W.L., '*They Made it their Home*, Njoro'.
3. Johansen, *The Kenya I Knew, 1904–1963*, pp. 50–7 (unpublished).
4. Interview with Dorothy Vaughan, Chipping Norton, 1983.
5. Johansen, *The Kenya I Knew, 1904–1963*, pp. 50–57.
6. Foran, *Cuckoo in Kenya*, p. 314.
7. Blencowe, *Kenya Recollections of a Sailor*, Rhodes House, Oxford. E.A.E.P.S. 6/16
8. Johansen, *The Kenya I Knew, 1904–1963*, p. 43.
9. Ibid.
10. Smart, *Nairobi: A Jubilee History, 1900–1950*, p. 28.
11. Interview with General Philips by Doria Block, Gilgil, 1979.
12. *The Leader*, 20 November 1909.
13. Interview with Dr Gerald Anderson, Nairobi, 1977.
14. Hemsing, *Old Nairobi and the New Stanley Hotel*, pp. 22–6.
15. Smart, *Nairobi: A Jubilee History, 1900–1950*, p. 32.
16. Hemsing, Old Nairobi and the New Stanley Hotel, pp. 22–5; Block family data.
17. Interview with the late Eddie Ruben by Doria Block, Nairobi, 1978.
18. My father's recollections.
19. Interview with Brian Burrows, Taita Hills, 1978.
20. Hemsing, Old Nairobi and the New Stanley Hotel, p. 10; and interview with May Stocker by Betty Kiggan, South Africa, 1978.
21. Ibid.

22. Farrant, *The Legendary Grogan*, p. 182.
23. Interview with May Stocker by Betty Kiggan.
24. Huxley, *White Man's Country*, Vol. 1, p. 309.
25. Binks, *African Rainbow*, p. 128.
26. Hunter and Mannix, *African Bush Adventures*, pp. 178–81.
27. Interview with the late Gertrude Alexander, Chester, 1978.
28. Huxley, *White Man's Country*, Vol. 1, pp. 312, 313.
29. Interview with the late Eddie Ruben.
30. Ibid.
31. Nicoll, *Mrs Haller—Woman of Faith*, in the series 'Pioneers of Kenya', *East African Standard* (undated).
32. Interview with the late Eddie Ruben.
33. Interview with Mr and Mrs Maxwell Nightingale, Njoro, 1978.
34. Alexander Davis papers.
35. Interview with the late Gertrude Alexander, Chester, 1978.
36. Alexander Davis papers.
37. Interview with the late Sarah Block, Nairobi, 1978.
38. Oates, *A draft History of Muthaiga Club*, pp. 1–4 (unpublished).
39. From a recording of the recollection of Freddy Ward.
40. ibid.
41. Interview with Anthony Seth-Smith.
42. Oates, *A draft History of Muthaiga Club*, pp. 1–4.
43. Huxley, Nellie, *Letters from Africa*, p. 34.
44. Thurman, *Isak Dinesen, The Life of a Storyteller*, p. 107.
45. Interview with the late Sarah Block.
46. Huxley, *White Man's Country*, Vol. 1, p. 313.
47. Miller, *The Lunatic Express*, p. 514.

Chapter 12

1. Huxley, *White Man's Country*, Vol. 2, p. 11.
2. Davis, 'The 1914–18 War in a Nutshell'.
3. Huxley, *White Man's Country*, Vol. 2, p. 32.
4. Ingham, *A History of East Africa*, p. 248.
5. Davis, 'The 1914–18 War in a Nutshell'.
6. Meinertzhagen, *Army Diary 1899–1926*, 16 April 1916.
7. Miller, *The Lunatic Express*, p. 521.
8. Interview with the late Sarah Block, Nairobi, 1977.
9. Ingham, *A History of East Africa*, pp. 245, 246.
10. Miller, *The Lunatic Express*, p. 521.
11. Trzebinski, *Silence Will Speak*, p. 106.
12. Miller, *The Lunatic Express*, p. 522.
13. Johanesen, *The Kenya I Knew, 1904–1963*, p. 89 (unpublished).
14. Davis, 'The 1914–18 War in a Nutshell'.
15. Huxley, *White Man's Country*, Vol. 2, p. 8.
16. Johansen, *The Kenya I Knew, 1904–1963*, p. 90.
17. Interview with the late Eddie Ruben, Nairobi, 1978.
18. Davis, 'The 1914–18 War in a Nutshell'.
19. Johansen, *The Kenya I Knew, 1904–1963*, pp. 66–7.

20. Huxley, *White Man's Country*, Vol. 2, p. 8.
21. Interview with the late Eddie Ruben, Nairobi, 1978.
22. Correspondence with Eve Pollecoff, 1983.
23. Interview with the late Eddie Ruben, Nairobi 1977.
24. Johansen, *The Kenya I Knew, 1904–1963*, pp. 71, 72.
25. Ingham, *A History of East Africa*, pp. 248, 249.
26. Huxley, *White Man's Country*, Vol. 2, p. 10.
27. Ingham, *A History of East Africa*, p. 249.
28. Huxley, *White Man's Country*, Vol. 2, p. 12.
29. Interview with Richard Wilson by Doria Block, Kilifi, 1979.
30. Squires, *The Army That Found Itself.*
31. Davis, 'The 1914–18 War in a Nutshell'.
32. Huxley, Nellie, *Letters from Africa*, p. 48.
33. Interview with Jock Rutherfurd by Doria Block, Nairobi, 1979.
34. Davis, 'The 1914–18 War in a Nutshell'.
35. Buxton, *Adventures of a Norfolk Lady.*
36. Interview with May Stocker by Betty Kiggan, South Africa, 1979.
37. Huxley, *White Man's Country*, Vol. 2, pp. 16, 17.
38. Ibid., p. 17.
39. Interview with General Phillips by Doria Block, Gilgil, 1979.
40. From a recording of the recollections of Abraham Block made by Doria Block, Nairobi, 1955.
41. Interview with Sam Weller by Doria Block, Nairobi, 1979.
42. Interview with Brian Havelock Potts, Havant, 1979.
43. Letters of Arnold Paice, 1914.
44. Interview with the late Sarah Block, Nairobi, 1978.
45. Gregory, *Under the Sun*, p. 80.
46. Huxley, *White Man's Country*, Vol. 2, pp. 21, 22.
47. Ibid., p. 24.
48. Davis, 'The 1914–18 War in a Nutshell'.
49. Interview with Sam Weller by Doria Block, Nairobi, 1979.
50. Ingham, *A History of East Africa*, pp. 251, 252, 235.
51. Huxley, *White Man's Country*, Vol. 2, p. 20.
52. Ingham, *A History of East Africa*, p. 235.
53. Young, *Marching on Tanga*, pp. 33, 34.
54. Ibid.
55. From a recording of the recollections of Abraham Block (unpublished).
56. Meinertzhagen, *Army Diary 1899–1926*, pp. 96, 97.
57. Correspondence with the late Dicky Edmondson, 1979.
58. Johansen, *The Kenya I Knew, 1904–1963*, pp. 86, 87.
59. Young, *Marching on Tanga.*
60. Johansen, *The Kenya I Knew, 1904–1926*, p. 78.
61. Ingham, *A History of East Africa*, p. 255.
62. From a recording of the recollections of Abraham Block.
63. Johansen, *The Kenya I Knew, 1904–1963*, pp. 83–89.
64. Correspondence with Dr Gerald Anderson, 1980.
65. Ibid. and with Dr Pascal Imperato, 1980.
66. Johansen, *The Kenya I Knew, 1904–1963*, p. 96.
67. Interview with the late Eddie Ruben, Nairobi, 1977.

Notes

225

ccc
68. Interview with the late Sarah Block, Nairobi, 1978.
69. Interview with Mary and Alban Mitford Barberton, Nairobi, and *Drumkeys Year Book 1909*, p. 157.
70. Van Someren family data.
71. Huxley, *White Man's Country*, Vol. 2, p. 16.
72. Interview with Sam Weller by Doria Block, Nairobi, 1979.
73. Interview with Taj Ahmed, Nairobi, 1979.
74. Huxley, *White Man's Country*, Vol. 2, pp. 31, 35.
75. Best, *Happy Valley*, p. 99.
76. Ingham, *A History of East Africa*, p. 280.
77. Huxley, *White Man's Country*, Vol. 2, p. 37.
78. Ingham, *A History of East Africa*, p. 260.
79. Miller, *The Lunatic Express*, p. 522.

Chapter 13

1. Johansen, *The Kenya I Knew, 1904–1963*, p. 93 (unpublished).
2. Miller, *The Lunatic Express*, pp. 518, 519.
3. Huxley, *White Man's Country*, Vol. 2, p. 27.
4. Miller, *The Lunatic Express*, p. 519.
5. Huxley, *White Man's Country*, Vol. 2, pp. 26, 27.
6. Hemsing, *Then and Now, Nairobi's Norfolk Hotel*, p. 57.
7. Correspondence with Eve Pollecoff, 1983.
8. Rodwell, 'Covering the Waterfront', *Kenya Weekly News*, 5 May 1957.
9. Huxley, *White Man's Country*, Vol. 2, p. 51.
10. Interview with the Sunde family by Doria Block, Langata, 1979.
11. Ingham, *A History of East Africa*, p. 265.
12. Ibid., p. 290.
13. Huxley, *White Man's Country*, Vol. 2, p. 53.
14. Sorrenson, *Origins of European Settlement in Kenya*, p. 291.
15. Davis, *The Currency Question*.
16. Huxley, *White Man's Country*, Vol. 2, p. 74.
17. From a recording of the recollections of Abraham Block made by Doria Block, Nairobi, 1955.
18. Davis, *The Currency Question*.
19. Ibid.
20. Huxley, *White Man's Country*, Vol. 2, p. 75.
21. Gregory, *Under the Sun*.
22. Huxley, *White Man's Country*, Vol. 2, p. 104.
23. From the recollections of Abraham Block.
24. Gregory, *Under the Sun*.
25. Johansen, *The Kenya I Knew, 1904–1963*, p. 93.
26. Hemsing, *The Nyali Beach Hotel Story*: 'A record of my life in Kenya and how I came to start hotels there' by Eva Noon, p. 30.
27. Block family data.
28. Interview with Brian Burrows, Taita Hills, 1979.
29. Block family data.
30. Interview with Barbara and Pip Thorpe, Milford-on-Sea, 1980.

31. Huxley, *White Man's Country*, Vol. 1, p. 98.
32. Johansen, *The Kenya I Knew, 1904–1963*, p. 94.
33. Dinesen, *Letters from Africa, 1914–1931*, 26 February 1919.

SELECT BIBLIOGRAPHY

Alport, C. J. M., *Hope in Africa*. London: Herbert Jenkins, 1952.

Beard, Peter Hill, *The End of the Game*. New York: Viking, 1965; reprinted 1977.

Binks, H. K., *African Rainbow*, London: Sidgewick & Jackson, 1959.

Blixen, Karen, *Out of Africa*. London: Jonathan Cape, 1964.

Boyes, John, *John Boyes, King of the Wakikuyu*, London: Methuen, 1911.

Carlebach, Julius, *The Jews of Nairobi, 1903–1962*. The Nairobi Hebrew Congregation, 1962.

Chilver, E. M. and Alison Smith, *History of East Africa*, Edited by Vincent Harlow, Vol. 11. London, Oxford University Press, 1965.

Churchill, Winston S., *My African Journey*. London, Hodder & Stoughton, 1908.

Cranworth, Lord, *A Colony in the Making*. London, Macmillan, 1912.

Cranworth, Lord, *Sport and Profit in East Africa*, London.

Crawford, D., *Thinking Black*. London, Morgan and Scott, 1912.

Eliot, Sir Charles, *The East Africa Protectorate*. London, Frank Cass, 1905.

Gregory, J. R., *Under the Sun*. Nairobi, The English Press, n.d.

Hake, Andrew, *African Metropolis*. London, Chatto & Windus for The Sussex University Press, 1977.

Hardy, Ronald, *The Iron Snake*. London, Collins, 1965.

Hill, Mervyn F., *Magadi*. Birmingham, The Kynock Press for the Magadi Soda Company, 1964.

Hill, Mervyn F., *Permanent Way*. Nairobi, East African Railways & Harbours, 1949.

Hemsing, Jan., *Old Nairobi and the New Stanley Hotel*. Nairobi, Sealpoint Publicity, 1974.

Hemsing, Jan, *The Nyali Beach Hotel Story—Happiness Through Heartbreak*. Sealpoint Publicity and Public Relations, Nairobi, n.d.

Hemsing, Jan, *Then and Now: Nairobi's Norfolk Hotel*. Nairobi, Sealpoint Publicity, 1975.

Hemsing, Jan, *Treetops Outspan Paxtu*. Nairobi, Church, Rait & Associates, 1974.

Huxley, Elspeth, *No Easy Way: A History of the Kenya Farmers' Association and Unga Limited*. Nairobi, The East African Standard, 1957.

Huxley, Elspeth, *White Man's Country*. London, Chatto & Windus, 1935.

Farrant, Leda, *The Legendary Grogan*, London, Hamish Hamilton, 1981.

Farson, Negley, *Last Chance in Africa*. London, Gollancz, 1949.

Foran, W. Robert, *A Cuckoo in Kenya*: The reminiscences of a Pioneer Police Officer in British East Africa. London, Hutchinson, 1936.

Henry, J. A. and edited by H. A. Siepmann, *The First Hundred Years of the Standard Bank*. London and New York, Oxford University Press, 1963.

Ingham, Kenneth, *A History of East Africa*. London, Longman's, Green, 1962.

Imperato, Pascal James, MD, *Medical Detective*. New York, Marek, 1979.

Jackson, Sir Frederick, *Early Days in East Africa*. London, Edward Arnold, 1930.

Joelson, F. S., *Rhodesia and East Africa*, London, East Africa and Rhodesia, 1958.

MacFee, A. Marshall, *Kenya*. London, Ernest Benn.

MacMillan, H. F., *Tropical Planting and Gardens*.

Meinertzhagen, Colonel R., *Kenya Diary, 1902–1906*. London, Oliver and Boyd, 1957.

Meinertzhagen, Colonel R., *Army Diary, 1899–1926*. London, Oliver & Boyd, 1960.

Miller, Charles, *The Lunatic Express*. London, Macdonald, 1971.

Mitchell, Sir Philip., *African Afterthoughts*. London, Hutchison, 1954.

Morris, James, *Pax Britannica: The Climate of an Empire*. London, Faber, 1968.

Moxon, Robert J., Agricultural Innovation in Kenya. n.d.

Mungeam, G. H., *British Rule in Kenya*, London, Oxford University Press, 1966.

O'Shea, T. J., *Farming and Planting in British East Africa*. Nairobi, Newland & Tarlton, 1917.

Playne, Somerset, FRGS edited by Holderness Gale, *East Africa (British) Its History, People, Commerce, Industries and Resources*. Foreign Colonial Publishing Coy, 1908–9.

Preston, R. O., *Oriental Nairobi*. Nairobi, Colonial Printing Works, 1938.

Preston, R. O., *Genesis of Kenya Colony*. Nairobi, Colonial Printing Works, n.d.

Purvis, John B., *British East Africa and Uganda*. London, Swan Sonnenschrin, 1900.

Stewart, Desmond, *Herzl*. London, Hamish Hamilton, 1974.

Sorrenson, M.P.K., *Origins of European Settlement in Kenya*, Oxford University Press, Nairobi, 1968.

Swainson, Nicola, *The Development of Corporate Capitalism in Kenya, 1918–1977*. London, Ibidan, Nairobi, Heinemann Educational Books, 1980.

Thurman, Judith, *Isak Dinesen, The Life of a Storyteller*. New York, St Martin's Press, 1982.

Weisbord, Robert, *African Zion*. Jewish Publication Society of America.

Wilson, Christopher, *Before the Dawn in Kenya*. Nairobi, The English Press, 1952.

Young, Francis Brett, *Marching on Tanga*. London, William Heinemann, 1917.

Official documents, yearbooks, periodicals, private publications

Accumulation & Control: The Making of the Colonial State in Kenya, 1888–1929 by Bruce Berman and John Lonsdale. African Studies, Oxford, 1978.

Blackwood's Magazine, No. 1533. July 1943, Vol. 254.

Drumkey, Y.S.A., *Drumkey's Year Book for East Africa, 1909*. The Times Press, Bombay, 1909.

The East African Annual, 1941–42.

The East African Annual, 1950–1951.

The East African Annual, 1951–1952.

The East African Standard 'A Glance down the Years', 30 June 1945.

The Globe trotter, 1906.

Handbook of East Africa, 1912.

The Leader, 27 November 1909.
Oriental Nairobi compiled by R. O. Preston, Nairobi 1913.
The Reveille, Vol. 1, No. 3, December 1915. Nairobi, The Swift Press.
The Sunday Nation, 31 March 1963.
The Sunday Nation, 7 April 1963.
The Sunday Nation, 14 April 1963.
The Sunday Nation, 21 April 1963.
The Sunday Nation, 28 April 1963.
The Sunday Nation, 5 May 1963.
The Sunday Nation, 19 May 1963.
The Sunday Nation, 26 May 1963.
The Sunday Nation, 2 June 1963.
'Adventures of a Norfolk Lady': Miss Cara Buxton's Sport in East Africa, Cara Buxton.

Unpublished memoirs and diaries of the period

The Famous 1908 Boer Trek from South Africa to BEA: The memoirs of the ninety-year-old Mr Stoffel Roets taped by Danie Steyn in 1976.
Kenya Recollections of a Sailor by C. B. Blencowe.
Happy Days in East Africa, 1906–1919 by Hilda MacNaughton.
Blowing My Own Trumpet by Helen Mayers, 1910 *et seq.*
Memoirs of Richard Gethin, 1908–1941.
Nanyuki thirty-four years ago by Mrs R. Gascoigne.
The Kenya I Knew, 1904–1963 by Alfred Johansen.
Woodsmoke, 1907–1947 by Edit Klaprott.
A Train Journey in 1917 by O'Neill.
A Train Journey in 1904 by Kit Taylor.

Letters and diaries

Extracts from Richard Meinertzhagen's diaries, 1902–1916.
The diaries of John Ainsworth, East Africa 1895–1902.
The diary of Herbert Binks, Nairobi 1902–1905.
The diary of Brian Hook—Nairobi-Nanyuki January 1914.
The Langridge papers—Letters of Lucy Langridge 1909–1915.
The diary of Mary Mitford Barberton, Uasin Gishu and Mount Elgon 1914.
The diary of Edward Morton, 1903–1905.
The diary of S. H. Montagu, Kiambu and Nairobi 1910–1911.
The diary and letters of Arnold Paice to his mother, Naivasha, Nairobi and Nanyuki 1907–1920.
The diary of Helen Sanderson, Nairobi 1904–1908.
Extracts from the diaries of Lady Francis Scott, Nairobi, Makuyu and Nanyuki 1919–1937.
The diary of camps by Da Silva.
The diairies of Lord Francis Scott, January 1919.
Extracts from the diaries and letters of Donald and Martin Seth-Smith, Nairobi, Makuyu, Kiambu, Njoro 1908–1912.
The diary of Lady Whitehouse, Mombasa, Nairobi 1898.
The diary of Morgan S. Williams, Mombasa, Nakuru April to June 1900.
East African Society of Pioneers papers.
John Boyes's scrapbook.

INDEX

**New Directions for
Community Colleges**

Arthur M. Cohen
EDITOR-IN-CHIEF

Richard L. Wagoner
ASSOCIATE EDITOR

Gabriel Jones
MANAGING EDITOR

Policies and Practices to Improve Student Preparation and Success

Andrea Conklin Bueschel
Andrea Venezia
EDITORS

Number 145 • Spring 2009
Jossey-Bass
San Francisco

POLICIES AND PRACTICES TO IMPROVE STUDENT PREPARATION AND SUCCESS
Andrea Conklin Bueschel, Andrea Venezia (eds.)
New Directions for Community Colleges, no. 145

Arthur M. Cohen, Editor-in-Chief
Richard L. Wagoner, Associate Editor

NEW DIRECTIONS FOR COMMUNITY COLLEGES (ISSN 0194-3081, electronic ISSN 1536-0733) is part of The Jossey-Bass Higher and Adult Education Series and is published quarterly by Wiley Subscription Services, Inc., A Wiley Company, at Jossey-Bass, 989 Market Street, San Francisco, California 94103-1741. Periodicals Postage Paid at San Francisco, California, and at additional mailing offices. POSTMASTER: Send address changes to New Directions for Community Colleges, Jossey-Bass, 989 Market Street, San Francisco, California 94103-1741.

SUBSCRIPTIONS cost $89.00 for individuals and $228.00 for institutions, agencies, and libraries in the United States. Prices subject to change. See order form at the back of book.

EDITORIAL CORRESPONDENCE should be sent to the Editor-in-Chief, Arthur M. Cohen, at the Graduate School of Education and Information Studies, University of California, Box 951521, Los Angeles, California 90095-1521. All manuscripts receive anonymous reviews by external referees.

New Directions for Community Colleges is indexed in CIJE: Current Index to Journals in Education (ERIC), Contents Pages in Education (T&F), Current Abstracts (EBSCO), Ed/Net (Simpson Communications), Education Index/Abstracts (H. W. Wilson), Educational Research Abstracts Online (T&F), ERIC Database (Education Resources Information Center), and Resources in Education (ERIC).

Microfilm copies of issues and articles are available in 16mm and 35mm, as well as microfiche in 105mm, through University Microfilms Inc., 300 North Zeeb Road, Ann Arbor, Michigan 48106-1346.

CONTENTS

1

This chapter surveys the educational landscape to describe current policies and practices that affect student preparation for and success in community college, ranging from national trends and state-level policies to individual classroom projects.

The Landscape of Policies and Practices That Support Student Preparation and Success

Andrea Conklin Bueschel

Community colleges, which serve almost half of postsecondary students in the United States, are receiving ever-increasing attention from policymakers and researchers (Bailey, 2002). Although these institutions have always served a wide range of people in their communities, the number of students who enter community college requiring additional preparation before they can receive credit for college-level work has increased in recent years. Of course, there will always be returning students whose knowledge and skills need refreshing, but most of the students requiring developmental course work are recent high school graduates, a population that is unlikely to be rusty. (Many terms are used for the courses that precede the college credit level courses: *developmental, basic skills, precollegiate,* and *remedial,* among others. All appear in this volume.) Rather, these students never mastered the content and skills in these areas in the first place (Bueschel, 2004).

Given the low percentage of students who progress through the precollegiate course sequence successfully, documented in this volume and many other places, the focus of work by practitioners, policymakers, and researchers must be on how to better help students succeed from wherever they start. In most states, the question of access to the community college is no longer the most significant concern (though it is still an important one). Instead, it is clear that our obligation is to help ensure that students can persist and complete their educations successfully.

NEW DIRECTIONS FOR COMMUNITY COLLEGES, no. 145, Spring 2009 © 2009 Wiley Periodicals, Inc.
Published online in Wiley InterScience (www.interscience.wiley.com) • DOI: 10.1002/cc.351

1

This volume spans multiple levels and perspectives in its effort to share ideas and potential solutions to the challenge of improving the preparation and success of students entering two-year institutions. We are interested in what goes into practice and policy, what is campus based and what is national, and what is inside the classroom and what is outside. The volume is targeted at faculty and staff at community colleges, policymakers seeking to improve the structures and opportunities for students, and researchers interested in understanding and documenting what is happening on campuses. This chapter provides an introduction to the volume by offering a brief overview of the landscape of current policies and practices and providing context for the chapters that follow.

Brief History

The community college has been part of the postsecondary picture for over a century in the United States. Originally created to serve the function of delivering lower-division course work to university students, they were viewed as junior colleges (a name preserved by a few institutions today) and were often private. However, states soon entered the business of two-year postsecondary education. And "organizationally, most of the early public community colleges developed as upward extensions of secondary schools" (Cohen and Brawer, 2003, p. 8). This dual identity has persisted despite some efforts to clarify it. Various articulation plans in every state align the community colleges with the four-year systems, yet funding structures for community colleges can be similar to K–12 systems. This is still true in California. "In 1988, the California legislature passed a comprehensive reform bill that made many community college management practices correspond with those in the state's universities, but in the same year, a proposition was passed by public initiative that placed college funding under guarantees similar to those enjoyed by the K–12 system" (Cohen and Brawer, 2003, p. 20). And in some states, community colleges receive less per student funding than do K–12 schools ("Quality Counts Report," 2008; Delta Project, 2008).

Another aspect of the multiple identities of community colleges is in academic offerings. Community colleges offer college-level course work that is eligible for university transfer. At the same time, they also have extensive offerings of classes that include content usually delivered in high school or even middle school. The growth in the population of students who are underprepared for college level work calls greater attention to those precollegiate courses. The mission of community colleges has also shifted and broadened beyond traditional academic offerings. Although not the focus of this volume, the ever-increasing diversity of career and technical offerings ensures both wide opportunities and great challenge in balancing resources and priorities, among other issues. All community college programs require a certain level of academic preparation. A health care worker or a heating, ventilation, and air-conditioning repairperson, for example, cannot be successful without being able to read with comprehension or manage basic calculations.

Many community colleges embrace their broad, inclusive, occasionally schizophrenic missions (Bueschel, 2004). They want to be the institutions that welcome everyone regardless of background. However, there are some current trends that merit attention. Bailey and Morest (2006) highlight what they see as a potentially troubling shift in the academic mission of many community colleges. More and more students enter postsecondary education aspiring to a bachelor's degree, a generally positive trend. At the same time, however, tuition is increasing, and states are bearing a smaller part of that burden. Students must come up with the necessary fees instead, often especially challenged to cover costs at four-year institutions. As the authors point out, "These developments create an increasing motivation to shift institutional missions and activities toward better prepared students with more resources, resulting in relatively less emphasis on low-income and more poorly prepared students" (p. 30). One version of this shift is a focus not only on honors programs, but even the development of baccalaureate programs at the community college.

Current Context

Possible shifts in mission or priority are important because of the impact on students who need developmental sequences to prepare them for college-level work and because the populations overrepresented in developmental courses are growing. The U.S. Census Bureau estimates that about 85 percent of the growth among eighteen- to twenty-four-year-olds will come from minority and immigrant families over the next decade, and over 40 percent will come from low-income families (Kirst and Bracco, 2002). In some ways, community colleges are and will continue to be victims of their own success. They have communicated clearly that they are institutions that welcome anyone; students know they have access to community colleges. However, many students do not know what is required of them in order to succeed there (Rosenbaum, 2001; Bueschel, 2004).

It is not surprising that students are confused. In many ways, the policymakers and colleges themselves are not clear about expectations. Although courses are designated as college credit or not, access to them is not always consistent. In addition, being placed in developmental courses is no guarantee of college readiness due in large part to the fact that students often do not complete the developmental course sequence. There is much research documenting how few students persist and complete community college overall, let alone those who start in developmental courses. In fact, success in the first semester is a telling indicator. Students "who do well in their first semester classes and who manage to persist in their education and maintain their high aspirations after the first semester are much more likely to transfer than the majority of students who do not" (Driscoll, 2007, p. 2).

New Directions for Community Colleges • DOI: 10.1002/cc

In Chapter Two, Tom Bailey discusses these issues in much greater detail, but the issues highlight important failings at both the classroom and policy levels.

Programs at the National Level

There are many points of leverage for improving outcomes for community college students, including some national and state programs worth mentioning briefly here. The Achieving the Dream project is discussed in some of the chapters. This project, funded by the Lumina Foundation and others, has broad goals at both the community college campus level and the state and federal policy level. It hopes to "advance knowledge about improving outcomes" and has developed a wide network of community colleges using an annual cohort model. The participating campuses commit to use data "to guide institutional priorities and decisions" and to contribute their data to a national database for broader research (Achieving the Dream, n.d.). The overall goal is to help students, particularly those most underrepresented, to persist and complete their academic goals.

The California Partnership for Achieving Student Success (CalPASS) also uses data as a starting point. The data are submitted voluntarily and span elementary school through the university system with unique identifiers for individual students. Once institutions have joined CalPASS, they have access to information that can help them see not only what is happening on their own sites, but what happens to their students before and after they are enrolled with them. A key strategy of CalPASS has been to create Professional Learning Councils, "regional councils made up of teams of discipline-based faculty from elementary, middle school, high school, community college and university segments [which] collaborate to discuss curriculum, exemplar teaching practices, instructional materials, and performance measures which are shared and reviewed in light of transition data" (CalPASS, 2008). In the case of the transition from high school to community college, having the high school math faculty understand that the majority of their students are placed into a community college class that they have already passed at the high school is important, if difficult, information to have. There are a number of ways to try to respond to information like that, but the questions and responses these data prompt can have a direct effect on student preparation for college level work.

The Basic Skills Initiative in California is a state-funded project developed for "planning professional development, research projects, and activities to help our colleges better prepare our students for success" (*Basic Skills Initiative Newsletter,* 2008). Its goals include promoting research and data collection, professional development in effective practice, student equity, the transition from high school to college, and information through Web site and electronic sharing. Unlike the other programs described here, this is a project that is designed for all of the institutions in the state. Like the others, increased success for students is the central goal.

Researchers at the University of Texas started the Community College Survey of Student Engagement (CCSSE) following the success of the National Survey on Student Engagement (NSSE), which focuses on students at four-year institutions. NSSE's success at linking levels of engagement with academic outcomes prompted questions about whether engagement would play the same role on two-year campuses, where students, many of whom attend part time, are unlikely to live on campus. In fact, community college engagement—with the faculty, with other students, with academic work, and with other campus activities, among other things—has proved to be important in many ways. One of the more significant findings has been the importance of the first semester: "Longitudinal data show that community colleges lose many students before a second term of enrollment" (Community College Survey of Student Engagement, 2007, p. 21), a finding consistent with the persistence trend. If community colleges have the equivalent of only one term to improve a student's chances of success, there are clear and specific responses that campuses can take. Given that finding, CCSSE has developed a new initiative, the Survey of Entering Student Engagement (SENSE), in order to understand better what factors affect students most when they begin at the community college. They note that "those who drop out are, for example, disproportionately students of color, low-income students, and academically underprepared students" (Survey of Entering Student Engagement, 2008, p. 3). They want to build on their knowledge that "helping students succeed through the equivalent of first semester (12–15 credit hours) can dramatically improve subsequent success rates. Specifically, research shows that successfully completing the first semester improves students' chances of returning for subsequent semesters, reaching key milestones, and ultimately earning certificates and degrees" (p. 13). It is clear that students' entering experiences range from being able to find the admissions office to feeling engaged, supported, and challenged by their courses.

The chapters in this volume do an excellent job of describing and analyzing additional ways of improving outcomes for students. At the national and state levels, the broadest efforts have been initiated and supported by private organizations, often foundations. Although these groups do not make policy, they do hope to achieve other goals by experimenting with new strategies, generating data and information that can better inform decision making, documenting existing practices to better understand conditions on the ground, and bringing together constituencies to share ideas and generate solutions. In Chapter Three, Pamela Burdman describes some of these activities and the theory of change that informs them. As she says, "The foundation's theory assumes that in order to improve outcomes for students at community college, several change are required: changes in practice at the college level (including improved instruction, increased access to student services and financial aid, and increased ability to track student progress) and changes at the policy level that facilitate changes at the

New Directions for Community Colleges • DOI: 10.1002/cc

college level (including more resources for colleges, resources better targeted toward student success, and more financial aid resources for students)."

Nancy Hoffman, Joel Vargas, and Janet Santos discuss in Chapter Four national efforts to develop dual-enrollment programs, an alternative pathway to college attainment. The policies and structures that shape these programs have a significant effect on their ability to change outcomes for students. In Chapter Eight, David Spence shares not only the policy challenges but the politics around a specific state-level readiness initiative for four-year universities that serves as a possible object lesson for similar policies and programs at the community college level. Although not everything described here—or in the other chapters—is funded by foundations, many of the programs or policies were developed externally and brought to the community colleges. As the authors explain, an external force in many cases is a necessary catalyst for change.

Practice at the Campus Level

Although the policies in and around community colleges are no doubt important in terms of issues of everything from access to transfer, this volume also emphasizes the necessary attention to what happens on the ground. No one in community colleges needs to be told how urgent the issue of underprepared students is, but fewer acknowledge just how much this population of students affects the whole academic enterprise. On most campuses, students are required to take a placement exam (though there are ways to get around that). Then they are recommended for a certain level course in English or mathematics, though not all registration systems prevent enrollment in other levels, and some campuses' placement procedures are voluntary. In many cases, other departments are somewhat loath to have prerequisites for their courses (for example, completion of the developmental reading sequence) because it would depress enrollment. Finally, there are concerns that placement exams are not reliable or valid. One outcome is that students who may not have the skills to handle college-level reading, writing, or quantitative processes often enroll in college-level transfer classes like Psychology 1 or Economics 1. The presence of these students in nondevelopmental classes makes the issue of basic skills mastery everyone's business. Grubb and his colleagues (1999) talk about this "hidden remediation" (p. 198). They explain that it "comes in many forms, ranging from the worst cases—when an entire college-level course has been hijacked for the purposes of basic instruction—to the most deft instruction with basic skills embedded in other content as the need arises. None of this is planned by the college, and none of this can be recognized as remediation except by observing the classroom" (p. 198). Although attention to the curriculum and pedagogy of developmental courses is a necessary first step, it is important to acknowledge that the issue of helping basic skills students succeed goes beyond those classrooms.

The challenge, of course, is that there is no silver bullet even for the students who are in the right place. As Schwartz and Jenkins (2007) note, "Despite the prevalence of students who take developmental courses at community colleges, there is surprisingly little definitive research evidence on what makes for effective developmental education practice" (p. 2). There are some patterns about which students do well in different types of courses, but the one universal is that no single textbook, teaching style, or class structure is going to work for this highly diverse population of students.

Some programs, most notably learning communities, have yielded improved outcomes for students. The goal of learning communities is to create a community where students know and trust each other and the faculty, where faculty have a sense of what is happening in their students' lives, and that the material covered in both classes will have more meaning in this richer context. As most higher education practitioners are aware, learning communities can be as simple as coregistered courses with a shared student enrollment, the most common form on community college campuses. Often an English course (reading or writing) is paired with a social science or humanities course, and the faculty members coordinate their curricula and assignments to be reinforcing in some way. There may be a counseling or student success component as part of the learning community—either an additional low-credit student success type class or a designated counselor who works with students in that community.

Although these goals are not always met, there is some evidence that learning communities are making a difference for students. Scrivener and others (2008) found that students in learning communities had improved college experiences, improved some educational outcomes (though somewhat diminished with time), attempted and passed more courses, earned more credits first semester, and moved more quickly through developmental English. There was mixed evidence on program persistence, though other studies have found better outcomes on persistence than other achievement measures. Tinto (2008) also describes improved performance and persistence for students in learning communities. He and his colleagues found that students improve "in part, because of the way the courses that comprise the learning communities are aligned in their actions so that what is learned in a basic skills course can be applied in the other course or courses that make up the learning community."

In other studies, students have stressed affective outcomes of learning communities, including greater confidence in school, better studenting skills (like time management and organization that contribute to being a better student), and a greater connection to their classmates, professors, and the institution as a whole (Bueschel, 2008). As one learning community student said, "It empowers you so greatly. School is always something that hurt me, because I didn't know how to do it, and I felt so scared, and it could've stopped my college career because that's how bad it was. But now I feel very empowered in everything I do" (Bueschel, 2008, p. 11).

NEW DIRECTIONS FOR COMMUNITY COLLEGES • DOI: 10.1002/cc

Another on-campus program that has shown positive results for some students is supplemental instruction (SI), a strategy developed at the University of Missouri, Kansas City, and adapted widely at many community colleges: "SI is a peer facilitated academic support program that targets historically difficult courses so as to improve student performance and retention by offering regularly scheduled, out-of-class review sessions" (International Center for Supplemental Instruction, 2008). The instructor invites a student who has previously been successful in that class to attend all of the class meetings and to hold additional voluntary meetings with small groups outside class. The dual purpose here is not only to help students consolidate knowledge in a less intimidating setting, but also to have the student instructor model good student behavior in the classroom.

Some SI principles are reflected in other approaches as well. Many faculty have tried to create less intimidating settings by incorporating small group work, having more group discussions, or encouraging students to use tutoring centers or libraries. Helping students engage more fully in their courses—both with the material and with their classmates and instructor—is often the goal of these efforts. Although outcomes vary, "research shows that students who attend SI sessions regularly average one half to one full letter grade higher than their classmates who choose not to attend" (International Center for Supplemental Instruction, 2008). At their best, these innovations give students well-structured opportunities to articulate what they do and do not understand about the content and to share strategies for working through difficulties; they give teachers a better chance to find out what their students are really thinking and to plan their own next pedagogical steps (Bueschel, 2008).

The Strengthening Pre-Collegiate Education in Community Colleges (SPECC) project, an effort of the Carnegie Foundation for the Advancement of Teaching and the William and Flora Hewlett Foundation, takes a different focus on improving developmental courses. The project uses the idea of faculty inquiry as a starting point. It has worked closely with faculty members at eleven community colleges and encouraged them to ask questions about their teaching and their students' learning. The inquiry can be a teaching community committed to meeting regularly to question, discuss, and try to address a specific issue (for example, what foundational mathematics skill most elementary algebra students stumble on), or a research question that a faculty member wants to explore after noticing a pattern in her classroom (the students who drop out late in the term are not necessarily the ones with the lowest grades to that point).

Two chapters in this volume are from faculty at SPECC campuses. In Chapter Seven, Chris Juzwiak and Monette Tiernan write about the uses of technology in developmental English classes at Glendale Community College, and in Chapter Six, Brock Klein and Lynn Marie Wright describe a pre-algebra faculty inquiry group at Pasadena City College. In both cases, the faculty started with a question, or a pattern, or a hypothesis about why their students were not succeeding, designed a way to address that question, and have conducted inquiry to test their hypotheses. In addition, Chapter Five examines a reaccreditation process at Mississippi Delta Community College (MDCC) that triggered questions about the preparedness of entering students, with a specific focus on preparation at the high school level. As Renee Moore shares in that chapter, MDCC's English department changed its assumptions about how best to meet the needs of their developmental students. She, like other authors in this volume, suggests that teachers can be—and often are—underprepared too.

There are many more examples of approaches to improving developmental courses that have worked (or not), but the larger point here is that we need to continue to ask questions and challenge assumptions about developmental education and community colleges. Tom Bailey's excellent overview in Chapter Two stresses this point. It is also clear that we ignore one level at the peril of the other. The best policy in the world will not make a difference for the people in the classroom—teachers and students—if it does not make sense in their day-to-day lives. And we know the finest teaching will not matter at all if a student does not have access to that classroom. This volume seeks to balance these levels by sharing big picture trends, highlighting promising policies and programs at the national and state levels, and providing on-the-ground examples of how to help students succeed.

References

Achieving the Dream. "About Achieving the Dream." N.d. Retrieved Apr. 29, 2008, from http://www.achievingthedream.org/ABOUTATD/GOALS/default.tp.

Bailey, T. "Community Colleges in the 21st Century: Challenges and Opportunities." In P. A. Graham and N. G. Stacey (eds.), *The Knowledge Economy and Postsecondary Education: Report of a Workshop*. Washington, D.C.: National Academies Press, 2002.

Bailey, T., and Morest, V. S. (eds.). *Defending the Community College Equity Agenda*. Baltimore, Md.: Johns Hopkins University Press, 2006.

Basic Skills Initiative Newsletter. Mar. 2008. Retrieved May 16, 2008, from http://www.cccbsi.org/Websites/basicskills/Images/BSI-Newsletter.pdf.

Bueschel, A. C. "The Missing Link: The Role of Community Colleges in the Transition Between High School and College." In M. Kirst and A. Venezia (eds.), *From High School to College*. San Francisco: Jossey-Bass, 2004.

Bueschel, A. C. "Listening to Students About Learning." Stanford, Calif.: Carnegie Foundation for the Advancement of Teaching, 2008.

California Partnership for Achieving Student Success. webpage on professional learning councils. "Professional Learning Councils." N.d. Retrieved Apr. 29, 2008, from http://www.cal-pass.org/Councils.aspx.

Cohen, A., and Brawer, F. *The American Community College*. San Francisco: Jossey-Bass, 2003.

Community College Survey of Student Engagement. *Committing to Student Engagement: Reflections on CCSSE's First Five Years*. Austin, Tex.: Community College Survey of Student Engagement, 2007.

Delta Project. "Issue Brief #1: Who Pays for Higher Education? Changing Patterns in Cost, Price, and Subsidies." Washington, D.C.: Delta Project, Apr. 2008.

Driscoll, A. K. "Beyond Access: How the First Semester Matters for Community College Students' Aspirations and Persistence." Berkeley and Stanford, Calif.: Policy Analysis for California Education, 2007.

Grubb, W. N., and Associates. *Honored But Invisible.* New York: Routledge, 1999.

International Center for Supplemental Instruction. Information webpage. "Supplemental Instruction @ UMKC." Kansas City: University of Missouri, 2008. Retrieved June 10, 2008, from http://www.umkc.edu/cad/SI/.

Kirst, M., and Bracco, K. "Bridging the Great Divide." Stanford, Calif.: Bridge Project. 2002.

Moore, C., and Shulock, N. "Beyond the Open Door: Increasing Student Success in the California Community Colleges." Sacramento, Calif.: Institute for Higher Education Leadership and Policy, 2007.

"Quality Counts Report." *Education Week,* Jan. 10, 2008.

Rosenbaum, J. *Beyond College for All.* New York: Russell Sage Foundation, 2001.

Schwartz, W., and Jenkins, D. "Promising Practices for Community College Developmental Education." New York: Community College Resource Center, 2007.

Scrivener, S., and others. "A Good Start: Two-Year Effects of a Freshman Learning Community Program at Kingsborough Community College." Oakland, Calif., and New York: MDRC, 2008.

Survey of Entering Student Engagement. "Starting Right: A First Look at Engaging Entering Students." Austin, Tex.: Community College Survey of Student Engagement, 2008.

Tinto, V. "Access Without Support Is Not Opportunity." *Inside Higher Ed,* June 9, 2008. Retrieved June 9, 2008, from http://insidehighered.com/views/2008/06/09/tinto.

ANDREA CONKLIN BUESCHEL is a program director at the Spencer Foundation. She is a former research scholar and member of the Strengthening Pre-Collegiate Education in Community Colleges research team at the Carnegie Foundation for the Advancement of Teaching.

NEW DIRECTIONS FOR COMMUNITY COLLEGES • DOI: 10.1002/cc

2

This chapter provides a national context about how students progress in community colleges across the country. It includes data about students who take developmental education courses, how they move through the developmental course sequence, the obstacles they face when completing their intended course of study, and programs and practices that appear to help students meet their goals.

Challenge and Opportunity: Rethinking the Role and Function of Developmental Education in Community College

Thomas Bailey

Developmental education is one of the most difficult issues confronting community colleges. Community colleges are charged with teaching students college-level material, yet a majority of their students arrive with academic skills in at least one subject area that are judged to be too weak to allow them to engage successfully in college-level work. Thus, a majority of community college students arrive unprepared to engage effectively in the core function of the college. Colleges address this problem with extensive programs of developmental education, which are designed to strengthen skills so students can successfully complete college-level courses. (The terms *developmental education* and *remediation* are used interchangeably in this chapter.)

In this chapter, I first review evidence on the number of students who arrive with weak academic skills and the incidence of developmental education. Using longitudinal data sets that track students through their college

The work and research for this chapter were carried out as part of the Achieving the Dream: Community Colleges Count initiative. I thank Dong Wook Jeong and Sung-Woo Cho for analysis of the Achieving the Dream data and Pamela Burdman, Juan Carlos Calcagno, Davis Jenkins, Dolores Perin, Jeff Rafn, and Diane Troyer for many useful and insightful comments and suggestions.

experience, I then report on what happens to developmental students and review the research on the effectiveness of programs at community colleges designed to strengthen weak academic skills. The subsequent section briefly discusses the costs of these programs to students. I conclude by arguing that on average, developmental education as it is now practiced is not very effective in overcoming academic weaknesses, partly because the majority of students referred to developmental education do not finish the sequences to which they are referred.

This bleak picture of the developmental education landscape justifies a broad-based effort to reform and rethink the endeavor. But there is reason for optimism. In recent years, a dramatic expansion in experimentation with new approaches has taken place. There is now a growing commitment to better evaluation and quantitative analysis of student progression in community colleges that promises a more systematic and informed process of program and policy development. I suggest a broad developmental education reform agenda based on a comprehensive approach to assessment, more rigorous research that explicitly tracks students with weak academic skills through their early experiences at community colleges, a blurring of the distinction between developmental and "college-level" students that could improve pedagogy for both groups of students, and strategies to streamline developmental programs and accelerate students' progress toward engagement in college-level work.

Weak Academic Skills and the Incidence of Developmental Education

How many students arrive at community colleges with weak academic skills? Using data from the National Education Longitudinal Study (NELS), a sample of traditional college-aged students, Attewell, Lavin, Domina, and Levey (2006) found that among a sample of students who were in eighth grade in 1988 and were tracked until 2000, 58 percent of those students who attended a community college took at least one remedial course, 44 percent took between one and three remedial courses, and 14 percent took more than three such courses. A different sample suggests a similar incidence. Achieving the Dream: Community Colleges Count, a national initiative funded by Lumina Foundation and others, involves eighty-three community colleges in fifteen states. To participate, colleges are required to submit longitudinal data to a national database that contains detailed information on referral to remediation and enrollment and completion of developmental courses and sequences. In mid-2008, the Achieving the Dream database had information on 256,672 students. The entering cohorts of first-time college students at every participating college for each year the college participates in the initiative are tracked longitudinally for the duration of the college's involvement. In this chapter, I use data on over 250,000 first-time students for whom there are three years of data. According to these data, 59 percent of students in the colleges participating in the initiative enrolled in at least one developmental education course during the three years that students were tracked. Note that this is not a random sample of colleges since colleges with high proportions of minority students or Pell grant recipients were recruited for the initiative. (See www.achievingthe dream.com for more information.)

Although these rates of incidence of developmental education are high, nonetheless they underestimate the number of students arriving at community colleges with weak academic skills. Many students whose test scores suggest that they need some academic help to prepare them for college-level work do not end up enrolling in developmental education classes. In some states, California being the most prominent, students can enroll in college-level courses even if their scores on an assessment test suggest that they are not adequately prepared, so that enrollment in remediation effectively becomes voluntary. In other states, students, professors, and colleges often find ways around eligibility criteria: students whose assessment test scores fall below cutoff levels enroll in regular courses anyway using various formal or informal exceptions. In a study of fifteen community colleges, Perin and Charron (2006) found extensive enrollments of this type, and Calcagno (2007) reported significant enrollments of "ineligible" students in college-level courses in Florida, despite a policy in which remediation was mandatory for students whose test scores fell below the statewide cutoff point.

Data from the Achieving the Dream sample reveal this gap between referral and enrollment. Among the colleges in the Achieving the Dream initiative, about 21 percent of students referred to developmental math do not enroll in any remedial math course within three years of initial registration. For developmental reading, the comparable figure is 33 percent.

Moreover, even data on referral to developmental education may understate the extent of inadequate academic skills among community college students. Indeed, in some states or colleges and for some occupational courses, students are not required to take assessment tests that might refer them to remediation. Moreover, many students who are judged to be college ready struggle in their classes as well. Thus, it is reasonable to conclude that two-thirds or more of community college students enter college with academic skills weak enough in at least one major subject area to threaten their ability to succeed in college-level courses.

Progression Through Developmental Education

What happens to students who enroll in developmental education? Do they complete the sequence of developmental courses, do they enroll in college-level courses, and are they successful in those courses? According to NELS data, 68 percent of students pass all of the developmental writing courses in which they enroll, and 71 percent pass all of the reading courses. Students have much less success with math courses: only 30 percent pass all of the math developmental courses in which they enroll (Attewell, Lavin, Domina, and Levey, 2006).

These data concern pass rates for individual courses. However, students are often referred to a sequence of developmental courses comprising two, three, or even more levels below the entry-level college course in a given area. Thus, some students are judged to need three or more semesters of course work before being prepared to learn college material.

Among the Achieving the Dream colleges, for students in colleges that offer three levels of developmental math, about one-third of all entering students are assigned to the lowest level of math remediation. In colleges that offer two levels of developmental math, 28 percent of the students are referred to the lowest-level course. Students in the sample arrive at community colleges with skills in reading that are relatively stronger than those in mathematics. 34 percent are referred to any developmental reading course, but only about 11 percent are referred to the most elementary course, which is two or three levels below the entry-level college course.

How many students complete the sequences of developmental courses to which they are referred? The first conclusion to note is that many simply never enroll in developmental classes in the first place. In the Achieving the Dream sample, around one-fifth of all students referred to developmental math education and one-third of students referred to developmental reading do not enroll in any developmental course within three years.

Of the students referred to remediation, how many actually complete their full developmental sequences? Within three years of their initial assessment, about 44 percent of those referred to developmental reading complete their full sequence, but this accounts for two-thirds of those who actually enroll in at least one developmental reading course. These numbers are worse for math: only 31 percent of those referred to developmental math complete their sequence. And this accounts for only 44 percent of those who enroll in any developmental math course. Few students who start three levels below college level ever complete their full sequence within three years—just 16 percent for math and 22 percent for reading. In addition, many students who successfully complete one or more developmental courses do not show up for the subsequent course. For example, about one-quarter of all students referred to three levels below college level for both math and reading drop out between courses.

Degree completion for remedial students is also rare. Less than one-quarter of community college students in the NELS sample who enrolled in developmental education complete a degree or certificate within eight years of enrollment in college. Another 14 percent transfer to a four-year college without having completed a degree or certificate. In comparison, almost 40 percent of community college students in the NELS sample who did not enroll in any developmental education course complete a degree in the same time period, and 14 percent transfer without having completed a degree or certificate.

NEW DIRECTIONS FOR COMMUNITY COLLEGES • DOI: 10.1002/cc

The Effectiveness of Developmental Education

Students who enter community colleges with weak academic skills face significant barriers. As we have seen, students who enroll in remediation are less likely to complete degrees or transfer than nondevelopmental students. But this comparison does not suggest that developmental education itself causes or leads to worse outcomes or even that it does not increase student outcomes. After all, students enrolling in developmental education have, on average, weaker skills, and in some cases much weaker skills, than other students. So these data suggest that remediation is not able to make up for the deficiencies, but it is possible that developmental students would have even weaker outcomes if these services were not available. Indeed, research that controls for entering academic skills and other demographic characteristics finds that developmental students in community colleges do as well as students who never participate in developmental education (Adelman, 1998; Attewell, Lavin, Domina, and Levey, 2006).

But if these analyses show that taking developmental education does not hurt students, they also suggest that these courses do not help them either. Since these studies control for measures of academic preparation, they seem to conclude that among students with equally low assessment tests scores, those who take developmental education do no better than those who enroll directly in college-level courses. It is a serious problem if developmental students do no better than similar students who enroll directly in college courses. Developmental education costs students, the colleges, and the public sector real resources, and in any case, it exists to strengthen the outcomes for students—concluding that developmental students do as well as similar students who go directly into college courses is not good enough and suggests that remediation wastes money and time.

There are still some methodological problems with the studies that compare developmental and nondevelopmental students after controlling for measured student characteristics, which may make their results unreliable. It is possible that unmeasured differences between remedial and nonremedial students might account for the outcomes rather than any influence of the developmental classes themselves. For example, if among students with low test scores, the more motivated and aggressive find ways to avoid remediation and enroll directly in college courses, then that might reduce the measured effect of remediation, since those who avoid remediation could be systematically different (they could be more motivated, for example).

While few studies address the problem of unmeasured differences or selection bias, there are now three groups of studies based on large, longitudinal state data sets that use quasi-experimental methods to derive more reliable causal estimates of the effects of developmental education: studies of Ohio by Bettinger and Long (2005), of Florida by Calcagno (2007) and Calcagno and Long (2008), and of Texas by Martorell and McFarlin (2007). All of these used data from the late 1990s and early 2000s.

Bettinger and Long (2005) used differences in placement policies among colleges in Ohio to compare similar students who are and are not enrolled in developmental education. Because of differences in institutional place-ment policies, a student placed into developmental education at one college may be otherwise similar to a student placed into college-level courses at a different college (one that has lower cutoff scores). This methodology would be threatened if students change colleges in pursuit of more sympathetic placement policies. Bettinger and Long addressed this problem by using the reasonable assumption that students are more likely to go to colleges close to where they live. Thus, combining the differences in placement policies and students' tendency to attend colleges closer to home allowed the researchers to estimate causal effects of remediation on student outcomes.

In their study, Bettinger and Long (2005) analyzed first-time degree-seeking community college students who were eighteen, nineteen, or twenty years of age and who had taken the ACT assessment test. They found posi-tive outcomes for students placed in math remediation. Those students were found to be 15 percent more likely to transfer to a four-year college, and they take approximately ten more credit hours than similar students not placed in remediation. The analysis showed no positive effects for developmental English classes. It should be noted that the conclusions of this study apply primarily to students who are very close to the cutoff point for determining assignment to remediation and therefore are less relevant for students who face serious academic deficiencies. It should also be noted that remediation for older students was not considered in the study. Older students may have a different type of developmental need than the younger students included in the sample.

The Florida and Texas studies used a regression discontinuity approach (Shadish, Cook, and Campbell, 2002). Regression discontinuity can be used when there is a fixed cutoff that determines in a reliable way who gets assigned to a program or initiative. In the case of remediation, the strategy is most straightforward if everyone who scores below a fixed cutoff point enrolls in remediation and everyone who scores above that cutoff enrolls in college-level courses. The contention is that students just above and just below that cutoff point are essentially identical, yet only the students who score below the point enroll in remediation. Thus, by comparing outcomes for students just above (college level) and just below the cutoff (remedia-tion), one can derive a reliable estimate of the effects of remediation.

A regression discontinuity analysis was possible in Texas because the state had a common mandatory statewide cutoff score for placement in developmental education on the Texas Academic Skills Program (TASP) test at the time the sample was collected. According to the policy, students who tested below that cutoff score were required to enroll in developmental edu-cation, while those with test results above the cutoff score were able to enroll in college-level courses. Martorell and McFarlin (2007) found some weak evidence that remediation improves grades in the first college-level math course (for developmental students who took such a course), but they found no effect on the probability of passing a college-level math course, transferring to a four-year college, or completing a degree.

Similarly, in Florida, Calcagno (2007) and Calcagno and Long (2008) compared outcomes for community college students who scored just above the statewide cutoff score for developmental education on the College Placement Test (CPT) to those who scored just below it. Florida requires students who score below the cutoff to enroll in remediation. The researchers found that students scoring just below the cutoff for the math test are slightly more likely to persist to their second year than those who scored just above the cutoff. They also found that developmental math students accumulate more total credits (remedial and college level) over six years. However, they found no effect on the completion of college-level math (nonremedial) credits. And developmental education had no positive effect on passing subsequent college-level English or math courses. Finally, they found no statistically significant effect of math remediation on completing a certificate or associate degree or on transferring to a public four-year college. Results for reading were more negative. Assignment to remediation had a statistically significant negative effect on completion of the first college-level course, associate degree completion, transfer to a four-year university, and total nonremedial credits earned.

Figure 2.1 presents a visual depiction of these results for math. The horizontal axis in each panel displays scores on the CPT with the statewide cutoff score set at zero, and the vertical axis displays the probability of achieving a particular outcome within six years after enrollment: passing the first-level college course, associate degree completion, total credits earned, fall-to-fall retention, transfer to a four-year college, and total college-level credits earned. The circles are the average outcome for students with a given CPT score. If developmental education is effective and if students are following the developmental assignment policy, then the circles just to the left of the cutoff line should be higher than those to the right of it. The top right panel (illustrating the total number of credits earned) shows the expected pattern with a clear break at the cutoff score. This is strong evidence that over six years, developmental students accumulate more credits (developmental and college level) than similar students who go directly into college-level courses. But the bottom right panel indicates that the additional courses are accounted for by remediation itself. Developmental students do not earn any more college-level credits than do students who scored above the developmental education cutoff score. The bottom left panel shows the slightly higher probability that developmental students will persist into the second year. The other panels, which show results for passing the first college-level course in the relevant subject, transfer, and completion of a two-year degree, all show a gap in outcomes at the cutoff point that suggests a negative effect

Figure 2.1. Educational Outcome by Math College Placement Test Score and Estimated Discontinuity in Florida, 1997–2000

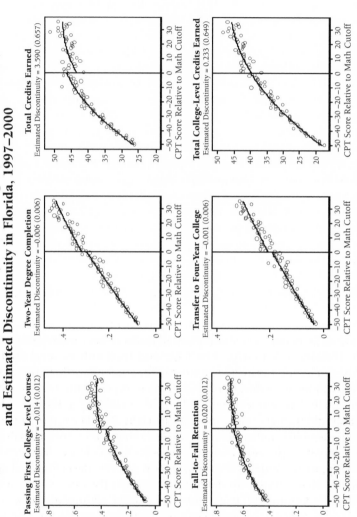

Note: Each graph corresponds to a different educational outcome. The circles are the mean of the binary dependent variable for students with a given CPT score. The fitted lines are predicted probabilities from a linear probability model for the educational outcome on the assignment to treatment variable and quadratic polynomial terms in the CPT score. Entering cohorts were tracked for six years.

Source: Calcagno and Long (2008).

for developmental education, although these differences are not statistically significant. Martorell and McFarlin (2007) display similar graphs of the relationship between scores on the TASP test and several outcomes, generally showing no statistically significant gap at the cutoff point.

There are two other studies of developmental education that use a regression discontinuity design. Lesik (2006) studied three cohorts of first-time, full-time students at a large state university and found that developmental education improves the chances of completing a first-level college math course on the first try. Moss and Yeaton (2006) studied students at a large community college and concluded that students who took developmental English do as well in subsequent college courses as students who scored above the developmental cutoff score. Only students who enrolled in a college-level course were in Moss and Yeaton's sample, so they could not measure any effect of developmental education on that enrollment. Moreover, both of these studies make use of relatively small samples—fewer than two thousand students. Since the samples include students with scores throughout the range of possible scores, there are few students close to the cutoff scores. As a result, the authors needed to make strong assumptions about the relationship between assessment test scores and subsequent outcomes, making these results less reliable than those from the Texas, Florida, and Ohio studies. (See Calcagno, 2007, for a more detailed criticism of the Moss and Yeaton study. He concludes that their estimates of the effectiveness of developmental education are biased upward.)

Thus, these studies give mixed results: the Texas and Florida studies suggest students gain little from developmental classes, and the Ohio study shows some positive results. Nevertheless, there are several important points to emphasize with regard to these studies. First, the results for all three studies are most reliable for students whose assessment results lie near the cutoff score. They do not provide much insight into the effectiveness of developmental education for students with very weak skills. The methodological problem is simply that there are very few such students in college-level courses who can serve as a comparison group for low-scoring developmental students. Second, these studies provide an average statewide picture that obscures institutional-level variation: if the average effect is zero, then undoubtedly the developmental programs at some individual colleges will have a positive effect. Educators could certainly learn from these programs if they are identified. Third, some subgroups may benefit more from remediation than others. The Ohio study found positive results using a sample of traditional-aged students who were oriented enough toward college to have taken the ACT. Calcagno (2007) found some positive results for older students. Fourth, as we have seen, many students who are referred to remediation either never enroll in or fail to complete their developmental sequence; thus, many students do not receive the full developmental treatment. This could weaken the measured effects of developmental instruction.

It also suggests that in order to improve remediation, educators will have to improve the experience in the classes *and* get students to enroll and stay in those classes. Finally, these longitudinal results are all from the late 1990s or early 2000s and therefore do not reflect any effects of the growing reform movements of this decade.

These studies measured the average effects of all of the developmental education offered in a state. The developmental courses included in the studies therefore represent a wide variety of remedial programs and pedagogies. What do we know about the effectiveness of different approaches to remediation? In practice, there is no consensus about how to carry out developmental education most effectively. As a result, the content and organization of remediation also vary widely. In her analysis of remediation in fifteen colleges in six states, Perin (2006) found more approaches than colleges. Indeed, many colleges use several approaches. For example, most colleges offer remedial courses in which students gather with a professor in a classroom a given number of times over the course or a semester. The surveys of the incidence of remediation count these types of remedial classes. But within that structure, there is wide variation in the pedagogical strategies used. These range from traditional lecture formats to more interactive approaches based on active student participation (Grubb, 1999; Perin, 2006). However, colleges also use other forms of developmental education that rely on student access to assistance in learning centers or through special tutors.

Research appears to offer some general guidance, but definitive evidence on the effectiveness of particular strategies is scarce. Based on their reviews of the literature on academic achievement in college, Pascarella and Terenzini (1991, 2005) suggested that institutions can aid the academic adjustment of poorly prepared students by providing extensive instruction in academic skills, advising, counseling, and comprehensive support services. They contended that their findings have been replicated in several national studies and that the results hold even after controlling for important student and institutional characteristics. Unmeasured factors, however, are generally not considered in the studies that they reviewed.

The National Center for Developmental Education carried out a large project on developmental education in the 1990s, and its conclusions, along with conclusions from other projects, were summarized *What Works: A Guide to Research-Based Best Practices in Developmental Education* (Boylan, 2002). These conclusions are generally consistent with the Pascarella and Terenzini summaries, advocating counseling and support, mandatory assessment and enrollment, and specialized programs for developmental students. While many of these conclusions are reasonable, the studies on which they are based are primarily descriptive or correlational, so causal inferences are difficult to establish. In any case, if these practices are effective, the disappointing research on the overall effects of remediation suggests that they have not so far been widely adopted.

Researchers have been particularly enthusiastic about learning community formats for remediation. In his review of research on developmental education, Grubb (2001) argued that learning communities appear to have positive benefits on student performance in subsequent college-level courses. Bailey and Alfonso (2005) also found some support for the model in community colleges based primarily on quasi-experimental and correlational research. There is extensive research on learning communities in four-year colleges, although these efforts are not primarily designed for developmental students (Taylor, Moore, MacGregor, and Lindblad, 2003).

A random assignment study of a learning communities program at Kingsborough Community College in Brooklyn, New York, provides some evidence for the effectiveness of learning communities (Scrivener and others, 2008). This study, carried out by MDRC, found that students in the learning communities are more likely than control group students to attempt and pass both English and writing assessment tests during their first semester. This advantage persists, but does not grow, in subsequent semesters. But with the exception of this MDRC study, there is little research that reliably measures the causal impact of different approaches to remediation.

Thus, there is a general consensus in the field about some characteristics of developmental education: for example, assessment should be mandatory, appropriate counseling and support services should be available, and developmental faculty should have adequate preparation and be committed to the particular mission of developmental education. These suggestions are based primarily on the experience of developmental educators and administrators and in some cases on suggestive evidence. So far, there is only a meager harvest of research that reliably measures the benefits of either developmental education compared to simply enrolling students in college-level courses or of different types of program designs or pedagogies.

The Costs of Developmental Education

The modest benefits of developmental services need to be evaluated in relation to their significant costs to the state and the institution and especially to the student. The most common citation for the financial cost of remediation is Breneman and Harlow (1998), who found a decade ago that colleges spend more than $1 billion annually on developmental education. A more recent study calculated the annual cost of remediation at $1.9 to $2.3 billion at community colleges and another $500 million at four-year colleges (Strong American Schools, 2008). State reports from Florida, Arkansas, and Ohio cite expenditures of tens or hundreds of millions of dollars annually (Florida Office of Program Policy Analysis and Government Accountability, 2006; Arkansas Department of Higher Education, n.d.; Ohio Board of Regents, 2006).

Perhaps more important, developmental education carries significant financial and psychological costs to the students. While in developmental classes, students accumulate debt and spend time, money, and, in many cases, financial aid eligibility while not earning credits toward a degree. Even if no tuition is charged, remedial students bear the opportunity cost of lost earnings. In practical terms, taking developmental courses lengthens the time required to complete a degree, and factors that lengthen the time to degree, such as attending part time or interrupting enrollment, also tend to reduce the probability of degree completion (Horn and Nevill, 2006; Horn and Carroll, 1996). It is also the case that students referred to developmental classes, most of whom are high school graduates, are often surprised and discouraged when they learn that they must delay their college education and in effect return to high school. A recent survey of remedial students found that a majority believed that they were prepared for college (Strong American Schools, 2008). This unexpected gap between their understanding of their own skills and the discouraging results of assessment tests can cause students to become frustrated and to give up and leave college (Deil-Amen and Rosenbaum, 2002). Student resistance to remediation requirements may help explain the low enrollment rates and high attrition rates. Faculty and advisors often collaborate with students in an effort to avoid remediation, using loopholes and exceptions that can be found in many regulations and guidelines (Perin, 2006).

What Differentiates a Developmental from a College-Level Student?

Developmental education assessments are in reality high-stakes tests. Failing such tests often leads to enrollment in remediation with attendant costs and delayed progress for students. Yet those services have dubious benefits, at least in the way that developmental education is currently carried out. But despite the importance of the test outcomes, there is no national consensus about what level of skills is needed to be college ready or how to assess that level. (There is currently an ongoing discussion aimed at defining what knowledge and skills are needed to succeed in college. See Conley, 2005. But this discussion so far has not resulted in widely used assessments to determine whether students should be referred to developmental education.)

Many different tests are used to determine developmental need, although versions of Accuplacer and Compass are the most common. More than one hundred tests are used in California alone (Kirst, 2007; Brown and Niemi, 2007), although most colleges choose from a much smaller number of tests. For example, for math, the large majority of California community colleges use one of three assessments (Task Force on Assessment, 2008). Even when the same test is used within a state, institutions are often free to choose their own cutoff scores. Attempts to develop statewide standards often meet resistance. For example, the Texas policy that set a statewide test and cutoff point that provided the methodological basis of the Martorell and McFarlin (2007) study has since been altered to allow much greater local autonomy.

NEW DIRECTIONS FOR COMMUNITY COLLEGES • DOI: 10.1002/cc

One source of resistance to standardization is that the assessments measure only some of the skills needed for a successful college experience. Indeed, attempts to articulate a comprehensive understanding of what skills and knowledge are needed to succeed in college, such as the work done by Conley (2005), highlight the narrowness of the assessments used for remedial placement. Even students who pass the placement assessments may lack many of the skills and knowledge that Conley argues are essential "college knowledge."

The wide variation in various outcomes for students with the same assessment test scores illustrates the gap between the skills measured by the assessments and the skills needed to be successful in college. While the graphs displayed in Figure 2.1 do show a positive relationship between test scores and various outcomes, they indicate the average outcome for each test score and therefore give a false sense of regularity. Data referred to earlier from the Achieving the Dream database support this claim. They show that some students who were referred to developmental math but never enrolled in a developmental math course nevertheless took and passed a college-level math course. And findings from a series of validation studies carried out between 1990 and 1992 on the Accuplacer assessment show considerable variation in the correlation between scores and course grades. For example, the average correlation between reading comprehension test scores with grades in developmental reading was 0.18 (the lowest reported correlation was 0.03, the highest was 0.38). Average correlations for arithmetic test scores and grades in developmental math courses (such as general mathematics, arithmetic, elementary algebra, and intermediate algebra) ranged from 0.31 (arithmetic) to 0.38 (general mathematics and intermediate algebra). The statistical significance of these results was not reported (College Board, 2006). The College Board does advise that colleges should combine Accuplacer scores with other information to decide on the most appropriate placements.

Despite the uncertainty that results from the variation of outcomes for any given score, educators must decide where to set the cutoff point. It is clear from Figure 2.1 that there is no obvious point of discontinuity where a dividing line could be reasonably set. Within a relatively large range around the cutoff score, there is little difference between students who are assigned to developmental education and those who are encouraged to enroll in college-level courses. Similar graphs from the Texas study show the same continuous relationships (Martorell and McFarlin, 2007).

To a large extent, the distinction between developmental and nondevelopmental students is arbitrary—the dichotomous categorization does not match the underlying continuity. Thus, some students placed in remediation do succeed in college-level courses even when they do not enroll in remediation, while many students who score well above the cutoff scores struggle in their college courses. In Florida, average associate degree completion rates are under 50 percent for students who score well above the

CPT cutoff score, and these rates occur in a state that has strong incentives for associate degree completion for students who wish to transfer and earn a bachelor's degree. Because of generally weak skills found among community college students, professors in many college-level classes must teach in such a way as to address the needs of students with weak skills. Grubb (1999) refers to this widespread phenomenon as *hidden remediation*.

To be sure, developmental education assessments are not designed to predict future college outcomes, but rather to determine the appropriate course into which a student should be placed (there is a relationship between whether a student knows precollege math and how well that student will succeed in college math and in college generally, but they are not the same thing). Yet even in terms of determining appropriate remediation in particular subject areas, assessment scores may do little to reveal what help students need to be successful in college. Students with the same low score on a mathematics placement test could face very different problems. For example, some students may have learned math successfully but scored poorly because they had been out of school for many years; other students may never have learned in high school the math being assessed; others may have taken the appropriate courses but failed to learn the material nonetheless; still others may be immigrants who had trouble understanding the English used in the math placement test. Each of these four groups of students, all with the same assessment test scores, probably need very different types of services to prepare them to be successful in college-level mathematics.

Given the current confusion, lack of consensus, and weak outcomes for developmental students, the existing approaches to assessment for developmental placement should be reconsidered and perhaps replaced with an approach that tries explicitly to determine what a student will need to succeed in college generally rather than one that aims to identify a somewhat narrow set of skills a student possesses at a given point.

Discussion and Conclusion

Stepping back and taking in the broad picture of developmental education shows an extensive system that involves thousands of dedicated counselors and professors carrying out a crucial function. But at the same time, that system is characterized by uncertainty, lack of consensus on the definition of college ready or of the best strategies to pursue, high costs, and varied and often unknown benefits. Many students who are referred to developmental education never enroll in it. Many who complete one remediation course fail to show up for the next course in the sequence. Overall, fewer than half of students who are referred to developmental education complete the recommended sequence. What is more, many students who do complete their developmental courses do not go on to enroll in the associated college-level courses. The evaluation data concerning developmental education are equally discouraging. Much of the research on developmental education is suggestive but cannot reliably measure the effect of remediation or differentiate among different approaches. The handful of more definitive studies shows mixed results at best.

This picture is complicated by the lack of consensus about what constitutes being college ready and by assessments that have only a weak relationship with subsequent educational performance. This uncertainty is reflected in the bewildering plethora of assessments and cutoff points used around the country. And perhaps even more important, there is no break or discontinuity in assessment test scores that clearly differentiates developmental from college-level students. Many students who test out of remediation nonetheless struggle in their college courses, and educational outcomes for such students are too low. Thus, a sharp distinction in the services received by these two types of students is not justified.

Although this portrays a pessimistic picture, there are some reasons to temper that pessimism. Some positive findings from Ohio and several studies of individual colleges show more positive results. Also, it may be that students make significant progress in developmental education, but their skills still do not reach the college-level standard. Getting a student from a sixth- to a tenth-grade math level is a valuable social undertaking, even if it is not enough to provide a solid foundation for a college education. Moreover, the aggregate results reported in this chapter can obscure strong programs at individual colleges.

The above caveats notwithstanding, it is difficult to escape the conclusion that the developmental function in community colleges is not working well. What direction should reform take? The analysis presented in the chapter suggests some promising areas for exploration and innovation. I suggest that any comprehensive strategy to improve the developmental function in community colleges should include a reform and research agenda focused on three recommendations.

First, rethink assessment, focusing on understanding what students need in order to be successful in college rather than simply concentrating on placement within the sequence of a curriculum. Two students with the same score on an assessment test may need completely different types of assistance to be successful in college-level courses. This is consistent with the weak relationship between test scores and subsequent measures of student success in developmental and college-level courses. And the blizzard of assessments and cutoff scores suggests no consensus about what constitutes college ready or how to measure it. The growing national movement for better high school–college alignment may offer a framework within which we can make progress on answering these questions (Achieve, 2006; Kirst and Venezia, 2004).

Second, abandon the dichotomy between developmental and college-ready students for a wide range of students above and below current developmental cutoff scores by opening college-level courses to more students and incorporating academic support assistance for all students who need it into college-level courses. The current formal policy makes a distinction between developmental and college-ready students. Yet the discouraging evidence about the effectiveness of developmental education (especially for students who score around the cutoff point), the uncertainty about assessment, and the absence of any clear discontinuity in the relationship between student assessment scores and student outcomes suggest that a policy based on categorizing students as developmental or college ready is misguided. Students who score below the cutoff point, especially those near the top of the developmental range, are asked to spend time and money on services of dubious value, while those who score above it are assigned to college-level courses without special help, even though many of them have weak academic skills. A policy based on the recognition of these ambiguities would blur the distinction between different classes of students.

Analysis of developmental education shows that students near the cutoff scores gain little from their experience in developmental education. This at least suggests that such students would not be any worse off if they enrolled in college-level courses without spending time and money in remediation. But in most cases, they do need additional help to engage successfully in college course work, as do many students placed directly in college-level courses. Thus, it does not make sense simply to enroll students currently referred to developmental education directly into college courses as those courses are, for the most part, taught now.

There are a variety of approaches to incorporating extra support into regular courses. Perhaps the best-known strategy for doing this is the supplemental instruction model, which relies on peer tutoring. There is some evidence that this can be effective for first-level college courses (International Center for Supplemental Instruction, 2006). Another approach is used by the Digital Bridge Academy at Cabrillo College in California. This program uses a variety of experiential learning and other pedagogical strategies to incorporate learning into the pedagogy of actual college-level courses (Navarro, 2007). This approach, which is consistent with the accelerated learning strategy used in the K–12 sector and has been found to have positive effects, eschews special programs for weaker students, maintaining that good pedagogy for those students is the same as it is for advanced students (Bloom and others, 2001). The principle of dual enrollment or early college is also based on the notion that students benefit from being pushed to achieve at levels that traditionally were not thought to be appropriate for high school students. Preliminary assessments of the effect of dual enrollment on postsecondary outcomes are also encouraging (Karp and others, 2007).

Third, for students whose skills are so weak that they could not be successful even in augmented college-level courses, explicitly work to minimize the time necessary to prepare students for entry into those courses. While students with skills that are relatively close to current cutoff levels benefit little from developmental courses, we know less about the effects of remedial courses on students with very weak skills, although we do know that very few students who are referred to developmental courses two or three steps below the college level rarely complete introductory college courses and are even less likely to complete degrees.

Since the mission of community colleges holds that they accept this type of student, they need to provide developmental services. One objective should be to get such students to college-level courses as soon as possible in order to minimize the expense and discouragement associated with remediation. The suggestions that I have outlined will facilitate this process. First, more comprehensive assessment will help staff understand exactly what services a given student will need. Second, if college-level courses include extra support for students who continue to have difficulties, then preparing students for those courses will be easier than preparing them for less hospitable courses.

Many colleges are now experimenting with accelerated strategies. These include intensive bridge programs in the summer. The Digital Bridge Academy includes a two-week intensive immersion program (Navarro, 2007). At the Community College of Denver, students can combine two levels of developmental math, reading, or writing to accelerate their progress (Baker and Brancard, 2008). Initial comparisons with a sample of similar students show encouraging results for both of these programs—although they are still quite small and definitive evaluations have not been carried out. It is also the case that many students who complete one level of remediation fail to show up for the next level. Thus, another simple way to accelerate movement through various levels of remediation would be to combine levels or eliminate any elapsed time between levels.

Contextualization of developmental education is another way to engage students and allow them to make progress in their areas of interest while they are still in remedial classes. And some research suggests that teaching to adults is more effective when it is linked to meaningful applications (Rubenson and Schutze, 1995; Sticht, 1995). Similar conclusions have been reached about adolescents—that connecting literacy instruction to content areas is advantageous (Conley, 2008).

Introducing these and other needed reforms will be an extremely difficult task, but this is a good time to work on improving the developmental education function of community colleges. The past few years have seen a dramatic growth of interest in strengthening weak academic skills of college students and indeed in college learning of all types. The promising practices discussed here are products of that increasing interest. Several states, including California, Texas, Tennessee, and Kentucky, are organizing comprehensive initiatives to improve their developmental programs. A growing number of private foundations and the federal government have turned their attention to this problem, and colleges all over the country are trying new approaches to developmental education. Developmental education is a core part of Achieving the Dream, a $100 million initiative, funded by Lumina Foundation for Education and many other funders, to improve student success at eighty-four community colleges (www.achievingthedream.org). The U.S. Department of Education's Institute of Education Sciences has funded the National Center for Postsecondary Research (NCPR, www.post secondaryresearch.org) whose research is focused mainly on evaluating initiatives (primarily but not exclusively in community colleges) to improve outcomes for students with weak academic skills. The Bill and Melinda Gates Foundation has started a major initiative designed to improve college opportunities for low-income youth and young adults. These illustrate the growing focus on developmental education in policy, practice, and research. Moreover, there is also a growing commitment on the part of colleges, state agencies, and researchers to more detailed analysis of student progression through college and more systematic and rigorous evaluation of program interventions. The increasing interest in using state longitudinal unit record data sets provides a tremendous opportunity to increase our understanding of the barriers that students with weak academic skills face. Most of the best research that I have discussed in this chapter was based on these state data sets. All of these developments provide an opportunity for a major and much-needed effort to strengthen and rethink developmental education.

References

Achieve. *Closing the Expectations Gap*. Washington, D.C.: Achieve, 2006.

Adelman, C. "The Kiss of Death? An Alternative View of College Remediation." *National CrossTalk*, 1998, 6(3), 11.

Arkansas Department of Higher Education. *2003–04 Arkansas Academic Cost Accounting System: A Strategic Management Tool for Higher Education Planning and Campus Decision-Making*. Little Rock: Arkansas Department of Higher Education, n.d.

Attewell, P., Lavin, D., Domina, T., and Levey, T. "New Evidence on College Remediation." *Journal of Higher Education*, 2006, 77(5), 886–924.

Bailey, T., and Alfonso, M. *Paths to Persistence: An Analysis of Research on Program Effectiveness at Community Colleges*. Indianapolis: Lumina Foundation for Education, 2005.

Bailey, T., Jeong, D. W., and Cho, S. *Referral, Enrollment, and Completion in Developmental Education Sequences in Community Colleges*. New York: Columbia University, Teachers College, Community College Research Center, 2008.

Baker, E. D., and Brancard, R. "FastStart at CCD." Presentation at the Breaking Through Peer Learning meeting, Denver, Colo., Apr. 2008.

Bettinger, E., and Long, B. T. "Remediation at the Community College: Student Participation and Outcomes." In C. A. Kozeracki (ed.), *Responding to the Challenges of Developmental Education*. New Directions for Community Colleges, no. 129. San Francisco: Jossey-Bass, 2005.

Bloom, H., and others. *Evaluating the Accelerated Schools Approach*. New York: Manpower Demonstration Research Corporation, 2001.

Boylan, H. *What Works: A Guide to Research-Based Best Practices in Developmental Education*. Boone, N.C.: Appalachian State University, Continuous Quality Improvement Network with the National Center for Developmental Education, 2002.

Breneman, D., and Harlow, W. "Remedial Education: Costs and Consequences." Paper presented at the Remediation in Higher Education: A Symposium, Washington, D.C., July 1, 1998.

Brown, R., and Niemi, D. *Investigating the Alignment of High School and Community College Assessments in California.* San Jose, Calif.: National Center for Public Policy in Higher Education, 2007.

Calcagno, J. C. "Evaluating the Impact of Developmental Education in Community Colleges: A Quasi-Experimental Regression-Discontinuity Design." Unpublished doctoral dissertation, Columbia University, 2007.

Calcagno, J. C., and Long, B. T. *The Impact of Postsecondary Remediation Using a Regression Discontinuity Approach: Addressing Endogenous Sorting and Noncompliance.* New York: National Center for Postsecondary Research, 2008.

College Board. *ACCUPLACER Online: Technical Manual.* New York: College Board, 2006.

Conley, D. *College Knowledge: What It Really Takes for Students to Succeed and What We Can Do to Get Them Ready.* San Francisco: Jossey-Bass, 2005.

Conley, M. "Cognitive Strategy Instruction for Adolescents: What We Know About the Promise, What We Don't Know About the Potential." *Harvard Educational Review,* 2008, 78(1), 84–206.

Deil-Amen, R., and Rosenbaum, J. "The Unintended Consequences of Stigma-Free Remediation." *Sociology of Education,* 2002, 75(3), 249–268.

Florida Office of Program Policy Analysis and Government Accountability. "Steps Can Be Taken to Reduce Remediation Rates; 78% of Community College Students, 10% of University Students Need Remediation." Tallahassee: Florida Office of Program Policy Analysis and Government Accountability, Apr. 2006.

Grubb, N. *Honored But Invisible: An Inside Look at Teaching in Community Colleges.* New York: Routledge, 1999.

Grubb, N. *From Black Box to Pandora's Box: Evaluating Remedial/Developmental Education.* New York: Columbia University, Teachers College, Community College Research Center, 2001.

Horn, L., and Carroll, C. D. *Nontraditional Undergraduates: Trends in Enrollment from 1986 to 1992 and Persistence and Attainment Among 1989–90 Beginning Postsecondary Students.* Washington D.C.: National Center for Education Statistics, 1996.

Horn, L., and Nevill, S. *Profile of Undergraduates in U.S. Postsecondary Education Institutions, 2003–04: With a Special Analysis of Community College Students.* Washington, D.C.: National Center for Education Statistics, 2006.

International Center for Supplemental Instruction. *Supplemental Instruction/Video Supplemental Instruction: Annotated Bibliography.* 2006. Retrieved Sept. 2, 2007, from http://www.umkc.edu/cad/si/.

Karp, M., and others. *The Postsecondary Achievement of Participants in Dual Enrollment: An Analysis of Student Outcomes in Two States.* St. Paul: University of Minnesota, National Research Center for Career and Technical Education, 2007. Retrieved February 25, 2009, from http://ccrc.tc.columbia.edu/Publication.asp?uid=547.

Kirst, M. "Who Needs It? Identifying the Proportion of Students Who Require Postsecondary Remedial Education Is Virtually Impossible." *National CrossTalk,* Winter 2007. Retrieved Sept. 10, 2007, from http://www.highereducation.org/crosstalk/ct0107/voices0107-kirst.shtml.

Kirst, M., and Venezia, A. (eds.). *From High School to College: Improving Opportunities for Success in Postsecondary Education.* San Francisco: Jossey-Bass, 2004.

Lesik, S. "Applying the Regression-Discontinuity Design to Infer Causality with Non-Random Assignment." *Review of Higher Education,* 2006, 30(1), 1–19.

Levin, H., and Calcagno, J. C. "Remediation in the Community College: An Evaluator's Perspective." *Community College Review,* 2008, 35(3), 181–207.

Martorell, P., and McFarlin, I. "Help or Hindrance? The Effects of College Remediation on Academic and Labor Market Outcomes." Dallas: University of Texas at Dallas, 2007.

Moss, B. G., and Yeaton, W. "Shaping Policies Related to Developmental Education: An Evaluation Using the Regression-Discontinuity Design." *Educational Evaluation and Policy Analysis,* 2006, 28(3), 215–229.

National Center for Developmental Education. *N.C.D.E. National Research Project on Developmental Education.* Boone, N.C.: Appalachian State University, National Center for Developmental Education, n.d.

Navarro, D. J. *Digital Bridge Academy: Program Overview.* Watsonville, Calif.: Cabrillo College, 2007.

Ohio Board of Regents. "Costs and Consequences of Remedial Course Enrollment in Ohio Public Higher Education: Six-Year Outcomes for Fall 1998 Cohort." Columbus, Ohio: Ohio Board of Regents, Aug. 2006.

Pascarella, E. T., and Terenzini, P. T. *How College Affects Students: Findings and Insights from Twenty Years of Research.* San Francisco: Jossey-Bass, 1991.

Pascarella, E. T., and Terenzini, P. T. *How College Affects Students: A Third Decade of Research.* San Francisco: Jossey-Bass, 2005.

Perin, D. "Can Community Colleges Protect Both Access and Standards? The Problem of Remediation." *Teachers College Record,* 2006, *108*(3), 339–373.

Perin, D., and Charron, K. "Lights Just Click On Every Day." In T. Bailey and V. S. Morest (eds.), *Defending the Community College Equity Agenda.* Baltimore: Johns Hopkins University Press, 2006.

Rubenson, K., and Schutze, H. G. "Learning at and Through the Workplace: A Review of Participation and Adult Learning Theory." In D. Hirsch and D. A. Wagner (eds.), *What Makes Workers Learn: The Role of Incentives in Workplace Education and Training.* Cresskill, N.J.: Hampton Press, 1995.

Scrivener, S., and others. *A Good Start: Two-Year Effects of a Freshmen Learning Community Program at Kingsborough Community College.* New York: MDRC, 2008.

Shadish, W., Cook, T., and Campbell, D. *Experimental and Quasi-Experimental Designs for Generalized Causal Inference.* Boston: Houghton Mifflin, 2002.

Sticht, T. G. "Functional Context Education for School Places and Workplaces." In D. Hirsch and D. A. Wagner (eds.), *What Makes Workers Learn: The Role of Incentives in Workplace Education and Training.* Cresskill, N.J.: Hampton Press, 1995.

Strong American Schools. "Diploma to Nowhere." 2008. Retrieved Oct. 8, 2008, from http://www.edin08.com/.

Task Force on Assessment. "Report of the Consultation Task Force on Assessment to the Board of Governors of the California Community Colleges." Sacramento: Task Force on Assessment, 2008. Retrieved Oct. 24, 2008, from http://www.cccco.edu/Portals/4/Executive/Board/2008_agendas/january/3-5_Assessment%20TF%20Report%2001-08.pdf.

Taylor, K., Moore, W. S., MacGregor, J., and Lindblad, J. *Learning Community Research and Assessment: What We Know Now.* Olympia: Evergreen State College, Washington Center for Improving the Quality of Undergraduate Education, in cooperation with the American Association for Higher Education, 2003.

THOMAS BAILEY *is the George and Abby O'Neill Professor of Economics and Education at Teachers College, Columbia University, and the director of the Community College Research Center and the National Center for Postsecondary Research.*

3

This chapter explores various theories of change for community colleges and examines how external agencies and funders have sought to support reforms that improve success for diverse groups of students. The author provides a preliminary scan of how successful institutionalization attempts have been, including national and regional examples, and suggests ways that community colleges can sustain reforms over time.

Sustaining Changes That Support Student Success in Community College

Pamela Burdman

Recent efforts to improve student success at community colleges around the country have been driven in part by the investments of numerous private foundations. Investing large amounts of money in community colleges is a relatively new philanthropic endeavor. Until recently, more attention was given to four-year institutions. Some of these foundations operate nationally and fund projects around the country. The largest single project is probably Achieving the Dream, a national initiative launched by Lumina Foundation and seventeen other funders. With several partners, including the Community College Leadership Program at the University of Texas at Austin, the Community College Research Center at Teachers College, and the American Association of Community Colleges, the project now reaches out to eighty-two colleges in fifteen states. So far, four cohorts of colleges have joined the endeavor, which entails a five-year commitment to improving outcomes of disadvantaged students, aided by the Achieving the Dream partners and about $100,000 a year. Lumina and the other funders together have invested nearly $100 million in the project.

Another national project, the Ford Foundation's Bridges to Opportunity, has worked with community college systems in six states to integrate the academic and workforce missions of colleges in order to help low-income and nontraditional students meet their goals. Since 2002, Ford has invested more than $10 million in the Bridges project (C. Driver, personal communication, December 10, 2007).

NEW DIRECTIONS FOR COMMUNITY COLLEGES, no. 145, Spring 2009 © 2009 Wiley Periodicals, Inc.
Published online in Wiley InterScience (www.interscience.wiley.com) • DOI: 10.1002/cc.353

Many more foundations focus their efforts on particular regions, whether in a single state, a group of states in the same region, or a specific urban or rural area within a state. For example, the Joyce Foundation concentrates its investments in the Great Lakes, the Mott Foundation has a particular emphasis on the state of Michigan, and the James Irvine Foundation and the William and Flora Hewlett Foundation are supporting efforts to improve opportunities for students at community colleges in California.

Because of the increasingly prominent role of foundations in supporting improved opportunities for community college students, it may be helpful to understand how foundations set priorities and make decisions. Some foundations engage in responsive grant making, whereby they outline priority areas and then respond to proposals received from the field, approving those they judge to be the best. Increasingly, though, large U.S. foundations pursue strategic grant making, whereby they specify not just priorities but also specific goals and strategies for pursuing them. Engaging in strategic grant making typically causes foundations to become more explicit about the theory of change that drives their strategy (Brest, 2003).

A theory of change entails a causal analysis of the underlying problem, the leverage points for addressing it, and the strategies and approaches it deems most likely to effect change. Thus, it provides a framework for explicitly distinguishing among activities and their effectiveness in addressing the underlying problem. It is imaginable, even likely, that a funded activity may produce its intended output using the available resources within the allotted time without a noticeable impact on the problem that is being addressed. Such instances may be explained by dosage or duration, that is, the activity requires a broader reach or longer time frame. But they also may reflect a break in the causal chain, or theory of change. Thus, the theory of change can be a valuable tool to assist foundations in clarifying their goals and assumptions and working with grantees to assess not just their specific accomplishments but ultimately their impact. "The theory of change is a powerful driver of change," noted Ralph Smith, vice president of the Annie E. Casey Foundation, in a recent address. "It forces us to see whether what we're doing can work" (Smith, 2007).

When foundations choose to invest in work to improve education generally or community colleges specifically, this decision often evolves from a high-level foundation-wide theory of change. In turn, the theory of change that drives the investments in the community college area is derived from that higher-level theory. To illustrate how this works in practice, this chapter uses the example of the William and Flora Hewlett Foundation, a private foundation based in Menlo Park, California, which engages in strategic grant making on an international level. After situating the foundation's community college grant making within a foundation-wide theory of change, it looks at the specific theory of change that is driving the foundation's investments in community colleges.

Situating Grant Making Within a Theory of Change

In its vision statement, the William and Flora Hewlett Foundation says that it "makes grants to address the most serious social and environmental problems facing society, where risk capital, responsibly invested, may make a difference over time. The Foundation places a high value on sustaining and improving institutions that make positive contributions to society" (Brest, n.d.). As ways of addressing the most serious social and environmental problems facing society, the foundation has chosen two missions: promote a sustainable environment and promote human well-being. As part of its goal to promote human well-being, it has selected the broad goals of improving the well-being of the world's poorest people and the well-being of U.S., California, and Bay Area residents (Brest, n.d.). The goal of improving outcomes for community college students falls under the latter goal.

An implicit theory of change is rooted in the notion that improving educational outcomes is necessary to improving the well-being of California residents. Before discussing the specific theory of change for community colleges, an explanation for the focus on community colleges is in order. The goal derives from numerous analyses that have highlighted the need to raise the education level within the state. Studies by the Public Policy Institute of California and others reveal that the needs of the twenty-first-century California economy for an increasing number of college-educated individuals will not be met if the state continues to educate residents at the current pace. According to the Public Policy Institute of California, California will face a shortage of college-educated workers in the year 2020 and will have twice as many high school dropouts as the state will be able to employ (Hanak and Baldassare, 2005). Failure to increase overall education levels could have dire consequences for the state: economic stagnation, increased need for social services and prisons, decreasing civic participation, and growing inequality. Although the dilemma is a nationwide one, California's demographics suggest that an uneducated workforce could cost the state more in per capita income than any other state, according to the National Center for Public Policy and Higher Education (Jones, 2006). Based on data that both reveal the educational pipeline problems in California and indicate that those problems will worsen over time if changes are not made, the foundation developed its strategy. In a memo on its education strategy, the foundation states:

> The ultimate goal for our work on Improving Educational Outcomes in California is to improve success for students in California to enable them to contribute effectively to their families, their communities, and to a robust California economy. Though ultimately we seek to improve opportunities for all students to succeed at the highest levels, including bachelor's degrees and beyond, we focus our investments on the students who face the greatest barriers to reaching those goals: those attending California's public schools and

community colleges. In particular, to keep pace with demographic shifts, we seek to improve educational outcomes for low-income students, Latino and African American students, and English language learners.

Currently California falls behind most other states in students' chance of attending college by the age of nineteen, reflecting both low high school graduation rates and low rates of college enrollment directly from high school (National Center for Higher Management Education Systems, n.d.). While Hewlett's investments in K–12 education reform seek to improve outcomes for students in the state's public schools, strengthening opportunities for students to attend and complete college is also an essential component in meeting the long-term goal.

In California the majority of students pursuing postsecondary education attend one of the California community colleges. The state's master plan for education directs that the majority of high school graduates have only one option for attending a public higher education institution: one of the state's 109 community colleges. In fact, the colleges enroll nearly 75 percent of all students in public higher education in California, well above the national average, making the two-year institutions indispensable to meeting the goal of increasing educational attainment in California (Shulock and Moore, 2007).

The analysis that improving outcomes for community college students would be necessary to the broader goal of improving educational outcomes generally explains the initial decision of the Hewlett Foundation in 2002 to explore work to improve outcomes for community college students. Another California foundation, the James Irvine Foundation, also has a focus on California community college students. However, Irvine came to this emphasis from a somewhat different direction. Historically, Irvine makes grants only in California, and one of its focus areas is youth, with an emphasis on multiple pathways to college and career.

Community Colleges in California

The theory of change begins with an analysis of the underlying problem—the barriers that inhibit greater student success. Although California has one of the best-funded public research university systems in the country, its community colleges are chronically among the worst funded, leaving the two-year institutions ill-prepared to address many of the challenges they face (Zumeta and Frankle, 2007). At the same time, many students in California are also less well equipped for the demands of college. Besides the large number of students with poor K–12 preparation and the large percentage of very low income students, students in California often delay entry into college (Hill, 2008).

As it stands, California ranks forty-eighth in direct entry into college from high school, and California's community college students attend part time at greater rates than students in other states. At 29.4 percent, the CCC share of full-time students was substantially below the national community college figure of 41.6 percent (Zumeta and Frankle, 2007). This array of barriers facing both institutions and students inhibits degree completion, certificate completion, and transfer to four-year institutions. While precise completion rates vary depending on the choice of denominator, Shulock and Moore (2007) found that only 26 percent of community college students who are seeking a degree, credential, or transfer achieve one of those outcomes within six years. The Public Policy Institute of California (Zumeta and Frankle, 2007) found that 24 percent of students seeking to transfer do so within six years, and the National Center for Higher Management Education Systems states that only 9.6 percent of community college students enrolled in 2005 earned a credential, compared to a national average of 14 percent (Shulock and Moore, 2007; Sengupta and Jepsen, 2006).

Open door policies, including the lowest fees in the nation, have given many students a chance to attempt college in California (Zumeta and Frankle, 2007). Indeed, college participation rates in California are high—about 10.6 percent of Californians age eighteen to sixty-four are enrolled in college, making California the eleventh-ranked state in this measure. These low completion rates reveal a fundamental dilemma for higher education policy in California: community colleges' open door policies, including some of the lowest fees in the nation, have given many students a chance to attend college in California (Zumeta and Frankle, 2007). However, that access to college has not translated into college success for enough students. For that reason, the Hewlett Foundation has chosen to focus its efforts on ensuring that more students can succeed in a program of study leading to further education or career path employment. In particular, while recognizing the need to preserve broad access to higher education, it seeks to make investments that will help ensure that more students have the opportunity to reach outcomes including degree completion, certificate completion, and transfer.

Using the Theory of Change to Improve Outcomes

Insufficient preparation for college is one of the major barriers preventing students from succeeding at community colleges. Because lack of preparation is such a significant barrier for students in succeeding at community colleges, the William and Flora Hewlett Foundation has chosen to place particular emphasis on improving opportunities for underprepared students. This emphasis complements the foundation's extensive work to improve outcomes in K–12 schools through an emphasis on informing policy change.

The foundation's theory assumes that in order to improve outcomes for students at the community college level, several changes are required: changes in practice at the college level (including improved instruction, increased access to student services and financial aid, and increased ability to track student progress) and changes at the policy level that facilitate changes at the college level (including more resources for colleges, resources better targeted toward student success, and more financial aid resources for students). However, simply outlining what needs to change is not an effective approach. The foundation's theory assumes that colleges and policies without will not be transformed without significant momentum from within and heightened external expectations.

In accordance with that theory, Hewlett's strategy for strengthening community colleges as avenues for lifting postsecondary attainment operates on multiple levels. First, the foundation seeks to help strengthen colleges' capacity to increase student success by replicating effective instructional programs and building capacity for colleges to track student performance in order to improve instruction and support services. One premise of the theory is that changes and innovation must be locally developed or locally embraced in order to have ultimate traction statewide. California has a strong tradition of local governance and college professionals; faculty especially play a prominent role in the shared governance system.

As colleges deepen their efforts to improve student success and a valuable knowledge base is developed and shared across colleges, the need emerges for a second type of change: systemic improvements at the college, system, and state levels. That is, changes in individual classroom practices or the addition of programs that serve groups of students are not sufficient to achieve necessary improvements. Barriers that prevent such improvements from reaching more students or being scaled up at the college need to be addressed; these range from bureaucratic structures, insufficient funding, and restrictive regulations to the lack of time for faculty and counselors to meet with each other. Together these policies have an impact on the availability of counseling, financial aid advising, and the ability of faculty and counselors to strengthen their professional practices. Ultimately the resources and regulations needed to support systemic change depend on state policy as a lever. Therefore, the foundation places a significant and increasing emphasis on informing state policy decisions through research, dissemination, and public engagement.

Operating on multiple levels, the theory assumes that change will not happen without good data well analyzed, research in the hands of practitioners and policymakers, and capacity building to help colleges learn from the research and make changes that best help students. Therefore, the strategy is supported by three types of investments: (1) research and analysis to deepen understanding of the problems faced by colleges and potential solutions to those problems, (2) advocacy and awareness building among stakeholders inside and outside the system to build shared knowledge and momentum for change, and (3) technical assistance, capacity building, and tool development for practitioners and policymakers. Below are descriptions of the theory behind each of these areas as well as examples of grantees working in each. In practice, many of the grantees work in more than one area.

Research and Analysis. Research and data analysis must occur on an ongoing basis to continually provide evidence that can be used to improve both practices and policy, according to Hewlett's analysis. Quantitative and qualitative data about students and institutions should be central to discussions about change, whether at the classroom, college, system, or state level. Therefore, this research needs to occur locally at colleges, by the college system itself, and by independent researchers who are well positioned to reach key audiences inside and outside of the system. Examples of two Hewlett-funded projects in this area follow:

- The Institute for Higher Education Leadership and Policy at California State University, Sacramento, conducts research on community college policy based on California community college data, state policies, interviews with community colleges insiders, research literature on student success, and other resources. Three reports issued by the institute in 2007, with funding from the Hewlett and Irvine Foundations, played a large role in shaping policy discussions within the community college system and in Sacramento.
- The California Benchmarking Project at the University of Southern California's Center for Urban Education (CUE) works directly with colleges to help them analyze student outcomes data in order to uncover equity gaps in outcomes such as transfer. CUE then works with colleges to help facilitate a research process to discover underlying causes of equity gaps and surface approaches for addressing them. The research is also used to inform other colleges, the college system, and policymakers about best ways of serving minority students at community colleges.

Ensuring the quality and availability of relevant data for use from the classroom to the state capitol is an essential piece of this strategy. So are feedback loops in which the data analysis—for example, on students' mastery of material—informs decisions in the classroom. In the spirit of continuous improvement, feedback loops ensure that the data and research findings can regularly be updated and used to track progress and inform decisions, whether about how to teach math or about how the state should distribute financial aid most effectively. Indeed, data analysis and research findings form the basis of the other two investment areas.

Advocacy and Awareness Building. Advocacy and awareness building among stakeholders inside and outside the system is another key element of Hewlett's strategy. This is based on the assumption that institutional change and policy change are unlikely to occur without both internal momentum and external pressure. The strategy is predicated on the assumption that engaging practitioners in focusing on student success will provide needed support for the policy changes that are ultimately necessary to significantly improve student outcomes. Although this theory has yet to be proved, it is undoubtedly true that policy changes that are opposed by practitioners, even if adopted into law, are unlikely to achieve their desired effect.

New Directions for Community Colleges • DOI: 10.1002/cc

At the same time, significant change is unlikely to occur without the support of external stakeholders such as advocacy groups interested in improving opportunities for underserved students. Within Hewlett's strategy, these stakeholders have a dual role: they advocate at the state level on behalf of more attention to and resources for community colleges, while also expecting colleges to improve their practices so that more students can succeed, especially populations that have historically not been well served by the state's education system. This external support and pressure can support college faculty and leaders in changing the status quo in ways that best improve student outcomes. Although their agendas are not identical, a degree of collaboration among internal and external stakeholders is essential to ensuring that community colleges can play the central role in higher education policy that they were assigned under California's master plan.

The Hewlett Foundation has made grants to organizations including the Campaign for College Opportunity, a coalition-building effort to build support for more funding and better policies for higher education; California Tomorrow, a project to advocate for policies to help improve outcomes for minority and immigrant students; the California EDGE campaign, a coalition of labor, workforce, industry, and community colleges working to enhance access to postsecondary education and training in California; and the Los Angeles Area Chamber of Commerce Foundation, a new effort to unite California businesses to prioritize increased funding and improved policies within the community colleges.

Technical Assistance, Capacity Building, and Tool Development. Technical assistance, capacity building, and tool development support colleges in making improvements in student success, even within the constraints of existing policies and resources. The professionals who work with students on a daily basis are the front lines in supporting students' progress. Therefore, according to Hewlett's analysis, a strategy to improve student outcomes must marshal the strengths of those practitioners, in particular providing opportunities for the most dedicated and creative faculty to examine evidence of student learning, use it to improve their teaching, and engage in inquiry with their colleagues. The same is true of other practitioners, such as counselors. This work relies less on specific best practices than it does on the principle of using data of various kinds to build knowledge and spark improvement at each level: classroom, department, college, district, system, and state.

Structures such as faculty inquiry groups, professional learning councils (which involve high school teachers together with community college instructors), and multicollege learning networks are central to this work. One example is the Strengthening Pre-Collegiate Education in Community Colleges (SPECC) network, a project with the Carnegie Foundation for the Advancement of Teaching that involves eleven colleges in using faculty inquiry approaches to strengthen classroom practice. CalPASS, the California Partnership for Achieving Student Success, facilitates professional learning councils that bring high school and community college instructors together in their disciplines to eliminate curricular disjunctures.

Other learning opportunities include training sessions offered by Cabrillo College's Digital Bridge Academy to enable faculty at other colleges to replicate the curriculum. In addition, several tools are being developed to aid colleges in their work to improve student outcomes. Multimedia Windows on Learning in the SPECC project offer online resources and exemplars of good instructional practices, and a Web-based data tool helps assist colleges in analyzing cohort data.

Though building capacity and developing resources can have an impact on student success at the college level, large-scale improvement based on expanded professional learning and increased availability of services for students may require policy changes or additional investment. Many decisions about deploying resources, though made at the local level, are constrained by state laws and regulations. For example, state laws and regulations provide dedicated streams of funding (categoricals) for certain priorities but not others and dictate things like the ratio of classroom instruction to noninstruction in the college payroll. Sometimes such state policies are outmoded, serving as barriers to approaches that might better serve students. Changes in policy, then, may be necessary to maximize colleges' ability to help students succeed.

Although foundation dollars can directly support changes in programs or practices at individual colleges, they cannot legally be directed toward influencing legislation. Foundations can support work to inform state policy decisions, but ultimately such changes occur outside the direct scope of foundation investments. Capacity building at the policy level involves disseminating research through briefings, media coverage, policy briefings, and other avenues to inform state policymakers about the barriers to student success and ways of removing them. This work includes educating those who develop policy so that they grasp the central role of community colleges in providing postsecondary opportunity in California. Because of term limits affecting state lawmakers as well as high turnover among college leadership, capacity to analyze information, identify problems, and propose solutions is quite limited. An evaluation conducted for the foundation identified providing timely and effective technical assistance for policymakers as an important role the foundation can fill (William and Flora Hewlett Foundation, 2007). In addition, Hewlett grantees' work with colleges across the state to strengthen student success, if successful, will ultimately provide the most useful information for policymakers about needed changes in policy.

Conclusion

Where there was once a vacuum of knowledge about community college policy issues in California and nationally, a series of research reports generated by Hewlett grantees and others in the field are helping to fill this void.

New Directions for Community Colleges • DOI: 10.1002/cc

Because Hewlett is one of only two foundations in California with a statewide emphasis on community colleges, this research would be less likely to be conducted absent Hewlett's investment. In addition, a series of projects at colleges across the state, while helping individual students succeed, are also building the knowledge base and capacity to improve outcomes for larger numbers of students.

The Hewlett Foundation seeks to "address the most serious social and environmental problems facing society, where risk capital, responsibly invested, may make a difference over time." It also seeks to use its funds to leverage existing strengths and expose existing weaknesses along with solutions for minimizing them. Hewlett seeks to supplement, not replace, state investment. By the end of 2008, the foundation had invested close to $30 million in efforts to strengthen community colleges.

Although the strategy operates at multiple levels, including the level of institutions and state policy, the nexus between policy change and institutional change may provide the most fertile ground in which dynamic improvement can occur. One example may help to illustrate this possibility. California's community colleges have embarked on a strategic plan that includes improving access and success among its goals. One initiative that has emerged from the plan, the statewide Basic Skills Initiative, is a systemwide priority supported in the state's budget. Similar to the Hewlett Foundation's goal of improving outcomes for underprepared students, the initiative seeks to improve the success of students who enroll in basic skills courses.

State policy created the Basic Skills Initiative with a system proposal and a state-level budget decision. But it cannot succeed without leveraging the resources locally. Resources are only part of the picture however. As part of the Basic Skills Initiative, the college system commissioned research on effective practices. The research has been distributed to colleges. Colleges then receive technical assistance or professional development through a state-funded effort. The initiative, if successful, can be a powerful tool for awareness building related to the important role of community colleges as avenues for improving the prospects of Californians who have not been previously well served by the education system. Investments by the foundation to research barriers to the success of underprepared students, raise awareness and understanding of the community colleges' important role, strengthen instruction for underprepared students, and improve colleges' ability to use data to improve student success all have the potential to leverage the investments of the Basic Skills Initiative.

References

Brest, P. "Update on the Hewlett Foundation's Approach to Philanthropy: The Importance of Strategy, 2003." 2003. Retrieved February 25, 2009, from www.hewlett.org/Programs/Philanthropy/presidentstatement2003.htm.

Brest, P. "Update on the Hewlett Foundation's Approach to Philanthropy: The Importance of Strategy." William and Flora Hewlett Foundation. N.d. Retrieved February 25, 2009, from http://www.hewlett.org/Default.htm.

Hanak, E., and Baldassare, M. *California 2025: Taking on the Future.* San Francisco: Public Policy Institute of California, 2005.

Hill, E. *Back to Basics: Improving College Readiness of Community College Students.* Sacramento, Calif.: Legislative Analyst's Office, 2008.

Jones, D. "State Shortfalls Projected to Continue Despite Economic Gains." San Jose, Calif.: National Center for Public Policy and Higher Education Policy Alert, Feb. 2006.

NCHEMS Information Center. "Ratio of Degrees and Credentials Awarded to the Number of Students Enrolled." N.d. Retrieved February 25, 2009, http://www.highered info.org/dbrowser/index.php?submeasure=62&year=2002&level=nation&mode=graph&state=84.

Sengupta, R., and Jepsen, C. "California's Community College Students." In California Counts: Demographic Trends and Profiles. San Francisco: Public Policy Institute of California, Nov. 2006. Retrieved February 25, 2009, http://www.higheredinfo.org/dbrowser/index.php?level=nation&mode=graph&state=84, 2006.

Shulock, N., and Moore, C. *Rules of the Game: How State Policy Creates Barriers to Degree Completion and Impedes Student Success in the California Community Colleges.* Sacramento: California State University-Sacramento, Institute for Higher Education Leadership and Policy, Feb. 2007.

Smith, R. Keynote address to the Community College League of California Annual Convention, Nov. 16, 2007.

William and Flora Hewlett Foundation. "FSG Social Impact Advisors Retrospective Evaluation of The William and Flora Hewlett Foundation's Strengthening Community Colleges Portfolio." Oct. 22, 2007.

Zumeta, W., and Frankle, D. *California Community Colleges: Making Them Stronger and More Affordable.* San Jose, Calif.: National Center for Public Policy and Higher Education, 2007.

PAMELA BURDMAN *is a program officer with the Education Program at the William and Flora Hewlett Foundation.*

4

This chapter provides a national picture of innovative learning options, such as dual enrollment and early college high schools. These options prepare high school students for college-level course work by providing supported early immersion in college. The chapter also discusses how such programs can help a wide range of students and highlights the importance of state policy in encouraging these efforts to create stronger connections among high schools, post-secondary institutions, and the workforce.

New Directions for Dual Enrollment: Creating Stronger Pathways from High School Through College

Nancy Hoffman, Joel Vargas, Janet Santos

There are a number of ways to increase high school graduation rates and put more students on the path to and through college. Most states are trying to do so by increasing the academic rigor of all their high schools. A first line of attack is to boost the academic requirements for high school graduation. Fifteen states are instituting a core curriculum that ensures that the default pathway through high school is a college preparatory sequence (American Diploma Project, 2007).

Moreover, a substantial number of states are aligning high school graduation standards with the standards required to advance directly into non-remedial, college-level work. For example, thirty states are at work on such alignment through Achieve's American Diploma Project Network (2007), and other states are engaged in aligning standards themselves. Some states use tenth- or eleventh-grade assessments to provide students with information about their readiness for college. And some states and school districts are mounting programs to recover high school dropouts and students who fall behind in earning credits: these students too need intensive academic work to meet the more rigorous standards required to complete high school and succeed in a community college.

An emerging body of research and practice suggests that providing college-level work in high school is one promising way to better prepare a wide range of young people for college success, including those who do

New Directions for Community Colleges, no. 145, Spring 2009 © 2009 Wiley Periodicals, Inc.
Published online in Wiley InterScience (www.interscience.wiley.com) • DOI: 10.1002/cc.354

not envision themselves as college material. Increasing numbers of young people are taking advantage of such opportunities. In some states, such as Florida and Rhode Island, as many as 17 percent of high school students graduate with college credit (Vargas and Hoffman, 2006; Fletcher, 2006).

If designed well, this college-level work in high school can:

- Increase the pool of historically underserved students who are ready for college.
- Provide realistic information to high school students about the knowledge and skills they will need to succeed in postsecondary education.
- Improve motivation through high expectations and the promise of free courses.
- Decrease the cost of postsecondary education by compressing the years of financial support needed.
- Create a feedback loop between K–12 and postsecondary systems around issues of standards, assessments, curriculum, and transitions from high school to college.

Across the country, increasing numbers and more varied students are taking part in accelerated learning options that provide college-level credit during high school. These options increase the likelihood that students currently underrepresented in higher education will enroll in postsecondary education. Data from the U.S. Department of Education (Adelman, 1999, 2006) indicate that the accumulation of twenty college credits by the end of the first calendar year of college is a strong predictor that a student will successfully earn a college credential. If the accelerated high school program is intensive—that is, if students gain twenty or more credits—it is our estimation that such credit attainment should also be highly correlated with the student's likelihood of earning a postsecondary credential. In addition, such credit attainment is a strong indicator that the student is college ready—the goal increasingly set by states as the only sufficient outcome of high school. Some accelerated options also have the potential to better link secondary and postsecondary institutions and to point to better ways to integrate financing, data systems, and accountability mechanisms across K–16.

Community colleges lead the way in making accelerated learning options available. First, their missions include outreach to high schools and service to their immediate neighborhoods and regions. Second, in many of the forty-two states with dual-enrollment policies, public community colleges, not four-year institutions, provide such opportunities. When they are not mandated to do so, community colleges are encouraged and supported in doing so. Ninety-eight percent of public two-year institutions had high school students taking courses for college credit, compared to 77 percent of public four-year institutions, 40 percent of private four-year institutions, and 17 percent of private two-year institutions (Kleiner and Lewis, 2005).

NEW DIRECTIONS FOR COMMUNITY COLLEGES • DOI: 10.1002/cc

In this chapter, we describe three such options: traditional dual enroll-ment, dual-enrollment pathways, and early college high schools. We then present cases of states and community colleges that have particularly inter-esting models for these options and review the evidence that such options can do what they claim: increase college success.

Our organization, Jobs for the Future (JFF), has worked over the past five years with several states and intermediary organizations that are imple-menting early college schools and strengthening their dual-enrollment poli-cies. Based on this experience and national research, we discuss the lessons learned about practice as well as policy barriers and opportunities posed by the options. In each section, we highlight the key role played by commu-nity colleges as the leaders in facilitating these options.

One final note is that dual enrollment is also called *dual credit, concur-rent enrollment, college in the high school,* and *joint enrollment. Dual enroll-ment, joint enrollment,* or *concurrent enrollment* typically refer to high school students taking postsecondary courses, no matter what credit they receive. *Dual credit* refers to dual-enrollment course taking that results in both high school and college credit. *College in the high school* usually refers to college courses that are offered on the campus of a high school. Any of these pro-gram variations can fall under the umbrella of what some states call post-secondary, or accelerated, learning options.

Accelerated Learning Options: Definitions and Prevalence

The term *accelerated learning options* covers a continuum of designs and approaches. Another common name for these options is *credit-based transi-tion programs* (Bailey and Karp, 2003). The most intensive of these, early college schools, move students through at least the critical first year of post-secondary education and often through the second year. Dual-enrollment programs, although not as intensive, also provide exposure and access to college-level work to a large number of high school students.

The most familiar of these accelerated learning options is dual or con-current enrollment. These programs allow high school students to enroll in college-level course work and earn credit for it while they are still in high school. Students typically enroll in college courses in their junior and senior years. In most programs, courses result in dual credit: the college course replaces a required high school course, and the student earns credit for both. In some programs, however, students must choose between high school or college credit. Most dual-enrollment programs offer free or discounted tuition, providing some savings for families who otherwise might not afford to send their children to college.

In 2006, the National Center for Education Statistics (NCES) published the first national study to attempt to capture the number of students partic-ipating in exam- and course-based college-level learning in high school.

According to key NCES findings (Kleiner and Lewis, 2005) for the 2002–2003 school year, there were an estimated 1.2 million enrollments in courses for dual credit. If a student took multiple courses, schools counted the student for each course in which he or she was enrolled. Thus, enrollments may include duplicated counts of students. Overall, approximately 813,000 high school students took college-level courses through postsecondary institutions, either within or outside dual-enrollment programs. Using Kleiner and Lewis's figures (2005), over 15 million students were enrolled in public and private high schools in the United States in fall 2001 (the last year for which data are available). Thus, dual enrollees represent about 5 percent of all high school students. If we assume most course takers are juniors or seniors, the percentage of dual enrollees among these students rises to approximately 13 percent.

The NCES data are not state specific and therefore do not capture growth in dual enrollment in states that have a history of providing such opportunities and keeping dual enrollment data. In Florida, for example, participation has increased 100 percent between 1995 and 2003 (Florida Board of Education, n.d.).

Although participation in community college dual-enrollment programs has existed for several decades, some states and community colleges have made changes in their purpose, structure, and visibility—previously they had existed as an escape from high school for advanced students—and reconceiving them as a path to college and technical education for a wide range of students. In this new configuration, dual enrollment becomes a central strategy for increasing college-going rates of local high school students. The expectation is that students will receive help in course selection and academic support as needed. In some community colleges, dual enrollees do not have to reapply once they finish their high school requirements. This sends a strong signal to students that if they succeed in their first course, they can go right on in the host community college.

Dual enrollment has another advantage in making college access more equitable. In rural and low-income areas where advanced courses may not be available to high school students, accelerated learning options may be provided virtually or by high school teachers or adjuncts certified by a community college. For these reasons, a number of states are making the opportunity to earn college credit in high school available to every high school student in the state.

A second structure for dual enrollment, and one for which there is not yet settled terminology, is what we call here *dual-enrollment pathways*. Within a traditional high school, students participate in a preselected sequence of two to four college courses, sometimes preceded by a "college 101" introduction to study skills. The pathway includes opportunities for those not likely to qualify for college courses before graduation—students who are at risk of graduating with weak preparation for college. In addition, such enhanced programs often reach out to middle school students, offering them programs that familiarize them with the demands of postsecondary education and the adventure of visiting a college campus.

In dual-enrollment pathways, courses are carefully chosen to meet postsecondary career certificate or general education requirements in two-year institutions and to be transferable. For example, high school students might be required to enroll in foundation or gatekeeper courses, such as the first college-level math or English courses, which when successfully completed are highly predictive of earning a credential. The expectation is that students will require and receive substantial academic support and that taxpayers will receive a return on this investment as more young people enter the labor market with a credential, contribute to the state's economy, and pay taxes.

In terms of scale, dual-enrollment pathways are not as prevalent as traditional dual enrollment. To qualify as a true dual-enrollment pathway, students would graduate from high school with anywhere from one to four semesters worth of college credit. These programs are in very early stages of development and thus not yet widely known. Nonetheless, visible models exist. With over twenty thousand enrollments in college courses by high school students in 2004–2005, the City University of New York's College Now program is the largest and most developed example of which we are aware (Meade and Hofmann, 2007). Middle colleges similarly build pathways, as do some tech prep programs.

While also relatively small in scale, the third accelerated option, early college high schools, is proliferating quickly and garnering considerable attention nationally. Early college high schools currently serve over fifteen thousand underrepresented students in integrated pathways and will eventually reach over ninety-five thousand students. Like dual-enrollment pathways, they align and integrate course sequences across the sectors with the goal of promoting postsecondary completion. But unlike dual-enrollment pathways, early colleges are small, autonomous schools. They are designed so that students underrepresented in postsecondary education (low-income students, student of color, and first-generation college students) can simultaneously earn a high school diploma and an associate degree or one to two years of credit toward a bachelor's degree tuition free. Each school is developed in partnership with a postsecondary institution whose courses make up the college portion of the student's education. Students begin college-level work as early as ninth grade.

Beginning in 2001, the Bill and Melinda Gates Foundation, in cooperation with state and local education departments, philanthropies, and nonprofit partners (including JFF, which coordinates the national initiative), have supported the growth of a national network of over 160 early college high schools in twenty-four states. Sixty-four percent of these schools are partnered with a community college and are on or near a community college campus; another 7 percent have both community college and four-year partners (Jobs for the Future, 2009). In addition, a number of states are creating additional early colleges without external funding, largely in partnership with their community colleges; several states are using the early college model to reinvent career and technical education.

Early colleges have three designs: grade 6 to 12 schools that incorporate two years of college within the same time as a student would complete a high school diploma; four-year programs that incorporate up to thirty college credits by the end of twelfth grade; and five-year programs that start in ninth grade and incorporate up to sixty college credits by the end of the fifth year, which takes place entirely on a community college campus.

Community Colleges and Accelerated Learning Options: Cases

To demonstrate the variety of ways that community colleges are leaders in enabling the growth of accelerated learning options, we describe how two states and one system have implemented accelerated learning options. For dual enrollment, we turn to one of the most extensive statewide programs: Florida's comprehensive articulated acceleration array of choices for high school students. For dual-enrollment pathways, we turn to CUNY's College Now program with an emphasis on its implementation in the six community colleges among the twenty-three CUNY institutions. For the most extensive network of early college high schools within a state and one encompassing both transfer and career preparation, we look at the forty-two currently open Learn and Earn schools in North Carolina, thirty-seven of which are partnered with a North Carolina community college.

Traditional Dual Enrollment: Florida. Florida has one of the most highly articulated and centralized public education systems in the country. In terms of accelerated learning options, Florida provides multiple means for secondary school students to accumulate college credit—Advanced Placement (AP), International Baccalaureate (IB), and dual enrollment. However, dual enrollment is perceived as a path to a postsecondary degree or credential not just for gifted students, but for those considered middle achievers or on a career or technical track. Dual enrollment grew from 27,689 students in 1988–1989 to 34,273 in 2002–2003. The growth in participation for African American and Latino students was especially high during this period (Florida Board of Education, n.d.).

Florida legislation mandates that all twenty-eight community colleges and specific four-year institutions offer dual-credit courses (Florida Statutes, Chapter 1007.27, 2002). Approximately 80 percent of all dual-credit courses take place at the community college (P. Cisek to Janet Santos, pers. communication, November 2007). Students may attend courses during the school day, before or after school, or during the summer, thereby relieving overcrowding in high schools and maximizing flexibility to participate. Students can access Web-based information that provides guidance in choosing college courses. In some community colleges, dual enrollees do not have to reapply once they finish their high school requirements, a strong signal to students that if they succeed in their first course, they can go directly on in the host community college.

The state provides incentives for postsecondary degree completion through its lottery-funded Bright Futures Scholarship Program (Florida Department of Education, n.d.). The Bright Scholars Program is a merit-based academic scholarship awarded to students based on high school transcript and standardized test scores (SAT or ACT). The program consists of three scholarship awards: the Academic Top Scholars Award, the Florida Medallion Scholars Award, and the Florida Gold Seal Vocational Scholars Award. Participation in dual enrollment receives the same weight as participation in AP and IB for the purposes of evaluating a candidate's scholarship application.

Dual enrollment is open to all public, private, and home-schooled students. The state has established eligibility guidelines recommending that general education students have a 3.0 grade point average (GPA) and that students pursuing a career certificate have a 2.0 GPA in order to qualify for dual enrollment. Florida also provides dual-enrollment funding for high school students enrolling in college-level English or math if they have passed the College Entry Level Placement Test (CPT), the math and English admissions exam for the state's college system (Florida Statutes, Chapter 1011, 2002). Additional admission criteria are included in the articulation agreement between the community college and the local school district.

Florida's only restriction on course taking is that courses count simultaneously for college and high school graduation. The state's Articulation Coordinating Committee (ACC), whose members are appointed by and report to the commissioner of education, is responsible for ensuring a smooth transfer of credit from high school to college. The ACC comprises representatives from all levels of public and private education: the state university system, the community college system, independent postsecondary institutions, public schools, and applied technology education. It also includes a student member and a member at large. It meets regularly to coordinate the movement of students from institution to institution and from one level of education to the next by evaluating high school courses, including AP, and assigns them equivalency prefixes and numbers that match comparable college courses. Standing committees are charged with such issues as postsecondary transitions and course numbering.

Despite the prescriptiveness of Florida's legislation, the implementation of dual enrollment varies by institution: some provide college in the high school, and others bring large numbers of high school students onto college campuses. Dual-enrollment students are exempted from paying tuition, matriculation, and laboratory fees (Florida Statutes, Chapter 1009, 2002). Each district and its community college partner negotiate how they will share the cost of dual enrollment (transportation, faculty salary, advising, and student support) through their articulation agreement. The state subsidizes the purchase of textbooks and other instructional materials only for public high school students, not for private or home-schooled students.

Florida's comprehensive K–20 education data warehouse is the nation's leader in the linking of student-level data across K–12 and postsecondary institutions. The gathering of such information allows the state to generate reports analyzing the effectiveness of its dual-enrollment policy (and its implementation) in helping students meet set educational goals. For example, a 2004 descriptive analysis conducted by the Florida Department of Education found that high school students who participate in dual enrollment were enrolling in colleges and universities at rates significantly higher than students who did not participate. In addition, Hispanic and African American students who took dual-enrollment courses were enrolling in higher education at higher rates than whites or any other ethnic group (Florida Department of Education, 2004a, 2004b). The news is encouraging considering previous findings reporting that only 32 percent of this population of students go on to college within four years of ninth grade (Ewell, Jones, and Kelly, 2003). Such encouraging results led to a much more extensive study published in 2007 (Karp and others, 2007).

Dual-Enrollment Pathways: College Now. New York State has no dual-enrollment legislation. But the City University of New York, the largest urban postsecondary system in the country, and the New York Department of Education, the largest urban school district in the country, have established a high school–postsecondary partnership that rivals in size those of entire states. CUNY's College Now, widely recognized as a national model for an integrated K–16 system, is the country's most extensive dual-enrollment partnership (College Now, n.d.). Between the 2001–2002 and 2006–2007 academic years, enrollment for high school students seeking college credit at City University of New York's College Now program increased by 109 percent, from 7,084 to 14,380 students. In 2006–2007, high school students completed 20,650 credit courses, and 68 percent of total college credit enrollments took place at the community colleges (T. Meade to Nancy Hoffman, pers. communication, January 2005; S. Cochron to Nancy Hoffman, various communications between October 2004 and March 2005).

The CUNY colleges have long opened their doors to students prior to their completion of high school diplomas—sometimes to help them complete the diploma or GED program. CUNY's Collaborative Programs comprise a continuum of college preparation approaches serving students at different developmental stages and with different needs: early college high schools, university-affiliated high schools (there are fifteen on or near CUNY campuses), and Gear Up serving cohorts in single schools. College Now is another example and offers a range of programs: summer arts and theater activities that acquaint students with college faculty, college culture, and college campuses, and, of course, dual enrollment.

College Now's mission is to help students meet high school graduation and college entrance requirements without remediation and to be retained through a degree. Begun in 1984 at Kingsborough Community College, College Now expanded in 1999 when the CUNY board voted to end remediation at CUNY's senior colleges. The program was designed specifically to serve students who might not otherwise be able to attend postsecondary institutions and who receive inadequate college preparation in the city's high schools. Most CUNY students are poor (average family income is $28,000), and retention and graduation rates are low even at six years from college entry.

The centerpiece of College Now is its free, credit-bearing college courses. College Now differs from most other dual-enrollment options in that courses are not offered at random but are provided in a structured sequence with academic supports as needed. All credits are transferable within the CUNY system, but college courses do not necessarily replace high school courses.

In 2006–2007, 29,040 students participated in the program, with 46,888 course and activity enrollments. (Activities include noncredit prerequisites to specific college courses and content-rich workshops, such as an English language learners history course, to aid in the statewide Regents exam preparation.) College Now models vary, but the largest, at Kingsborough Community College with 7,699 college credit enrollments in 2006–2007, teaches almost all its courses in high schools. Other College Now programs taught courses on college campuses.

Student eligibility for credit courses is based on Regents exam scores, high school records, and other measures, including substantial personal advising. While the College Now philosophy is to be stringent about admission to credit courses, the rigor of courses, and the standards of exit assessments, the program provides multiple and widespread opportunities for students to prepare for these courses. Some College Now programs also help prepare students for English and mathematics Regents exams and offer noncredit developmental college preparatory courses.

Early College High Schools: North Carolina Learn and Earn. North Carolina's leaders are making dramatic changes to the state's education system. A major thrust of these efforts is to prepare more young people for high-skills jobs by encouraging them to complete some college before high school graduation. This is a response to the decline of the state's long-time economic engines—tobacco, textile, and manufacturing jobs—that used to provide family-sustaining wages for workers without postsecondary training or education. As the state tries to reinvent its economy and attract innovative, knowledge-intensive industries, it must strengthen the educational attainment of its workforce.

To meet the challenge, the state has invested in early education, raised high school graduation standards, and increased K–12 accountability. It is also aggressively starting new high schools, creating or redesigning 150 schools designed to produce more graduates—and graduates who are on a path to complete college. Early colleges, most of them on community colleges campuses, are central to this effort.

Since 2004, North Carolina has opened forty-two early college schools, known in the state as Learn and Earn schools. These currently serve about fifty-one hundred students, and the state plans to open thirty-three more (G. Coltrane to Joel Vargas, pers. communication, January 2008). Learn and Earn schools enable students to earn up to two years of college credit or an associate degree (A.A. or A.A.S. in some cases), along with a high school diploma, within five years. Students are reflective of local school district populations, and Learn and Earn targets students not normally found on a college path.

In 2007–2008, the state invested $15.2 million in Learn and Earn. Starting in 2007, it also made college courses available at no cost to any North Carolina high school student using the Internet through Learn and Earn On-Line. Thirty-seven Learn and Earn schools are partnerships between community colleges and local K–12 districts; four work with four-year institutions (G. Coltrane to Joel Vargas, pers. communication, January 2008). Given Learn and Earn's extensive reach into the public college system, it represents both a large-scale high school redesign initiative and a significant investment by the higher education sector in preparing a world-class workforce ion North Carolina.

North Carolina has long permitted dual enrollment through community college courses offered exclusively to high school students, and through a concurrent enrollment policy allowing juniors and seniors to take college courses with other college students. (These dual-enrollment courses are known as Huskins classes, named after the North Carolina Huskins bill that provided the enabling legislation.) These programs were designed to provide supplemental educational opportunities, particularly for students from rural communities.

Without altering those programs, the state took steps that allowed Learn and Earn to design dual enrollment as an improved pathway from grades 9 to 14. For example, the state created the Innovative Education Initiatives Act in 2003, which authorized state support of cooperative education programming between high schools and colleges, including for accelerated programs such as early college and dual enrollment. This laid the groundwork for state approval of several policy exemptions for Learn and Earn schools. Thus, Learn and Earn schools have avoided policy barriers confronted by early colleges in other states that stem from uncoordinated secondary and postsecondary education policies. For example, Learn and Earn schools have received a waiver from a state restriction, sometimes found in other states, on dual-crediting college courses toward nonelective high school course requirements.

North Carolina is also supporting the capacity of its early college schools to build and sustain strong partnerships vital to their design. Learn and Earn schools must use some state funds to support a liaison between the high school and college partners. The New Schools Project, funded with private and public funds, supports Learn and Earn school implementation and sustainability through leadership trainings, instructional coaches, cross-site peer learning, and other services. The project also facilitates data collection, advises on research efforts, and reports to policymakers about the progress of the initiative. Given the size of North Carolina's effort, Learn and Earn will hold instructive lessons for other accelerated learning options nationally.

Research About the Benefits of Accelerated Learning Options

What is the evidence that accelerated learning options are a means of improving college success? It is promising but still nascent. Many states and programs do not track or report dual-enrollment outcomes. Fewer have unit-record longitudinal data systems that are capable of telling whether dual enrollees have better education outcomes compared to nonparticipants who are otherwise similar in social and academic background. However, some studies that use longitudinal data are available, including recent research on each of the three accelerated options discussed here. The research strongly suggests that dual enrollment can prepare high school students for college and give them momentum in completing a degree or credential. Moreover, it shows that these benefits extend to groups who are typically underrepresented in college.

Traditional Dual Enrollment. Researchers from the Community College Research Center studied Florida's large statewide program (Karp and others, 2007). The state's P-20 data system allowed the researchers to examine the postsecondary outcomes of 36,214 dual-enrollment participants from the high school graduating classes of 2000–2001 and 2001–2002 and compare them to similar students who did not participate.

Dual enrollees who entered college were more likely to continue for a second semester and be enrolled two years after high school. At both milestones, former dual enrollees had higher GPAs than classmates with no dual-enrollment experience. Dual enrollees also had earned 15.1 more college credits on average than nonparticipants three years after high school. Although it stands to reason that some of these credits were earned through dual enrollment, the researchers deduced that "it is also likely that some were earned after matriculation into postsecondary education" (Karp and others, 2007, p. 7).

The Florida data shed light on the benefits of dual enrollment for underrepresented students because the program serves a wide range of students. Although participants must meet some academic requirements, they vary in their academic and social backgrounds. This variation enabled researchers to look at dual-enrollment outcomes for subgroups such as low-socioeconomic-status (SES) students, African American and Latino students, and students with lower academic achievement.

In terms of positive effects on first-year and cumulative college GPA, low-income students and those with the lowest high school GPAs benefited to a "greater extent than their dual enrollment peers who enter[ed] college courses with more social, economic, and educational advantages" (Karp and others 2007, p. 63). Low-income students also seemed to benefit more in terms of greater college credit accumulation.

Dual-Enrollment Pathways. There are similarly positive outcomes from CUNY's College Now. CUNY cooperates closely with the New York City Department of Education, including sharing data across the two systems. Using these data, CUNY's office of Collaborative Programs Research and Evaluation has studied the postsecondary outcomes of College Now students who became first-time freshmen at a CUNY college during the fall of 2002 or 2003. The research compares participants to nonparticipants who otherwise had similar academic achievements when starting college (Michalowski, 2006).

The evidence suggests that College Now puts students on a path toward college completion. Among first-time freshmen, participants were more likely on average to enroll for a third semester and had higher GPAs on average than their classmates with no College Now experience. They also earned more credit on average than nonparticipants by the end of their first year. First-time freshmen in 2002 and 2003 with College Now experience earned an average of 1.08 credits more at the end of their first year versus nonparticipants. These figures do not include credits acquired through pre-college dual enrollment or AP programs, which conceivably would have increased the number of college credits reported for the participants of College Now. Most of these positive effects held for College Now students across achievement levels among those admitted to a CUNY campus.

Other findings are notable from the Community College Research Center's study, which included both data from Florida and CUNY. In addition to positive effects on retention and GPA, dual enrollment was positively related to enrollment in college for Florida students and was positively related to enrollment in a four-year institution for CTE students in CUNY College Now.

Early College High Schools. JFF and the intermediary organizations supporting early colleges have been collecting data about early college students, but as the newest of the accelerated options, early college schools still have limited longitudinal data. These efforts include JFF's development of a Student Information System for the Early College High School Initiative and the national evaluation of the initiative being conducted by AIR (American Institutes for Research) and SRI International. The oldest schools have just graduated their first classes of students (about nine hundred in all), permitting a glimpse at early outcomes.

The data suggest that the schools reach underrepresented student populations and graduate them with considerable momentum toward a postsecondary degree. Early college schools overall serve students who are representative in race and SES of their local communities. National figures show that low-income students comprise at least 60 percent of all early college students, based on free and reduced-price lunch eligibility—a conservative estimate of the number of students from low-income families since they rely on self-reporting by students and their families.

If credit accumulation is indicative of eventual degree attainment, then early college schools have put many graduates on a promising path toward a degree. The vast majority (85 percent) accumulated between a semester and two years of college credit by graduation. The Middle College National Consortium, which supports some of the longest-running early colleges in the nation, reports that its students accumulate an average of thirty-one credits by twelfth grade and pass their college courses at rates of 92 percent with an average GPA of 2.78 (Middle College National Consortium, 2008).

Lessons Learned and Looking Ahead: Policy and Practice

Beyond the benefits to the students themselves, accelerated learning options point the way to practices and state policies that can improve the alignment of the secondary and postsecondary sectors. The options are most likely to be supported and spread in states with certain policies and by the same token exemplify practices for improving college readiness and success that states may choose to expand through policy changes.

Policies that are supportive of all accelerated learning options—early college schools, dual-enrollment pathways, and traditional dual enrollment—are guided by the recommendations of a state-level P–16 council, roundtable, or other body representative of secondary and postsecondary education. An essential starting point for policymaking is agreement on the purpose of these programs: ideally, to serve as a bridge to college for underrepresented students as well as a head start on college for those already on their way. A clearer purpose gives guidance to local partnerships and lends coherence to other policy decisions. Other policies that support local accelerated learning options include:

- Encouraging dual crediting and the smooth transfer of college credits to other institutions of higher education
- Ensuring tuition is not an obstacle for dual enrollees
- Holding colleges and high schools harmless in financing dual enrollment so that they can provide joint support of dual enrollees, including through special efforts that recruit and prepare academically underprepared students for dual enrollment
- Setting eligibility criteria that are agreed on by the secondary and postsecondary sectors and allow students to take college courses in subject areas for which they have demonstrated readiness based on a variety of measures
- Promoting quality through policies that set minimum instructor qualifications and support teacher training

- Collecting and reporting data on dual-enrollment participation and outcomes—best done with longitudinal, student-level data across high school and college

At the level of practice, strong accelerated learning programs require several key elements to create feedback mechanisms and structures for collaboration across K–12 and higher education:

- Formal structures that link a high school and a partner college such as a renewable partnership agreement; a person serving as liaison between high school and college; and a decision-making body to design, monitor, and collect data about the program
- A feedback loop to high schools from postsecondary on student success: high school and college transcripts include college course grades and call attention to how well courses are sequenced between high school and college and how well high schools are preparing students for college work
- Shared responsibility (financial and otherwise) by leaders in secondary and postsecondary education institutions for the continued collaboration

From a narrow perspective, these practices and policies support promising accelerated programs that use dual enrollment. To be more speculative, if research continues to show that these programs have positive effects, they might be seen as indicative of broad-scale changes needed in practice and policy to build a more seamless P–16 education system for all students.

Would not all local high schools and colleges benefit from regular collaboration to review and improve the efficacy of course sequences in preparing students for postsecondary? How could state finance and accountability systems be more integrated and engender joint responsibility for the successful transition of all students, especially underrepresented youth, through high school and college?

That said, dual enrollment is no panacea and is not necessarily easy to implement. Dual-enrollment pathways and early college schools require that high schools and colleges work in close partnership, negotiating financing across the two systems and using dual enrollment as a laboratory for aligning standards across secondary and postsecondary education. These partnerships are challenging to build and sustain precisely because the country's secondary and postsecondary systems are, by design, disconnected and uncoordinated. Their differing academic calendars, course schedules, crediting systems, and organizational norms can make partnership difficult. Accelerated learning programs have the potential to reconcile these divisions but are also constrained by them.

These strategies also entail unique costs. Districts, colleges, or states must cover tuition and fees for college courses if dual enrollment is to be made accessible to lower-income students. There are also costs associated with maintaining the high school–college partnership such as employing a liaison who coordinates the alignment of curriculum, supports, and professional development across grades 9 to 14.

Another challenge is that college courses offered through dual enrollment are only as good as regular courses offered by the college. Because there are no common content or learning standards across postsecondary institutions nationally or statewide, course quality takes special effort to monitor in accelerated programs.

Despite these challenges, accelerated learning options are an important strategy for increasing the nation's high school and college success rates because of their potential for bridging the secondary-postsecondary divide. Given their support of such programs, community colleges are well positioned to remain at the forefront of these efforts.

References

Adelman, C. *Answers in the Tool Box: Academic Intensity, Attendance Patterns, and Bachelor's Degree Attainment.* Washington, D.C.: U.S. Department of Education, 1999.

Adelman, C. *The Toolbox Revisited: Paths to Degree Completion from High School Through College.* Washington, D.C.: U.S. Department of Education, 2006.

American Diploma Project. *Aligning High School Graduation Requirements with the Real World: A Road Map for States.* Washington, D.C.: Achieve, 2007.

Bailey, T., and Karp, M. M. *Promoting College Access and Success: A Review of Credit-Based Transition Programs.* Washington, D.C.: U.S. Department of Education, Office of Adult and Vocational Education, 2003.

"Early College Overview." Middle College National Consortium. Retrieved Oct. 15, 2008, from http://www.mcnc.us/earlycollege_overview.htm.

Ewell, P. T., Jones, D. P., and Kelly, P. J. *Conceptualizing and Researching the Educational Pipeline.* National Information Center for Higher Education, 2003. Retrieved February 25, 2009, from http://www.higheredinfo.org/suppinfo/Pipeline%20Article.pdf.

Fletcher, J. "Dual Enrollment." Presentation to the Florida House of Representatives, Jan. 11, 2006. Florida Legislature Office of Program Policy Analysis and Government Accountability, 2006. Retrieved February 25, 2009, from www.oppaga.state.fl.us/reports/pdf/1–11–06_Dual_Enrollment_House.pdf, 2006.

Florida Board of Education. *Florida Dual Enrollment Participation Data.* N.d. Retrieved Dec. 26, 2007, from http://www.flboe.org/news/2004/2004_03_10/DualEnrollment_Pres.pdf.

Florida Department of Education. *Dual Enrollment Students Are More Likely to Enroll in Postsecondary Education.* Tallahassee: Florida Department of Education, Mar. 2004a.

Florida Department of Education. *Impact of Dual Enrollment on High Performing Students.* Tallahassee: Florida Department of Education, Mar. 2004b.

Florida Department of Education. "2008–09 Florida Bright Futures Scholarship Program Fact Sheet." Office of Student Financial Assistance, N.d. Retrieved Oct. 15, 2008, from http://www.floridastudentfinancialaid.org/SSFAD/factsheets/BF.htm.

Florida Statutes, Title XLVIII, K–20 Code, Chapter 1007, sec. 1007.27. 2008. Retrieved Oct. 15, 2008, from http://www.flsenate.gov/Statutes/index.cfm?StatuteYear=2004&Tab=statutes&Submenu=1. n.d.

Florida Statutes, Title K–20 Code, Chapter 1009, sec. 1009.25. N.d. Retrieved Oct. 15, 2008, from http://www.flsenate.gov/Statutes/index.cfm?StatuteYear=2004&Tab=statutes&Submenu=1.

Florida Statutes. Title XLVIII, K–20 Code, Chapter 1011, sec. 1011.62. 2008. Retrieved online from http://www.flsenate.gov/Statutes/index.cfm?StatuteYear=2004&Tab=statutes&Submenu=1.

Jobs for the Future. "A Portrait in Numbers." In *Early College High School News*. Boston: Jobs for the Future, 2009.

Karp, M. M., and others. *The Postsecondary Achievement of Participants in Dual Enrollment: An Analysis of Student Outcomes in Two States*. New York: Community College Research Center, Teacher College, Columbia University, Oct. 2007.

Kleiner, B., and Lewis, L. *Dual Enrollment of High School Students at Postsecondary Institutions: 2002–03*. Washington, D.C: U.S. Department of Education, National Center for Education Statistics, 2005. Retrieved February 25, 2009, from http://nces.ed.gov/pubsearch/pubsinfo.asp?pubid=2005008.

Meade, T., and Hofmann, E. "CUNY College Now: Extending the Reach of Dual Enrollment." In N. Hoffman, J. Vargas, A. Venezia, and M. Miller (eds.), *Minding the Gap: Why Integrating High School with College Makes Sense and How to Do It*. Cambridge, Mass.: Harvard Education Press, 2007.

Michalowski, S. *Preliminary Interpretation of Regression Analysis on the College Now Program Conducted in Conjunction with Jobs for the Future*. New York: City University of New York, Office of Academic Affairs, 2006.

Vargas, J., and Hoffman, N. *Dual Enrollment in Rhode Island: Opportunities for State Policy*. Boston: Jobs for the Future, 2006.

NANCY HOFFMAN *is vice president of Youth Transitions and director of the Early College High School Initiative at Jobs for the Future.*

JOEL VARGAS *is program director at Jobs for the Future.*

JANET SANTOS *is program manager of district, state, and national policy at Jobs for the Future.*

5

In this chapter, the English faculty at a rural community college used part of the school's mandatory reaccreditation process to investigate the increasing lack of readiness among incoming students and discovered a serious disconnect between the new challenges and the school's traditional English program.

Ready or Not?

Renee A. Moore

The stated mission of Mississippi Delta Community College (MDCC) is "to provide quality educational experiences that include intellectual, academic, vocational, technical, social, cultural, and recreational opportunities, at a nominal cost to those who qualify for the courses of study offered" (Mississippi Delta Community College, 2008). The phrase "those who qualify" captures both the unique history and the complex challenges of this institution.

Mississippi Delta, one of the oldest community colleges in the country, is located in Sunflower County, Mississippi, which was home to both the infamous White Citizens Council and civil rights heroine Fannie Lou Hamer. It serves one of the poorest areas of the country; the unemployment rate in the district is higher than that of any other community college in Mississippi. The Delta population is nearly 65 percent nonwhite, and almost 40 percent of the population live in poverty. While Mississippi ranks fiftieth in the country in per capita income at $12,830, the Delta ranks even lower at $12,432. Mississippi has the highest illiteracy rate of any state in the nation, and the Delta has the highest rate in the state: over 40 percent of adults.

Since 1995, MDCC has aggressively worked to increase access to college for as many residents of the Delta as possible. The college established satellite campuses, increased its online course offerings, and has energetically pursued the newly approved dual-enrollment program with area high schools. As a result of the attention to access, MDCC's minority population has grown rapidly (from 48 percent in 1995 to 60.4 percent in 2006). Also during that period, female students moved from being a minority to a majority group at the college, averaging 60 percent of enrollment each year.

NEW DIRECTIONS FOR COMMUNITY COLLEGES, no. 145, Spring 2009 © 2009 Wiley Periodicals, Inc.
Published online in Wiley InterScience (www.interscience.wiley.com) • DOI: 10.1002/cc.355

At the same time, an increasing number of freshmen were entering the college without appropriate language and computational skills. In response, MDCC established a general education (developmental) program for students needing academic help and the College Center of Learning to improve retention of students through academic success.

These conditions of challenge and change converged as we began to prepare for the college's reaccreditation process through the Southern Association of Colleges and Schools. As part of the process, the college developed a faculty-led initiative, the quality enhancement plan, that focuses on improving some student learning. The development of this plan has shown that both the students and the college were underprepared for twenty-first-century educational realities. That same inquiry process, however, has helped us explore and initiate meaningful changes in our writing program to best serve the needs of our students and the communities that depend on their success.

Student Readiness

One reason for the increased need for remediation is the increased enrollment of students who may not have previously considered postsecondary education. More of the students with lower high school grade point averages and a lower range of ACT scores are enrolling out of compulsion, expectation, or desperation. As noted in other chapters in this volume, approximately 70 percent of high school students will enter some form of postsecondary education (National Center for Educational Statistics, 2007). Nationally, 50 to 70 percent of those entering college freshmen require some type of remediation, and 25 percent have learning disabilities (McCusker, 1999). The percentage of students at MDCC requiring remedial services grew from approximately 5 percent in 1993 to 60 percent in 2000 and has remained near that level for the past eight years.

In MDCC's seven-county service area, poor performance has been a constant fact of academic life. Since 2000, Mississippi's mandatory testing program has required all students to pass an exit exam after completion of tenth-grade English. Students may repeat the test up to four times per school year, but they must pass it in order to receive a diploma. Passing in this case means a score above 300 (which is considered minimal according to the scoring categories) on the multiple choice section and a score of at least 2.0 (on a scale of 0 to 4) on the essay-writing section. Students must pass both sections to graduate from public high school in Mississippi. Students graduating from the predominantly white private academies are not required to take the state exams.

Since implementation of the federal No Child Left Behind (NCLB) legislation, the Delta high schools have consistently scored far below the state average on the multiple choice section of the test; however, they have remained almost even with the state average on the essay portion. Delta schools are nowhere near the proficient level (scores of 346 or better) that NCLB mandates all students must reach by 2014. In fact, after a slight peak to the Basic category (312–345) in the 2004–2005 school year, most of the scores have dropped well back into the Minimal (311 and below) category (Mississippi Department of Education, 2006).

The quality of English instruction in the high schools of the Delta ranges from challenging to nonexistent. Being in a chronic teacher shortage area, Delta school districts are more likely to resort to hiring less-qualified staff on emergency certificates, assigning teachers out-of-field, or using long-term substitutes in key academic courses. A few schools offer Advanced Placement English, but it is more common to find dual-enrollment agreements with the local colleges. The Delta boasts some of the finest and most highly recognized veteran teachers in the state, yet it also has extremely high teacher vacancy and turnover rates each year. Although the state is fifth in the nation for number of National Board Certified Teachers (over twenty-five hundred), only a fraction of those teach in Delta schools, and attracting more of these highly accomplished teachers to the Delta's high-needs schools remains a challenge (Berry and Rasberry, 2008).

Like most other Mississippi state colleges, MDCC uses student scores on the English section of the ACT to determine placement of students within its academic program. A long and bitter federal lawsuit against the state's higher education system (*Ayers v. Fordice*) resulted in a leveling of general entrance requirements across the predominantly white public colleges and the historically black public colleges. However, there are no limitations on the use of test scores as placement criteria. Consequently a student with a score of 18 (on a scale of 1 to 36) on the ACT English subtest may be admitted to a credit-bearing Freshman Composition I course at one college or placed into a remedial English class at another. Most of the four-year colleges require a score of 21 or higher on the English test for placement in Composition I, while 18 is acceptable at most of the community colleges.

As with the state high school tests, students at the public schools in the Delta score consistently lower on the ACT. While the statewide average on the ACT has hovered around 19 (out of a possible 36), the average score at schools in the counties served by MDCC is 16 and falling (Mississippi Department of Education, 2007). To compensate for this, MDCC admits students into Composition I with ACT English scores of 16 or higher.

Teacher Readiness

While the composition of the student body at MDCC has rapidly changed, that of the English faculty has not. Except for the occasional white male and the lone black female, the members of the English faculty remain primarily white women. In the past, most of the teachers came to the community college from the private K–12 academies in the surrounding counties.

Although mostly well intentioned, some of the college faculty could not help but make a causal connection between the increasing number of minority students and the simultaneous increase in the need for remediation.

Nevertheless, the instructors attempted to instruct each new crop of students using traditional instructional methods, with mostly disappointing results.

Just prior to the beginning of the college's reaccreditation process, the English department went through several significant changes. First, the department was dissolved as part of a schoolwide restructuring and folded into a larger division. Next, the administration cut the English course offerings at MDCC to two freshman-level composition courses and two semesters of world literature. The administration also indicated that English faculty in the new humanities division would be expected to help teach the remedial English courses (and those in the general education or developmental division would help teach the composition and literature courses).

The retirement and resignation of most of the existing faculty followed these changes. The number of full-time English faculty dropped from ten to five, and most of the positions were not replaced for budget reasons. Meanwhile, the college was expanding its online, satellite campus, and dual-enrollment offerings. The relatively new English faculty soon found themselves stretched geographically as well as pedagogically. The use of adjunct faculty increased dramatically. Communication and coordination among the faculty was seriously impaired. The newer teachers were hesitant to assume what had formerly been the department chair's role of facilitating basic tasks such as textbook selection, course scheduling, professional development, and department-wide assessment of student writing.

Checking the Mirror

This time of internal upheaval, however, proved an advantageous moment for self-examination. At a faculty meeting near the start of the fall 2005 semester, several teachers commented that fewer students were successfully completing freshman composition and more were experiencing difficulty meeting writing requirements.

The teachers were successful in getting their concerns about student writing adopted as the focus of the reaccreditation's new quality enhancement plan process. A team of thirty faculty members from across disciplines spent the next two years examining and questioning the effectiveness of the MDCC's English program. The process included a painstaking review of over twenty-five hundred student transcripts, which confirmed the teachers' suspicions that many students who began in the developmental courses were not going on to complete the writing program. The team's analysis revealed a need for better reporting systems and closer monitoring to follow the progress of students through the English program.

The data clearly showed that the major stumbling point was the transition from the developmental program to Freshman Composition I. Why were so many students unable to complete the credit-bearing composition course? Team members questioned the validity of using ACT scores to determine the writing ability of incoming MDCC students. Some members suggested an

NEW DIRECTIONS FOR COMMUNITY COLLEGES • DOI: 10.1002/cc

introductory composition class for all students except those with the very highest ACT scores. Others argued that we not only needed to provide background knowledge and skills in the remedial courses, but also to help students develop the stamina and motivation to complete their English program. Teachers shared concerns about the challenge of taking students who have been through disheartening experiences with English instruction and rekindling a love of learning. What training, preparation, or experiences did we as college teachers need to be effective at each level in the composition program?

The quality enhancement process revealed how dependent the college had become on course grades alone as the sole indicator of student performance and the lack of alignment of learning outcomes from one level of English composition to the next. While individual teachers were using learning outcomes at the classroom level to determine grades, these outcomes were not consistent across classes. As one teacher commented, "I do not think instruction is equal among all sites, instructors, or mediums." Another was even more pessimistic: "I think MDCC is in dire need of change in the English [class] format." Several teachers lamented "stale teaching, unchanged over years and years. . . . We need to look for better ways to do things, but we don't have to all do it the same way. . . . We have to evaluate constructively what's been going on and what we want to do about our own teaching and across divisions."

When Boylan and Saxon (1999) summarized thirty years of research on college remedial education programs around the nation, they listed key characteristics of the most successful programs. Compared to that list, a glaring weakness in the MDCC English program over recent years had been the lack of any systematic professional development for the faculty. In fact, most of the newly hired teachers were not yet active in any state or national professional organizations. Since we saw each other only in passing between classes, there was little dialogue about instruction. Armed with the sobering data, the team spent the second year of the process researching and debating how best to address each of these inconsistencies.

Fitting into New Realities

One big issue was placement. The quality enhancement plan team had found that ACT English subtest scores alone were not a reliable indicator of student performance, particularly for African American students. More disturbing was the revelation, through data analysis, that passing one or both of the developmental English courses did not correlate to success in Freshman Composition. The new quality enhancement plan developed by the faculty team aligns the placement and progress of students according to performance on specific learning outcomes for each course. Incoming students are more carefully placed using a combination of test scores and writing samples. Using the combined performance data, trained faculty advisers now assist students in selecting the appropriate course along the English composition sequence.

NEW DIRECTIONS FOR COMMUNITY COLLEGES • DOI: 10.1002/cc

Researchers have found that students, particularly younger ones, are adversely affected by being placed in remediation at the college level, both in their subsequent academic performance and in their perseverance toward their educational goals (Calcagano, Crosta, Bailey, and Jenkins, 2006; MacLellan and Gandy, 2002). To mediate those effects, we decided to counsel students about the placement process and the importance of gaining college-level proficiency in written communication. By basing placement on performance on specific learning outcomes, we can help students better understand the benefits of the remediation courses and set realistic targets for their own academic performance.

During its analysis of student transcripts, the quality enhancement plan team noted that many students did not begin taking English courses immediately. In fact, some did not begin the English sequence until their second year. The team also found that large numbers of students did not move through the English program systematically, sometimes waiting a year or more between attempts at English courses. Over the four-year period the team studied, the percentage of students who started in Intermediate English (the midlevel remedial English course) and went on to complete Freshman Composition steadily declined to a low of 29.33 percent. The quality enhancement plan calls for a reversal of this trend, so that by 2012, at least 75 percent of remediated students will go on to complete Freshman Composition successfully. Toward that end, the plan not only encourages careful initial placement of students, but also recommends that all degree-seeking students be required to take an English course every semester until they have completed Freshman Composition. Under the quality enhancement plan, students will be more closely monitored to ensure timely completion of the English composition requirements relevant to academic or career programs.

We believe the most important determinant of student academic success is the quality of classroom instruction. Therefore, pivotal to the success of the plan are the development, calibration, and use of a schoolwide writing rubric for evaluating student work. The process of creating the rubric was itself a rigorous and enlightening learning opportunity for the faculty members. The first step in developing the rubric was getting instructors to agree on specific learning outcomes for the entire writing program, sequenced by course. These outcomes were then correlated with appropriate evaluation criteria. For example, the group came to consensus that level A writing would exhibit the following qualities:

- Is original and thought-provoking
- Is well organized with clear thesis and topic sentences
- Clearly illustrates all key ideas with sufficient examples
- Uses a highly effective tone for audience and purpose
- Is highly fluent in diction and range of sentence types
- Is free of major errors in grammar and mechanics

Next, calibration of the rubric required the teachers to use the new instrument to score student work samples. Instructors debated the relative importance of the outcomes and how students could best demonstrate them. Surprising to some, the expectations and evaluations of instructors in the developmental program were often more stringent than those of the regular Fresh███ Composition instructors. By the end of the intensive session, one teacher noted, "It was encouraging how consistent our results were; I thought my scores would be really out-of-step with the others." The English faculty are working together now on a specific plan for faculty development relative to the student learning outcomes.

Given the changing student demographics and the challenges of preparing students to communicate effectively in the twenty-first-century workplace, the teachers wrote into the plan support for quality professional development in the areas of cultural diversity and differentiated instruction, multiple intelligences, learning styles, and expanded integration of technology in the teaching of composition, as well as other areas directly relevant to the student learning outcomes in English composition. The administration has also been making a more conscious effort to recruit teachers with some experience in the predominantly black K–12 public schools.

Looking Ahead

Huber and Hutchings (2005) observe, "There is a need to establish more and better occasions to talk about learning. This sounds simple but it isn't. Campus conversations about learning often take place on the edges of campus life, and in ad hoc ways that cannot be sustained or built on. Structures and occasions are needed to bring people together on campus for sustained, substantive, constructive discussions about learning and how to improve it" (pp. 118–119).

One of the most successful structures for this type of professional dialogue and growth on college campuses has been the development of faculty learning communities (FLCs), counterparts to the professional learning communities that have become increasingly popular in many K–12 schools. In order to be truly effective, creation and participation in a faculty learning community must be voluntary. Therefore, the team did not mandate establishment of an FLC. Rather, we are seeking to create conditions favorable to emergence of such communities. One step was to bridge the gap between full- and part-time faculty. Although often ignored in past professional development efforts, adjunct faculty are being fully integrated into the quality enhancement plan training and implementation. Meanwhile, the team established the English Advisory Committee and a dedicated Web site to improve communication among the widely dispersed English instructors. We hope the camaraderie generated by our research process will mature into full faculty learning communities during our five-year implementation period.

An unexpected benefit of the process was how it helped the faculty move into new levels of comfort with educational technologies such as online chats, e-mail, message boards, and webinars, many of which are now used regularly in the classroom with students. We did not realize it at the time, but our work was also helping us develop into a learning community, not just a group of professors who all happened to teach for the same school.

The planning is finished, but our process of transformation has just begun. Statewide, English professionals from higher education and from the public PK–12 schools are working on how to smoothe out the transition between levels of education by aligning standards and expectations. Had we continued to focus only on what we perceived as students' unreadiness for college, we would not have uncovered our own learning needs. The inquiry-based, quality enhancement process has energized the English faculty members to pursue a more collaborative, research-based approach to improving our writing program rather than remain in the defeatist cycle of passing blame for poor student performance.

References

Ayers v. Fordice, 111 F.3d 1183 (5th Cir. 1997).

Berry, B., and Rasberry, M. Every Child Deserves Success: Recommendations from Mississippi's National Board Certified Teachers on Supporting and Staffing High Needs Schools. Center for Teaching Quality and Mississippi Association of Educators, Jan. 2008. Retrieved February 25, 2009, from http://www.teachingquality.org/pdfs/MSNBCT summitl.pdf.

Boylan, H. R., and Saxon, D. P. What Works in Remediation: Lessons from 30 Years of Research. 1999. Retrieved Sept. 8, 2006, from EBSCOhost: ERIC database.

Calcagno, J. C., Crosta, P., Bailey, T., and Jenkins, D. Stepping Stones to a Degree: The Impact of Enrollment Pathways and Milestones on Community College Student Outcomes. New York: Community College Research Center, Teachers College, Columbia University, 2006.

Huber, M., and Hutchings, P. The Advancement of Learning: Building the Teaching Commons. San Francisco: Jossey-Bass, 2005.

MacLellan, A. M., and Gandy, K. H. The Stanford Bridge Project: Maryland Community College Extension. 2002. ERIC Report. (ED 464 675)

McCusker, M. "ERIC Review: Effective Elements of Developmental Reading and Writing Programs." Community College Review, 1999, 27(2), 93–105.

Mississippi Delta Community College. College Catalog and Student Handbook. 2008. Retrieved February 25, 2009, from http://www.msdelta.edu/catalog/index.html.

Mississippi Department of Education. Retrieved February 25, 2009, from http://www.mde.k12.ms.us.

National Center for Educational Statistics. U.S. Department of Education. Retrieved February 25, 2009, from www.nces.ed.gov. 2007.

RENEE A. MOORE is on the English faculty at Mississippi Delta Community College. She is a 2001 Milken Family Foundation Educator of the Year and Mississippi's 2001 Teacher of the Year.

NEW DIRECTIONS FOR COMMUNITY COLLEGES • DOI: 10.1002/cc

6

In this chapter, the authors describe their efforts, as codirectors of Pasadena City College's Teaching and Learning Center, to increase success rates in prealgebra and address issues of equity and access through a faculty inquiry-based process.

Making Prealgebra Meaningful: It Starts with Faculty Inquiry

Brock Klein, Lynn Marie Wright

Community college instructors of basic skills math and English face a daunting task every day of every semester, engaging students who see little or no value in writing essays about essays or finding the value of the ever-elusive x. Whether or not students felt any differently about essays or x's in the "good old days," we know that the students sitting in basic skills English and math classes back then were very different ethnically, economically, and socially from the students in those same seats today. In California, for example, the community college student population has changed dramatically in the past twenty years (Hayward, Jones, McGuinness, and Timar, 2004). At some point, without many educators realizing it, California community colleges acquired a new "typical" student, and the transformation to a student body that is predominantly of color, immigrant, low income, and underprepared for college appears to be permanent. In addition to a more diverse student body, we also have a larger one. According to the nonprofit advocacy group California Tomorrow, the state's college-age population is steadily increasing, with more than half a million additional students projected to attend California community colleges in the next five to ten years. Because the student population is becoming larger, more diverse, and less prepared, issues of access and equity are more troubling than ever before.

A Call to Action: It's Not Just About Programs

While much discussion about student success as it relates to access, equity, and underpreparedness at the collegiate level is taking place nationally (for

NEW DIRECTIONS FOR COMMUNITY COLLEGES, no. 145, Spring 2009 © 2009 Wiley Periodicals, Inc.
Published online in Wiley InterScience (www.interscience.wiley.com) • DOI: 10.1002/cc.356

example, the Lumina Foundation-funded Achieving the Dream Initiative) and statewide (for example, the California Community Colleges' Basic Skills Initiative), a strong and specific concern prompted some of us at Pasadena City College (PCC), a large urban community college located northeast of downtown Los Angeles, to address the issues head-on. Students in the summer bridge/first-year experience program were staying in school and their classes, but an unacceptably large number of them were failing their courses, particularly math. In 2006, analysts in the college's Institutional Planning and Research Office reported specifically on underpreparation for transfer-level math: over 85 percent of new students at the college place into precollegiate math; success rates have been on a downward trend for more than ten years; less than 15 percent of all students will ever complete the three-course basic skills math sequence, and on average it will take them six years to do so; and Latinos and African Americans are overrepresented in basic skills math courses. We desperately needed a swift and effective intervention.

At PCC, the Teaching and Learning Center was created specifically to develop innovative programs to provide greater access to higher education for underprepared students. These programs are based on a learning community model and include .XL, a summer bridge/first-year experience (SB/FYE) program that we—the center's codirectors, the authors of this chapter, and, notably, composition rather than math instructors—designed for young, underrepresented first-generation college students taking precollegiate-level English and math classes. Students begin the program with a six-week summer bridge that includes a prealgebra math class, a study and student success skills course, and mandatory homework labs. They continue in the fall and spring semesters in two cohorts to complete their English and math requirements before moving on to general education courses. The first-year pathway has always been filled with challenges, but particularly troubling was the consistently high failure rate in math. After several years of program modifications based on evaluation findings and recommendations, we realized that focusing solely on program design was not enough. We needed to turn our attention to what goes on in the classroom, specifically with our underprepared teachers.

Identifying the Problem: The Genesis of the Inquiry Process

It has been standard practice during the summer bridge portion of the .XL program for the math instructors, mentor/tutors, counselor, and program coordinator to meet weekly to discuss group dynamics and students' individual academic progress, as well as to determine any needed interventions. Initially these meetings were simply a community of teachers and staff getting together to talk on a regular basis, a precursor to what we now call a faculty inquiry group (FIG), broadly defined as a team that works together over time to understand students' needs and develop strategies to address them. Early on in these meetings, we recognized a misalignment between the summer bridge math instructors' espoused teaching philosophy and their practice. These instructors, Ann Davis and Jay Cho, were caring individuals dedicated to helping basic skills math students succeed, yet their actual teaching practices often ran counter to their intentions. They understood, for example, how important it is to address nonmath issues, such as reading, writing, and study skills, in their classes, but they struggled to integrate them into the curriculum and at the same time cover the required topics and concepts.

Through our weekly summer meetings, we realized that our deeply committed math instructors were stuck in a traditional math teaching paradigm and unable to recognize the problem on their own, let alone do anything about it. They felt powerless to change the basic skills math curriculum at PCC, which is influenced by both tradition and textbook writers and publishers. Math instructors generally teach the way they were taught and use their textbook as a script. In addition, a tacit sink-or-swim sentiment persists among many in PCC's math department; if students do not make it through the fast-paced, concept-packed basic skills courses, perhaps they do not belong in college.

We thought that actively engaging faculty (specifically, Ann and Jay) in creating more meaningful curriculum would solve the problem of poor student engagement and success. However, our ongoing dialogues about teaching practice soon revealed a greater challenge: effective curricular transformation relies on significant faculty transformation. The prealgebra curriculum would not change without faculty first changing notions about themselves and their students. It became clear that we needed to be faculty development coordinators as much as program directors. We needed to create a place for the scholarship of teaching and learning, a place in which faculty could be empowered so that they in turn could empower students. Our first official FIG (faculty inquiry group) soon followed.

The Inquiry Process and Outcomes

The inquiry process is an effective tool that teachers can use to become scholars of teaching and learning and ultimately provides increasingly diverse groups of students access to greater academic, personal, and professional success. In essence, FIGs constitute collaborative self-study research "in which teachers examine their beliefs and actions within the context of their work as educators and explore pedagogical questions. It allows professors to renew their instructional tools as well as discover new tools" (Louie, Drevdahl, Purdy, and Stackman, 2003). The process we describe here began with a group of instructors who identified a problem (low success rates in our summer bridge prealgebra classes) and hypothesized that meaningful math would lead to greater student engagement and that greater engagement would lead to greater student success. The process they followed was structured, sustained, and faculty led; it was also "designed down," that is,

NEW DIRECTIONS FOR COMMUNITY COLLEGES • DOI: 10.1002/cc

participants began by defining their outcomes. We view the FIG process as an iterative one of research, discussion, reflection, piloting, evaluation, and modification. Critical to success and legitimacy is the fact that the FIG process and outcomes rest on a culture of evidence.

Ann and Jay, the .XL prealgebra instructors, were the obvious leads for this first FIG because they were teaching the course that needed change and had been prepared for it through both their .XL summer bridge teaching collaboration and their active participation in previous TLC professional development opportunities. (Since 2005 there have been FIGs for instructors at all three levels of the basic skills math sequence, at the first level of the basic skills English sequence, and in the natural sciences.) With a clear initial outcome in mind—curriculum reform (including the development of prealgebra learning outcomes and assessment instruments)—and a deadline (the .XL summer bridge prealgebra courses were only nine months away), they recruited six of their colleagues, created agendas, facilitated discussions, led research, and provided lunch. Brock or Lynn, or both of us, attended most of their meetings, took notes, helped create agendas, and led debriefing sessions with Ann and Jay.

Although this FIG was clearly outcomes driven, Ann began indirectly by helping the inquiry participants negotiate an understanding of the FIG individually and collectively. What is inquiry? Why is it an effective tool? What did the participants expect to occur? When does the process end? Interestingly, several instructors came to this first meeting with feelings of trepidation, suspicion, and fear. What was the agenda? Were the participants being blamed for students' poor success rates in math and criticized for what they thought they did well? Were standards and rigor going to be thrown out the door? Ann posed several questions to her colleagues to allay their concerns:

- What should a PCC student know about math to function well in life?
- What should a prealgebra student know and be able to do at the end of the course?
- How much time should a prealgebra instructor spend on nonmath issues such as time management and test anxiety?
- How much do reading and writing skills relate to success in math courses?
- Do tests measure the learning instructors expect and value?
- Are there forms of assessment other than traditional tests that can and should be used to measure learning?

Rather than blame the instructors for the low success rates in math or allow them to turn the FIG into a series of unproductive gripe sessions, at this crucial first meeting Ann deftly challenged her colleagues to develop effective practices, learning outcomes, and alternative forms of assessment. She focused on empowering them to implement short, easy-to-accomplish classroom activities (what we call "small, doable things"). For example, the group set ground rules (participate actively, respect your colleagues by listening to them, and state a problem only if you can offer a potential solution) and completed a reflective writing assessment (What do you believe is the main objective of this project? What is the main benefit for your students, yourself, the math division, and the college? Why did you agree to participate in this FIG? How effective was this first meeting?). The participants decided on a day and time for the next meeting, and Ann assigned homework, asking the instructors to make a list of what they wanted their prealgebra students to know and to be able to do on completion of the course. (This was our first foray into working with faculty on the development of student learning outcomes.) She also asked them to bring in one effective practice to share with their colleagues. The meeting ended with pizza, and we were on our way. A community of math teachers and learners had been formed.

The prealgebra FIG met every two or three weeks throughout the sixteen-week fall and spring semesters, and although Ann and Jay's specific intention was to revise the curriculum for the .XL program, the participants found value in the constructive and collegial process. In addition, as program directors, we slowly began to understand that the transformation of the instructors themselves was more important than, and critical to, the transformation of methodology and curriculum.

Faculty Transformation and Evaluation

We know from our experiences as instructors that among any group of learners, some will engage actively, take risks, and transform significantly. Unfortunately, we also know that some learners will be peripheral participants who take small, hesitant steps, and others will remain unmotivated and uninterested and may eventually drop out. Of the eight instructors who participated in the FIG process, four clearly had a powerful experience; they attended all the meetings, participated actively in all the activities, engaged in research, made changes in their teaching practices, and are now powerful advocates for basic skills math students in their department and on campus. These instructors no longer see themselves just as content specialists but as community college professionals engaged in the dynamic process of teaching and learning precollegiate math. They identify themselves as change agents in their students' lives, a powerful responsibility that challenges them to engage their students and make math meaningful to them. They can no longer be simply the sage on the stage and expect students to "get" math, and they can no longer see themselves as filters who "weed out the students who don't belong in college." Key to identifying themselves as change agents has been getting to know their students, embracing them for who they are, and seeing precollegiate math instruction as an intellectually challenging and rewarding endeavor that requires them to move beyond the traditional and clearly ineffective math instruction paradigm and embrace nonmath curriculum, such as reading, writing, and other student success topics, such as time management, note taking, and techniques to reduce test anxiety. As a participant astutely pointed out during a FIG session, "It's not so much about teaching math as it is about teaching students that they can do math."

The actively engaged instructors employed several methods in order to get to know their students and understand how they learn. For example, Jay used think-alouds, a process by which students are videotaped speaking out loud what they are thinking while working through math problems. Jay videotaped several of his students working on word problems that involved negative numbers while thinking aloud and showed the tapes to the FIG participants, who discussed what they had seen and heard.

The think-alouds provoked great discussions among the math instructors about diverse learning styles, cognitive load, reading, critical thinking, problem solving, and motivation. They argued about the value of rote learning, shortcuts, and manipulatives. Most important, they all began to question their assumptions about how students learn math. The math FIG participants were surprised by many of the comments that the students in Jay's think-alouds made. Among their discoveries:

- Students often rely on mathematically unsound strategies that they have acquired informally rather than correct or appropriate ones provided by their instructors.
- They often "go wrong" early in the process, and even if they feel that something is not making sense, they are unwillingly to stop, assess, and try something else.
- When they discover that their answer is incorrect, they often begin guessing and eventually lose interest. ("Just tell me what x is.")
- Students struggle with word problems. Their calculations may be correct, but they often arrive at an incorrect answer because they are unable to decode the language.

Clearly there are great differences between the ways math experts and novices solve word problems. In addition, what is transparent for math instructors is opaque for many of their students.

The FIG participants' valuing of the think-aloud process is one measure of the effectiveness of the FIG process. Other evidence is that FIG participants have become leaders within the math department and advocates for precollegiate math curriculum reform. Ann, for example, is an active participant in the California Community Colleges' Basic Skills Initiative on our campus and mentors other math faculty who are interested in improving basic skills math success. Ann and Jay together have given campuswide presentations on the process they used to understand, implement, and assess student learning outcomes. In addition to documenting the prealgebra FIG process and his action research for the Windows on Learning project on the Carnegie Foundation for the Advancement of Teaching Web site,

Jay has presented campuswide for "The Passion for Teaching and Learning Workshops," helping nonmath faculty understand the value of the inquiry process and how they can start their own. In addition, several of Ann and Jay's math colleagues have formed inquiry groups at the two higher levels in the basic skills math sequence, beginning and intermediate algebra; one has resulted in yet another online Windows on Learning project as well as a common final for intermediate algebra. Finally, there is now a powerful core of math faculty who are looking at data; questioning the efficacy of the curriculum and their practices; beginning to understand the value of creating and assessing clear, attainable learning outcomes; and sustaining a dialogue about student success.

Curriculum Transformation and Evaluation

As program directors, we have learned that faculty transformation is paramount to achieving student success; it is an essential predecessor to curriculum revision, but it is no guarantee that significant curricular or methodological changes will immediately occur. For example, although the faculty engaged in the inquiry process now see value in incorporating nonmath topics into their daily lessons, they still struggle with the issues of content and coverage. Throughout the FIG process, participants grappled with several questions: Is our curriculum pedagogically sound? Can we expect students to master over three hundred concepts in one course and apply them to concepts at the next higher level? If not, what are the essential concepts a student needs to know in prealgebra to succeed in elementary algebra?

Not every FIG participant has resolved these questions of coverage, but several have come to terms with the fact that as algebra is usually taught, it has little relevance in the lives of many community college students. Although PCC's basic skills math program is calculus tracked, the vast majority of our students declare majors that do not require calculus for transfer or degree completion. (In fact, college data have revealed that less than 0.5 percent of the students who enter the math sequence at Level One, prealgebra, will ever enroll in the beginning calculus course, and only half of them will pass it.) The college's commitment to provide diverse communities within its service area access to certificate and degree completion and transfer opportunities appears to have been unwittingly undermined by course sequence and articulation policies.

Although faculty members have little initial control over these policies, they can make immediate changes in what goes on in the classroom. The revised prealgebra curriculum that eventually did result from this guided inquiry process reflects the FIG participants' belief that making math meaningful to students will lead to greater student engagement and eventually greater student success. They have reduced the number of essential prealgebra concepts by approximately a third and increased the time they spend helping students make connections between the math they are studying and life outside the classroom. Their goal is greater mastery of fewer concepts. XL summer bridge prealgebra instructors now introduce each chapter with a basic concept that includes a real-life application: asking students to perform meaningful math tasks, such as balancing a checkbook, budgeting for a party, and hanging photos equidistantly, for example. These activities are clearly connected to Ann and Jay's student learning outcomes for the .XL prealgebra course, and they have created pre- and postassessments to measure outcomes achievement.

Assessment: A Work in Progress

Outcomes-based assessment has helped relieve faculty anxiety about reducing the number of topics covered in a semester, but assessment was, and remains, a formidable challenge. Faculty who participated in the inquiry process have developed and implemented many new and innovative practices, yet they still struggle to see beyond the traditional, and often unfair and inappropriate, tests and quizzes that determine their students' final grades. They fret about what to do with students who repeatedly demonstrate their understanding of a specific math concept in class activities but fail to do so on a test. Several instructors admit that their logic about testing is circular, and therefore flawed: "I give tests because math students have to take tests. That's what you do in math." Unfortunately, using multiple assessment measures appears to many to be an excuse for "dumbing down" the class and passing more students, and FIG participants still rely heavily on tests. A breakthrough for Ann and Jay, however, came when they created prealgebra pre- and posttests as part of their action research and asked us to edit them. As English and English as a second language instructors, we had red pens in hand in a flash: fragments, syntax problems, redundancies, misspelling. Then came our admonition: "Since you rely predominantly on tests, make sure they're well written and well formatted, not to mention fair and appropriate." What might have been an embarrassing professional moment was instead a powerful teaching and learning moment: two math instructors and two composition teachers working together to write and format a couple of prealgebra exams.

The FIG participants' research into the effects that the inquiry process has had on student performance in basic skills math is promising. Preliminary findings reported by Ann and Jay about the impact of the FIG on student performance in prealgebra (see Table 6.1) show a significant increase in retention and a modest increase in success. The FIG's impact on .XL summer bridge prealgebra courses can be seen in Table 6.2. In summer 2005, after completion of the FIG and revision of the curriculum, retention and success rates increased 8 percent each.

Perhaps most important, research conducted in 2006 by PCC's Institutional Planning and Research Office revealed that .XL students who succeed in prealgebra (Math 402) succeed at the next higher level of math (beginning algebra) at significantly higher rates than their non-.XL counterparts

Table 6.1. Impact of FIG on Student Performance in Prealgebra

Prealgebra	Retention	Success
FIG participants	88%	56%
Non-FIG particpants	77	53

Note: Data for summer and fall 2005.

over time. As Figure 6.1 reveals, 40 percent of the .XL students in Cohort 4 (.XL 4) succeeded in beginning algebra within one year after successfully completing prealgebra, as compared to 10 percent of all PCC students and 8 percent of Hispanic students at the college. A similar relationship is seen for cohort 3 (.XL 3) two years after successfully completing prealgebra and cohort 2 (.XL 2) three years after. We will continue to monitor the impact of these curricular changes on .XL students' subsequent success in math.

Even though in this, our first FIG, we urged inquiry participants to create student learning outcomes, as program directors, we were slow to recognize that we also had to identify key outcomes for our "students," that is, the faculty participants. (Program directors take note: practice what you preach!) Our own conversations about the inquiry process that we were coordinating became more regular and structured as we worked with the FIG leads and our external program evaluators. In addition to understanding what Ann and Jay were learning through their FIG process, we became more reflective about our role as coordinators and organizers through debriefing sessions with them. For instance, in our role as math outsiders, we observed that faculty were relying on quick fixes, such as an extra hour of instruction per week, a better textbook, and teaching assistants, to address retention and success problems in math. The faculty's desire for quick and easy solutions for students was the same as our initial outcome for the faculty: we simply wanted faculty to "fix" their curriculum so that

Table 6.2. Impact of FIG on .XL Summer Bridge Prealgebra Course

Prealgebra	Retention	Success	Persistence (Summer to Fall)
.XL5 (summer 2006)	100%	74%	95%
.XL4 (summer 2005)	100	76	93
.XL3 (summer 2004)	92	68	93
Matched comparison group (age, ethnicity, course)	80	53	68

Figure 6.1. The Power of Inquiry: Implications for Professional Development

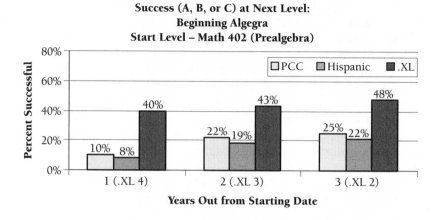

Success (A, B, or C) at Next Level:
Beginning Algegra
Start Level – Math 402 (Prealgebra)

Years Out from Starting Date

students would be successful in the course. In fact, for all participants (ourselves included), the real outcome should be the development of self-motivated and reflective lifelong learners. The challenge for FIG participants was to understand how students learn and to align that understanding with the way that they themselves teach. Our measure of success was whether faculty participants could identify a problem that was in their power to solve, be open to fully exploring it, implement a change confidently, and evaluate its success (or lack thereof).

Since the end of the prealgebra FIG, two of the participants have documented some of their action research for the Carnegie Foundation for the Advancement of Teaching Web project Windows on Learning ("How Jay Got His Groove Back and Made Math Meaningful," n.d.; and "No Longer Lost in Translation: How Yu-Chung Helps Her Students Understand (and Love) Word Problems," n.d.). It is significant to note that their curricular revisions and research have continued well beyond completion of their FIG and Web projects.

Implications for Institutions

What does all this mean for the institution? Our work so far has been with small numbers of faculty and students, but college administrators want to have an impact on the most people in the most cost-effective way possible. Although we understand their desire to scale up effective programs, resources, and services, we have also come to understand the value of intimacy and intensity, that is, working very hard with a small group for an extended period of time. We believe that the process that we have created and followed was necessary to effect deep transformation. Intense, small-scale inquiry tailored to specific concerns and interests is as important to faculty development as it is to student success. As Carnegie Foundation for the Advancement of Teaching scholar Mary Taylor Huber (2008) notes, "Working with others who share a local context is not only more efficient and pleasurable; . . . collaborative inquiry and shared responsibility . . . is particularly important for basic skills education" (p. 9). Access and equity come by nurturing a right-to-success environment, and creating that environment starts with transforming faculty identity, moves to methodological changes and curriculum reform, and ends with student success.

Inquiry has led us well beyond faculty development. We are now thinking more broadly about what influences equity, access, and success, including institutional policies. We have begun an inquiry group with our basic skills deans, and other administrators on campus are considering forming one of their own. We see inquiry groups as a way of developing a community of scholars of teaching and learning throughout all areas of the campus, a transformation perhaps long overdue.

References

"California Tomorrow: Vision and Action for a Just and Inclusive World." Retrieved February 25, 2009, from http://www.californiatomorrow.org/.

Hayward, G. C., Jones, D. P., Mc Guinness, Jr., A. C., and Timar, A. *Ensuring Access with Quality to California's Community Colleges.* San Jose, Calif.: National Center for Public Policy and Higher Education, 2004.

"How Jay Got His Groove Back and Made Math Meaningful." Windows on Learning. Stanford, Calif.: Carnegie Foundation for the Advancement of Teaching. Retrieved February 25, 2009, from http://www.cfkeep.org/html/stitch.php?s=2814408673732& id=55737225670123.

Huber, M. T. "The Promise of Faculty Inquiry for Teaching and Learning Basic Skills." Stanford, Calif.: Carnegie Foundation for the Advancement of Teaching and Learning, 2008.

Louie, B. Y., Drevdahl, D. J., Purdy, J. M., and Stackman, R. W. "Advancing the Scholarship of Teaching Through Collaborative Self-Study." *Journal of Higher Education,* 2003, 74(2), 150–151.

"No Longer Lost in Translation: How Yu-Chung Helps Her Students Understand (and Love) Word Problems." Windows on Learning. Stanford, Calif.: Carnegie Foundation for the Advancement of Teaching. Retrieved February 25, 2009, from http://www.cfkeep.org/html/stitch.php?s=2814408673732&id=55737225670123.

BROCK KLEIN *is an associate professor of English as a second language and a codirector of Pasadena City College's Teaching and Learning Center.*

LYNN MARIE WRIGHT *is an associate professor of English and a codirector of Pasadena City College's Teaching and Learning Center.*

NEW DIRECTIONS FOR COMMUNITY COLLEGES • DOI: 10.1002/cc

This chapter shares the experience of several English faculty members of Glendale Community College in their efforts to improve student outcomes in developmental composition classes through extensive use of technology in the classroom. Their pedagogies of visibility—of literacy, of learning, and of research—have allowed them to better understand not only how their students learn, but also how to continue to document progress in ways that can be useful to others.

Pedagogies of Visibility: The Full E-mersion and Beyond

Chris Juzwiak, Monette Tiernan

In the year 2000, what started as an isolated pedagogical gambit at Glendale Community College (GCC) in Southern California has evolved into a program-wide initiative to revise the developmental composition curriculum and boost student learning outcomes. One instructor, frustrated with poor student motivation and success in his precollegiate writing workshops, asked: What would happen if we infused the instruction with as much technology as possible? From this premise, several colleagues joined forces to explore the possibilities of an electronic pedagogy for developmental composition, generating and assembling a database of original, technology-based instructional materials along the way. The result was what has become known as the "Full E-mersion" pedagogy.

In 2004, the Carnegie Foundation for the Advancement of Teaching recognized the work with a three-year grant, and the Glendale faculty became participants in a California-based initiative to Strengthen Pre-Collegiate Education in Community Colleges (SPECC). This funding allowed a broader and more systematic evaluation, revision, and implementation of the Full E-mersion pedagogy at Glendale College; moreover, Carnegie's SPECC-related activities linked the faculty to the International Society for the Scholarship of Teaching and Learning community. Out of this contact grew a more expansive mission for the Glendale team, dubbed Pedagogies of Visibility. The research now includes a tripartite investigation of visible literacy (making instruction transparent for students), visible learning (making student learning transparent for instructors), and visible

NEW DIRECTIONS FOR COMMUNITY COLLEGES, no. 145, Spring 2009 © 2009 Wiley Periodicals, Inc.
Published online in Wiley InterScience (www.interscience.wiley.com) • DOI: 10.1002/cc.357

research (making outcomes transparent for a wider academic audience). This chapter defines these concepts and narrates their trajectories.

Visible Literacy: Making Instruction Transparent for Students

Through almost a decade of innovation and inquiry, the Glendale team has continually revisited an abiding question about the Full E-mersion: What is it that this pedagogy does more effectively than other pedagogies? At this juncture, we believe that the pedagogy makes the literacy of our discipline, academic writing, highly transparent for students. This transparency involves not only the instructional content but the instructor's role and rationale as well, representing a full disclosure of the instructional process. We recognize that academic writing can seem nebulous and amorphous to many college students and to developmental learners—those students unprepared to do college-level work—in particular; hence, the notion of a visible literacy has become our guiding principle in the ongoing augmentation and refinement of the instructional apparatus.

Currently, the Full E-mersion pedagogy has five overarching applications: (1) interactive PowerPoint lessons, (2) a robust class Web site or "living textbook," (3) the computer classroom as a transformational learning environment or "cyberspaceship," (4) the Internet as a primary resource for high-interest writing prompts and supports, and (5) rapid student-response devices. Our fullest realization of the pedagogy has been in our paragraph-to-essay-level composition course, as the following narrative recounts; however, individual instructors apply the features selectively according to their particular requirements and level of proficiency with the technology.

Interactive PowerPoint Lessons. Through regular student interviews, we have identified two recurring themes about the "graphic dimension" of instruction: first, handwriting on a chalkboard or whiteboard is generally inefficient and ineffective; second, bullet-pointed slide shows projected in a darkened classroom are anathema to student engagement. Instructors who write large amounts of expository content (as opposed to performative, calculation-based content) on the board must sacrifice important face-to-face interaction with students. This lag time can be especially pronounced in developmental instruction where lots of written examples are required. Furthermore, many students report that they have frequent difficulty deciphering instructor handwriting and are generally too embarrassed or deferential to ask for clarification. Finally, handwritten graphics may create a monotonous, monochromatic visual landscape that provides scant stimulation for strong visual learners. Early PowerPoint graphics offered a remedy to these inadequacies, but the ubiquitous bullet-pointed content soon quashed the promise inherent in the technology. Instructors who routinely read from a bullet-pointed slide risk the same sort of student disengagement as instructors who have their backs to the class while scrawling reams of informational content on the board.

NEW DIRECTIONS FOR COMMUNITY COLLEGES • DOI: 10.1002/cc

Our response to this instructional challenge has been to develop a new generation of PowerPoint slides that are highly visual, dynamic, and interactive. In six years of trial and error, we have honed our design principles to optimize the transparency and interactivity of the material. We use simple fonts and strong contrasting colors; keep slide content economical and unencumbered; incorporate diagrams, images, sound effects, and video clips in moderation; use strategic animation of content (sentences break apart and come back together, elements of an outline dissolve and are replaced with other elements, individual components of a body paragraph grow and shrink, and so on); use an inductive, problem-solving approach to content delivery, starting with (flawed) examples and models that require student feedback; and deliver content incrementally. Although we have experimented with more elaborate content that mirrors professional Web design, we believe that our students thrive on clear graphics and literacy-driven content, and strong contrast among the design elements permits projection in a dimmed, rather than a darkened, classroom. Finally, the more dynamic and interactive the slides are, the more likely students are to review them voluntarily on the class Web site.

An unanticipated dividend of the slides has been their rich potential to teach instructors about student learning. With each subsequent use of a given slide show, the instructor is able to recognize specific gaps or glitches in a learning sequence and address the problem by fine-tuning the material. In addition, a healthy sharing of PowerPoint lessons among our faculty means that these teachable moments routinely become the subject of collective inquiry. Our database of slide shows now serves as an archive that facilitates our reflection on student learning, the curriculum, and our pedagogical evolution.

The Class Web Site, a "Living Textbook." In its infancy, our first class Web site was little more than a smattering of grammar quizzes and documents loaded onto a WebCT platform. We developed these quizzes in response to gaps in the textbook exercises where struggling students would become confused and give up when doing their homework. We tailored the content to the specific needs of our students and wrote feedback for all answers; in addition, we programmed the quizzes to randomize the order of the questions and the answers within each question. We then instructed students to take each quiz as many times as necessary until they received the score they desired. As a result of these simple innovations, the students tackled the grammar homework with unusual alacrity and determination. In fact, the demand for these electronic materials was so strong that the faculty felt compelled to develop more of them. Several years later, after such great momentum, we have multiple Web site templates containing original instructional materials for our three levels of developmental composition. Individual instructors use these templates to build and customize their own Web sites, and any new content they create may be added to the databases within the templates, allowing a healthy cross-pollination of best teaching practices and materials. The collective content is now so robust that some faculty use a class Web site in place of a textbook, and the college's learning center has adapted content for specialized workshops to assist students in writing across the curriculum.

Prior to receiving the SPECC grant in 2004, our production of new materials relied on the initiative of several instructors in their spare time. Early on, we researched free-access online resources that we might incorporate in the pedagogy. However, most of these materials proved too broadly conceived for our purposes; even the publishers' supplemental online resources mirrored the pedagogical limitations inherent in the textbooks. With the Carnegie funding, we were able to enlist more faculty in the effort, and our production of original resources grew markedly. Working collaboratively, we have honed our understanding of why the class Web site, a "living textbook," is pedagogically superior to a conventional textbook. As suggested, it renders the literacy more visible to students, both literally and cognitively. We base our conviction on eight observed attributes of the electronic media: (1) superior interactivity, (2) augmented quantity of examples, (3) greater correspondence to diverse learning styles and paces, (4) increased personalization of content and public recognition, (5) improved student accountability, (6) better connectivity and collaboration among students, (7) greater element of surprise and power of choice, and (8) enhanced critical thinking through multitasking.

It became clear early on that electronic media are interactive in a manner that a conventional textbook could never be. Foremost is the element of immediate and ample feedback that the Web site provides at every opportunity, allowing students to adjust their knowledge and repeat their practice. Learners participate in an instant and continuous dialogue with the content, eliminating the detrimental lag time associated with textbook homework when students must wait hours or days to confirm and correct their understanding. We also use extensive hyperlinking to help students get inside texts—everything from the course syllabus to "X-Ray Essays" and exercises on paragraph construction. For example, a sample descriptive paragraph might allow students to click and see "verbs with energy," "colorful adjectives," "transitional expressions," and so on. With simple color-coding or highlighting, these elements—the guts of good writing—become dramatically and compellingly transparent to students.

In an exercise on paragraph unity, students might be asked to identify details that do not fit with the governing idea of the paragraph. With a conventional textbook, students working alone have no recourse when they are stumped about how to proceed. With an electronic version of this exercise, we can offer students a graduated sequence of hyperlinked clues to help them proceed; when the digressive details are finally exposed, the learner may click on each one and be hyperlinked to an explanation of why the particular detail is inappropriate. Hence, we move from a "blob" of unresponsive text on the printed page to an interactive gamelike learning sequence that engages and assists students of diverse skill levels.

Developmental learners benefit from a rich resource of writing samples that they can peruse and contemplate throughout the semester. Conventional textbooks are limited in the quantity of examples they may provide, and because these books are designed for a broad audience, much of the content may not be optimal for a specific cohort of students. The class Web site allows us to post a plethora of writing samples that are a valuable resource for students. For example, in "Passing the Torch," the first online journal assignment of the semester, students are invited to read journal entries written by former students in the class offering detailed advice to incoming students about what to expect from the class and how to succeed. Since we have collected these exit testimonials for several years, there are scores of them that students may select from. This modest assignment illustrates the virtually inexhaustible capacity of the technology for archiving and posting sample work. Our students rely on these resources, reporting that access to multiple samples makes the expectations of the literacy more transparent.

This storage capacity also allows us to offer greater choice to students in determining the particular content of their writing. In a descriptive writing assignment, for example, students are shown fifteen photographs each of individual red cars, exotic masks, dolls' heads, unusual chairs, or other items. They are instructed to select one photograph and write a description that is so precise that the instructor will be able to identify the object being described from one of the lists. The spate of engaging images delights and surprises our students, and the power of choice affords real agency in the cognitive process, rendering the object of their inquiry more visible.

Unlike a conventional textbook, the class Web site incorporates course management tools that prompt unprecedented levels of student accountability. Standard features such as the electronic calendar, grade book, and e-mail are powerful lures for developmental learners who want to succeed but may drop the ball when provided the slightest opportunity to do so. Posting detailed homework instructions on the calendar eliminates the possibility that students will not hear or understand the homework instructions. The grade book, or "My Progress," feature allows students to track their grades, attendance and punctuality, and intermittent performance evaluations. Online quizzes are graded and posted automatically, and failing or missing grades are highlighted in red to alert students. We have observed that our students track their scores assiduously, promptly reporting errors and requesting permission to eliminate "red alert" marks. In exit interviews, our students routinely remark that the transparency of their progress is empowering and motivational; apparently, in other classes, grading remains a rather nebulous dimension of the academic experience. Finally, we have designed a biweekly online status report that requires students to evaluate their own performance in the class through a series of multiple choice and short-answer questions. Although these reports take very little time to complete, the awareness they elicit is profound.

The Computer Classroom, a "Cyberspaceship." An early gambit in our pedagogical exploration was to move a developmental composition class entirely into a computer classroom. Our guiding metaphor was that of a "cyberspaceship": we wanted to discover whether the electronic media could transport our students to new cognitive and imaginative galaxies. We wanted a transformational learning environment that might disrupt student expectations about instructional space, time, and content. We wanted to tap into the physical and creative energy of the technology and propose it as an alternative to fossilized instructional approaches and "dead" classroom space: scattered desks, littered floors, and drab walls. We wanted learning challenges so engaging that students would become oblivious to time. And we wanted them to rediscover English instruction as a universe of unexplored possibilities. In short, we sought to thwart the mind-numbing associations with academic English instruction that frequently plague our developmental learners.

This move was not without concerns. How would we accommodate students who were uncomfortable with the technology? How would the fixed, linear seating in the computer lab affect small group work? How would we respond to system crashes, lost data, and other unforeseen mechanical problems? How could we avert our students' compulsion to browse the Internet, send personal e-mails, and the like? As it turned out, these challenges proved eminently manageable. For example, we partnered technosavvy students with technoresistant students to reduce the discomfiture of the latter, and year by year we witnessed the refinement of the technology so that even novice users—often older, returning students—were able to adapt to the environment within a week or two. We found that collaborative learning succeeded with pairs or triads of students seated next to one another. In the event of a server crash or a viral attack, exceptionally rare occurrences in our labs, we learned to keep a backup of nonelectronic activities and materials to proceed with the instruction. Finally, to counter the distractions of the Internet and keep our students on task, we sought to make our assignments irresistibly compelling, incorporating a range of engaging online resources.

In the computer classroom, the class Web site becomes the primary portal for instructional activities and materials, complementing or replacing the textbook. Many students arrive early and log onto the Web site, completing assignments, checking their scores, and reading the writing recently posted by their peers. The instructor may dim the lights and play meditation music to create a relaxed and contemplative ambiance—small adjustments that send a powerful message to the students that this is an out-of-the-ordinary place where unexpected opportunities will occur. The daily vocabulary quiz is programmed to open on the hour when class begins; students who arrive late may miss the window of opportunity to take the quiz. Others may view the results of their attempt immediately, making special note in their online notepad of words that have given them difficulty. Class proceeds with a number of e-learning sequences in which dynamic PowerPoint demonstrations are interspersed with online exercises, quizzes, chatroom discussions among students in different parts of the room, and brainstorming exercises. The outcome of each learning sequence is clearly defined, and implementation and testing of each skill is immediate. Even the most advanced students must stay focused in order to complete the concatenation of tasks.

Students work with a wide range of resource materials, including photographic, panographic, video, audio, and textual. Moreover, they are able to manipulate this content by scrolling, grabbing, dragging, dropping, zooming, highlighting, copying, pasting, and juxtaposing, and even beginners pick up these simple techniques quickly with the help of their peers. Unlike the linearity of textbook content, electronic content is layered and vertical, allowing students to navigate among multiple resources and delve more deeply into individual resources. Clearly the pedagogy can appeal to a full range of learning styles; furthermore, it enhances cognitive visibility and critical thinking opportunities, permitting students to access and know the subject of their inquiry in multiple ways.

The electronic classroom also promotes self-paced and autonomous learning. Early in the term, we emphasize the benefits of time management to our students. Although we encourage methodical attention to the composition process, we also direct students to use downtime efficiently, updating, completing, or getting a head start on outstanding or upcoming assignments. Increasingly we are amazed at how little prompting it takes to engender this behavior in our students; the gamut of available tasks on the Web site seems to have a magnetic draw for them. Faculty visitors have noted the unusual involvement of the whole class, even as the minute hand on the clock creeps past the end time for the session.

The Internet as Instructional Resource. In our quest for high-interest writing topics, we look increasingly to the World Wide Web for inspiration and resources. We employ a variety of free-access Web sites and subscription databases to craft innovative, resource-rich assignments. For example, to prepare for a journal entry on prejudice, students are required to visit Tolerance.org, where they are directed to specific links and a questionnaire. This brief perusal jump-starts their personal associations with prejudice, motivating them to explore and articulate their experiences and opinions. For other journal topics, students may be required to visit Web sites on happiness, parenting, multiple intelligences, or fallen service personnel in Iraq.

For formal essay assignments, students receive a more systematic introduction to Web sites such as the UNESCO World Heritage List, the Project for Public Spaces, *Time* or *Newsweek* Photos of the Year, Los Angeles murals, or user-friendly databases such as the Biography Resource Center or Opposing Viewpoints. Even simple resources such as an online dictionary and thesaurus can serve as conduits to exciting writing opportunities. For example, from a narrowed list of terms devised by the instructor, students select a term of their choice and write a definition essay; however, they must incorporate as many synonyms as possible from the thesaurus, also relying on the dictionary to investigate range and nuance in meaning. Not only does this assignment reveal the thesaurus and dictionary as powerful repositories, it also reinforces the importance of precise vocabulary and the sheer fun of semantic exploration and discovery. Other ostensibly simple resources such as online lists of colors or emotions can be enlisted as supporting materials for writing activities. Students learn to keep these resources open as tabs on their screen, consulting them intermittently for guidance and inspiration during the composition process. A glance at any of the lists should convey the considerable transparency that they afford to student cognition and imagination.

While we are invigorated by the success of these applications, we offer the following caveats: (1) significant time and patience are usually required to locate and evaluate optimal source materials, (2) time and ingenuity are usually required to incorporate these resources seamlessly into writing assignments, and (3) time and hard-won foresight are usually required to develop effective navigational directions for students. Internet resources are not an easy fix for the instructor: when used strategically, they can promote exceptional learning outcomes, but when applied thoughtlessly, they can generate confusion and disappointment for students.

Rapid Student-Response Devices. The latest addition to our instructional repertoire comes in the form of rapid student-response devices. With funds from our grant, we purchased a set of clickers and a GamePro software license. The individual student-response clickers are devices that let the students respond electronically to a question posed by the instructor. The instructor can tally the responses to determine what content or concepts students are still struggling with. Clicker applications and their benefits are well documented, but it may be worth noting that developmental learners are especially energized by the interactivity and accountability inherent in the technology. When response data are projected intermittently during instruction, students see learning in new ways: the patterns and pitfalls experienced by their peers are made transparent, disclosing commonalities and dispelling a sense of isolation. The elegant and user-friendly GamePro software allows faculty to load course content into five different game show platforms based on popular TV game shows such as *Family Feud, Jeopardy*, and *Tic Tac Dough*. A host of visual and audio features, plus three "slapper" units, simulate the televised competition and appeal to a range of learning styles. Our students respond with wild enthusiasm to the game shows, and when used in moderation, these events represent a powerful complement to the Full E-mersion pedagogy. In developmental composition, the content for a game show can be based on grammar or vocabulary, outlining, paragraph unity, developing details, critical reading, and so on. The time required to develop the content will vary according to discipline and topic; in our experience, two or three instructors working together can create a basic show in about an hour. The content is stored in a communal database and may be redistributed for other shows.

The Full E-mersion pedagogy appears to work best when the five overarching applications are integrated and balanced. However, given the protean nature of student populations, human learning habits, and pedagogies themselves, such integration and balance require an ongoing effort.

NEW DIRECTIONS FOR COMMUNITY COLLEGES • DOI: 10.1002/cc

Visible Learning: Making Student Learning Transparent for Instructors

The development of new instructional materials and the discussion about the pedagogical rationales for these materials prompted a more systematic and rigorous investigation into student learning. We wondered what a closer look at the students might reveal, not only about the strengths and short-comings of the pedagogy but also about the students themselves—about what it means to be a developmental writer and learner. Despite the unavoidable problems of mediation and of the metaphors "visibility" and "transparency" when it comes to something as elusive as the learning process, we embarked on an attempt to get inside students' minds.

From the outset, we had been observing the students as a whole and marking their successes and failures through their engagement in class and evaluations of their written work, but these familiar modes of student assessment gave us little in terms of understanding the intricacies of developmental learning habits: Where and why, exactly, were students making significant strides or encountering difficulties? Might their difficulties be addressed by fine-tuning certain features of the pedagogical materials? Or did roadblocks result from personal distractions, outside difficulties, or affective resistances? If so, how might those be addressed? Ultimately we decided to focus deeply and specifically on four students. Our intention was to gather as much information as possible about how these students were learning (that is, how they were responding to the pedagogy) but also to attempt to know them as learners more intimately than is generally possible in a typical classroom setting.

The four students we tracked came into the course among the weakest in terms of their writing skills. Three of them, although we did not know it at the time we selected them, had been diagnosed with learning disabilities and had previously failed the course, two of them twice before. The fourth had significant grammar errors characteristic of many English as a second language writers. From each, we collected hard copies of every writing assignment, from brainstorming to outlining to the final revised product. In addition, we videorecorded the students in the acts of brainstorming, outlining, and writing, filming the computer monitor as they composed. During these sessions, students were sometimes working independently and sometimes in small groups. Finally, we interviewed the students on videotape following each writing assignment and at the entrance, midterm, and exit of the course.

The Collected Writing. English 191, the paragraph-to-essay-level developmental course, is a credit or noncredit course. Each written assignment is graded in three areas: organization, development, and grammar. For a piece of writing to be considered satisfactory, it must receive a passing score in all three areas. By collecting the writing of the four students from the beginning to the end of the writing process for each prompt, we were able to make useful observations and suggestions to the students as they moved from assignment to assignment and, at the end of the semester, to graph their progressions or regressions in the three graded areas.

Visibly mapping student progress enabled us not only to see how the writing was changing but also at times to ascertain why it was changing in the ways that it was. For example, we noted that scores in the area of organization regressed when the students tackled an assignment requiring only a slightly different structure from that to which they had become accustomed. In other cases, we found that as students improved in one area, they simultaneously backslid in another. One student, for instance, began the course with development of supporting detail as his primary area of difficulty. In following his written trajectory, we found that as his development of detail increased, so did his difficulty with sentence structure and his rate of grammatical and mechanical error. These problems suggested that perhaps his primary difficulty was not so much development but rather an acute awareness of his difficulty with the language: in trying so hard to say it right, he was virtually bringing himself to a halt.

Other features of the writing took our inquiry in different directions. We were able, for example, to analyze specific aspects of the writing much more closely than is generally possible in the typical rush to mark and return papers in a timely manner. We could often ascertain at what stage in the writing process students went awry. Did the problem have to do with generating relevant ideas during brainstorming? With creating a coherent outline? Or with neglecting to follow the outline carefully while composing the essay? And having access to entire archives of student work meant that we could compare essays and identify some of the overarching obstacles and compositional patterns of specific students, whether grammatical, syntactical, structural, or developmental. Finally, we were at times given brief glimpses into the affective dimensions of our students, which, though always present and operating in complex ways on students' composing processes, are rarely accessible and never ultimately knowable with certainty. For example, a close look at one student's brainstorming and outlining pages over the entire semester corroborated our sense that he had tremendous difficulty committing himself to his ideas, a problem that resulted in his repeated inability to finish assignments in the allotted time. His brainstorms and outlines were written so lightly in pencil as to be barely legible and had been erased and rewritten numerous times, often with changes in word choice that made little, if any, substantive difference.

We found that many of our observations of the four students were often more or less applicable to other students in the class and to developmental students generally. We thus were prompted to ask new questions about the pedagogy in an attempt to address the difficulties we were observing. How, for example, might we make the move from one assignment to another more seamless for students? How might we help students navigate the demands of written development and grammatical correctness so that consciousness of one does not occur at the stake of the other? And how do we, and can we, raise our awareness of students' conscious and unconscious resistances to writing in order to help them over affective hurdles?

Videorecordings of Students at Work. Over the semester, we also attempted to capture the learning process by videorecording our four students as they participated in various activities, such as completing online grammar quizzes, brainstorming (alone or in small groups), outlining, and writing. If this process was a bit intrusive in the beginning, the students quickly overcame their camera shyness, and as the instructors became more adept at setting up and manipulating the equipment, recording soon became a seemingly normal part of the classroom setting for everyone involved.

Starting out on this leg of our venture, we were not sure what we would see or whether we would find anything that proved useful. Our concern, again, was to attempt to make visible the learning process and to come to a more in-depth understanding of our students, and we were approaching that challenge from every angle we could think of. Surprisingly to us, our recordings of students composing at the computer, which seemed at first an entirely fruitless, even silly, endeavor, gave us some of our most poignant and dramatic footage. Underscoring the extent to which developmental writers come into writing classes accompanied by myriad difficulties (both present, in terms of the writing task they are immediately working on, and past, in terms of their own writing histories), the recordings provided us with a starting point as to the nature and prognosis of those difficulties. And because the recordings were generally conducted separately from the regular classroom and in the presence of the recording instructor, the students often asked more questions and received more feedback than would typically be possible in a regular classroom setting. This of course raised a number of questions for us: To what extent were we elevating these students' self-consciousness by isolating them from the others and holding them under such immediate scrutiny? How much in-process assistance to them was too much assistance? How could we avoid creating instructor dependency in this setting? But we were also able to gain tremendous insight, not only from watching the choices students made as they composed or the points in the writing process that inspired them or slowed them down, but also from the kinds of questions they asked, did not ask, or did not think to ask.

In reviewing the recordings after the semester ended, we were repeatedly astonished at how compelling it was to see the writing unfold on the screen and to witness what seemed to be the thinking process made visible. With one student, we were struck by the agonizing slowness of his writing process. For his first assignment, he was able to produce a paragraph of only four sentences over a two-hour period. As we watched him compose, several reasons for that slowness became apparent. For one, he was endlessly distracted by the colored underlining generated by the grammar and spelling assistance program: as each mark appeared, he would stop for long periods in the attempt to correct the problem. Most important, we noted that when prompted to develop his paragraph more, he typically struggled to embed new details into already constructed sentences, often causing his syntax to go awry and also causing the time-consuming colored underlines to appear to him once again. It was as if developing the paragraph meant to him primarily the lengthening of sentences rather than the generating of additional information in the form of new sentences.

Another student grappled with chronic organizational problems throughout the semester. We knew that she made coherent outlines with clearly articulated topic sentences and appropriate subpoints, yet her final papers often seemed randomly patched together, as if she had done no prewriting at all. In reviewing our recordings of her composing process, we were again able to ascertain some of the sources of her difficulty. For example, in several instances, as she attempted to follow her outline, she transcribed the entire outline at the beginning of her paragraph so that the topic sentence and subpoint sentences followed one after the other with no supporting details in between. She then began adding supporting details, not understanding that specific details needed to be inserted under the appropriate subpoints.

Instances such as these, which enabled us to take a close look at the writing process in action, brought us a renewed understanding of the extensive range of learning difficulties confronted by developmental writers, as well as a heightened awareness of the kinds of individualized assistance they often need in order to succeed, even when they are working in the context of immense pedagogical support.

Interviews. Throughout the semester, we conducted two sorts of student interviews. First, following the completion of each writing assignment, we interviewed and recorded the students, asking questions regarding the interest and difficulty levels of the assignments, their sense of how they had done with the assignments, and whether they would do anything differently if given the chance to rewrite them. In part, we simply wanted to know how the students were responding to the assignments themselves, but we were also interested in getting to know something about the students' levels of consciousness concerning how well or how poorly they might have performed on the assignments. Occasionally, in fact, we also interviewed the students after returning graded assignments to them to see how well their sense of accomplishment meshed with how they had been evaluated and, more important, to see if, once having problematic portions of an essay pointed out to them, they understood and could articulate how they might address problems in future assignments.

It was not surprising to us that these students sometimes had difficulty communicating orally in the official context of the interview. To glean what we thought might be useful insight, we often needed to read between the lines of their responses to learn how to hear what they were saying. And often the insights we gathered had little to do with the questions we asked. For example, in questioning one student about organizational problems in her essays, we learned two things. First, since we reviewed several postwriting interviews at once, we were able to see that with each new writing assignment, she seemed to face the same organizational problems anew, as if she were unable to abstract what she had learned in one assignment and apply it to another. We also saw how easily she could be thrown off track organizationally. A gregarious conversationalist, she easily launched into lengthy digressions during interviews, entirely losing sight of the question she had started out to answer. Still at other times, our observations reminded us that in assessing student performance, we can never think too deeply or lose sight of the progress that students have made, whatever their remaining obstacles might be. This was driven home to us during one interview when a student explained to us the organizational logic of a paragraph that we had deemed as entirely disorganized. Her explanation clarified for us that the problem with the writing was not truly organizational but was, rather, a simpler problem to address: she had not employed the proper transitional cues that would enable an audience to follow the direction of her thought.

In addition to the postwriting interviews, we also conducted more overarching interviews at the beginning, midterm, and exit of the course. During these sessions, we questioned students about their response to the course in general—the technology, the assignments, the computer lab, the course Web site—and about their own sense of their progress as writers. Again, we were struck by the kinds of information with which these interviews provided us, information that often went beyond the particular data we were seeking and provided us access to the ways in which the practical and affective dimensions of our students intersect in remarkable ways. In response to the question, "Do you think that your writing has improved this semester," one student responded quietly, "On my last assignment, I wrote almost three pages." When asked how he might account for writing so much, he simply repeated that he had written three pages, adding, "That's almost a thousand words." Despite the considerable writing challenges still facing this student by the end of the semester, his immense pride at what he had accomplished in the course brought us pause and prompted us to consider more fully the idea that what seems to us to be small, incremental steps from assignment to assignment can be huge cognitive leaps for our students.

In short, making these processes more visible has helped us to understand the complexity of our students' difficulties and to raise questions regarding how we can come to know and address more fully the endless variety of our students' conscious, unconscious, cognitive, and affective resistances.

Visible Research: Making Outcomes Transparent for a Wider Academic Community

With the Carnegie funding, we proposed to systematize our collection and dissemination of evidence for the pedagogy. To this end, we created a Full E-mersion Web site (http://courseweb.glendale.edu/thefullemersion) where we posted descriptions of the research, participants' biographies, instructional materials, faculty reports, student interviews, statistical data, and more. Determined to make the Web site an exemplar for online documentation, we set ambitious goals for its content. For example, we videotaped every weekly faculty inquiry meeting and included these on the Web site. For each session of the pilot Full E-mersion course, we collected a written rationale from the instructor and written observations from two visiting instructors; these narratives are posted alongside the instructional materials for each class meeting. In this way, outside faculty can follow an intricate mapping of the pedagogy, accessing and downloading instructional materials for their own use. From our end, maintaining the site required a herculean effort that we sustained for three semesters before moving on to alternate documentation methods.

By year two of the grant, the Carnegie Foundation began an initiative among the eleven SPECC campuses to encourage meaningful documentation and dissemination of the research. Two special seminars were planned to address these objectives. At the first session, participants evaluated the relative merits and deficiencies of exiting online offerings, then brainstormed the parameters for a new generation of online instructional support that might elicit greater use by faculty in search of such support. Following this general discussion, individual campus teams generated storyboards for their proposed projects; subsequently, the storyboards were subject to collaborative critiques by all the participants. Finally, the Carnegie's technical staff assisted the teams with the nuts and bolts of transferring their visions to electronic format, "Snapshots," using the Carnegie's in-house, public access software, the KEEP Toolkit (http://www.cfkeep.org/static/index.html).

The campus teams returned several months later to the second seminar to unveil their projects. Another round of collaborative critique enabled the teams to hone the work, moving it closer to public launch. Out of the initiative came the Carnegie's Windows on Learning portal where the projects are showcased (http://www.cfkeep.org/html/stitch.php?s=2814408673732&id=94404660812025). Glendale's first contribution to the portal was a snapshot of a single technology-based lesson for a developmental composition class. Our guiding principle was a lesson that faculty could grasp conceptually and download with minimal effort (Glendale Community College, n.d.-a).

From our experience in documentation with Carnegie we undertook a new phase of research that would culminate in a second Windows on Learning Snapshot. Our initial goal was to expose the learning trajectories of four developmental composition students. In assembling the snapshot, however, we realized that a full representation of the pedagogy alongside the trajectories would make for a more coherent rendering. Hence, we refashioned the snapshot as a "course portfolio" that gives equal weight to the scholarship of teaching (visible literacy) and the scholarship of learning (visible learning). The portfolio offers visitors ample rationale, materials, and tools for implementing the pedagogy and capturing their own students' learning habits (Glendale Community College, n.d.-b).

We also believe in the power of personal networking and dissemination. Hence, our faculty has kept up a demanding schedule of presentations at ISSOTL (International Society for the Scholarship of Teaching and Learning), the League for Innovation, ECCTYC (English Council of California Two-Year Colleges), California Strengthening Student Success Conference, California State Academic Senate, the Hewlett Foundation, and elsewhere. We have conducted workshops on our campus and at other community colleges, and we are sharing our original instructional materials with other campuses and nonprofit organizations such as the Monterey Institute for Technology and Education. We encourage our colleagues in the field to modify and implement these resources according to their needs; eventually we hope to benefit from their experiences and feedback and the fruits of their labor.

Finally, the pedagogical innovations have found their way into conventional textbook form as well: *Stepping Stones: A Guided Approach to Writing Sentences and Paragraphs* (Juzwiak, 2009) and *Cornerstones: Constructing the Academic Essay* (Juzwiak, in press). Reviewers have commented that these textbooks represent a much-needed watershed in developmental composition pedagogy.

Profusions

Our research has exposed rich veins that compel us to think in terms of profusions rather than conclusions. Nevertheless, two salient questions must be addressed before we end: What evidence of student success have we gathered? Where do we go from here?

Evidence of Student Success. Anecdotal evidence collected from students and faculty speaks with comparative unanimity to the effectiveness of the Full E-mersion pedagogy. While preliminary statistical data do not contradict these testimonials, many of the data are deemed insignificant at this early juncture when implementation of the pedagogy varies greatly from instructor to instructor. More recent data may be tracked at the Full E-mersion Web site.

Where Do We Go from Here? Within the developmental composition program at Glendale College, we have witnessed a recent profusion of interest in the pedagogy and a collective momentum to render student learning transparent, measure the success of this learning, and find fresh pedagogical approaches to facilitate this success. We do not endorse electronic pedagogy as an exclusive approach, but we do acknowledge its seemingly ineluctable capacity to reinvigorate our instruction and our students' learning. In 2004, the proposed scope of the Carnegie grant was to involve four full-time faculty in the evaluation, revision, and implementation of the pedagogy; by the end of the three-year grant period, nine full-time and five adjunct faculty were using various applications of the pedagogy, and other faculty had expressed an interest in joining the discussion.

NEW DIRECTIONS FOR COMMUNITY COLLEGES • DOI: 10.1002/cc

We are hopeful that the research, specifically the faculty partnerships and the habits of inquiry, might be a unifying force among other initiatives that support our at-risk English students. Many of the faculty and the courses involved in these programs are linked to the Full E-mersion pedagogy and research. Hence, we have applied for California Basic Skills funding that will allow us to build on this nexus, potentially consolidating and fortifying our efforts and our students' learning outcomes.

Finally, our latest Windows on Learning snapshot is now live on the Internet. Through the painstaking endeavor of capturing and documenting the intricacies of our students' cognition, we maintained a "build it and they will come" optimism. We eagerly await, and invite, a profusion of discussion from our colleagues in the field.

References

Glendale Community College. "Powerful Uses of Technology in Developmental Education." N.d.-a. Retrieved Oct. 29, 2008, from http://www.cfkeep.org/html/stitch.php?s=37472228740782&id=60455143414862.

Glendale Community College. "The Full E-mersion: Electronic-Based Pedagogy in Developmental Composition." N.d.-b. Retrieved Oct. 29, 2008, from http://www.cfkeep.org/html/ stitch.php?s=37472228740782&id=60455143414862.

Juzwiak, C. Stepping Stones: A Guided Approach to Writing Sentences and Paragraphs. New York: Bedford/St. Martin's, 2009.

Juzwiak, C. Cornerstones: Constructing the Academic Essay. New York: Bedford/St. Martin's, in press.

CHRIS JUZWIAK is on the faculty of the English department at Glendale Community College and former chair of the Developmental Composition Program.

MONETTE TIERNAN teaches developmental and transfer-level composition and is chair of the English Division at Glendale Community College.

NEW DIRECTIONS FOR COMMUNITY COLLEGES • DOI: 10.1002/cc

This chapter traces the author's work in developing California State University's Early Assessment Program, an initiative that aligned eleventh-grade performance standards, new English and mathematics curriculum, and teacher education and professional development opportunities to prepare students to meet the state university entrance requirements.

State College Readiness Initiatives and Community Colleges

David Spence

Many states are working on efforts to improve student transitions between high school and college or career to ensure that students are graduating from high school well prepared for college or career training. This is a daunting task. ACT, an independent nonprofit organization that provides assessment, research, information, and program management services in the areas of education and workforce development, estimates that up to 70 percent of high school graduates are not ready for college or career study as measured by meeting readiness benchmarks in reading, writing, and mathematics.

Greater attention to the college and career readiness problem by state leaders and policymakers could drastically boost the numbers and percentages of students who graduate from high school ready for college and career study. This chapter discusses lessons learned from a major college readiness initiative, the California State University's (CSU) Early Assessment Program (EAP). It also makes the argument that community colleges could benefit from joining with regional universities in developing college readiness initiatives.

This chapter describes a comprehensive statewide initiative that sought to raise attention in college readiness while protecting existing open or less selective admission policies. This distinction between college admissions or entry and readiness is critical. A concern about access—the tensions between access and sending signals about readiness (or placement)—is a major reason that community colleges have been reluctant to join statewide college readiness initiatives across the nation.

NEW DIRECTIONS FOR COMMUNITY COLLEGES, no. 145, Spring 2009 © 2009 Wiley Periodicals, Inc.
Published online in Wiley InterScience (www.interscience.wiley.com) • DOI: 10.1002/cc.358

The CSU experience illustrates both the strengths and weaknesses, and the successes and failures, of statewide readiness initiatives. On one hand, the EAP program reached statewide to all high schools in California and established significantly high readiness standards in reading, writing, and mathematics. The EAP also developed, jointly with the California public schools, diagnostic test items for high school students, a revised or new school curriculum to help students meet these standards before graduation from high school, and new professional development opportunities for teachers to learn how to teach to the CSU's standards.

The California Community Colleges were not originally included in the EAP. After the inception of the EAP in the CSU, legislation passed to do a pilot of the EAP in the CCCs. Policymakers, educators, and researchers who support this pilot hope that the EAP will signal to prospective community college students that there are academic standards at the CCCs, while not limiting access. Only when a state's community colleges work as one with regional universities can the same powerful, specific messages be sent statewide to all high schools about what it means to be ready for college. This severely limits the impact of the readiness initiative given that most high school graduates in California attend community colleges and look to these institutions for readiness signals. Only when a state's community colleges work as one with regional universities can the same powerful, specific messages be sent statewide to all high schools about what it means to be ready for college.

While many are concerned that sending clearer signals about academic preparation could diminish community colleges' traditional open-access mission, "diagnostic signaling," when done correctly, will not discourage students from attending. In the tradition of precollege outreach programs that provide information about and supports for the rigors of postsecondary education, providing high school juniors with specific information about their college readiness and how to remedy any deficiencies before graduation will improve their chances of success in community college.

State College Readiness Initiatives

The EAP work begun at the California State University in 2001 has generated theory and practice that yields a series of steps states can take to implement successful statewide college readiness initiatives:

- Identification and agreement by all public schools and higher education institutions statewide on one set of academic readiness standards in reading, writing, and math—the skills needed to learn at higher levels
- Diagnostic assessment of high school students' performance on the academic readiness standards to enable them to get further help during high school

- Inclusion of readiness performance as part of the state's public school accountability process, ensuring that high schools emphasize college readiness
- High school developmental courses, other learning activities, and supports focused on college readiness
- Intensive focus on postsecondary readiness during the senior year of high school
- Provision of preservice and in-service activities that help prospective and practicing teachers provide courses that focus on the specific learning skills associated with college readiness

The CSU added items to California's preexisting high school tests so that the testing burden for students was not increased. We realized, though, that simply testing students without providing additional academic and social supports will not help students prepare for college. The real advancements in student preparation come with the development of new courses, forms of supports, and professional development opportunities to promote readiness. While most popular attention is directed to the eleventh-grade assessment, the core of the EAP—and most of the current activity—centers on the provision of new courses and professional development opportunities. The key is not just telling students about their readiness for college-level work, but to make sure that students have every opportunity to become ready while still in high school.

The EAP's design team believed that the manner and quality with which states carry out the generic steps are equally or even more critical to success. Our experience in California strongly argues that a successful statewide readiness initiative must include the following implementation characteristics. These characteristics are derived from our work in developing the EAP and in observing the implementation statewide. We believe they are likely generalizable for other states and regions that are developing similar reforms:

- Accurate and strong focus on where the action needs to be—on high school classrooms and teachers. All decisions regarding how to carry out the technical implementation steps need to be considered in light of how to create the conditions in which high school teachers can make postsecondary readiness a top priority and can teach effectively.
- Improving readiness should be approached on a statewide basis, involving all public high schools and all public community colleges and universities. Higher education needs to band together to send readiness information to all high schools. Having this single message about specific standards will enable all high schools and their teachers to focus on and give priority to college readiness with the necessary strength. Currently too many uncoordinated and unclear signals are sent from a variety of colleges and universities.

- Focus on reading, writing, and mathematics (through algebra 2). These are essential skills needed to learn. In the case of academic readiness, less is more as long as the core skills are identified at the right performance levels.
- Establish a statewide understanding of what increasing readiness means and what it does not mean, stressing that access and admissions to post-secondary education will not change. In broad access institutions, readiness should be separate from admissions.
- The readiness standards need to be adopted and applied through common placement procedures in all public community colleges and four-year institutions.
- To ensure that the statewide readiness standards have maximum priority with all high school teachers, the standards need to be key components of the official state high school standards.
- Teachers and students need to give high priority to the assessment of high school juniors' (rising seniors') performance on the readiness standards. To make this assessment a high priority for teachers, the assessment needs to directly address the explicit readiness standards and be part of the statewide public school-based assessment program valued by the state school accountability program. Relying on surrogate or correlated standards and assessments (ACT, SAT, Accuplacer, Compass) lessens the priority for teachers.
- Significant weight needs to be given to college readiness performance in the statewide school accountability program.
- Cap, cement, and institutionalize the statewide college readiness initiative with robust state-supported statewide programs to strengthen the role of the senior year in improving college readiness and to prepare prospective and practicing teachers.

Why Such Slow State Progress?

Groups such as Achieve and the American Diploma Project have worked effectively to help a number of states develop college readiness standards. However, no state has succeeded in implementing a statewide college and career readiness initiative that fully involves the pre-K–12 public schools and public sectors of higher education. Of the few states that have defined readiness standards, most have not fully embedded them into state-adopted K–12 school academic standards. No state has brought its entire public higher education system to agreement on specific college and career readiness standards that can be shared and applied by all state two- and four-year colleges and universities. The EAP is an important piece of this work in California, but much is left to be done to implement the EAP in the California Community College system, and the EAP does not include career readiness signals.

   Moreover, only a few states have addressed effectively the need to develop school-based tests that measure students' progress on state-defined readiness standards. Some states rely on the ACT and SAT, national college admission tests that do not measure student achievement with direct reference to state-recognized college and career readiness standards.

Finally, no state has made college or career readiness a formal component of the state school accountability system. Only California has taken steps to focus the senior year of high school and teacher professional development on readiness standards. State education agencies, boards, officers, education sectors, and legislative and executive government branches have been slow to unite completely around common readiness goals or a specifically defined readiness agenda. Slow progress can be traced to several reasons, some concerning a lack of needed understanding and commitment by state policymakers and some related to the fears and self-interest of education sectors. Overall there is a strong need at the state level for a greater public understanding of the readiness problem and its impact and importance.

Progress in many states has been slowed by a concern that the open access mission of public postsecondary education, and particularly the community colleges, will be constricted. This is not and need not be so. The public cherishes and wants to protect access to community colleges and broad access institutions. These missions must stay intact, and students must never be dissuaded from attending. It is too easy currently to confuse admissions or entry with readiness. The public does not appreciate the difference between readiness (or placement) standards and admission standards and does not realize that both can be applied at the same time. They often do not know that admission standards are different and may be higher or lower than readiness standards. The public has no idea of the vast extent of the lack of readiness according to even moderate standards of reading, writing, and math.

Finally, the general public just now is beginning to make not just access to, but completion of, postsecondary education pathways, certificates, or degrees a priority. As this priority takes hold, there will be great pressure on postsecondary schools to increase completion rates, which will in turn press postsecondary education to work with K–12 to improve the readiness of incoming students. In short, the oncoming public move to hold colleges accountable, and perhaps even tie state funding in some way to these results, will create the imperatives needed for colleges to make academic readiness a priority.

Why Is It in the Interest of Community Colleges to Promote Statewide College Readiness Initiatives?

The short answer, of course, is that it is in the students' and state's interests: more students ready for college or career preparation on graduating from high school, with the consequent increase in completing pathways, certificates, and degrees. All of this makes better use of student and state resources and promotes individual and state social and economic success, in contrast to a situation in which students drop out of postsecondary education before completing their goals. Another answer recognizes that statewide readiness initiatives cannot succeed without full commitment of all community colleges. Only when all of postsecondary education sends one set of readiness signals can all high schools receive a strong and focused message.

Community college leadership in state readiness initiatives also will increase the leaders' effectiveness and reputation. Indeed, community colleges, more than any other postsecondary education segment, have more to gain. These benefits particularly will help buttress, substantiate, and protect the open-access mission in three badly needed ways.

First, leading efforts to define college readiness standards, which both four-year institutions and community colleges identify and apply statewide, will do much to make tangible the quality of community colleges and especially of their baccalaureate transfer programs. Unfair or not, the community colleges' dedicated association with open-door admissions can lead to a public perception that community colleges lack standards. Of course, the truth is that while admission criteria are open, readiness standards— through placement—are applied after entry. Establishing this distinction between admission and readiness standards by adopting common and significant statewide readiness standards (at least similar to those of regional universities in the state) would do much to prove community college quality.

Second, these readiness standards, especially if built with regional universities, would help to allay concerns over the quality of transfer programs. Few if any state higher education systems have good ways to oversee the quality of such programs, either through objective program exit criteria (beyond course content and grades) or—on the front end—substantive placement standards in the community college that rise to the level expected in many senior institutions. As unfair or unfounded as these perceptions are, establishing significant standards (comparable to four-year college placement standards) for beginning baccalaureate degree-creditable study would go a long way toward confirming the quality of community college transfer programs.

Third, full participation and leadership in statewide readiness initiatives would fortify community colleges' efforts to raise associate degree completion and transfer rates. The increasing public recognition of the relationships of associate and bachelor's degree attainment to a state's economy and to individual success is causing state policymakers to rethink how state funding and accountability mechanisms can be reworked to emphasize degree completion.

We know that any concerted commitment to increase completion must lead with higher readiness levels of incoming students, arguably the most important factor in completion. Identifying and applying common and higher readiness standards is crucial in two ways.

First, these standards and the associated high school assessments—as well as the increased focus of the teachers and curriculum on them—will result in higher percentages of high school graduates ready to begin college-level study.

Second, establishing the right kind and level of readiness standards is key to ensuring that developmental education programs effectively are preparing students to complete degrees. It is very likely that the current standards are not strong enough or are not applied as criteria to exit developmental education. These readiness standards, as adjusted to reflect the levels of reading, writing, and math actually required to complete degrees, can guide developmental education programs whose value will only increase with the higher premium accorded completion.

The CSU's experience with the development and implementation of the EAP provides many lessons for other states. K–12 and postsecondary institutions must speak with a unified voice to prospective college students and families. They need to agree on a set of readiness standards and on the measures to be taken, in partnership, to help students improve their preparation. And the most appropriate policy lever must be used to embed expectations into the classroom. Finally, much of the work takes time, and capacity needs to be built for schools and teachers to meet new expectations; courses must be aligned with readiness expectations and teachers must know how to help students prepare—particularly students who are not traditionally in college-bound curricular tracks.

DAVID SPENCE is president of the Southern Regional Education Board. Previously he served as executive vice chancellor and chief academic officer of the California State University system.

NEW DIRECTIONS FOR COMMUNITY COLLEGES • DOI: 10.1002/cc

9

The many projects, policies, and practices discussed in this volume suggest promising ideas for improving student success both before matriculation and in developmental education in community colleges. Ideally, improvement in the former will reduce the need for the latter, but until that happens, the goal will be to promote effective strategies for both. In this concluding chapter, the editors combine the information learned from the two strands within this volume to pose some final thoughts and next steps for future work in this area.

Looking Ahead: Synthesizing What We Know About National, Regional, and Local Efforts to Improve Student Preparation and Success

SuJin Jez, Andrea Venezia

As Chapter One discussed, the structure of this volume is split between chapters with campus-based and national perspectives. We believe this division parallels what needs to be happening in the field: reforms at the campus level must be supported, and sometimes spurred and documented, by others at the state, local, and nonprofit levels.

Focusing on reform in community colleges is different than it is in other education entities. Community colleges are unique in that they are completely open access; they each have different missions and goals, often tied to local economics and needs; they are usually locally autonomous; and their students are extremely diverse and, unlike students at other postsecondary institutions, do not share common goals. Moreover, community colleges must provide a multitude of educational options to diverse student populations with few resources, often little political clout, limited capacity, and a largely part-time or adjunct faculty.

Given the variety of student intents, programs, pathways, and courses offered at a given community college, it is almost impossible for community colleges to provide general information to all prospective students about how to prepare for all the courses offered. But if community colleges seek

New Directions for Community Colleges, no. 145, Spring 2009 © 2009 Wiley Periodicals, Inc.
Published online in Wiley InterScience (www.interscience.wiley.com) • DOI: 10.1002/cc.359

to help students reach their goals, they must improve the academic readiness signals they send to prospective students. This volume highlights the difficulty of sending these signals to even a single population of students: students who are degree- and transfer-seeking. As the authors in this volume describe, many of these degree- and transfer-seeking students are ill informed of the academic standards of community colleges, and they discuss some of the consequences. Without community colleges and their partners creating and distributing information on standards, the situation will not change, and students will enter expecting either that they are prepared or that the community college will prepare them.

However, many students find that their expectations about rectifying their academic weaknesses in college are not always fulfilled. As Bailey discusses from a national perspective in Chapter One and Moore reinforces in Chapter Five with her experiences at the campus level, the key academic support of developmental education is not working as it should. Institutions and systems are not succeeding with a core function if students who take developmental education, by and large, do no better than those who enroll directly in college-level courses. Either the advising, assessment, and placement processes are broken, or the courses are not effective, or both. Bailey and Moore make compelling arguments for revamping all of those policies and practices and figuring out better ways to determine what community college expectations are and to measure all the skills necessary for a successful educational experience.

While improving developmental education is one way to improve student success, the other route is to focus on ensuring that students are prepared by the time they enroll at a community college. An innovative and promising model provides college-level course work to traditionally underserved high school students. As Hoffman, Vargas, and Santos discuss in Chapter Four, a variety of promising ways can integrate college-level work into high school. The three options they describe range from least to most intensive integration of high school and college: dual enrollment (also known as dual credit or concurrent enrollment), dual-enrollment programs or pathways, and early college high schools. Regardless of intensity, these programs show early signs of providing first-generation college students with the academic and nonacademic supports to graduate from high school and enroll in college in higher numbers than their peers in traditional education programs. This promising reform affects not only the developmental education issue but also issues of college access and success for traditionally underrepresented students.

The dual credit and early college high school phenomena are but two indicators of a growing interest in community colleges. Over the past five to ten years, funders such as philanthropic organizations and the federal government have turned a great deal of their attention to these open-access institutions. Ten years ago, it was virtually impossible to find funding for a large-scale study focused on community-college-specific issues. Now, as Burdman outlines in Chapter Three, hundreds of millions of dollars are supporting both small- and large-scale efforts.

Working in the community college field and seeing these efforts, Burdman posits that "the nexus between policy change and institutional change may provide the most fertile ground in which dynamic improvement can occur." This volume speaks to this intersection. Colleges, state and local governments, foundations, businesses, and other community groups must work collaboratively to build capacity and create initiatives addressing local needs. But community college administrators and faculty members might not realize that local needs are often not just local or that their community college may not be so unique. Outside entities such as government and foundations can help community colleges build capacity and assist with replication and scale. While outside, and often nonlocal, entities have an important role to play in advancing the role of community colleges, Spence clearly highlights in Chapter Eight the delicate balancing act that must happen in this relationship. His example of California State University's Early Assessment Program shows that it is possible to develop effective large-scale reforms from the top down, but such reforms would likely be much more difficult to accomplish with community college systems given their history and culture of local autonomy. But if community colleges and their respective systems at the state level take the time and effort to find the lever that will get the most buy-in—one that builds off existing infrastructure or knowledge—they will create the most positive change for students.

This volume also delves into the intricacies of classroom-level reform. Each of the local perspectives highlights the importance of data-driven decision making. While several of the initiatives discussed in this volume are too young to have a significant amount of longitudinal data and thus cannot undertake rigorous outcome-focused evaluations, Klein and Wright showed in Chapter Six how the effective use of data can assist in making shorter-term decisions, as demonstrated when their frequent and continuing analyses of the data led them to veer an ineffective effort in an entirely different direction from what they originally intended. From analyzing the data, they learned that the program design itself was not the primary problem; instead, the instructors' teaching practices often ran counter to the philosophies that served as the foundation of the program. From closely studying the data, they learned that effective curricular transformation depends on effective faculty transformation. Their project also reinforced several tenets that are important for anyone involved in this work:

- Standards and rigor should not be thrown out the door when equity and access issues are addressed.
- An understanding of what a community college student should know to succeed in college and to function well in life is needed.

- An understanding of what the nonacademic skills and knowledge that community college students must know and have to succeed in college and in life and what the most effective ways to teach and measure those knowledge and skills is also needed.
- There must be constructive and frequent reflection on our own work.

Like Klein and Wright, Juzwiak and Tiernan, in Chapter Seven, also used data in their decision-making process, along with sharing a long commitment to the reform process, involving faculty, learning from mistakes, and constantly refining practices. Juzwiak and Tiernan also developed important constructs about transparency. Policy transparency is often viewed as a one-way street; policies must be transparent to the stakeholders who supposedly benefit from them, and the stakeholders are seen as one amorphous entity. But Juzwiak and Tiernan realized that policy transparency acts better as a two-way street: a transparency feedback loop exists. Instruction must be visible to students, student learning must be visible to instructors, and outcomes must be transparent for a wide audience. Furthermore, the visible literacy component can be part of a signaling process for prospective students, providing them with information about community college expectations.

While Moore's data in Chapter Five confirmed suspicions regarding students' difficulty advancing past developmental courses, they also highlighted how large the problem was and where students were faltering. From these data, the college developed better placement exams and student assessments and created faculty learning communities to enhance faculty teaching and student learning.

As evidenced by the chapters in this volume, people are jumping at the opportunity to figure out the best ways to meet community college students' needs and help ensure that more students persist in their course work and pathways, graduate, and are prepared to live a fulfilling life in which they can support themselves and their families. These reforms are happening at the classroom level, the state level, and every level in between. Moreover, interest in community colleges is growing. Everyone from policymakers and foundations to the general public shares an interest in how community colleges are faring with the millions of students who enter their doors every year.

SUJIN JEZ is a research associate at WestEd.

ANDREA VENEZIA is a senior research associate at WestEd.

INDEX